The Myth of the Ruling Class

The Myth of the Ruling Class

Gaetano Mosca and the "Elite"

With the first English translation of the final version of
The Theory of the Ruling Class

BY JAMES H. MEISEL

Ann Arbor: The University of Michigan Press

Manufactured in the United States of America
by H. Wolff Book Manufacturing Co., Inc., New York

PREFACE

This unabashed, old-fashioned exercise in cogitation—performed without the benefit of any task force or research team—was originally prompted by curiosity about the lesser known and untranslated works of the Italian, Gaetano Mosca, whom the Anglo-Saxon academic reader has met only as the author of *The Ruling Class*. That work summed up the intellectual labors of a man who had been the contemporary of both Marx and Mussolini.

As *The Ruling Class* was merely the elaboration of ideas conceived forty years before, I have treated at some length the work of Mosca's youth, the germinal, peremptory *Teorica*, so as to contrast it to the conciliatory later master work. The purpose—of what had been intended as a monograph—is to show how Mosca began as a champion of contemporary antidemocratic thought (because the democratic way as he conceived of it led straight into the Marxist bog), and how he ended up by shrinking from the consequences of his own ideas when the Duce, an ex-Marxist, took him at his word.

In the course of this investigation, other untranslated writings of the author were consulted, in particular the works of his old age, for it was then that Gaetano Mosca gave his doctrine of the ruling class

v

its final form, the brief and lucid piece which is here presented as a special Supplement (pp. 382 ff.).

Whoever speaks of Mosca cannot remain silent about Michels and Pareto, or about Karl Mannheim, Joseph Schumpeter, and C. Wright Mills. The theory of the elite has indeed been "a dominant theme in the history of Western thought in the last three generations." [1] Thus, the study grew into something else besides. No comprehensive survey and evaluation of elitist thought has been aimed at, but some of its most disturbing implications are considered and some tentative conclusions offered.

It is still true that all roads lead to Rome, but it is also true that some of them are better paved than others. It was Professor Mario Einaudi who pointed out to this researcher the particular road which led him into the Quirinal. There Minister Bernardo Mosca proved to be much more than helpful: he was a true friend. Without him, this commentary on his father's work could never have been written. From the inner recesses of the palace came additional support, for which the struggling stranger was most grateful to the lifelong friend of Gaetano Mosca: the distinguished second president of the Republic, Professor Luigi Einaudi. Another friend and colleague of Mosca, Professor Emilio Crosa of the University of Turin, was most gracious in conveying needed information.

On this side of the Atlantic, thanks are due the University of Michigan for granting a sabbatical leave of absence, and the Horace H. Rackham School of Graduate Studies for a generous travel subsidy. A special acknowledgment is owed Dr. Bernardo Mosca for permitting me to translate and quote from the Italian editions of Mosca's works, and to McGraw-Hill Co., publishers of *The Ruling Class*, for their permission to quote freely from that text.

Finally, I wish to state for the record that this study was completed in spite of my wife's abounding interest and patience. As for the debt I owe to other authors, the responsibility for my conclusions must remain entirely theirs.

JAMES H. MEISEL

Ann Arbor, July, 1956

CONTENTS

The Myth of the Ruling Class

INTRODUCTION

Elitism—at its crudest the notion that The Few should rule because they do in fact rule, and less crudely the contention that, since only a few can rule, The Many do not and never will—is, of course, no longer a novel notion. It has become if not the new creed —our secular religion of popular sovereignty is still too vigorous for that—then in any case the common parlance among those who like to think of themselves as members of Arnold Toynbee's Creative Minorities. The New Conservatism, of which one hears so much nowadays, surely derives much of its *raison d'être* from the very sense of importance which the elitist writers assign to this secondary stratum of the ruling class: the all-important subelite which rationalizes what the rulers do today and articulates what will be public opinion tomorrow.

This study is not meant to be "objective." It is inspired by the hope that this country will remain immune to the new creed—a formidable creed, because it can lay claim to a high degree of factual truth. To deal with that truth we shall do well to accept, with the least possible amount of fuss, what seems to be fairly valid in the elitist argument. There really is no point in denying the historic evi-

3

dence showing that The Many hardly ever rule, in the sense that major policy decisions could be called the direct result of the will of the majority.

What is proposed, then, is to do battle on the ground claimed by the elitist offensive (if it is indeed an offensive and not a mere rear-guard action). Acknowledging most of the points made by the New Machiavellians (an honorific term bestowed upon the "defenders of freedom," Sorel, Mosca, Michels, and Pareto, by James Burnham [1]), we will, in the following, understand elite rule to imply the collective manipulation of the masses by a small leadership group or by several such groups. We shall assume that all the members of the elite are alert to their group interest or interests; that this alertness is in turn caused or affected by a sense, implicit or explicit, of group or class solidarity; and last, that this solidarity is expressed in a common will to action. Even such a novel phenomenon as the bureaucracy that manages the Soviet Union under the direction of the Party shall be given the elitist benefit of doubt, although "we know about it too little to be able to gauge accurately its strength and outlook, the degree of its social unity, cohesiveness, and consolidation, or the extent to which it has or has not crystallized into a distinctive, self-centered, self-disciplined, self-conscious, and self-perpetuating social body." [2]

To put it into a facile formula, all elites shall be credited here with what we should like to call the three C's: group consciousness, coherence, and conspiracy.

What still remains to be weighed is the validity of the elitist contention that minority rule (Michels' "iron law of oligarchy") makes democracy inoperative, shows it to be "an illusion engendered by a false illumination ... an effect of mirage." To be sure, the same writer, Robert Michels, grants that "the democratic principle carries with it, if not a cure, at least a palliative for the disease of oligarchy." We note with interest the word "disease." There is at work, we are assured, "the *ideological* tendency of democracy toward criticism and control." Social education, as a by-product of oligarchic leadership, may "counteract oligarchic tendencies." [3] Indeed, most theorists of the elite will concede that democratic aspirations lead "in the direction of an ever greater approach toward equality." But as one man they will insist that the fruits of social and political progress are, and never will be more than, the left-overs from the tables of "educated malcontents leading, or aspiring to leadership of, the dissatisfied masses." [4] The victories in the perennial struggle for rights thus are won by default only: they are concessions granted to the people by elites competing with each other for predominance.

The great majority of the elitists end their search on this note of discouragement; most of them are disappointed liberals or democrats; Robert Michels was a disappointed socialist.

We shall start on the same gloomy note, but propose not to end on it.

Two Types of Myth

Title and subtitle of this study call for explanation. The belief in elite rule is taken to be a myth the same way as our notion of "the democratic way of life" has, of late, been called a myth by some—a myth in the Sorelian sense of a conviction based not necessarily on empirical fact but on faith, a confidence impervious to the remonstrations of critical reason.

Now, not even the most fervent advocate of democratic methods will claim that their virtues are efficiency, consistency, and boldness. What he will say is that they are less arbitrary, less crude, and less dangerous than those of other known systems of government. From the imperfections of the democratic process, the admirer will appeal to its perfectibility, to the ability of its practitioners to learn from experience. Beyond that, he will put his trust in the general principles of fair play and equity which inform the democratic practice. At this point, the democratic school splits into two (although most democrats remain blissfully unaware of any split).

The majority opinion holds that any attempt to define democracy in terms other than those of a technique results in vagueness or absurdity; objectives, ends are general, and some ends which one might want to call specifically democratic can be shown to be pursued and achieved by nondemocratic polities, by means that cannot be called democratic. It is, therefore, the means that count. Against this view some will hold that if democracy is merely a technique, a method, then no matter what kind of decisions are made, they will have to be called democratic if the democratic forms have been observed. This must result in vagueness or absurdity. You, the minority writ runs, accuse us of too broad a notion of democracy; we suggest that yours is too narrow.

Without taking sides in this debate,[5] one might say that when we speak of "the democratic way of life," we do have in mind something more than just a way of doing things: we are thinking about goals. We have a general idea about ends, objectives that are "democratic"; our judgment seems to function more precisely in the absence of fulfillment: we are sure that some decision is "not democratic." Thus understood, "the democratic way of life" is the name for an attitude of mind for which distinctions between form and content, between technique and objectives become purely academic, practically nonexistent. Thus understood, the democratic method will suggest itself as the most likely way to realize democracy. Behind all democratic reforms lurks that general passion for equality which in our time has "acquired the fixity of a popular prejudice." [6] The observation of rules alone would not explain the moral fervor of the democratic myth. Rules are rational, whereas the great strength of democracy is, as Pareto would say, its nonlogical, messianic nature. With the tradition of Stoic-Christian ethics behind it, equalitarianism represents the most potent socio-political solvent of modern times. It is stronger than the urge for liberty; it is annexing to itself the various forms and forces of fraternity. The power of the democratic myth not even its perverters will deny.

The myth of the elite has no such appeal. It is based on the demonstrable natural fact of human inequality. Whether we apply Pareto's "logico-experimental" or Mosca's historical method, whether the political system is labeled democratic or not, this is what, according to that school, we find: subjection.

Clearly, elitism finds itself at a grave disadvantage: it seems rather difficult if not impossible to conjure up much moral ardor out of the biological fact that some men are stronger, or cleverer, than most. Hence the age-long obscurity and the still limited appeal of the elite doctrine, a fact which Gaetano Mosca deplores and tries to explain.[7] But then, we may be asked, why worry about something that can never command the allegiance of the many, running counter to their innermost desires? And why call the elitist theory a myth? Is not its claim to scientific truth the very evidence of an attempt to shun the myth, all myths? Yet, history abounds with creeds and thought systems which are contemptuous of human self-respect, which make demands of utmost harshness and yet enlist the devotion and enthusiasm of many millions. "Scientific" certainty, as the success of Marx has shown, holds an uncanny appeal even for those who, in the event of a proletarian victory, have everything to lose.

The example of Marx seems to prove the very point we try to make, for with all his scholarly, deliberate detachment he could never quite suppress the truth that he was *morally* engaged in the "objective process." While talking economics, he meant freedom. The living Marx was the indignant revolutionary,[8] not the author of highly technical tomes on capitalist accumulation and surplus value. How could writers who, instead of freedom, talk subjection, ever captivate the minds of those who would have to form the mass of the subjects unless that subjection were being made somehow attractive? And that feat would remain impossible unless the scientist of The Few and The Many, of The Rulers and The Ruled, himself believed that the acceptance of the facts, his facts, will make society more rational, less hypocritical, and therefore better, freer. If he believed all that, his faith might be infectious.

To demonstrate the hidden moral bias, the potential myth-making aspect of elitist writing, is one major purpose of this study. Closely bound up with it is the additional objective: to show that the elitist facts and the elitist myth cannot be logically reconciled. This contradiction cannot faze the charismatic leader, the inspired religious genius, or a revolutionary demagogue, but it can and does disconcert, as we intend to show, a writer honestly devoted to his scientific principles.

The myth-making *intent* is not easy to discover. In Pareto's work it is explicitly denied. The sharp distinction which that author makes between what we deem true and what we deem to be desirable and useful socially applies to his conceptions of the myth (which he calls "derivations") as well as of the elite: the objective findings of the scientist may be completely at odds with the common interest.

To act according to a known truth (such as the knowledge that The Many never rule) is, therefore, not always commendable, and it was certainly Pareto's view that any real science, such as his, could have no traffic with political or social propaganda. It is true that he frequently forgot his own injunction, but there was, in his mind, never a doubt as to its correctness. Like Flaubert, Pareto thought that he was following the precept, *Je ne propose rien, je n'impose rien—j'expose.* His exposures were based on the quantitative method only; nothing was assumed, least of all any principles that smacked of transcendence; normative values were excluded, or were simply the object of scientific interest.

And yet, even this stern relativist is not immune to the infection of the normative Ought. We are informed that, under optimal conditions, that is, in a society of unimpeded social mobility, those elements which reach the top will, by definition, be the best in their field—in a society of thieves, the elite will be composed of the most talented pickpockets and burglars. But later, when Pareto treats of historical societies in which the "circulation of elites" is not completely free, he suddenly instructs us that those at the top may not be The Best after all; the latter may be kept out of power by entrenched, inferior men. But how, then, we may ask, are we to measure superiority or inferiority of an elite without possessing, or assuming to possess, some standard other than the factual one of success? Such a standard does not follow from the scientific premise which Pareto wants us to adopt; it is an intruder from the despised world of absolute, ahistoric values.[9]

Karl Mannheim, who perfected and refined the theory of the elite (and pointed out the self-defeating tendencies of the elitist process), also fell victim to the normative infection. Starting with a concept (his *Sociology of Knowledge*) which logically should yield a Thrasymachean view of society as a battlefield of ideologies all equally transparent and epiphenomenal to the observing social scientist, he ends up with the theory of an enlightened ruling class of social scientists whose task would be to integrate and reconcile the various clashing interests according to Right Reason, which in our time means the planned society. Plato's philosopher kings in charge of economic rationalization; Plato's justice setting the limits of individual freedom.

Mannheim's theory of the elite thus derives its appeal not from the well-observed facts of subjection and pre-eminence, but from the author's urge to provide a new rationale of obligation extrapolated from contemporary tendencies toward the welfare state. It is the transformation of the elite doctrine into a melioristic creed that generates the elusive and seductive glow of the myth.[10]

Elite Is a Middle Class Concept

In no author's writings does the dilemma between science and morality, between the obligation to describe what is and the urge to find out what ought to be, become so apparent as in those of Gaetano Mosca. And that is perhaps why he is humanly the most appealing figure of the school. He is not satisfied with a morality that merely takes elites for granted; he cannot suppress the wish for an elite that satisfies morality. Unlike Pareto, Mosca does not look on all elites with equanimity. Why not? Because as a *homo politicus* Mosca is forever making value judgments which the scientist in him could not accept and must be made to overlook. But it is precisely because of this contradiction that we may find Mosca more rewarding and more of a challenge to our intellectual curiosity than the much more consistent and acute Pareto. The latter took, with a determination which can only be called passionate, the line of absolute indifference toward all ends. Under his chilly scrutiny, the pretenses of all creeds and programs crumble into dust. He took his Archimedean stand in an elaborately contrived system from which neither advance nor retreat is possible. When fascism came, the Marquess Pareto (who died the next year) was vindicated because he had foretold that a government of foxes could not long endure against the revolt of the lions. In consequence, his reputation became tainted: world opinion damned him as a protofascist. "Marx of the bourgeoisie," he had been called. But in addition to being considered the bourgeoisie's answer to Marx, Pareto could claim to have been, like Marx, one of its most effective gravediggers.

Gaetano Mosca, too, did spadework for that grave. But when he saw, at the last moment, that the grave was meant for him, that it meant living death, Mosca refused to dive into the trap. What may be called his inconsistency, the moral passion underneath his "scientific" crusade against democratic freedom, made him choose that freedom after all, although the ambiguity of his position remained unresolved.

Yet in another sense he never had to make a choice. What looks like ambiguity was logically predicated by his historical location.

"Elite" was originally a middle-class notion. Carlyle's "captains of industry" were the first bourgeois to claim, and to claim successfully, the right, assigned to them by Saint-Simon and Comte, to rule instead of the old landed aristocracy. The new industrial and business elite based its claim on "achievement" or, as Mosca prefers, "merit." But barely had that class consolidated its position when it found itself between two fires; while still battling the rear guards of the old regime, the third estate had to face a still younger class. In view of the fast-growing proletariat, the elitist formula had to be given a new, antiproletarian twist. "The history of all hitherto-existing societies is the history of class struggles"? And the proletariat is to be the ultimate class which will usher in the classless society? Not so. Rather, the history of all societies, past and future, is the history of its ruling classes.[11] It is also true that history is the graveyard of aristocracies,[12] but from that graveyard arise, phoenix-like, forever new elite formations to eternalize the cycle of domination. No matter whether the economy remains capitalistic or becomes the plaything of equalitarian levelers, there will always be a ruling class, and therefore exploitation. The Associations of the Free Producers cannot prosper anywhere but in Utopia.

This is the antisocialist, specifically anti-Marxist, bent of the elitist theory as it unfolds in the last decade of the nineteenth century. It is the argument by which the middle-class intelligentsia tries to silence the triumphant propaganda of the revolutionary Left—as well as its own doubts. Elitism is a defensive doctrine, a new Dismal Science aimed at the naive optimism of eighteenth-century enlightenment. The Marxists had inherited that naive confidence, and did not destroy it conclusively in the minds of the bourgeoisie.

In order to achieve that wrecking job, elitist critique had to turn against the very bourgeois tenets which had helped to enlist the—still disenfranchised—working class against the old nobility. Again

Carlyle, so savagely contemptuous of middle-class mediocrity, points the way. In particular, the attack had to be directed against the new democratic institutions which seemed to make possible the peaceful conquest of the state power by the Red International, the vertical barbarian invasion.[13] Confidence in the wisdom of the common man was misplaced; therefore its rationale, the doctrine of popular sovereignty, had to be expunged from the middle-class canon.

Although that argument was offered in perfectly good liberal faith, it is easy to see why it failed to persuade the great majority of liberals. They continued to think of themselves as good democrats and moderate progressives while carrying on their uneasy two-front fight against both revolutionaries and reactionaries. It is equally easy to see how the antidemocratic aspects of the elite theory could become useful to feed the resentment of the social groups hemmed in between Big Labor and Big Capital. It was the petty bourgeoisie which furnished the first recruits for the antisocialist *and* anticapitalist mass movement of fascism. It was, ironically, that plebeian stratum which provided the elitist aspirations with the basis they could not find in the middle class proper. Only in the "classless" party movement of the Duce and the Fuehrer, which became a cross-section of all the social groups and classes, could the myth of the elite become a revolutionary force, a mass revolt which at the same time was an act of mass submission.

Most of the elitist thinkers were left high and dry by the all-too-complete success of their profaned and brutalized idea. Like Molière's Georges Dandin, they could be told, with some degree of justice, "Well, you asked for it!" And although, in a strictly political sense, the accusation was inaccurate (even Pareto's sympathy with Fascism must be called highly unorthodox), in a deeper sense the whole elitist school, by throwing overboard democracy together with Karl Marx, had indeed become guilty of collaborating with the New Barbarians.

Their "collaboration" begins with the attempt to turn the tables upon Marx, as Marx himself had turned the tables upon the Ricardian classical economists. The Marxian doctrine of the class struggle, its proletarian teeth extracted, furnished the materials for both Mosca's and Pareto's theory of the "circulation of elites." From Saint-Simon, Mosca derived his two-class scheme of dominant minority and ruled

majority; he developed it along the lines defined by Ludwig Gumplowicz. Now, Saint-Simon was a utopian socialist besides being,
as Auguste Comte's teacher, the first positivist. Gumplowicz, too,
although highly critical of Comte, considered it his task to write
"the natural history of mankind": the struggle between classes is
preceded by the struggle between races; conquest is the origin of
states and nations.[14]

In denying the identity of natural and human history, by taking
over Saint-Simon's class theory without the socialism and the Gum-
plowiczian version of that theory without the racial angle, Mosca felt
that he had reached the scientific terra firma. His historical approach
seemed to align him with Marx—the Marx who had written that
"men make their own history." But Mosca had been careful to
demarxify the element adopted from the Marxian system: his own
version of the class struggle lacked the substratum of materialism;
no more was production the unique and ultimate determinant. Or
so it seemed.

The way seemed free for Gaetano Mosca to elaborate a social and
political philosophy immune to the corroding influences of contemporary socialist and bourgeois ideologies. However, the book that
would have expressed such a philosophy of independence Mosca
never wrote. His liberation from materialist and positivist thinking
remained incomplete. He had rejected the *idées maîtresses* of nineteenth-century progressivism, but had not been able to get rid of the
assumptions on which those rejected values and conclusions rested.
The civilization he observed was still unfolding and advancing,
although showing danger signs of imminent decay; the "social forces"
which made up society, although not "classes" in the Marxian sense,
he still thought of as representing interests. Their struggle should,
and could, be normalized—yet only on the basis of a mutual power
check. Mosca's "ideal state" would be one in which the "balance of
the social forces" would make possible "juridical defense": a government of law dispensing "relative justice." [15]

Relative justice as the result of a power equilibrium between competing groups—all absolutism is alien to the mind of Gaetano Mosca.
He could never have adopted any neo-idealist, organicist position;
his liberal background was too strong to permit him that solution.

Although he was too polite to take up Voltaire's war cry, *Ecrasez l'infâme!*, his anticlerical dislike of Vatican infallibility remained outspoken.

His habitat was not Pareto's nihilistic no man's land but the domain of doubt, his attitude one of watchful but undaunted scepticism. There was no reason why such a position could not be maintained. There is that side to Gaetano Mosca; it can be discovered in his work. But it is not the whole man. There is still another Mosca who did not feel comfortable in his half-way house placed on pragmatic territory; the moralist in him wished to build on firm ground, but that ground his epistemology could not provide for him. In fact, it sternly vetoed all escape into a world of constant values which, his mind told him, were inimical to his scientific premises. So he remained uneasy; what had officially to be denied became a subterfuge.

Officially, he was an antidemocratic liberal—to be precise, a neoliberal in the sense that he professed to give a realistic reinterpretation of the liberal *mystique*. But if we look below the surface we discover that he did not actually advance into the twentieth century. His nostalgia seems to belong to the liberal society in its Victorian heyday, but his intellectual arsenal, all the critical sallies against Spencerism and Comtism notwithstanding, is replete with weapons that belong to even earlier times. He recoiled from his own nineteenth-century youth into the fastidiousness of the enlightenment, where he calls Montesquieu to order, only to indulge him in the end, if surreptitiously. He clashes head on with his bogeyman, Rousseau, and yet shares with him the dislike of groupings, parties in particular, which intervene between the sovereign and individual subject. And that is not yet the end of the secret, retrograde quest for a justice more than relative. In the end, Mosca even condones Aristotle whom he defied as a youth, and he meets with Plato's class of the disinterested educators, whom he salutes bashfully but fondly.[16] The old bourgeois virtues which were so dear to that French revolutionary Georges Sorel rank equally high on the list of the conservative Italian, Gaetano Mosca.[17] Austere and passionate, he is an ancient stranded in an alien age. No son of Italy has been less kin to Machiavelli, than this "Machiavellian" who, indebted though he was, not to the author of *The Prince* but to the writer of *The Discourses*, greatly preferred to Machiavelli his contemporary, friend, and critic, the judicious Guicciardini.[18]

Habent Sua Fata . . .

The Latin proverb that tells of the strange way fate arranges the lot of books, bestowing fame on one, while relegating to oblivion other by no means inferior works—that proverb comes to mind as one considers Gaetano Mosca's reputation as an author. Firmly established in all serious textbooks, it presents a puzzle to the student of "world history as the world court of justice." That the modern formulation of the theory of the elite was first presented by the author of *The Ruling Class* nobody will deny. Yet today, thirty years after completion of his major works Mosca's name is known only among the initiated few. He is the great forgotten man of the elitist triad. Pareto is disparaged by the most advanced sociologists but is still studied in their seminars. Robert Michels, the avowed disciple and epigonus of Gaetano Mosca, has his editors and commentators.[19] Mosca, who died as late as 1941, has still to be discovered.[20]

Why is that so? Many dismissed Mosca in a more or less extended footnote as the man who played The Baptist to Pareto. Granted that *The Ruling Class* cannot compare in scope and depth with the *Trattato*. But assuming that the writer of the first was to the writer of the second what in music Liszt had been to Wagner, the task would still be to judge our Liszt on his own merits. Mosca's worth—Mosca's unworthiness—must be explained by Mosca's work, not by the greater glory of him who came afterwards.

The relationship between the two men is a matter of embarrassment to the beholder. The offending part was without any doubt Pareto's. His refusal to acknowledge Mosca's earlier "discovery" of the elitist key to history drew blood. The furious outburst of the older man was all the more remarkable as he conceded willingly that his own theory had a distinguished ancestry.[21] Mosca was extremely modest in his claims, which he used to make in the name of "the new school" rather than in his own. His already noted tendency to whittle down the sharpness of his argument (Saint-Simon, Gumplowicz and Marx without their sting) contributes much to keep out of his findings all sensationalist elements, but also robs them of their possible effect. And there are other penalties that go with the rewards of caution. As some of his friends said, Mosca evokes the impression that he did not much care for intellectual clarification. Or worse: that he was constitutionally unequipped for it.[22] Indeed, if the French saying that *le style, c'est l'homme* applies to scholarly production, then a reading of *The Ruling Class* and other works by Mosca will reveal some baffling traits: the writing is agreeable enough; the style, manly yet graceful, has the grand manner without the pomposity. Yet that magistral ease does not seem to result from a deliberate and controlled effort; there is no evidence of powerful ratiocination going on under the even surface. Problems are posed but not really pursued; or we are given answers where we would like to hear questions. There is in the very style an element of elision: the narrative slides from one topic to the next, and what seems to us to be the main business, the specific problem of the elite, is submerged in a wealth—and it must be added, in a welter—of the most general and varied historic information. The result is an impressive miscellany, from which is missing the arresting quality that would force us to stop and think.

These strictures would be fair if Gaetano Mosca had called his great work or any other of his books *The Ruling Class*. But he did not. The work so named had as the original Italian title *Elementi di scienza politica*, which indicates that there was much more in the author's mind than a specific theory of the elite. The English title is unquestionably more effective, but also misleading. In fact, not more than roughly one-third of the chapters deal specifically with the ruling class. It is a trying game to round up and unite those scattered parts into some systematic order. In so doing we may discern outlines of a system which, however, Mosca might not recognize as his own brain child. It would be a construction tidier than his own sprawling sketch, but also poorer, less evocative. Sometimes the very failures and omissions of one work are more productive than a perfect blueprint, painstakingly executed. Some of the most inspiring art is torso, fragment.

Gaetano Mosca's work ought to be understood as such a fragment. The approach to it demands restraint—a restraint not easily maintained in scholarly research, which insists on perfection in its subject. This writer offers in advance his most sincere apologies for attempting to force Mosca's thought into a mold for which it was not made. The reader will have to condone occasional outbursts of academic petulance; he will condone them if convinced, as am I, that the critical severity with which our author will be treated more than once is only the reverse of great if misplaced expectations inspired by respect and love.

The first among those misdirected expectations is connected with our wish to find out how elites come into being, how elites are formed. By what process do elites consolidate and attain what has been referred to earlier as the three C's: group cohesion, consciousness, conspiracy—the unity of being, thought, and purpose? It would be exaggerated to say that none of these questions ever gets an answer from the author. Indeed, he tells us how elites arise and why there must be ruling classes. But on the whole, the nature and existence of such groups is taken for granted rather than investigated; Gaetano Mosca was emphatically not engaged in the kind of empirical research such as is being carried out at the Hoover Institute. He was alert to Harold Lasswell's pioneer work and in sympathy with it.[23] Yet Mosca's own work, although branching out into the neighboring fields of sociology and comparative history, remained essentially within the pale of theory—a theory which takes its data completely for granted and erects its structure over trusted ground. That trust in facts is Mosca's positivist heritage; his confidence that all the necessary information for a genuine social science is available at last knows of no doubt. He did not think of his own doctrine of the ruling class as just another ideology. It was based on a *fact*, it was a fact. To doubt, to deny, as most Americans would, the existence of the ruling class would have caused more amusement than annoyance on the part of Gaetano Mosca.

Another question to which we must not expect an answer from him has to do with the means of control which the elite exerts over the masses. Again we are presented with a "fact," this time a fact of popular psychology. All ruling classes justify their domination by a "formula" acceptable to the majority; this formula, or myth, will more or less reflect the character and function of the ruling class in charge. Beyond that the myth will express the "spirit of the time," the whole, or a prevailing, interest of a particular society.

So far, so good. But how a formula is generated, why it assumes this specific form and not another—that is of no interest to Mosca. To give an example (not discussed by him): what made the educated Frenchman of 1660 accept with enthusiasm the myth of the Sun King, and with equal passion reject the same *Roi Soleil* three decades later? Mosca might have answered, sensibly, that economic destitution in the wake of costly foreign wars had undermined the prestige of the monarchy. But that explanation, good as it would be, still begs the question, which concerns the *process* by which events, actions are translated into states of mind and vice versa. Why is it that sometimes, as Mosca notes, a formula retains its influence long after it has lost its *raison d'être*, while at other times it dies a premature death? A rudimentary form of Pareto's "circulation of elites" is Mosca's answer: ruling classes may fail to adapt their formula to the changed demands of society; or ruling classes may renew themselves or be renewed. In the first case, failure to renew the formula may signal the end of the ruling class; in the second case, the formula might be retained (the British crown would be a good example). What Mosca fails to study is the possibility that the succession of elites does not account for the succession of ideas. That the ruling classes may owe their existence and position *in the first place* to the social need for sublimating the harsh facts of power and subjection never occurred to that foe of historical materialism. Mosca never could have written that a "system of ideas as expressed in an ideology is not, as Marx would have it, merely a superstructure or an epiphenomenon; it is the formative force which molds and shapes into total subjection those whom it touches." [24]

No. For Mosca the ruled mass remains the humus out of which grow leading groups; the ruling class must never be considered as an isolate. Its ideology remains, if not epiphenomenal, an aspect of the total social process until, at some point of class differentiation, the myth of the ruling class obstructs the evolutionary flow and becomes a mere "class ideology."

All this he knew. And yet, he did not quite avoid creating the impression that a ruling class may be considered by itself alone, confronting rather than reflecting the rest of society. But that impression is not due to a neglect on Mosca's part of social history. If anything, he gave it too much room, and not enough to his own theory. In fact, he missed not a few opportunities to reinterpret the past in the light of his new method. Mosca never created his doctrine large enough to cover the whole canvas. He was too much of a scholar and too little of a doctrinaire to push his own theory to the extreme. The result was a disjunction between Mosca's historiography and Mosca's doctrine. Thus, the Ruling Class was thrown into a disproportionate relief and became, on the surface, much more isolated and important than the author may have wanted it to be.

Did Gaetano Mosca sense an incongruity in his design? The fact that he wrote one and the same book three times may lead us to suspect as much. Was it dissatisfaction with his work, a fear that something was eluding him that forced him to return to the theme of his firstling decade after decade, annotating, expurgating, adding, buttressing?

I doubt it. Nothing in the work of Gaetano Mosca reveals the sentiment of insufficiency. That great and good man, humble in his pride, said what he had to say, no less, no more. If he felt any limitations, he accepted them in good grace as a matter of course. Rather than rebel against them, he would remain silent—as he did during the last decade of his life, seeing the final editions of his books through the press and otherwise observing the regime of *Il Fascismo* with an outward show of patriarchal calm. His was the calm of a good conscience, after he had, in 1925, made his last speech in the Italian Senate.[25]

Nulla Apologia Pro Vita Sua

Mosca's last speech, that valedictory of one who refused to bow to the dictator, only dramatized the gradual change that had transformed his attitude toward democracy from execration to indulgence. Like the Hebrew prophet, he had started out to curse and ended on a note almost of blessing. It was no belated *Gran Rifiuto* of totalitarian tyranny; he had predicted long before that the type of executive dictatorship which Mussolini was establishing would be the end not only of the system he had criticized, but also of the values he had loved. Thus he had nothing to apologize for when he took his leave from public life. He had been right: the democratic regime had to end the way it did because it had lost sight of the need for those virtues which, Mosca believed, had been the greatness of nineteenth-century liberalism. There he stood, a vindicated prophet. But it was a tragic day for him. Was he a gravedigger of freedom after all? But he had never had much faith in the influence and power of the intellectuals. He had spoken his piece; scattered applause greeted his exit into political oblivion. With him, an entire generation joined the "graveyard of the aristocracies."

That Senate session was the one spectacular event in an otherwise quiet life. At the same time it was a life of intense and diversified activities. There was the scholar Mosca, the professor of distinguished universities; there was the public servant, with a long distinguished record as a deputy, and later as a member of the upper house. It was in that career that he acquired the practical experience that gives even to his more abstract speculations a down-to-earth quality. Born in 1858, before his Italy became one nation, he died in 1941 in his eighty-third year, just too soon to see Mussolini's fall. A portrait which I saw in Gaetano Mosca's home in Rome shows the imposing figure of that vanishing type, the paterfamilias. The expression indicates both stern and benign qualities. It is a passionate face of great dignity and seriousness, of scholarly absorption blended with patrician self-assurance. He seems to have been a man of strong convictions who would not tolerate opposition. But his features also reveal a defensive element, a brooding loneliness. His "drive" may be ascribed to his Sicilian origin: he was born in Palermo. Like many other sons of that poor island, he soon left for greener pastures. His migrations encompassed the very poles of the Italian geographical and national character. After some years in Rome, where he served on the staff of the Italian equivalent of the *Congressional Record,* and after some ill-fated attempts to establish himself in the academic field, he finally received, in 1895, a call from the University of Turin. The Sicilian became a Piedmontese and married a young lady of that region, which was to the rest of Italy what Prussia had been to the German Reich. As a professor of constitutional law, and later also of political theory and political economy, Gaetano Mosca remained in Turin until 1923. Then, at long last, the University of Rome gave him his due, appointing him to the chair for public law. Piedmont once more conquered Rome—too late this time, for Mussolini had already conquered her in the preceding year.

But now the academic honors came, the memberships in the societies of learning. Again too late to erase that trace of bitterness still visible in the portrait. It had not been all smooth sailing, as one source would have us believe.[26] It seems that invidious colleagues managed to block the path of the young instructor for a considerable time. Not being able to denigrate his splendid gifts, they made much of the fact that he, whose specialty was constitutional law, had dared to write and publish a book on contemporary politics.[27] In other words, he was not solid. There are some audible notes of political fanaticism in the solid *cantus firmus* of the book reviewers that young Mosca's concern with the dubious aspects of Italian parliamentarianism bordered on the morbid.

It did not in any case prevent him from serving his Sicilian district as a deputy (from 1908). In 1919 he became a senator. Before that, during the war, Gaetano Mosca had been a member of the Salandra cabinet as an assistant secretary for colonial affairs. He spoke frequently and wrote for the press on the questions of the day. No southern orator, he always found a most attentive and respectful audience. Behind the soberness of his official utterances some, at least, of his listeners and readers must have felt that quality of the disinterested public servant of whom Mosca had written so nostalgically in *The Ruling Class*.

After his senatorial swan song, he withdrew into a privacy that remained undisturbed by the regime. The man was too big to be touched by the Fascist *squadristi*. But then he did not, as did Benedetto Croce, anger them by an unceasing if veiled opposition. Crafty allusions were not in the line of Gaetano Mosca. He would have fought the New Barbarians bluntly if at all. I had hoped to unearth, among Mosca's private papers, some showing what he had thought of that twentieth-century phenomenon, fascism, in the years of its spectacular success. But there were no such papers. The infirmity of old age is not too conducive to the writing of philippics. Write he still did, only it was no longer politics that interested him. The moralist in him had in the end completely gained the upper hand. His last known utterance (published posthumously) is a series of meditations on such problems as the nature of goodness, truth and falsehood, and the passion of revenge.

Sermonizing *in excelsis*? Not quite. For when the old author thinks of hatred, the name of that formidable hater, Marx, intrudes. Another section is devoted to The Crisis of Civilization. Like all jottings in this copybook—for that is what these ultimate meditations are—the text is made up of quotations, with hardly a comment added. Corroboration from dead witnesses is preferable: their ripe wisdom is more edifying; it is also safer—just in case the diary should fall into the wrong hands. What could be more innocent than the lament of the Abbé Galliani (1778) over the fact that "so much of what our forebears believed to be true was found out to be false by us. And thereupon we are left with a feeling of great emptiness. That emptiness is the true reason for our sadness."

These words have a familiar ring to Gaetano Mosca. Presently it comes to him: long, long before the learned Frenchman wrote in the prescience of the coming end of his civilization, Ecclesiastes had already expressed the same thought, thus: "He who adds to knowledge, adds to sorrow." [28]

The ancient is still ruminating his great subject, his great sorrow. To the very end, his mind remains preoccupied with the theme of his great society, its rise, its glory, and its end.

Part One: Early Approaches

1

EXIT ARISTOTLE

No less than four of his other works, all published before 1896, the year in which the first part of *The Ruling Class* appeared in the original Italian, heralded the theory with which the name of Gaetano Mosca has become associated.[1] The first and most important of these sketches, the *Teorica dei governi e governo parlamentare*, suffered the fate of all forerunners eclipsed by a mature achievement. Some Italian writers have treated it as the preamble to the later master work; elsewhere it remained just a title. Arthur Livingston, in his authoritative introduction to *The Ruling Class*, mentions the germinal work in a few lines that give us no information whatsoever. It was left for H. Stuart Hughes to outline, in a study published recently, the argument of the *Teorica* in a few illuminating pages.[2]

There are various reasons for this all-but-total neglect of Mosca's impressive firstling. One is that the text is almost unavailable today. Even the second edition, which followed the second part of *The Ruling Class* by two years, has been out of print for a long time.[3] Another is that the author himself thought his youthful effort superseded by his major work. In his preface to the new edition, he treats the *Teorica* as a historic document mirroring "the political conditions

25

of Italy around 1882 in a sufficiently exact manner." He considers the first, theoretical, part of the work to be much more important than the rest. He is still proud of the first chapter which develops "the doctrine of the political class," as he will continue to refer to the elite, and he cannot help registering that "this doctrine has spread throughout Italy, and is beginning to become known even abroad." But he modestly qualifies that boast by saying: "It would be puerile to affirm that the *Teorica dei governi* has already brought the method sketchily employed in that work to its full fruition." Otherwise, he asks, why would its author have deemed it necessary to write two more volumes on the same subject?

While conceding, in so many words, that the *Teorica* is dated, Mosca ends on a note that puts even the work which replaced it in *its* place: "There is not the slightest reason to believe that the arduous task has been accomplished." And he adds, hopefully: "Once the new direction will have led us to the goal, then, perhaps, the youth will be remembered who, as a mere graduate, intuitively and spontaneously had a glimpse of it." [4]

To return to the beginnings, to the early stirrings of a powerful idea, will be, in our case, more than an act of philological piety. We will behold Mosca's *idée maîtresse* already formulated with astounding clarity. It is, like newly born birds, still without its feathers: the rich ramifications and embellishments of the full-fledged elitist doctrine are still missing. Like all innovators, Mosca overstates his case; he seems obsessed with his discovery, it becomes a fixed idea to which everything else has to be sacrificed. The argument of the "mere graduate" is as crude and direct as is the way of youth; it is provocatively flaunted. At the same time, the assurance with which it is carried to its ultimate conclusions is impressive in such a young man.

The young man has obviously read a great deal at a precocious age, as becomes evident from his source references. He confesses owing much to "an alert and most tenacious memory, which, strange in a boy, recalled facts rather than words." Historical literature he eagerly devoured, until he was old enough to sense that history was being made right around him. Italy had just been unified under the Savoyan dynasty, which family, one of his friends assured him, was

one of law-abiding gentlemen with no tyrannical ambitions whatsoever. The same friend argued the vast superiority of constitutional
monarchies over republican regimes. Young Gaetano Mosca did not
see the light at once because the fires of the *risorgimento* had not
died yet; the spirit of Mazzini's national revolution, defeated though
it was, still had not given up the ghost. Mosca remembers that most
of his friends used to be liberal republicans and "even a bit on the
pinkish side." [5] Like them, he alternated between being a republican,
a liberal, a democrat, until at last he became reconciled to the Savoyan Victors and Emmanuels.

So now he was a monarchist with his *galantuomo*, law-abiding king
in Parliament. But how did he acquire that loathing for the parliamentary regime that is so marked in the *Teorica?* Most instrumental
to that end was perhaps that ability of his to retain facts rather than
words. How could he help noticing that the facts of liberal democracy did not agree with its enticing words? This typical discovery of
early adulthood in Gaetano Mosca's case coincided with Italy's coming of age. It was the sad awakening from the dream to the threadbare reality of the eighties and nineties, culminating in a national
disaster: the defeat administered to the Italian army by the Negus
Menelik of Abyssinia in the battle of Adowa (1896). Young Mosca
and his generation must have felt as many of the older Bolsheviks did
when the great experience of the revolution and the heroism of the
civil war years had worn thin and the order of the day was no longer
the conquest of communism but the struggle on the wheat front
or the sewage front. The Rubashovs of the *risorgimento* too had
had their day, and now it was the turn of the Italian Gledkins to
take over.[6]

It was a good time for cynics, but the young Sicilian was not one
of them. He felt outraged, insulted. Surely it was possible to reform
the New Italy. What it most needed was another Machiavelli,
though the problem was no longer unification of the country, but a
thorough overhauling of its government. But in what way, in what
direction? In order to discover it, the first requirement was for the
traditional Italian realism to assert itself, to name the facts with
brutal bluntness.

Not that our author could be called a leader of the protest movement. On the contrary. His voice was only one in a mass chorus of most telling arguments against a liberal regime superimposed upon a backward populace, with the results, inevitably, of corruption and a government manipulated by small cliques.[7] Were the *Teorica* not more than that: another denunciation of the parliamentary regime at its worst, we would hardly pay attention to the work, be it ever so brilliant. What makes it stand out is its theoretical equipment. Mosca may have conceived his law of the ruling class in order to clinch his argument against the way his Italy was being governed in his day. But, the reader of the nineteen-fifties will, with more or less impatience, plow through chapter after chapter analyzing the Italian constitution and practice of the eighteen-eighties only in the hope of understanding the doctrine of the ruling class, and to no other purpose. What may have been a mere means to the author has become an end to us. Our interest is in the history of an *idea* rather than of any, ever so important, *institution*, such as representative government.

By that approach, however, we do violence to Mosca, who was never able to draw a sharp line between the study of ideas and the study of important institutions. To him, the forms of and the notions about government are but two aspects of one and the same phenomenon: civilization in a state of flux. Even the one of his works specifically dedicated to political doctrines [8] reverts over and over again to the political and social facts and factors underlying doctrinal justification or critique.

One sees that our author will not easily be labeled. To be sure, he spoke the language of the political scientist and accepted that name, as the Italian title of his main work proves conclusively. But there are many elements of the sociologist in him. No doubt Mosca would have frowned upon that word, because sociology, when he began to write, was still considered an upstart science. Right at the outset, in the first chapter of the *Teorica*, Mosca declares that his method of looking at facts would "expose, in all its nakedness, the primitive state of the political science which is also called sociology." [9] Best of all he might have liked the title of social historian or psychologist: "For a great many years," he wrote at the age of sixty-four, "it has been my conviction that there is only one way for man to control, up to a certain point, his passions and to improve his lot—through the study of individual and collective psychology." [10]

Considering the period in which Mosca started his studies, it is remarkable how strongly the young scholar felt the need to base his research on the study of people. He gathered his materials for the work in progress almost as a social scientist would do today, if less systematically: by many individual interviews—the term "sample" was as yet unknown to him—talking "as a student to other students and to my professors; later, as a soldier in the barracks, to everybody; to members of the so-called good society as well as to employees, civil servants, deputies, workers, peasants—traveling, engaged on pleasure or on business, I always kept in mind ... to find out what importance the one I was talking to, had in society." [11]

The author does not, of course, claim that he learned from experience only. He gratefully lists all the thinkers who helped him find his own intellectual bearings: "Fischel, Gneist, Stuart-Mill [sic], Bluntschli, and, above all, Taine." To all but one of these men Mosca insists he owes merely the facts they relate in their works, while the interpretation, he claims in the hallowed academic terms, is his alone. The one exception is Hippolyte Taine: "from him, I must confess, I borrowed many views and judgments scattered throughout the stupendous volumes dealing with the origins of modern France." [12]

The Method

Like so many before him—and after him—Gaetano Mosca deplores how much the so-called science of politics lagged behind the natural sciences in precision, or, as we would say in the age of opinion polls, in measurability. Without claiming as much as that natural scientist of humanity, Ludwig Gumplowicz (whose name does not appear in the *Teorica*), Mosca is convinced that, at long last, the social sciences are on their way to producing exact results. He quickly disposes of some naive misunderstandings: the greater glory of the natural sciences has been ascribed to the use they are making of "common and vulgar observation," while their discoveries are in fact quite frequently in perfect contradiction to sense evidence. If that is so, why have the social sciences, which can rely on a great mass of ready-made sense evidence, not made more progress than they have until now? Mosca answers that "in the natural sciences we deal with a certain number of phenomena which it is possible to reproduce at will and to analyze with relative ease..." The macrocosm can be reduced to a laboratory experiment, while "in the social sciences that never happens; all observation must be based... on the study of phenomena as they naturally unfold, under the conditions as they present themselves, which frequently are not the most opportune." Precisely because he has to rely on "common and vulgar observation," the social scientist, unlike his colleague in the natural sciences, will get results more slowly. His task of gathering all the materials needed for his work is actually the more difficult one.

Mosca grants that this sounds like a highly paradoxical conclusion. After all, the social facts happen under our very nose; they are, more or less, our own direct concern and therefore ought to furnish us much better means of observation than the natural phenomena. And yet we find: it is not so. The natural scientist is able to rely on method and experiment. Whether his data be derived from sense impression or calculation, he can always study them; whereas "the study of social phenomena demands an age-long experience well informed about the vicissitudes of the various human societies; it presupposes the ability to distinguish which of these events is really important, substantial, and worthy of our attention..." We are, as Hegel wants us to do, to sift out that which is "real" from the mere mass of the "actual."

Now, until recently, "the authors in the social sciences did not possess the necessary vast historic knowledge," for the simple reason that the necessary information was not yet available to them. They had to make do with the scraps of superficial and distorted records, mostly limited to the orbit of the Graeco-Roman and Judaeo-Christian traditions. "If they distinguished themselves, it was due to their acumen, ingenuity, and zest" rather than to the solidity of their assumptions. Giambattista Vico, in whom Mosca might have found an at least partly congenial mentor (the history of all mankind is written in the record of its man-made institutions)—Vico is curtly dismissed in an aside as "an unquestionable genius" whose theory of cycles is, however, unacceptable, since it depends "on the scant historical knowledge available in the author's time." In the same breath, Mosca censures Montesquieu for over-emphasizing, from the same lack of reliable data, the importance of climatic influences; and Rousseau had, "in addition to his lack of positive knowledge, a defective sense of reality; his mind was made up of the paradox." [13]

But not all this ignorance was caused by lack of information; to an at least equal degree it must be blamed on human prejudice. At a time when the churches had long ceased to obstruct the research of the natural scientists, the social scientist's mind was still faced with deeply ingrained human prejudices which had managed to survive. Mosca cites approvingly an utterance of "Stuart-Mill" from his *Political Economy*: each epoch succumbs to some major error, the absurdity of which becomes apparent to anyone a generation later. But until then, nobody remains immune from it unless he makes an extraordinary effort, straining to the utmost his intelligence and courage.[14]

The prospects for a comprehensive and objective social science would seem rather poor so far. But that is not at all Mosca's conclusion. He suddenly turns optimist: "If no true social science did exist up to the present moment, it can now come into being." If not in the nineteenth century, then in the twentieth. No longer could the failure of the social sciences be blamed upon a lack of correct information. We moderns know not merely all or most of what there is to be known about Greek, Roman, medieval history, we also have at our disposal now the histories of the oriental monarchies, of China, India, and Japan; we have modern archeology, prehistoriography, ethnography, and furthermore, philology to help us in our task. "The facts are all there, we do have the knowledge; all that remains for us to do is to act in accordance with the saying: 'He who has eyes, let him see!'" [15]

The question of whether or not Gaetano Mosca stands convicted of the positivist heresy will be disputed in a later chapter.[16] At this point it looks bad for him. Had he not, with complete approval, cited Mill on human prejudice? What made him suddenly hope that the fading century or the as yet unborn one would produce a different kind of humanity? At any rate, it would have to be a humanity receptive to the "extraordinary efforts" of those who can muster enough intellectual strength and courage to establish the true facts of life. The older Mosca will no longer be so confident as to believe that his new message will be received as glad tidings. The young Mosca still sounds rather like a latter-day illuminato from the eighteenth century who, like Voltaire, dismissed the past as a tragicomedy of error and blind passion. Miraculously, it will make way for the age of reason. The mists hiding the truth will dissolve under the piercing scrutiny of scientific observation. Historic facts will no longer be in dispute and can, therefore, be subjected, like any physical data, to objective analysis. The same applies to political science—provided, of course, we first get rid of the master superstition that has so long dominated that field: the Aristotelian classification of governments.

The Argument

In zoology, Mosca submits, animals are not classified according to the color of their skin or to their weight, but on the basis of their anatomic structure. Likewise, plants are not classified as fruit-bearing or non-fruit-bearing, but again according to their structure. He goes on:

Now, when we come to the classification of governments which goes back to Aristotle and is still in our day universally accepted: into democratic, aristocratic, or monarchic types, depending on whether supreme authority rests with a majority of citizens, a limited class, or else is vested in a single person—then we should expect that classification also to be based on the most important, the essential characteristics of government and not on mere trivialities and appearances.

Suppose, asks Mosca, we were able to show that this time-honored scheme is inspired by altogether superficial criteria? And suppose further we could, "without replacing it by another scheme, nevertheless establish other, much more substantial and significant criteria." [17]

This bold bid is followed by the celebrated formulation which appears here in the *Teorica* for the first time:

In all regularly constituted societies in which something called a government exists, we find that all authority is being exercised in the name of the entire people, or of an aristocracy, or of a single sovereign ... but besides that fact we find unfailingly another: the ruling class or, rather, those who hold and exercise the public power, will be always a minority, and below them we find a numerous class of persons who do never, in any *real* sense, participate in government but merely submit to it: these may be called the ruled class.[18]

Compare with this the following passage from the *Elementi*, eleven years later:

> In all societies . . . two classes appear—a class that rules and a class that is ruled. The first class, always the less numerous, performs all political functions, monopolizes power, and enjoys the advantages that power brings, whereas the second, the more numerous class, is directed and controlled by the first, in a manner that is now more or less legal, now more or less arbitrary and violent . . . [19]

The latter statement is much more inclusive (covering both constitutional and arbitrary power systems); it has more nuance and is more elegantly written. But essentially it does not go beyond the older statement. Nor was there any need for it: both formulations represent first propositions, a device to sort out things for further, more elaborate analysis. What may be called Mosca's First Law of the Ruling Class is in itself the opposite of startling. Mosca himself tries to avoid giving the impression that he has made an earth-shaking discovery. He hastens to observe that mankind has, intuitively, always been aware of the fact that The Few rule The Many. We speak, Mosca reminds us in another writing, of "those on high, who have their finger in the pie, who make the good and the bad weather." [20]

Yet the harmlessness of Mosca's formulation is deceptive. The truism has a disturbing implication—disturbing not only the Aristotelian, but the willing follower of Gaetano Mosca. The source of trouble is located, quite innocuously, in the very middle of the statement where the author says that all authority is being exercised *in the name of* whoever has the legal claim to sovereignty. And that, looking at first sight like a reassertion of, and a concession to, the old Aristotelian triad, is in truth its *absolute* negation. Mosca will have none of it. His ruling class, it seems, is not even identical with Aristotle's aristocracy.

Now that is startling. One can understand why he excluded the democratic demos from his definitions, since, according to our author, the majority never rules. Nor is there any real need to question his contention that, with rare exceptions, the monarchic power, even of the formally most absolute regime, is exercised not by the ruler himself, but by others in his name.[21]

But why insist on aristocracy, too, ruling by name only? There seems to be no reason to include it among the rois fainéants. Aristocracies are usually not very large; nobody ever heard of an aristocratic majority of the people. Why then not simply contract Aristotle's three types of rule into one and say that all democracies and monarchies are in fact aristocracies—no matter whether they be of plebeian or noble origin? Did Mosca's pen just slip? But there is nothing casual about the whole passage; it has all the earmarks of a carefully composed and pondered piece. The answer to our question must be sought elsewhere.

When we speak of aristocracy, we may employ the term in a pragmatic sense and label certain groups aristocratic because they effectively control the state. In that case, we do not inquire into their origins or into their specific claim to power; we are satisfied with the accomplished fact that certain people are in charge, whom we will, for convenient reasons, call aristocrats, although they may not at all act the part. That will be particularly true of a new aristocracy; in that case, there is reason to expect that, even if the fathers are still boors, the children will, with the appurtenances of aristocratic privilege, acquire, if not the virtues then at least the attitudes of their exalted status. But that expectation is already influenced by the traditional interpretation of the term "aristocratic."

The older notion, the by far more influential one, is the reverse of the pragmatic view: aristocratic status is not understood as the mere attribute of rulership; on the contrary, the right to rule is conceived as an attribute of aristocracy, as a claim, absolute or relative, to power based on some true or imaginary excellence. This is, of course, precisely the view which the Stagirite took in his Politics, and one should think that Mosca would reject it with the rest of Aristotle's theory of government. But we shall learn, to our surprise, that this is not the case. Occasionally, Mosca will feel the attraction of the power theory of politics; he may be said to straddle both interpretations. But he is not, consciously, a trimmer. It is just that he is not a pragmatist.

And though his anti-Aristotelian bark will prove to be worse than his bite, our author has no use for Aristotle's aristocracy. That may have been personal whim or mere oversight. But I think not. The ruling class, in Gaetano Mosca's definition, cannot be equated with any old or new aristocracies, and for good reason. It is argued at some length and with considerable power of conviction: Mosca starts out by observing sensibly that under primitive conditions, in a savage tribe, a strong man is quite likely to emerge and to impose his regiment on the community (the author obviously does not refer to primitive, but to postprimitive, small-scale society). However, in a state comprising millions of inhabitants such a thing would be quite impossible. Now, Mosca's Law applies precisely to the latter case, to a "populous, orderly, and civilized human society."

But granted our exceptional man could propel himself, in an unusual situation, into a place situated centrally enough to serve him as a pivot from which to set the entire vast and complex machine of government in motion, "that machine would still not be identical with him but be a human organism determined by a multitude of historical and social factors which a single man could neither create nor radically modify."

The same is true of "democratic" states; there too "a governmental machine is bound to be in existence," which machine will again "naturally" be composed of a minority in charge of all activities of government.[22] In consequence:

> That special class of persons forms the government, and it is in that class entirely ... The masses, the majority, to be sure, furnish [that class] with the means by which it sustains and justifies its action, and they do so either voluntarily, because they see the benefits that flow from it, or else they do it under duress.

In any case, the impact of the dominant minority is irresistible, and that is due to two unquestionable facts of social human nature:

> Superior moral fibre will in the long run prevail over superior numbers and brute force; and, secondly, far more important yet less noted than the first: an organized minority, acting in concert, will forever triumph over a disorganized majority of people without common will or impulse.[23]

The indebtedness to Machiavelli is too obvious to need special emphasis. We note for future reference that Mosca's dominant minority owes its position to its higher moral caliber. But we note also that the moral superiority of the elite needs, in order to become effective, a collective form: *organization*. Whether the morality of the elite is, in the author's view, a mere effect of organized existence, that is, an *esprit de corps* distinct from individual moral qualities, or whether he believes that moral superiority explains the irresistible strength of all organized minorities, explains the power of organization—all that remains to be seen. For the time being, Mosca confines himself to listing the names by which the ruling classes of all ages and civilizations were known to the majority of subjects. Whether these paid homage to the barons, clergymen, and communal officials in the Middle Ages, to the bureaucrats and courtiers of the age of absolutism, to the mandarins in China, to the samurai and daimios in Japan, to the Tchinovniks of old Russia; whether their betters were the English landlords and capitalists or, in America, the "Politicians" (*sic*)—always and everywhere did the power to dispose and to exercise authority and to assume responsibility rest with a special class. Its elements may vary according to place and time, but that class will invariably confront and control the mass of the governed: "This special class we are hereafter going to call the political class." [24]

The question of why Mosca refused to equate his political class with Aristotle's aristocracy seems to resolve itself, although our author is not very helpful in the process. His list of "ruling classes" is, to say the least, confusing. No American will agree that his "Politicians" constitute the ruling class—assuming that there is, in this republic, something like a ruling class in Mosca's sense. The Chinese mandarin class fits the definition better, and so does the Russian Tchin. The English "landlords and capitalists" will hardly do. The influence of Marx seems to have misled Mosca momentarily. Marx indeed could identify both social groups as ruling classes. But those classes never were, in their totality, identical with the political "machine," the *organized* minority of Mosca's political class. Nor will the medieval barons, clergymen, and city consuls qualify. The feudal system lacked, as Mosca will inform us later on, precisely the co-ordinating powers of large-scale administration. Perhaps he thought of the feudal lords gathered in parliament, or of the continental great estates deliberating with the king or emperor. But Mosca's entire emphasis is, at this point, so much on integrated action (alien to the feudal age), the argument so intent on executive controls and mechanisms, that this explanation hardly satisfies.

Inconsistencies aside, the meaning of the definition is quite obvious. What Mosca tries to say is that his political class is, as a rule, distinct from, although of course in most cases (but less frequently than one would think) derived from, the traditionally so-called ruling classes. Mosca might have spared us—and himself—a great deal of trouble had he only spoken of the ruling classes in the Marxian sense as upper classes, thus distinguishing between them and his own ruling class which constitutes the *organized* core of the upper strata, exercising control as, or else over, the government. (He later does distinguish between an upper and a lower stratum of the political class, but that is something else again, because both strata, the first very small, the second larger, do partake in government, in a directing and executive capacity, respectively.)

If this is so, any member of an upper class—a baron or entrepreneur—will hold superior rank in his society, but he will not, in Mosca's meaning, necessarily govern. The French aristocracy which did not meet the rising power of its first peer, the king, with a tightly knit organization will be overwhelmed by his machine, composed of commoners, in the belated struggles of the *Fronde*. Where the aristocrats were in control, in Venice for example, they had to distill from their own class the tightly integrated group of actual rulers. But even had the political class of that city coincided with the total number of Venetian nobles, Mosca would have still insisted that the actual power of the dominant minority was based on its organization, not on its status. A nobility could hobnob with its government, it could use pull, exert all kinds of pressure, but it would still not necessarily belong to Gaetano Mosca's ruling class.

Power then is always power organized. It would be going too far to proclaim that power *is* organization, but unless I have entirely misread our author, there cannot be, according to him, any lasting power without at least a modicum of what Weber has called "bureaucratization." This is merely one more way of indicating what we know already: Mosca's Law is applicable only to societies that have reached advanced stages of civilization.[25]

The Genesis of Ruling Classes

So far we have been shown that elites do exist. But how do they come into being? Mosca appears baffled by that question. "How they are formed, or, rather, how they have been formed, we generally do not know." He blames this ignorance on the scarcity of records left behind by earlier societies. About the formative stage of the Graeco-Roman city-state and the postmedieval nation-state we know a great deal more, but still not enough to advance a general theory of elite origins. What we can ascertain, with reasonable certainty, is just this: "Brutal force, necessity rather than rational consideration or free will prompted the aggregation of men into great societies."

We are most anxious to hear more about the role of force as the great unifier, but for reasons which will only emerge slowly, Mosca is unwilling to say more about the subject and proceeds to state that integration was a gradual process moving from initial anarchy to first small and then ever larger groupings. "A large group always arises out of several small ones. There is the constant tendency of these small aggregations to reconstitute themselves whenever a large social group dissolves—and that occurs particularly in the case that the autonomy of the old subgroup has not been completely abrogated."

Again, we note for future reference that Mosca, known for his view that the best state will be one in which the "social forces" are in balance and do not lose their autonomy completely—that the same Mosca, at the outset of his writing career, seemed to frown upon autonomy and seemed to equate the articulation of society in vigorous small groups with anarchy. But lest his reader assume that he holds with that fabulous creature, the solitary anarchist of the old contract theory, Mosca, as it behooved the social scientist of his age, reassures us that the evolution of the human race starts with the group. More specifically, it starts with the family, a unit composed of "at least ten members." [26]

This figure might suggest that Mosca follows Gumplowicz, who argued against Aristotle that the family could not possibly have existed "prior in time" to the state, since, as the Stagirite himself assumes, the family already contained slaves, the management of whom required the prior institutionalization, legal and political, of slavery: "Hence the existence of a family of this kind presupposes the existence of the state." And that means, *pace* Aristotle, the state prior not only "by logic" but also "in time." [27]

But of that there is no trace in the *Teorica*. Mosca is satisfied that the original family nucleus already reveals the division into dominant and dominated elements—the dualism which, by the process of slow integration, leads from smaller groupings to the supergroup, the state. The family heads band together in the primitive organization, which develops, through millennia, until it becomes Mosca's political or ruling class. In the beginning came the patriarchs, then the stern heroes, and then the aristocrats, our author might have written, quoting Vico. Indeed, he says something very similar: "As social aggregations take form among the vicissitudes of strife, the strong, the rulers and chiefs, draw together and thus come to form the ruling, or political, class, while the others, the ruled elements, melt into a mass of subdued and governed individuals." [28]

There is in this passage still no hint that the position of "the strong, the rulers" might not be merely an incident, but *the direct result* of "strife" as the "efficient" and not merely the "material" cause of power. But that would make war and conquest, the subjection of one human unit by another, the root of the state and ruling classes. It would be, in one word, Gumplowicz, not Mosca, whose "strife" has merely the effect of making the strong ones close ranks; the ruling class arises from within one social group instead of being imposed on it from without. And there is, certainly, enough historic evidence available to show that some, if not all, ruling classes did arise that way: through an internal process of elitist integration.[29]

The question poses itself why our author, dedicated antisocialist that he was, chose to adopt the socialist, specifically Marxist, theory of class differentiation after having rejected out of hand the conquest doctrine of the origin of social classes as developed by the bourgeois thinker, Gumplowicz. The answer to that puzzle has to be deferred; all we can say here is that Mosca does not recognize brute force as the prime mover of civilization. The struggle for predominance is, as he sees it, merely incidental to the union and solidification of elite spearheads already in existence. For him, power—at this stage in any case—is not the collective product of a social process which endows the leadership of a few men with seemingly outstanding strength; rather it is leadership that seems to generate the social, the collective power. The Few are not The Strong because they rule—no, The Few rule because they are The Strong. Or even better: they can be so strong because they are so few. Once more, the essence of the political class is not status, but organization. Ruling bodies are co-ordinated groups. But the consolidation of minorities has a disintegrating effect upon the majorities: the larger group from which a new elite has issued loses its old solidarity; it dissolves into individual atoms. Later Mosca will inform us that this mass of individuals remains the source of ever new articulations (meaning new elites); for the time being he seems content with establishing a clear dichotomy between those who are subjects and those who are merely objects of decision-making power.

2

FORCES AND FORMULAS

The fusion of the leader elements may remain incomplete; in that case, the authority of the political class will remain precarious. Individual strong-man action will go on in force, whereas when and where integration is complete, it will be truly "irresistible." The charisma of one man or a number of men gives way to routinization, to use the expression of Max Weber. In our author's terminology: the coming of age of the political class signifies the end of personal rule.

By what is it replaced? Mosca could, with Rousseau, say: by the rule of law. But he is not yet ready for that answer. He first introduces us to still another of his major concepts when he observes that the dominant minority "absorbs a great many of the existing social forces." [1] He will presently explain the term "social force" as comprehending all pursuits and interests of social relevance at any given stage of cultural development. Such qualities as best meet the demand of a civilization will be at a premium. In a primitive society, the preferential type will be the able fighting man and hunter. In more settled times, it will become the feudal lord, and still later, the landlord. Long before that, he and his like will have found a rival—

41

and an ally—in the servant of The Lord of Peace who ministers to the emotional and spiritual needs of the people, incidentally protecting them, to some extent, against the men of war. Lastly, mercantilization and urbanization will bring into play another "social force": the middle class.

To say, as Mosca does, that organized minorities "absorb" the social forces is only another way of stating that each social force tends to assert itself in the perennial struggle for predominance. If there is not more than one social force that matters, it will furnish the entire assemblage that constitutes the ruling class. If there is a plurality of potent social forces, the political class will do well to mirror at least those that cannot be repressed. If they do not find recognition, the political class, not being fully representative, is likely to lose power, since unabsorbed social interests are apt to find their own "strong men," prepared to challenge yesterday's monopoly of power.

In that situation, the political class will discover that repressive measures do not work and must be supplemented by persuasion. More important still, the rulers will find it advisable not to repulse but to attract new personnel. Mosca is quite explicit on these points, although some of his early formulations give the wrong impression: as if all activity took place exclusively within the ruling class, as if power had, like water, only one direction, downward. But that is not Mosca's view at all, not even in his early work. The power flow as seen in the *Teorica* is clearly circular; its thrust is channeled and its upward pressure has to pass through locks impeding its velocity, but there is never a suggestion that it ought to be dammed up.

Mosca finds almost solemn words to declare that whoever is a member of the ruling class must never be coerced by those above him. Free co-operation within the entire controlling group is the condition for the proper exercise of power. This sounds like a mere reminder of Plato's ironical remark that there must be honor even among thieves.[2] But there is more to it: "Not constraint, but man's natural passion for power and such advantages as adhere to it must be and is the incentive for entering the dominating class." [3]

Unless this is a mere slip of the pen, Mosca's ideal ruling class is not to be construed as a closed corporation but as open toward and accessible to members from among the dominated masses. To say ·

that the members of the elite are not to be coerced because they cannot function if coerced is one thing; advocating freedom from constraint of the elite as a means for attracting members of the nonelite, another. The idea, undeveloped in the *Teorica*, is a preview of Pareto's doctrine of the "circulation of elites." [4] And closely following the concept and connected with it we discover Mosca's version of the myth.

He links it to the well-known fiction of the social contract and is willing to find some slight merit in that notion. It makes it easier to explain and justify submission to political authority if we assume to have authorized it originally. Or we may hit upon some other formula in order to equate authority with superiority. We may find that the powers that be rule because they have some moral claim to rule: they are, or are assumed to be, in the literal sense of the word, our betters. Every one of them does, or should in any case, possess "a merit or a quality to which the group of which he is a part attributes great importance"—and the recognition by the group comes mainly, perhaps, because not all people have, or can have, superior quality. That moral eminence being one of the distinguishing marks of the ruling class, our acceptance or rejection of that class will be dependent on the evidence of or absence of it.[5]

But since that excellence is varying in character, depending on the period and the country, Mosca decides, just like Aristotle, that "no single criterion for the forming of, and the admission to, the ruling class can be established." The decisive factor is the paramount need of society at a specific stage of its development. Put differently: the specific "virtue" of the elite will be its ability to perform an essential social function, which, in turn, will be that of the most important *social force* or forces of society. The author is now ready to explain that term at length.

Physical prowess is the indispensable characteristic of elites in a civilization just emerging from horde anarchy. The more the habits of the group become refined, the more brute force loses significance. Nor must we confuse, as Mosca takes great trouble to inform us, primitive pugnaciousness with "military valor." Even savage man bows not so much to the material superiority as to the intellect and resoluteness of the masters. It is in those qualities that we must seek the explanation for authority, and for its correlates, obedience and respect.

The growing need for intellectual and moral nourishment begets a second social force and its particular elite: the clergy. It soon occupies the seats of power alongside of, or even ahead of, the military, who by now have settled down as the lords temporal. And as the market places for their manors graduate to cities, the third social force develops: money power, commerce. While there can be no doubt that in the dawn of society "the sole means to acquire and to preserve a fortune was the sword," in later times the causal nexus becomes less one-sided, and we can no longer say with certainty whether it is wealth that unlocks the gate to the manor of the noble, or whether riches accrue from armed force and with the riches, power. In a certain period of Graeco-Roman antiquity, "the wealthy classes furnished the main forces for the war and simultaneously controlled the state." In that connection, Mosca notes that the Athenian rich served in the cavalry and heavy infantry (as hoplites), while the middle class fought as light infantry (the peltasts), a branch of the armed services which prior to the second century B.C. was unimportant. The poorest citizens, we are told, were excluded from all military service. But, as Aristotle knew, the poor of the Piraeus district manned the ships, and they were "wholly democratic." [6]

As the economic factor asserts itself more and more, the military class becomes much less important. In times of trouble it may regain, for a while, its previous role, but on the whole our author, member of a generation for whom the Napoleonic wars were a thing of the remote past and our own world wars undreamed-of, is convinced that in his rich and civilized society the frequent wars of the past had become "an absolute impossibility."

If one says that today wealth is the main criterion of admission to the ruling class, that statement must be qualified at once to read that wealth is merely a prerequisite to more important attributes. Only insofar and inasmuch as it enables its possessor to acquire the culture and the knowledge necessary to direct a modern state can economic affluence and independence assume the proportions of social force. As our author dryly adds: "Those qualities are always much more easily acquired by a rich man." [7]

But, he says, whether the prerogative to rulership be based on birth (descent from the strong men) or wealth (inheritance), the ruling class will try to buttress and perpetuate its claims to eminence by legislation. The implicit or explicit purpose of all such enactments, civil or religious, is always the same: the permanent exclusion of the lowly born from the lists of the elect few.

Permanent exclusion? Did Mosca's pen slip after all when, a few pages earlier, he had written of the recruiting device "that must be and is the incentive for entering the dominating class"? No, because the whole context of that passage clearly refers to an *advanced* social stage. Closed ruling classes belong to the past, to the beginnings of civilization. Having said that much, Mosca is once more presented with the fatal question: how did those first ruling classes manage to establish their monopoly of privilege? Emerging from the anarchy of posttribal societies (for that seems to be Mosca's starting point), the primitive elite should have shown the characteristics of an open rather than a restricted corporation, with restrictive measures gradually affecting the original competitive selection.[8] Instead, we are told that the movement went from closed to open. Surely everything would have been simpler for our author if he had explained the origin of ruling classes and the state from conquest.

Mosca almost does so this time, but not quite. He is embarrassed, he equivocates and hedges when replying that the coming into being of a ruling class must be ascribed to the conditions of "primitive times, or to the fact that the process of social aggregation started with the submission of an inferior race to a superior one, or to some other reasons . . ."

The ghost of Gumplowicz still haunts him and cannot be laid to rest.

The ruling class, once it has legalized its privileges, may enjoy them undisturbed for a long time, "provided it retains the qualities through which it had achieved its power." In that case, the legal limitations will be willy-nilly acquiesced to by the subjects and will be resented only by "the one or other isolated individual who, though personally qualified for entry into the political class, finds himself ostracized by law." However, sooner or later that situation is bound to change:

When the aptitude to command and exercise political control is no longer the sole possession of the legal rulers but has become common enough among other people, when outside the ruling class another class has formed which finds itself deprived of power though it does have the capacity to share in the responsibilities of government—then that law has become an obstacle in the path of an elemental force and must, by one way or another, go.[9]

There are three things remarkable about this statement. One is its Marxist undertone: the striking similarity between the "obstacle" and the "integument [which finally] is burst asunder." Likewise, Pareto's "circulation of elites" makes here another of its prenatal appearances. Most startling perhaps is Mosca's avowal that a *whole class* other than the one in command may possess the necessary qualities for rule. But Mosca is, of course, not thinking of an entire social class in the conventional sense of the term but merely of its spearhead, crystallized into a new political class ready to take over. The French have a word for such a group: *les ministrables.*

But how could they become a crowd? If we take Mosca literally, then a ruling class which, to use Oswald Spengler's term, is still "in form," should be perfectly able to contain the commoners behind the hurdle of privilege, so that their superior individuals would remain few and far between. Why should that situation ever change? Why should "the aptitude to command" ever "become common among other people," unless we throw all elitist caution to the winds and assume that talent is more common after all than we had previously believed. The likelihood, not mentioned yet by Mosca, that a ruling elite resting on its oars will become decadent might help us to explain why the old ruling class is shrinking; it would not account for the growth of an out-elite.

But all this is mere quibbling. All Mosca has to do is to fall back upon his theory of social forces and assert that they are generally able to produce their own elites, no matter what repression, legal or illegal, the old rulers may resort to. Indeed, Mosca does say something of the sort, if only in a half-hearted aside. Remarking on the methods by which the patricians of the medieval German communes and the oligarchs of Venice blocked the access to their own charmed circle, Mosca writes: "When a class contains all the dominating elements of a society, it may act in that fashion with impunity; yet, in the course of centuries, it will have difficulty in keeping dominating elements from forming outside the existing ruling class and in excluding them legally from power without stirring up a struggle." [10]

That struggle will be fought between the old elite which has ceased to contain all *ministrables*, and new social interests which the "ins" have failed, or refused, to make their own while there was still time.

The Unwritten Law

The fall of legal barriers does not make possible right away that open ruling class implied in Mosca's thesis. Privileges based on birth will linger on long after their official abolition. By birth our author here means wealth—the useful contacts and the easy access to a plethora of information which is either totally denied or only made available to the poor at a disproportionate expense of time and effort.

In Mosca's day—and in this second half of the twentieth century as well—"we find many instances in which elective offices have constantly remained the property of one and the same family." To characterize that fact, Mosca makes use of the happy term of "infeudation." [11] Political jobs, and not only those bestowed by the electorate, become attached to certain "dynasties" by the right of heredity. The same names recur regularly, generation after generation—in the rosters of the diplomatic services particularly. Someone said that it is possible to write an English history by just consulting a few dozen chronicles of English families. The same is true almost to the same degree of the French Republic, where two family clans virtually owned the French Foreign Office before 1940, and of Mosca's Italy. As for the United States, with its deep distrust of Harvard men in high positions, one has only to evoke such names as Adams, Biddle, Holmes, Hoover, Lodge, La Follette, Taft, and Roosevelt, to mention a few families of national fame, in order to see Mosca's point.[12]

In the *Teorica* nothing is said to indicate the author's attitude toward that "infeudation" process in our democratic age. But we would guess that he looked on it sympathetically, even if we did not know it from his later works. A decade later he will repeat almost verbatim what we have just quoted, and add: "Qualification for important office ... is much more readily acquired when one has had a certain familiarity with it from childhood ... There is no eliminating that ... which the French call the advantage of *positions déjà prises.*" If this statement still has a factual ring to it, the laudatory note is frankly sounded in the second volume of the *Elementi*:

> It is not so certain ... that it would be altogether beneficial to the collectivity to have every advantage of birth eliminated in the struggle for membership in the ruling class and for high position in the social hierarchy. If all individuals could participate in the scramble on an equal footing, struggle would be intensified to the point of frenzy ... It may very well be that certain intellectual and moral qualities ... require, if they are to develop and exert their influence, that the same families should hold fairly high social positions for a number of generations.[13]

The democratic reader may not take too kindly to this notion, which, however, is essential to our author's outlook. Elites do not grow overnight, they need an incubation period which lasts longer than one generation. Since to Mosca the well-functioning of the elites is synonymous with the health of society, he is naturally inclined to look with favor upon any tendency that would slow down class mobility in our fast-moving time, and with disfavor upon any measures such as would "intensify the struggle to the point of frenzy." For instance, Gaetano Mosca was quite worried about the electoral and other reforms promulgated by the British Liberals before World War I, confiding to his son: "The English move too fast." Even the one and only ruling class which for so long had managed to absorb all comers without much harm to tradition seemed to have lost its firm touch. That boded ill for England's future.[14]

It is rather strange that Mosca, with his group concept of social evolution, should describe the "scramble" for high position in a thoroughly democratized society as one between "individuals." Does that mean that in a highly mobile and exceedingly competitive civilization groups and classes would forfeit their *raison d'être* and dissolve into their social atoms? One should think that, on the contrary, the very "frenzy" of the struggle would make for an even stronger and more rigidly enforced group solidarity or, rather for a multitude of such group solidarities, as the means of protection for the frantic, frightened individual. This Mosca did not see. Moreover, by describing the presumed effects of maximum acceleration in individualistic terms, he deprived himself of the chance to view that extreme situation as a competition between too many too-fast-moving elites. That task was, much later, performed by Mannheim.[15] Mosca's failure to cope with the problem is, of course, excusable. When he began to write, the necessary data were not yet available; by the time industrial society showed all the symptoms of a mass neurosis, Mosca's writing days were all but over. There remains the fact that the *Teorica* contains the materials from which others could construct the necessary framework for a study of elite formation in an open mass society.

For the study of that kind of society and nothing else is Mosca's intent when he introduces, after the military and economic criteria, achievement, personal "merit" as the "ultimate principle determining the recruitment for the political class." That term comprises all the special aptitudes enabling a man to discharge a public function properly: the quality of his knowledge, his intelligence, his character. Personal merit thus understood becomes the badge of admission to the ruling class in any markedly mature society: "And that is so not merely because in such society certain sentiments of social justice and equality, which by the way are innate in man, have become stronger, but also, and mainly, because the technical and scientific elements are now more developed."

Mosca's categorical aside about the innate sentiments of man, far from being a mere lapse into an older way of thinking, represents his true conviction: we shall see that social justice in his view is not, as one would assume from a casual perusal of his *Ruling Class*, the mere codification of a given power situation ("balance of the social forces"), but the sum of moral notions shared by all. Mosca's "justice" is a unitary concept, it is that which cannot be created by one group alone because it is the joint possession and creation of the whole. This is Mosca, the moralist. As pragmatist, however, he explains the increased prestige of the trained specialist from technological rather than moral reasons. Now that managerial know-how has become a must for an ever-growing sector of the ruling class, wealth, property alone will no longer provide the key to public office. They will, at least "to some extent be counterbalanced by another social force: knowledge."

Since it is easier to visualize a "social force" in terms of people, we will substitute for the word knowledge, the large, motley host of civil servants and white-collar workers, office managers and engineers, scholars and scientists. All, whether they aspire to high office or only to a routine job, must now undergo some kind of training that may last from six months to six years; they must produce more and more certificates attesting to the various "aptitudes" mentioned by Mosca. Their character and, lately even their associations, their opinions, all come under public scrutiny.

"Knowledge," the common denominator for the new social force, has indeed become the synonym for power. But it is too diversified, too specialized to give the New Clerks the distinctive character of a new class. Mosca seems to disown that offspring of his own thought, Burnham's doctrine of the Managerial Revolution, when he cautions against overrating the power potential of the new men of achievement. They labor under handicaps more severe than their predecessors on the social scene. As long as they still have to fight for recognition, "it is difficult if not impossible to see how wealth could lose its importance altogether." The reasons are too obvious to require restatement. Mosca adds that, in the long run, the new intelligentsia will, by hard work and will power, overcome the odds of poverty. More important is another handicap that slows down their ascendancy:

Personal achievement ... has the special trait that it does not impose itself of its own accord; it does not, as is the case with wealth or birth, become an active force by just existing: on the contrary, it becomes valuable only if it has already, in a more or less official way, found recognition.[16]

That is to say that the intelligentsia is, and is bound to remain (for some time? forever?) a subsidiary element of the political class. But that fact hardly detracts from the importance of the new elite of merit. For it is precisely from its ranks that the decisive second layer of the dominant class is composed.

We can read in the *Elementi*:

The Two Strata

In the last analysis . . . the stability of any political organism depends on the level of morality, intelligence and activity that this second stratum has attained; and this soundness is commonly the greater in proportion as a sense of the collective interests of nation or class succeeds in exerting pressure on the individual ambitions or greeds of the members of this class.

This concept does not yet appear clear-cut in the *Teorica*, but two assumptions already stand out: First, a small group of top leaders may lay claim to legal sovereignty in the state. In actuality, however, the small group depends on the skills and the good will of the larger subgroup, which is clearly more than a mere tool, since the continuity of the regime is predicated on the functioning of the secondary elite. If that substratum should break up, the top regime could no longer function either, although the disappearance of the top group would not necessarily result in disaster. Its personnel could probably be replaced from the reservoir of trained administrators and technicians of the lower stratum. As the author puts it in the *Elementi*: "Any intellectual or moral deficiencies in this second stratum, accordingly, represent a graver danger to the political structure . . . than the presence of similar deficiencies in the few dozen persons who control the workings of the state machine."

The higher stratum can be compared to the "generals and staff" of an army, and the lower stratum "to the officers who lead the rank and file in person under fire." There is no doubt in Mosca's mind which of the two groups would turn out to be the more important one if, "due to some unlikely accident," the one or the other "were to disappear at one stroke." His judgment echoes Saint-Simon's illustrious dictum which so deeply shocked the censor of post-Napoleonic France.[17]

In no sense, therefore, could Mosca's second stratum be considered secondary in importance to the first. Its officers do not merely implement the rules, they more than help in making and interpreting decisions. It is they who have to make those policies concrete and palatable to the public. They, and not the top men, are exposed to public counteraction: to that "pressure on their individual ambitions or greed," as Mosca put it, and to public censure of their public acts as well.

Second, that public reaction will be all the more effective as the subelite stands in a much closer relationship to the ruled people than to its superiors in the higher ruling stratum. At first glance this contention does not seem to be borne out by the appearances—particularly in countries where the administrative class has a special social status unknown in those countries which are democracies. But even in those which are not, the public functionaries are recruited for the most part from the people and remain, to some extent, susceptible to the pulls of their old milieu. To be sure, their new function and environment will weaken the old influences. But to some degree, at least those members of the subelite who come in daily contact with the people may be said, in an informal way, to represent them.

But how well? That will depend on the mode of selection. The importance of that factor is already recognized in the *Teorica*, although, again, spelled out only a decade later in the *Elementi*.

Civil service examinations, with those on high setting the standards and passing judgment, are one possible way of determining merit. Mosca finds the most perfect example of that method in prerevolutionary China. The mandarin class was recruited on the basis of elaborate entrance tests; each subsequent promotion was conditional on further stiff examinations. "China," Mosca writes three decades before Sun Yat-sen's republic, "is the country in which the criterion of achievement is most rigorously applied. If it does not yield the best possible results, the reason is assuredly not any lack of consequence and logic, but perhaps, so to speak, the very excess of these qualities." He was to write, in the same caustic vein, of democratic institutions that "they may be able to endure for some time yet if our *apparent* democracy is not fatally carried away by logic, its worst enemy." [18]

His second example, relegated for good reasons to a footnote, is the Russian Tchin. The Tsarist bureaucrats ruled the state like the Chinese mandarins, but birth and wealth played a far greater role in the selection process than did merit.

In the central and occidental Europe of his day, our author finds the mandarin type of administration side by side with the plebiscitarian method of creating public servants, whereby anybody becomes eligible for a pre-established number of positions; his examining board is the voting public. Still another, third type of officialdom was, when our author wrote, peculiar to England, where important offices, especially on the borough and county levels, were filled by governmental appointment without any great concern for qualifications other than good reputation: "Thus in that country many functionaries are neither elected by the people, nor are they bureaucratic employees, but are selected on the strength of their social position." Mosca does not hide his sympathy for that old-fashioned type of government by unpaid notables who seemed to be "more independent of both local influences and the central power." It seems Mosca remained partial to that system long after it had gone out of use in England, for his later concept of a disinterested ruling class has many of the features that distinguished the old British squirearchy.[19]

He is now ready to sum up his findings. But that summary is much more than a mere restatement of the principles established in his short but seminal first chapter: As a rule, he says, advanced societies, in the selection of their ruling sets, do not rely upon a sole criterion to the exclusion of all others. There is hardly a limit to the number of potential combinations, which in turn depend on the degree of civilization a people has achieved. "These combinations represent the variable element," the constant factor being "that in all times and in all societies political functions are entrusted to a special class." Enumerating once more the three elements, military valor, economic energy, and intellectual training, Mosca adds that once intelligence has broken away from its ecclesiastic moorings, it "imposes itself independently, like a natural force." This conflicts with his earlier assessment of achievement as a social force "that does not impose itself on its own accord ... it does not become an active force by just existing." I know of no way to resolve this contradiction, the kind of thing which would never have marred the work of a more logical— but also perhaps lesser—mind.

To leave no doubt in our minds that his principles are valid under all conditions, Gaetano Mosca declares solemnly:

The political history of mankind through the ages, in all nations and civilizations, may be summarized under two headings: we have to consider, on the one hand, the degree of co-ordination that exists between the various political classes, the amount of resources they have concentrated in their hands, and the effective strength of their collective action; on the other hand, the various forces that make up these classes, the specific methods by which they impose their rule, their struggles and their clashes, their maneuvers, shifts, and deals.[20]

In the first part of this iron law the stress is on homogeneity, in the second part on diversity. The unitary and the pluralistic elements are complementary, two aspects of one and the same phenomenon. The balance, the particular way in which equilibrium is brought about, determines the dynamics which the ruling class seen as a unit will be able to display: "The mobility of human societies depends entirely upon the continuous change in the relationship of the two factors." On the interplay, the blending, of the unitary and the pluralistic tendencies depends the fate of states, "whether they shall grow in strength or weaken; [and] their domestic agitations and dissensions which, in the majority of cases, will have salutary consequences but may also rend the social fabric and lead to collapse and dissolution."

This is admirable, and it would be admirable even in an older man. There is only one thing to regret: that Mosca did not yet elaborate his statement. There is a great deal that could be said about the two last lines alone, which show such superb insight into the ambivalence of social process, into the importance of the agonistic element as a creative as well as disruptive force, into the need for a dynamic balance—all these problems Mosca will develop later as ramifications of his central theory.

A Real Need of Human Nature

Having almost reached the end of the expository section, Mosca, rather suddenly, brings up a further point. It turns out to be his concept of the "political formula," well known to all students of *The Ruling Class*.[21] Twenty years before Sorel coined the term "myth" to circumscribe the vague but forceful images which may inspire The Ruled,[22] Mosca formulated the myth of The Rulers:

No political class, however constituted, will say outright that it rules because...its members are the ones most fit to rule. Instead, that class will always try to justify its power on the ground of an abstraction which we shall call the political formula. To say that all officials derive their authority from the official sovereign, who, in turn, derives it from God, is to make use of a political formula; another version is expressed in the phrase that all power resides in the people.

The notion at once recalls Marx and his "class ideology," it is as old as Plato's golden lie. But something new is added, which, in a way, takes the sting out of the Marxian and Platonic formulations: "At first sight, we seem to be confronted by a palpable mystification. Even so, however, the political formula would have its *raison d'être*, its importance ... Well documented as a constant fact by history, it must respond to a true need of human nature."

Mosca's formula, then, would imply more than "false consciousness" and its reflections in the class-bound human mind. And it would not, like the myth of Plato's ruler or Pareto's "derivation," merely denote a pragmatic truth, "social utility." It would do all these things, but also it would seem to satisfy, or to have satisfied at some point in the past, a common hunger for objective truth, a psychological demand transcending interest. The chant of the French Revolution, *liberté, égalité, fraternité*, our author might have said, was, to be sure, well suited to the class ambitions of the bourgeoisie, but it rang equally true to the lower class *canaille*.

However, that would have been more than Mosca wished to say. Unlike Sorel, he does not use the myth as a tool of liberation from the shackles of determinism and materialism; facts are facts, and though the concept of the "formula" deserves close study, it does not have, Mosca says, the same importance as the principles of the political class and the social forces.

The "true need of human nature" is, contends our author, "man's wish to believe that it is easier to submit to an abstract principle than to another man, who rules him because he knows how to rule." And that wish to believe, in turn, is aided by man's natural capacity to believe something in the teeth of stubborn facts. In short, the "formula" successfully exploits human credulity, and the true need of human nature is to be deceived. That justifies the golden lie to some extent; social utility becomes social necessity. Whereas Sorel's myth soars above the facts of life, Mosca's has the function to make these facts palatable. Marx's "ideology" distorts the facts and twists them so that they may fit class interests, while Mosca's "formula" accepts facts and makes them endurable by a semantic change that helps our self-respect. Beyond that Mosca would not go; not for him to proclaim the primacy of thinking man over acting man. He recognizes that our need for "abstract principles" has had, or may have had, some real influence on the development of human institutions, but he stubbornly refuses, as we shall see, to acknowledge mind as the prime mover. He limits himself to observing the fact that, with advancing civilization, personal rule shows the tendency to change into the rule of law, but he will also show what a precarious thing that rule is.

A survey of political formulas that have been in use through the ages demonstrates that "there have been many of them. But they may be easily reduced to two main categories: those based on a supernatural belief, and those founded on a principle of at least apparent rationality." According to that scheme, the doctrine of popular sovereignty would be of the rational type. "But once the will of the people ceases to be the expression of majority opinion and is credited with the authority of divine will ... it enters the first category." In other words, the statement: "letting the majority decide is an expedient way of settling issues," Mosca would call rational; the statement: "the majority is always right because it voices the will of the people," irrational. It would have been far simpler had he distinguished between supernatural and secular justifications. For all "formulas" address themselves to feelings, though they may, in many instances, draw strength from pseudorational argumentations. Our faith in a "formula" is never based on its essential plausibility; its plausibility is based on the fact that we happen to have faith.

The ruling formula is not always an imposition (in the literal sense of the word); whatever ruling class is in control will use a myth, but it may be the creation of the subjects:

The political components of society are never very stable; they are undergoing a continuous change as the level of civilization and the socioeconomic conditions of a people alter. Now, with new elements forever ready to become part of the ruling class and pressing their claims under the emblem of a new formula, it is quite easy to infer the changes in the composition of the ruling class from changes in the formula.

Examination of the myth informing the ascendancy of a new elite is important for the recognition and analysis of social change, but it must never lead to the assumption that the myth, and the belief in it, has caused that change to come about. Mosca is extremely anxious to remind us that "it is not the political formula which determines the formation of the ruling class, but, on the contrary, the ruling class always adopts the formula most advantageous to its needs." [23]

The reader is struck by the close resemblance of this statement to the famous dictum of Karl Marx that "it is not the consciousness of men that determines their being, but, on the contrary, their social being that determines their consciousness." [24]

The impression that our author is much closer to his great foe than he thinks is reinforced by Mosca's rather scornful attack on the theory of "innate rights," which occurs at the very end of the first chapter. Forgetful of the fact that, only a few pages earlier, he has called "certain sentiments of social justice and equality . . . innate in man," Mosca calls innate rights "more hypotheses of our mind. What matters in the social sciences is not speculation about the rights which man ought to have . . . but rather the discovery of what man can, and does, accomplish . . . Only then we may proceed from the things man knows how to do to finding out how he could do them better . . ." [25]

The Doctrine of the Ruling Class—a Myth?

No doubt about it, innate rights and ideologies as well as formulas in general are relegated to auxiliary positions. Mosca is here at his most consistent. We refer the reader to the passage quoted earlier in which the author assigns to the intellectual and moral element a signal role within the ruling class (the priesthood sharing power with the knights) but insists that the really decisive factor is organization.[26] That view Mosca is going to maintain in both parts of the *Elementi*. It is only in the ultimate restatement of his doctrine, following the second volume of the *Elementi* by ten years, that a change of emphasis will become evident. There we will read that "in all human societies which have reached some degree of culture, one can find two distinct types of forces operating which assure cohesion: one is intellectual and moral, the other material."

That is a literal restatement of Saint-Simon, who taught, according to the same work, that "two powers exist in every organized society: one exercising intellectual and moral, the other material control." [27]

Clearly, Mosca, at the end of his career, no longer holds the view that morals and intelligence are secondary matters. He still does not say that intellectual and moral ingenuity takes precedence over material power in the make-up of the dominant minority. The ideological and the material merely fuse. It is not a reversal but the abolition of the previous order of rank that takes place. Implied, however, is the recognition of the fact that mental and material power ought not be treated as separate elements in the first place—not even for the purposes of scholarly ratiocination. Organization is itself an intellectual and moral feat. As Mosca will express it in the last part of *The Ruling Class*:

> It is useless to argue whether moral forces have outweighed material forces to a greater extent than material forces have used the moral in their own service ... Every moral force tries, as soon as it can, to acquire cohesion by creating an underpinning of interests vested in its favor, and every material force tries to justify itself by leaning upon some concept of an intellectual and moral order.[28]

The ruling class thus has its formulas, its myths, which are an integral part of the power system. They are to be treated as *facts* by the social scientist, just as any other data he observes, although perhaps not easily measurable. In turn, the selection of these data was dictated by what Mosca took to be sound scientific theory, itself immune from any wishful, mythful thinking.

But what if that conception of the ruling class itself, besides being an extrapolation from acknowledged facts, should turn out to be a

Sorelian myth, a Marxian ideology transcending and ignoring certain other facts that contradict it?

On first thought, that suspicion seems to be unwarranted. For there is no good reason why the positivist universe should be marred by irrational considerations. The fact that the founding fathers of the school resorted to such dodges as the New Christianity of Saint-Simon and Comte's Cult of Humanity need not disturb us. A completely rational society would no longer have any need of formulas and derivations—they would disappear together with the terrors and frustrations of the past. With the environment brought under total control, no "false consciousness" need interfere with the correct "administration of things" and (Marx, forgive us!) people. The positivistic elite would be selected on the basis of anthropometric and other methods available for identifying those most fit to govern. The first of the chosen few might still develop a sense of elitist superiority and become higher beings to the masses, unaccustomed as yet to take a matter-of-course attitude toward all public function. In the long run, a myth of the ruling class could not survive; it would die out from lack of emotional nourishment. The "formula," if any, would have lost all poetry and would merely be a factual account of institutional arrangements.

In contrast, a myth is imagery of quite a different type of truth. It is unbearable reality transfigured by an act of intuition; on the action level it engenders a persistent heroism against which the gates of hell shall not prevail. Those partial to the revelation will develop, first, a sense of otherness, and then, of superiority. But it will be a superiority quite different in kind from that based on performance of a socially accepted public function. For the elite that cherishes a myth may be defined as a group with a claim that has not yet been publicly accepted and translated into concrete forms of social action. It will be the kind of claim which we call moral, a demand presented to, and made upon, the world on the strength of the sacrifice performed in the claim's service by the claimants. They will make it with that saintly pride that seems to go so well with the most deeply felt humility. But it would still remain a sentiment of superiority conditioned by a sense of mission. That kind of superiority would be most likely to appear in an instinctively impersonal disguise: it would be normative, not interested in what "man can and does do" but what he ought to do. Let us now consider Mosca's notion of the ruling class under this aspect. His point of departure is the dominant minority of our mature society and those groups which aspire to it. The composition of the "political class" reflects increasingly but not exclusively the contributions which are at a premium in a technological civilization. Those who can—or think that they can—make those contributions most effectively, a *classless* crowd of more or less well educated individuals belonging to all social strata, try to rise to the top of their contemporary *class* society. They desire the best of all worlds: the equality of Marx's chiliastic vision as well as the benefits of bourgeois class and status.

But what if the bourgeoisie should withhold those rewards, if the new class of merit should be pulled down by the democratic mob and its mediocre leaders? Then achievement of the technical or intellectual kind would by itself not be enough; it would need an additional justification: moral superiority. What better claim to power could the new nobility present than their ability to serve as umpires in a class-ridden society, what better promise could they make than to give the community truly disinterested leadership?

But could that plea be made by Gaetano Mosca? He will indeed raise his voice, and more than once, in favor of a new, disinterested ruling class. But each time his voice will trail off into an embarrassed silence. He cannot permit a myth to become the prime mover "which determines the formation of the ruling class" without reneging on his own conclusion which insists that "on the contrary, the ruling class adopts the formula most advantageous to its needs." [29] There is a real difference between an assertion that a moral force (the general wish for disinterested government) is being harnessed to an interest in power and an attempt to parley a moral force into material power, which without that moral force could, in all likelihood, not be attained. A disinterested ruling class would not only be justified but be the very creature of a myth, and Mosca, had he advocated it, would stand convicted as an inconsistent if amiable moralist. A ruling class of that kind, he knew, was not likely to arrive until philosophers are kings. If Mosca wanted to avoid the danger of utopianism, he had to magnify the actual power and homogeneity of his new class of "merit" and, in order to be logical, *of all other elites* as well. For the same reason he had to tone down the role played by brute force in the consolidation of past ruling classes and to stress their real and acknowledged moral superiority. Thus he would give historic backing to the claims to power of the one elite of which he himself was the—probably unconscious—spokesman.

3

THE HISTORICAL TEST I:
DEUTERONOMY TO DECLINE AND FALL

His principles established, Gaetano Mosca puts them, in the next two chapters, to the test of history. One could reverse that statement and say that the author subjects history to the test of his principles. Like Arnold Toynbee, Mosca takes his facts from the authoritative sources of his time. The section on the Greeks and Romans for example is "to a great extent based on the stupendous work of Foustel [sic] de Coulanges, La cité antique." [1] Through no fault of his own, our author was not always as well served as in this special case. For his review of Hebrew and Egyptian history, he did not have the information which we have today. The first volume of Wellhausen's great History of Israel had just appeared when he wrote the Teorica, but Dubnow's decisive work was still in the future, and so were Auerbach's and Goldberg's mythical investigations. The three Egyptologists of Mosca's period, Erman, Breasted, and Maspero, had not yet produced their standard works. [2]

Not that it matters. One is almost tempted to expect that the lack of sufficient information, the want of a great deal of conflicting detail, would be a help rather than a hindrance in the application of a doctrine of such sweeping generality as Mosca's in the Teorica. But nothing of the sort; if there is any cause for criticism, it is that the doctrine has not been put to sufficient use. This failure to exploit the potentialities of his own theory to the full cannot be attributed to youthful modesty or inexperience, because Mosca's later, mature works will show the same deficiency, the same halfheartedness in utilizing his historical materials.

Israel

Hebrew history is in Mosca's view a record of political failure. He recognizes the religious genius of the race but that is all. The nation of the Bible was no nation in the exact sense: it never graduated from a loose "agglomeration of tribes" to true statehood. Their leader elements never became a fully integrated political class.

In speaking of the early period "when there was no king in Israel: every man did that which was right in his own eyes," Mosca comments that the absence of a king would in itself not explain the existing anarchy; what caused it was "the lack of any form of regular government whatsoever." [3] Yet he concedes that even so, the ancient Hebrews somehow managed to retain a sense of national identity. What held them together was partly the religious bond, partly the ancestral myth of consanguinity, the affirmation of their common descent from the biblical patriarchs. In their cities we find so-called elders who continued to play a certain political role even in the times of Hebrew monarchy. Mosca does not hold that these notables were elected representatives; with considerable scorn he dismisses any notion of "popular sovereignty" for that period in which, according to him, certain members of the community exercised their natural prerogative on the basis of their wealth, the number of their slaves, and the size of their clientele. But he adds that some of the elders may have owed their great position solely to their "wisdom." [4]

The potential political class, then, contained from the first an element of "merit," plus the representatives of economic power. Mosca is curiously silent about the priestly class; he seems to be oblivious of the fact that political rule among the Hebrews always was a matter of dispute—as it was in the Christian Middle Ages— between secular elites and men of godly wisdom, and even among the latter, between inspired individuals and organized factotums of the Lord, Levites and priests. The history of these three dominant minorities and of their combinations, splits, and truces is an almost perfect subject for the theorist of the elite—beginning with that most dramatic of all stories, the first documented instance of one ruling group being forced to surrender power to a new, important social force. Max Weber was to make the most of that "change of the guard"; Mosca muffs his chance. He does not see that monarchy, the matter of contention between the old prophet, Samuel, and the crowd acclaiming Saul, had become a necessity when untrained levies, led by holy dervishes, were pitted against a superior war technology —that of the Philistines. The warnings against the concomitant evils of organized government, regimentation and taxation, which the biblical writer puts into the mouth of the old ecclesiarch, were of course (as Mosca shrewdly observes) an afterthought, belonging to a later period when the royal dragon had already shown his talons. [5] But that is all Mosca has to say about the famous story; he makes no attempt to read it in the light of his own theory. Had he done so it would have shown him that the rise of Hebrew monarchy was due to an *external* challenge, that the revolution which forced one elite out and raised up another had to be explained by foreign conquest or the threat of conquest—in one word: the result would have been Gumplowicz, not Mosca.

The resulting monarchy did not bring lasting unity, did not create a Hebrew nation. After just three generations, the great Solomonic empire breaks apart into the feuding states of Israel and Judah. Mosca's explanation of that split sounds plausible enough. The kingdom founded by Saul "never developed a real hierarchy of functionaries ... apart from the people, culminating in the king. Instead, the elders went on ruling in all cities; they retained all their judicial and administrative functions." More important still: those urban oligarchies retained control over the military units. In other words, the king did not have his own army. To be sure, a nucleus of royal bureaucracy existed; the king's household was quite large and made him, within limits, economically independent. But at no time was his power large enough to make him absolute. That situation remained virtually unchanged in the successor states.

Mosca regards the "absence of a solid organization among the ruling group . . . as one of the probable causes of the political decadence
of the Hebrews." He is quite "sure" that it was "a powerful contributing factor in the breakup of the Hebrew kingdom . . ." [6] But
since he does not offer any other reason, we remain with the impression that for him arrested growth was the decisive factor, that Hebrew society could not maintain its tenuous unity because the ruling
class never completed its own integration.

But suppose we reverse the causal chain and see the failure of the
ruling class to coalesce as an effect of national disintegration, or, to
be precise, as a mere aspect of a larger process which the theory of
the elite does not explain. The argument would be based on these
facts: The Solomonic kingdom was the imperial extension of a conquest by Southern, only partly national (Judaic) forces of the Northern (Israelitic) portion of the country. In that region the original
Hebrew conquerors or immigrants had merged with previous settlers
of Semitic origin. As the unceasing vituperations of the Prophets
show, that Northern peasantry never took to the cult of Jehovah
which the Southern desert dwellers had brought with them. It clung
stubbornly to its orgiastic worship of telluric deities.

The split between the two parts of the kingdom was in truth only
the reassertion of the economically stronger and religiously unrecon-
structed North against the temporary overlordship of a Southern
semitheocracy. The second book of Samuel makes quite plain that
David, a usurper and, technically, a traitor to his country, owed his
success to the clerical elite which helped him against "mad" Saul—
at a price: David the king was a good ruler as long as he did the bidding of the priests.

If this interpretation is correct, then the end of the United Hebrew
Kingdom would be not a case of national disintegration, but, quite
the contrary, one of integration along the natural lines of a national homogeneity which had been wiped out by despotic force.
Since Mosca does not recognize that factor of despotic force, he has
to blame the failure of the Hebrews to achieve a lasting union on the
—unexplained and unexplainable—shortcomings of the ruling class.
No ruling class, however, can work miracles and unify a country in
which the controlling social forces are at odds with one another

(priests against warlords) and divided within themselves by regional antagonisms (mountaineers against plainsmen, the Judaic God against the temple of Samaria).

Since Mosca ends his Hebrew chronicle with the Assyrian conquest and the Babylonian exile, he deprives himself of the chance to study later Jewish states with fully integrated ruling classes. His stated reason for not bothering with the theocratic government of the Ezra-Nehemiah restoration and the Hasmonaean and Herodian dynasties is that the first destruction of the temple marks the end of Hebrew independence.[7]

But a political class may continue to exist in a society although the state as such has lost its sovereignty. The measure of autonomy which Roman rule established in the province of Judaea, the satellite role thrust upon its aristocracy, made (all the internecine party struggles notwithstanding) for a higher degree of cohesion than had been existing in the times of freedom. External pressure forced the genius of that captive nation to develop new means of defense, new "formulas," new institutions, new elites to organize and to articulate the spiritual and social needs of a submerged community. The old elites, collaborators all, could not fulfill that function. It became the task of the dissenters: Pharisees led by a petty bourgeois—the artisan intelligentsia, and, departing from them, certain other sects. They formed societies within society, schools of theology contemptuous of political realities; they were the saved, twelve times twelve thousand, the elect, the last who will become the first. Under the impact of their formula—their new ecclesia—the great Roman empire will admit defeat, it will be conquered and, at last, give up the ghost.

Then there is the triumph of the Christian underground elite, literally rising from the catacombs to supreme power—what a subject for the theorist of the ruling class! But Mosca's treatment merely echoes Gibbon, and another chance to test the theory is missed, the likely reason being that the concept of the ruling class, as held in the Teorica, was still too rigid and too narrow to encompass such elusive and complex phenomena as a society that was, officially, not interested in the very problems of political and social power which Mosca intended to explore.

Enduring Egypt

As Mosca's glance turns from the Jordan river to the Nile, his tone becomes less negative, more confident in terms of his own theory, and this although our information about ancient Egypt is by far not as complete as our knowledge of Judaic history. Of the civilization of the Pharaohs, however, one thing, Mosca feels, can be said unequivocally: it developed its political organization to a degree of perfection never achieved by the Hebrews. The very oldest records already reveal a state of affairs far from primitive. The conquerors of the Nile valley, who came probably from Asia, unified the entire country, from the delta to the cataracts, under a feudal monarchy—monarchy, because the Pharaoh headed a system of central administration; feudal because the "seigneurs" of the small, local districts retained their hold over the land for a long time, concentrating in their hands all the juridical and administrative rights that go with infeudation. Although their powers were, in the end, all but absorbed by the central government, they somehow managed to survive and, whenever the central government lost its strong grip or broke down altogether, to recover their lost independence. The vitality of that provincial ruling class was perhaps due to the fact, noted by our author, that the functionaries of the Pharaoh were in the main recruited from its ranks. In other words, the national bureaucracy did not, at least under the Old Kingdom, represent a social force or forces different from, and antagonistic to, the feudal lords. Rather, one and the same class was in charge of both central and provincial governments.

On the basis of the evidence available to him, Mosca finds it impossible to say whether the Egyptian elite was at all open to aspiring members of the lower classes. But he finds a great deal of mobility within the ruling group, an easy interchange of personnel between the sections that compose it: "in one family, we may find one member to be a priest, another in the civil service, still another holding a commission in the royal army; frequently one and the same individual will successively occupy all three positions, usually starting as an army officer and ending as a priest." [8]

This flexibility of the elite did not, as we know, prevent serious conflicts between the lords secular and spiritual. But neither here nor later, when that very conflict occurs once more in the Christian Middle Ages, does Mosca pay enough attention to that crucial problem of elite infighting. He does say that the "enormous changes in the political structure which took place in the time of the Twelfth Dynasty" would indicate "a profound social evolution" which went on before that period. But the character of that great transformation does not become clear. What new social forces appeared on the scene? What other political classes made their bid for power? In the name of what new formula? Mosca does not say because he does not know. And he is too honest a scholar to indulge in speculation; unlike Vico he is not the man of the inspired guess. This much he can tell us: that the ruling class of the Twelfth Dynasty "was in all likelihood recruited, almost entirely, on the basis of merit," because the inscriptions preserved from the end of that period "refer distinctly to public offices awarded by way of examinations." [9] Examinations opened all doors to the literate; Egypt was now ruled by a bureaucracy much like the Chinese mandarins.

Then, of a sudden, utter collapse and disintegration, total anarchy. The country becomes the prey of the Hyksos and we do not know what other foreign marauders. Again, Mosca refrains from theorizing about the possible causes of such radical decline and fall. He might have attributed the end of the Old Kingdom to "infatuation with its master institution," to use Arnold Toynbee's term. He could, in short, have blamed disaggregation on the very bureaucratic superintegration that had preceded. Going further, Mosca could have asked whether civilizations break up because their elites become too brainy and cease to rely on force, and whether such an outcome is inevitable or can be arrested through a process of regeneration taking place in the old ruling class or through a new elite arising from society. But these are questions for Pareto and—to some extent—the older Mosca of the *Elementi*. In the *Teorica* he prefers silence, and we will respect him for it. Respect with a by-mixture of puzzlement: Why, if the history of Egypt was so little rewarding, contributing so little to his study of the political class, why did he bother to retell it in the first place?

Actually we would have been somewhat the poorer without it. For Mosca has some acute observations about the New Kingdom, which restored the bureaucratic order with a vengeance. Egypt became imperialistic; its army, now composed of professional soldiers, assumed an importance it never had before.[10] To what extent did this new element affect the composition of the ruling class? Was it a contributing factor in the following, second, catastrophe? And what about the split between the monarch advocating a new supernational religious formula and the traditionalist clergy? But the fourth Amenophis and Egyptian caesaropapism is Spengler's and not Mosca's kind of problem.[11]

The Perfect Proof

King, Council of the Elders, popular assembly—those three institutions would, "on the strength of the Aristotelian classification," make the government of the archaic Graeco-Roman city look like "a mixture of monarchical, aristocratic, and democratic elements . . . Yet, looking closer, we discover this impression to be wrong. The main, almost exclusive feature of political organization . . . is the absolute preponderance of the political class over all other social classes as well as the strictest separation between the two groups, so strict and absolute that it is hardly possible to find anything like it among other nations of a different civilization." [12]

The tone is firm and confident; our author has at last found home, back on familiar ground. Greek history will furnish him his perfect proof. The very cradle of democracy, the Athens of the Periclean Age, will vindicate his thesis: that The Many never ruled, can never rule.

It is a mighty challenge, but our author has no doubt that he can prove his point. For us it is hard to believe that the point needed to be made at all, so commonplace is it today. Or is it? How much of the Moscan doctrine do we actually accept unhesitatingly? A great deal of derogatory evidence has been unearthed that rather detracts from the glory that was Athens, drawing our attention to the seamy aspects of democracy. These we will not deny. The system was corrupt and, often, inefficient. In the end, it was defeated by the

Spartan oligarchs. Again, accepted. But when Mosca says that there was no such thing as democratic government in Athens—no. This we shall not believe, thus proving that a myth is stronger than all evidence refuting it. It is the kind of faith which, as Pareto puts it, must be judged not merely as to its truth content, which may be nil, but on the basis of its social utility, which may be of first magnitude. Modern democracy is such a myth. It has been moving mountains. It will even move an older, mellowed Gaetano Mosca. Still, he will never recant what he wrote, in the *Teorica*, about the sham democracy of Athens:

> If we understand by people the majority, then it is clear that they had never any share of power in the early Graeco-Italic city; if the form of government had the appearance of democracy, that was so because all the citizens took part in the decisions of the commonwealth, but they were only a restricted and exclusive class.[13]

The citizens were a *minority* to which the slaves, the clients, foreign metics, and those individuals who for some reason were considered illegitimate, could not belong.

In the early period, when the only kind of wealth was landed property, the domination of the ruling class, small as it was, could not be challenged by the poor and downtrodden plebeians. "In short: all elements capable of forming the political class were found among the full-fledged citizens." That situation changed with the development of trade and manufacture. New elements, partly former clients, became small but independent proprietors, somewhat like what today we would call *nouveaux riches*; they began to crystallize a new plebeian elite of their own, while at the same time the "true" citizens grew fewer and fewer in number. The ensuing struggle between the two elites, a universal fact of the whole Graeco-Roman world, ended almost everywhere (the only significant exception being Sparta) with the triumph of the plebs—in legal terms, with the abandonment of the aristocratic, gentilitian constitution.

And now Mosca moves up his big guns:

> That revolution . . . is commonly referred to by historians as a change from an aristocratic to a democratic form of government. In reality, if by democracy is meant majority rule, that interpretation is quite inexact. What happened was merely that the rule of one minority was superseded

by that of another—a larger minority, if you wish, and resting on a different social base.

Hand in hand with that factual change went the ideological: "The old political formula is given up and a new one adopted, admitting to citizenship and thereby to office all plebeians fit to direct public affairs."

The steely ring of this *pronunciamento* is as unmistakable as its apparent harmlessness. For what does Mosca say but that the governing majority does, under the conditions of Greek slave society, encompass the totality of the electorate, just as it does today. We are so pleased by this discovery that we are in no mood to question Mosca's statement in detail. What if he calls the ruling demos a minority, as long as he conceded that it is larger than the old minority of the aristocrats! If Mosca wants to quibble, we are satisfied that the majority of the Athenian *citizens*, by his own admission, were the government. And all plebeians could aspire to public office. To be sure, our author qualifies that statement: only those plebeians "fit" for office could partake in government. That sounds, does it not, as if the prerequisite for their admission was political fitness, whereas we know that it was the other way around: the granting of full civic equality to the plebeian class was the basis for their eligibility to public office.

That this was so can be shown easily enough. Suppose we accept Mosca's way of putting things: a certain number of potential leaders from the plebs were admitted to citizenship ("all plebeians fit to direct public affairs"). Then the question instantly arises as to how their fitness was established. By educational or other testing methods? That may have been the case when it came to actual appointment or even election to office; but we are talking about *eligibility* only. By what right did plebeians become citizens? The answer is by revolutionary right. This is so patently obvious that it takes no generosity to assume that Mosca's vagueness at this point is unintentional. He himself starts his statement by referring to a revolution that took place when the Athenian constitution became democratic.

In fact, he has quite a few eloquent lines to describe the savagery with which that "struggle for right" had been conducted in the seventh century B.C. In that connection he makes the acute remark that the rebellion against the patricians was preceded, and perhaps made possible, by the revolt of the patricians against their old royal "father." By deposing the archaic king or relegating him to a mere ceremonial role as keeper of the sacred flame they themselves "had dealt the first blow to the traditional order of things." [14] All revolutions, Mosca might have said with Plato, "begin in the head," that is, in the ruling class (the young timocrats resenting the old-fashioned mores of their fathers).[15] All revolutions, Mosca will say later, are, in this last sense, fought between elites, inside or outside the minority that governs.

Now, the picture of comparatively small groups fighting one another for the spoils of power, with the great majority of *hoi polloi* going about their business as usual, pausing occasionally to watch and cheer the protagonists—that picture has the charm of great simplicity, and Gaetano Mosca was no painter of historic forgeries. He knew too well that revolutions—distinct from mere palace revolts, military *Putsche*—possess historical significance only when masses are in motion, are engaged, when they do not merely do the bidding of their betters, to be dismissed when the shouting or shooting is over, but fight for some cause in which they fervently believe. That cause their leaders may betray the next day, but only at the price of being themselves swept away by other forces, although that may be a lengthy process.

The accession to power of any minority would thus reflect the impact, however delayed or limited, of some majority. More, the success of revolutionary elites will depend on a mass basis, or in Mosca's terminology: on a social force. He never claimed that it was otherwise. But frequently the light which the *Teorica* (and later on *The Ruling Class*) sheds upon the neglected role of dominant minorities obscures the major context in which those minorities make history.

This optical illusion is well illustrated by the author's treatment of that singular phenomenon of Greek civilization: the tyrant. In the well-known formula of Aristotle it was corruption of the worst, the oligarchic, form of government: the tyrant ruled without the benefit of any law. In Mosca's view, he is "a bold adventurer who, with a band of followers recruited mainly from the lower depth of society, makes himself supreme in power..." [16] Aristotle went still further when he wrote that revolutions break out "when opposite parties, e.g., the rich and the people, are equally balanced." Machiavelli's Prince, the great protector of the little people who performs the parasitical, Bonapartist function of the mediator between deadlocked classes, was already known to Aristotle when he said: "from mutual distrust, the two parties hand over the defense of the state to ... an arbiter between the two factions, who often ends the master of both." [17]

This *raison d'être* of the Greek tyranny does not emerge from Mosca's analysis. He does not seem to recognize that it too was the rule of an elite: a *lumpenproletarian*, negative elite to be sure, but an elite just the same, which played a temporary role essential for the preservation of the polis in travail.

Nor can it be said that Mosca's reading of the Solonian reform penetrates to the roots of the problem. He lists three parties, representing three conflicting social forces of the period: the patriciate (the big landowners), the class of depressed small farmers, and the wealthy merchants of plebeian origin who, so far, have been unable to satisfy their political ambitions. This time, Mosca's facts will not bear scrutiny. Our sources, more or less the same as those available to him, reveal that the commercial stratum mentioned in his text not only was not powerful enough to claim a share in government, but did not even exist as a class. It was Solon who created the conditions under which it could develop, by encouraging the change-over from " 'subsistence farming' to 'cash-crop farming' accompanied by a development of commerce and industry." [18] By assuming, for Solon's time, a tripartite class constellation which was actually that of Peisistratus' and Cleisthenes' period, Mosca fails to see what the Solonian reform was about. On the surface, it restored the disturbed balance of the two existing social forces—both agrarian: big landholders and their debtors. To the latter Solon granted, through his *Seisachtheia*, a reduction of their mortgage burden. Beyond that he did not go. His distinctly conservative bias disappointed the poor peasants. As a student of the period puts it: "They thought that a sweeping measure of land distribution must be the cornerstone of any edifice of reform." But "there is very little of the agrarian element in his legislation ... The deficiency of food supply ... was the evil he sought to cure . . . By laws encouraging trade and manufactures he provided a means of purchasing food from abroad . . . and produced at first a contented class of dwellers on the coast who got work and wages as craftsmen and sailors. Later [his reform] produced certain developments of a less happy nature which neither Solon nor any man of his time could have foreseen." [19]

It would appear, then, that the balance of the social forces, two in number, was restored by the addition of a third, or, to be quite correct, a third and fourth group, one of which became the new Athenian bourgeoisie; the *paralii*, the "dwellers on the coast," became the nucleus of what will later be the ultra-democratic proletariat of the fleet and the Piraeus port district. One might say that the Solonian solution consisted in a broadening of the class basis—except that this basis had to be created first. I can think of only one other example where the superstructure evolved faster than the basis and ahead of it: the revolution in the economic structure of the Soviet Union engineered by legal fiat from above in 1928. In that sense (and in that sense only!) the dictator Stalin of the five-year plans and agricultural collectives may be called a second Solon.[20]

Conclusions such as this could and should have been suggested by Mosca's thesis. That the twenty-six-year-old author did not himself draw them, does not, I believe, reduce the debt we owe him for his lead.

"Oligarchical Democracy"

Lest we forget, we are once more reminded of the fact that "though a bit enlarged, the political class always remains a minority." The use of the singular, political class, would lead us to expect that the leading elements of Athenian society had fused into a homogeneous group. But how are we then to explain the fact, brought out by Mosca himself, that "inside that very minority" of the elite "various factions and *camorras* did not fail to make their appearance." It was political gang warfare with all its ghastly epiphenomena of terror, confiscation, "liquidation." The only difference between the parties was their name: "if the clique was made up of rich people, it would call itself aristocratic; if of the poor, democratic." [21]

This is a clear avowal of the fact that "the" political class had failed to consolidate the "two cities" of the rich and the poor into one. "The" political class, in short, was simply a misnomer for at least two political classes: one very small, representing the old-time patricians; the other standing for the much larger class of smallholders and artisans who had once benefited from the economic policies of Solon, carried further by Peisistratus and Cleisthenes, and who were now the pauperized victims of advanced methods of manufacture based on cheap slave labor. This development, to quote once more that student of the period, led "to loss of employment by many of the old paralii, to such an extent that before the end of the Sixth Century, they, as a class which had earlier in the century been the middle, now became the extreme left in politics." [22]

How, in the face of these grave socio-economic contradictions, was it possible for Periclean Athens to achieve its celebrated democratic synthesis? This is, of course, not the term used by Mosca. He concedes that Pericles "placed poor and rich citizens on a footing of almost absolute equality," but he insists that "Athenian democracy was essentially a highly selected and carefully educated oligarchy." [23] How had the two warring classes become reconciled? For Mosca does not question that this was the case. No change in the composition and relative strength of the two social forces had occurred which would explain the slackening of the political or social tensions in that period. A study of the ruling class exclusively, then, will not yield the answer. Mosca himself does not try to find it there. He barely hints at the solution found: appeasement of the poorer classes without undue hardships imposed on the rich—that was the Periclean policy, made possible by economic and political imperialism.[24] The Athenian proletarians were fed and employed at the expense of the Greek "satellites" united in the Delian League. Colonialism (export of manpower by way of the cleruchies) and economic exploitation abroad in the service of a welfare state at home kept the indigent sovereign in line, much as, in Lenin's book, the English ruling class bribed its labor aristocracy by paying better wages out of surplus value wrested from Malayan coolies.[25]

In discussing the continuous social unrest of post-Periclean Athens, Mosca pays particular attention to the two successful if short-lived attempts of the old oligarchs to regain power. Curiously enough, he fails to give both counterrevolutions their identifying class and party label, speaking of their leaders merely as "The Four Hundred" and "The Thirty." Again the temptation to interpolate is irresistible. In speaking of the first attempt, made during the Peloponnesian War, after the Athenian expeditionary force to Sicily had been annihilated, Mosca mentions that the plotters "were backed by a nucleus of five thousand citizens," whom they had hoodwinked by the promise of a constitutional reform along moderate lines. Now those "five thousand" happened to be the five thousand citizens who served as heavy infantry, providing their own weapons and equipment. That middle-class group was known by the term, which also served as party label for the democratic moderates lead by Theramenes, the party of the hoplite census.

For a whole century, the oligarchic faction, much too small to rule alone, had been forced to lean on that center group which stood between them and the democratic ultras who were the war party. Sicily proved to be the undoing of the latter. The war party was deserted by the moderates, who veered toward the right and came out for the constitutional reform promoted by the oligarchs. The center was particularly pleased with the proposal to curtail the suffrage, limiting it to the middle class—themselves. Too late did they discover that they had been tricked: the city was in the grip of its first post-democratic tyranny. It did not last long; its fall was accomplished by a combination of the disenchanted moderates and the left democrats. The mere threat by a few Athenian naval squadrons to set sail for Athens was enough to bring about the bloodless removal of a government suspect of dealings with the enemy—a suspicion which had some foundation in the traditionally isolationalist and pro-Spartan leanings of the oligarchic party.

Back in the saddle, the left fought the war to its unhappy finish.[26]

About the second attempt to turn the clock back, the attempt of "The Thirty" to exploit the ultimate defeat, Mosca has even less to say. This time the oligarchs turned openly collaborationist, relying for support upon the Spartan garrison of Athens. For the rest, they had again their moderate allies, led by the same Theramenes of whom can be said: once a dupe, always a dupe. To that extent, history for once did repeat itself. But the changed circumstances of the city, which had lost an empire, gave the second counterrevolution that barbaric character which made the earlier attempt look like a comic dress rehearsal. Our author is shocked by the acts of wholesale confiscation and extermination which made the rule of The Thirty synonymous with political scoundrelism. Mosca concludes his indignant account with the words: "That government, which hardly deserves any other name but that of a criminal association, was finally swept out of office by the general discontent which stirred up an insurrection favored even by the Spartans." [27]

The sentiment expressed in these terse lines can only be called laudable, though they again fail to communicate some necessary facts. For the "general discontent" to become a successful insurrection, the moderates once more had to go over to the ultrademocrats. The "people" who defeated Critias, Plato's uncle, and his desperadoes in a street battle in the Piraeus had been stiffened by indignant troops who had come over from the heavily equipped Five Thousand.[28]

Mosca could have said that the counterrevolutions, both of them, were the work of a coalition between right and center of the ruling class, whereas the downfall of The Thirty and that of their predecessors was caused by a falling-out between the coalition partners, bringing the left-wingers back to power. The return of radical democracy brought in its wake a series of retaliative purges aimed at the collaborators of the tyrants. One of the victims happened to be Socrates, who belonged to the faction of Theramenes.

Mosca makes the point that scenes like those enacted by The Thirty never happened again in Athenian history, but that they were quite typical of Greek political life in general. He holds that "these distinctive traits of public life were some of the main reasons for the decadence of Greece." [29] But what are these distinctive traits if not an indication of the fact that the Greek ruling classes never managed to achieve cohesion? And if that were so, what good is it to say that "all societies are governed by minorities"? We are prepared to grant that much. But much more, if not all, depends on the shifts, combinations, disagreements prompted by the ever-changing situation of the year, month, day. To reduce all this confusion to a simple pattern which leaves the particulars untold will hardly do.

Rome Was Different and Yet ...

If the theory that all societies are governed by minorities is true, then one might say that the society called Greek did not exist because Greece was not governed. Roman history was quite another matter. Rome was governed. But that does not mean the difficulties to be mastered on the road to empire were less complex than those that confronted the Greek polis. On the contrary, as Rome outgrew her city boundaries until she became, in the end, coeval with the then known world, the strains of her internal growth process never abated. Only when expansion seemed no longer possible did the springs of extroverted energies recoil upon their point of origin and, at last, snap. The puzzle is not that Rome fell eventually, but that she lasted as long as she did.

For Rome may truly be called "The State as Permanent Revolution," to borrow a happy phrase from Bertrand de Jouvenel.[30] Rome became the byword for the greatest success story in political history precisely for the reason that hers was a conservative revolution. Fifty years before De Jouvenel, Mosca wrote: "What confers such a powerful mark of originality upon the Roman state is the fact that it was from the first more conservative and, simultaneously, more revolutionary than were all the other Graeco-Italian cities."

Mosca's brief account of Roman history is done with an astuteness singular in one so young. Disregarding for the moment some curious omissions which will be noted later, we shall not find much with which modern authorities would tend to disagree. To be sure, Mosca's task is made easier by the circumstance that the lack of cohesion in the ruling class, which had caused him so much trouble so far, was (for a long time at least) the very source of Roman strength. Nor was the theory of the elite faced with such chaotic moves and unaccountable shifts of the social balance as were characteristic of mercurial Greece. The struggles of the Roman ruling class show a much clearer outline: they were *institutionalized*. The flow of social dynamics was, with very few exceptions, kept within constitutional channels.

Much as he admires the pattern, Mosca, though displaying the erudition of the constitutional expert, tries to penetrate behind the institutional façade. Behind the framework of the two conjoint societies, patrician and plebeian, with their different assemblies and executive officers, he discerns a further bifurcation in the plebs into "a nucleus of rich plebeians who had the same education, the same means of influence as the patricians" on the one hand; on the other, "the great mass of poor plebeians who, like the poor of all times and in all countries, were less interested in political equality than in the betterment of their economic status." [31] What the dominant society of the patricians had to fear was not so much the revolt of the poor whom we have always with us, but the revolution of their political class. This important distinction, between the rebellion of the poor and the class struggle, seems to belong to Mosca although it has been ascribed to Georges Sorel.[32]

It was the genius of Rome that prompted the patrician upper class to make those timely if grudging concessions by which the out-elite of the plebeians was incorporated into the official ruling class *before* the commercial and financial revolution of the second century B.C. brought still new social forces to the fore. Mosca refers to that merger of the two elites into one senatorial aristocracy when he says that "the two cities, patrician and plebeian, became ultimately fused, and select elements of the plebs entered Rome's political class." And so he can once more triumphantly assert the precedence of political facts over political fiction. He might have added that legal proposals in the two assemblies (the mixed patrician-plebeian of the comitia centuriata and the separate consilium plebis) could never be initiated from the floor but were left to the discretion of the consuls and tribunes of the people, respectively. But then Mosca should have added further that in actuality the struggle between the two sectors of the ruling class went on, even after the plebeian elite had been absorbed into the old patrician class. That struggle was all the more embittered as it was now carried on throughout the entire hierarchy of government, up to the very diarchy of the decisive office. Whenever one of the two consuls chose to block an action of his colleague, the entire machinery of state was paralyzed.

Mosca's silence about this important aspect of Rome's institutionalized revolution is resounding. He prefers to look at the brighter side of things. He is impressed by the great vigor of the Roman ruling class and by its uncommon longevity, which he explains by the fact that "Rome was not too stingy in conferring citizenship ... upon strangers." That was "not the least reason for her grandeur." True, but Mosca forgets that extension of the franchise to non-Romans was one thing, inclusion of Italic and provincial city notables in the senatorial ruling elite quite another. Mosca himself testifies to the fact that the Roman ruling class before Augustus jealously protected its exclusive character: "the highest positions were always reserved to a certain number of families, mostly of patrician origin, with a sprinkling of plebeian elements ... In studying the lists of consuls and other high magistrates, we find certain names recurring frequently; wealth, family ties, and traditional loyalties as well as a historic name were the important factors in that technically democratic republic." [33]

And yet, republican *grandezza* becomes *decadenza*.

We do not expect, we cannot expect, Mosca to enrich the great debate about the causes of decline and fall by startlingly original discoveries. But we have every right to assume that he will try to understand the fall of the Republic in terms of his theory: as the effect of an affliction that befell the ruling class.

But once more Mosca shows a strange reluctance to apply the method which he had so proudly proclaimed. He had all the facts about the tragic transformation at his fingertips: how Italy went through the same economic convulsion which Attica had suffered three centuries earlier; how latifundia worked by slaves turned the free farmers into city proletarians selling their vote to the highest bidder; how high finance became the power in the state, completely altering the character of the political class. Rome is now governed by an "oligarchy composed of a tiny number of enormously rich families monopolizing for their members all high offices and keeping out those who could not afford to spend as much as they; . . . money became the sole arbiter of popular elections." [34]

The next paragraph informs us that "the Gracchi tried to stem the tide of evil . . ." He retells their attempts at agrarian reform but fails to introduce the social force which made and unmade their tempestuous movement. That force was not at all new; it had existed all along, becoming more important all the time. That Mosca did not even mention it is all the more incomprehensible because its existence was officially established by the constitution: as the equestrian order, the financial and commercial bourgeoisie was making headway, being the only class engaged in business—since patricians were forbidden by law to "make" money. In post-Hannibalian Rome the economic interests become a third force in the ruling class—the third force which our author always overlooks. We had occasion to notice that omission in the—less important—instance of the two Athenian tyrannies of The Four Hundred and The Thirty. There the situation was determined by a triune constellation in the ruling class: the right wing could not act without the center, and it was defeated when the moderates switched sides. Without stretching the argument we might say that the same argument holds good for the Gracchian situation, the only difference being that in the Roman case the business oligarchs, though they had partly infiltrated the patrician class, played the role of the Theramenean center. How they first used the "left" (a very loose description of the Gracchian faction which, to all intents, was a conservative group, its rebellion a belated attempt to arrest urbanization) for their own end, control of the judiciary, and how the equites, when they got what they wanted, dropped their allies, need not be retold here.[35] What concerns us is the fact that Mosca, by not telling it, missed still another splendid opportunity to demonstrate his theory to good advantage.

The only reason I can think of to explain a failure that is obviously not accidental is the rigid character of Mosca's scheme of classes. It reduces all political relations to a simple dualism: the ruling minority on the one hand, the ruled majority on the other. Mosca does not overlook the dualism within the elite itself: Athenians or Romans of patrician as well as plebeian origin are its constituent elements, competing for control over the government. But when a third contestant wants to join the game, our author stubbornly refuses to admit him. The dualism of the scheme does not permit him to acknowledge the existence of more than two ruling groups. The main conception, the dichotomy between the many and the few, is vindicated —but at what a price!

The Negative Elite

The period of the civil wars which signaled the advent of Caesar receives twelve lines altogether; Marius, Sulla, Crassus and Pompey are not even mentioned. From his viewpoint, Mosca may have been right to treat those great figures in such cavalier fashion. For though they were still able to appeal to real social *issues* (land for the veterans, to mention one), the social *forces* which they called upon were no longer articulated. Instead of authentic and autonomous organizations, there were only mobs and coteries left. Whether it was fighting in the streets, or Roman legion against Roman legion on a fratricidal battlefield, there were no longer real issues at stake. The question was not: what kind of Republic, but who was to rule. And Mosca names the only possible regime: "the government of plutocracy." [36] He does not honor it with the name of political class. That would indeed have been a belated recognition of the social force which he had never bothered to identify. But technically he was quite correct in not conferring any of his titles on the triumvirs. They were indeed not representative of any social force but masters over all. It was what Spengler called "the triumph of the sword over the money power." [37]

But this was not the end—not yet. The constitutional development of Rome had merely come full circle: from kingship to republic and back to imperial monarchy. It presents Mosca with the question: what new social forces made the reconstruction possible, a reconstruction whose spectacular success was undeniable? What new political class had emerged out of the chaos of the civil wars? In Mosca's wording: "the demoralized, exhausted Roman oligarchy, no longer able to govern what was then the entire world, had to yield to a new hierarchy, a new organization." Theoretically, a new hierarchy might have developed out of one or some of the old social forces, fast recuperating in the favorable climate of the Augustan peace. But that was not the "new organization" Mosca has in mind; it "was the Roman army; . . . the Roman empire was a military organism."

The new political class should have been, accordingly, recruited from the legions. Mosca knows of course that such was not the case under the early emperors. He mentions that the Augustan compromise left the old oligarchy in charge of the Senate, which retained some status; it admitted now the likes of Cicero from the provincial municipia. These municipalities in turn retained a measure of self-government. But lest we think that they were democratically governed, Mosca quickly adds that local power was the oligarchic privilege of the *curiales* who had to be very rich in order to be able to discharge their public duties. Below them, we find the by now large mass of enfranchised but in fact second-class citizens. What holds these clusters of home rule communities together is the military force of the imperial government. "It is the army which made and unmade the 'Sovereign,' controlled the highest judicial office of the Praefectus Praetorio, and furnished the governors of the provinces, thus exercising all authority, both in the administrative and the judicial branches."

Mosca's picture of that reorganization is, quite obviously, a sketch, and should be judged as such. Nevertheless, a few comments seem in order. The prevailing military character of the arrangement is correctly diagnosed. But Mosca's judgment that "history shows no other example of a similar concentration of social power in the military arm" calls for qualification. The army as a social force was neither so new nor quite so powerful as Mosca wishes to believe. It dated back to the "new model" introduced by Gaius Marius when Rome's citizen levies had to be replaced by professional armies. A distinct military class thus had affected and determined politics before the first Augustus institutionalized its coercive power and incorporated it into his state. But he was wise enough to anchor his authority in the tribunician office held for lifetime. Nor is Mosca correct in apportioning all the judicial and administrative powers to the army; surely the division of the empire into senatorial and imperial provinces must have been known to him. He could have made the point that those within the senatorial orbit were the less important ones. But even within the imperial domain proper the distinction between military and civilian jurisdiction soon developed, as the vast imperial household generated its own trained bureaucracy of educated slaves and freedmen. Mosca is not totally oblivious of that fact, for he states that "step by step a civil organization detached itself from the military, and a large administration was set up . . . which shed all military characteristics." [38] That is a devious explanation of the simple fact that from the first, the two organizations had existed side by side, although, to be fair to Mosca, it must be conceded that the military aspect was the more conspicuous of the two.

More important than these minor factual corrections is the question: Does the army of the Caesars really deserve the honorary title of a social force? We had occasion to take issue with our author because of his tendency to overlook amplifications in the ruling class. Now once more he spoils his own case by oversimplifying things. He first decided that the new imperial army was a genuine social force. His next step was to declare that it was the only social force remaining. Most historians, however, believe that Octavianus Caesar did succeed where his great-uncle Julius had failed precisely because he compromised with tradition. And tradition was synonymous with the prestige if not the power of the senatorial class. Its total eclipse is of a much later date; it is as late as Diocletian's *dominatus*, which completed the regimentation of society, absorbing all of it into the bureaucratic state.

It is then that the sharp division into the two ruling classes, military and civilian-administrative, becomes a consciously used and misused *arcanum regni*. Ultimately both organizations, the armed and the civil services, can be subsumed under the heading of defense; thus Mosca would be justified in singling out the military class as the new and decisive social force of the imperial Roman era. But one may wonder whether that term had by then not lost its former simple meaning. One has the impression that the author has reversed the process by which he arrives at his terminological conclusions. He finds a ruling class recruited from the army, which from the beginnings of the post-republican establishment has held the balance of imperial power and ends up holding it exclusively. Since ruling classes are recruited from one or more than one social force, it follows that the army was a social force. And who would question that that armed force once more fulfilled an eminently social function in a pacified *orbis terrarum* that was mortally afraid of the barbarian spoilsmen?

Yet, by attributing to the defenders of the Pax Romana the term social force, the author does short-change himself as well as us. For it obscures the true significance of the huge standing armies garrisoned from Britain to Mesopotamia. Who were these soldiers? Landless proletarians following their generals, who guaranteed their pay and booty and, perhaps, resettlement on conquered or sequestered land. Increasingly, the army became the sole vehicle of secular ambition; a lowly bourgeois engaged in the trucking business could become emperor because he could become a general: the name is Titus Flavius Vespasianus. If Rostovtsev is right, the destructive policies of Septimius Severus were a social revolution in disguise, directed against the superior culture of the urban aristocracies; the army of Severus was the rural proletariat in disguise, the general receptacle for former social forces, now mere frustrated, resentful energies which found their only, nihilistic, outlet in officially encouraged violence.[39]

The only other institution in which social mobility could be found was the underground organization of the Christian church. Mosca recognizes as much when he remarks that Christianity indirectly contributed to the dissolution of the empire because "it absorbed almost all material, intellectual, and moral energies of the time, constituting itself as a state within the state." [40] The armies and bureaucracies lost their best elements to a new ruling class that was as yet not interested in the things that belonged to Caesar.

But if Christian non-co-operation is, as Mosca says, not the sole cause of the catastrophe but only a contributing factor, then additional, and perhaps better, reasons should be looked for in the very make-up of the military ruling class. From a mere instrument *of* politics it had developed into a self-conscious group that was *in* politics. The commanding officer of the Praetorian Guard became kingmaker. He had all the power necessary, and the Senate could be easily enough persuaded to lend its authority. But one thing the praetorian *majordomi* did not have: a policy. It is sufficient to remember the pathetic scene in which they implored the bewildered conscript fathers to resume the supreme power that had once been theirs.[41] But even if that strong civilian had been found, what could have been the rallying point for a restoration of society? In Mosca's terms: Where was the political formula that could have held the many provinces together, after the God-Emperor myth had exhausted its old magic?

But Mosca's formulas and Mosca's social forces, it now becomes evident, are concepts that apply only to unfolding civilizations, not to one that was contracting. The last phase of Roman history cannot be understood unless we understand it as a process of such kind, accompanied, however, by its very opposite; systole and diastole were complementary. The best blood, the best energies of Rome had been drained off into the outer rim of empire, from where they sent back invigorating impulses to the great capital, which, however, as such had lost its function and its meaning. All it could do was to bid welcome to Iberian, Syrian and Illyrian emperors and their armed hordes. In some crude way these represented the new social forces of the romanized barbarians dwelling at the far perimeter of a defense which became self-defeating. The old centripetal tendencies were still mechanically emulated; crushing burdens were imposed on an enfeebled and anemic body politic for the sake of the unifying principle. But these exactions only promoted the new centrifugal forces. The political class dissolved into as many splinter groups as there were regional armed units fighting for supremacy. The selective process by which the ruling class was once constituted becomes reversed: the premium is no longer on superior contribution; what counts is the resilience of primeval instincts. As the shadows darken, we see the most brutal, the most cunning type win Caesar's wreath, a negative elite, denying in its acts and aspirations all the values which that concept stands for. In a circuitous way, Rome returned to her starting point: the not only so-called dark ages of civilization.

4

THE HISTORICAL TEST II:
CHARLEMAGNE TO BONAPARTE

By now we should have some idea of the fruitfulness of Mosca's method, of the use to which he puts, or does not put, his theory of the political class. So there is no further need to trail him as closely on his brisk peregrination through the past as we did up to this point. It will be enough for our purpose to retrace the outline of his narrative encompassing the period from the dissolution of the Roman Empire to the triumph of parliamentary government in the nineteenth century (Chapters III and IV of the *Teorica*). Twelve centuries of history are compressed into sixty-three pages, of which only fifteen are devoted to the Middle Ages. The remaining forty-eight pertain almost exclusively to the one country which serves Mosca as the perfect foil for his elitist theory. It is not Italy where he finds the political class most in evidence. The Holy Roman Empire with its dual ruling class of lords and priests, torn between centralizing and disintegrative tendencies, only receives a passing glance. Nor did England appeal to the author as a fitting subject of his pilot study, although it seemed better suited than most other countries to pursue the slow emergence, from the welter of anarchic localism, of the

87

master institutions dear to Mosca's heart: aristocratic parliament and liberal articulation of the social forces.

But Mosca's choice was France. To him, a Continental European, the British polity appeared as something alien and inimitable, precisely because its devices had been aped so often and with such spectacular lack of success. In contrast, the French neighbor inspired the Italian with that loving admiration mixed with jealousy which one can sense in Machiavelli's account of that nation.[1] The Italian attitude toward the Latin Sister had been always marked by strong ambivalence; deep gratitude for French assistance in the struggle for Italian unity had alternated with resentment—as, for instance, when the third Napoleon, after Solferino, stopped his intervention without liberating Venice. And so it goes, even to our days: France would evoke in the Italian a sneaking admiration punctured by outbursts of glee over the many failings and debacles of La Grande Nation.

In such a highly cultured man as Gaetano Mosca all these vagaries of native vanity were more than overcompensated by a sincere appreciation of the great French contribution to the progress of mankind. As a historian, he knew that France, ever since the first crusade, had displayed more vitality than any other part of Europe. More important, France was the first modern state kat' exochèn. Since the eighteenth century, France had served as the great laboratory of the revolutionary social and political ideas which, in various transmutations, are still agitating our minds. Thus Mosca's choice would seem in the main justified, since Mosca, like Lenin, was preoccupied with the twin problem of state and revolution.[2]

His curt treatment of the Middle Ages becomes intelligible once it is viewed in the light of his main doctrine. The political class as he sees it appears on the historical scene only when a sufficiently advanced stage of civilization has been reached, when many independent little groups have become integrated into a cohesive social whole. Conversely, just as long as social power remains fragmentized, distributed, as it was in the feudal era, among many petty "sovereigns," the political class cannot really fulfill its mission. However, Mosca does not say that such a class could not exist under conditions such as they existed before 1400, for he grants when speaking of the feudal class that "it was adequately homogeneous and compact, and what it lacked in solid organization it made up by the possession of a common spirit. Above all, it had acquired the habit of command, while all the other social classes had become accustomed to obedience."

Without question, that essential dualism of the medieval order with its sharp dichotomy between the rulers and the ruled seemed to meet at least some of the demands of Mosca's scheme. Also pertinent for him was the fact that that potential ruling class did "feel the need of rallying and organizing around institutions, symbols endowed with historical significance, and like the ruling classes of all times and places, it found it convenient to justify its material power by means of a political formula . . ." In the Middle Ages "that symbolic institution was . . . kingship; the political formula, feudalism."

But as long as the King was dependent on a system of relationships and services which fenced him off from all but a few of his subjects, all attempts at unified and centralized control were bound to fail, and the political class could not be more than a shadow of the substance. Feudalism and the state are mutually exclusive. If the former merits any interest, it is because the state develops out of medieval war society. The author pays some grudging tribute to the modicum of order feudalism was able to establish: "Everyone knows that honor exists even among thieves, and in the Middle Ages almost everyone was a thief. But the *Treuga Dei* was almost always scrupulously observed, and so were the pacts between the various lords and between lord and vassal." [3]

That was all to the good, but it is not quite good enough for Mosca. He is constitutionally unable to abide a social order in which power is so widely scattered and nobody is sovereign in the Austinian sense. Such a state of affairs may not be, strictly speaking, anarchy—as the four centuries between 500 and 900 A.D. were anarchic—but it would still not deserve the name of civilization. The character of Mosca's scheme could not be clearer: his political class is the ruling class of the contemporary, centralized, and bureaucratically governed nation-state, informed by the example of imperial Roman unity. Whatever intervened between that archetype and its recurrence is ephemeral; the lesson of the Middle Ages can at best have only limited, preparatory value.

So much granted, there remains the question of why our author paid such scant attention to the other medieval master institution which, in the face of tremendous obstacles, upheld both the traditions and the methods of the Roman state. The genius of the second Rome is not ignored by Mosca: "We see the union of all Christians in one word: the Church, steadily strengthening and centralizing its own hierarchical organization," he writes.[4] The men who built that Church formed a true ruling class. They extricated themselves from the feudal network in a famous clash with a Teutonic emperor who was not yet a real king. One wonders why that celebrated event, why Canossa, is not even mentioned in the text. The question as to why the Church failed to transform the union of all Christians into one great Christian empire under a Pope-Caesar should have been a challenge to the theorist of the elite. For what else was the argument about investiture with all its consequences but a falling-out between two social forces and their ruling classes which had been welded to each other in a spurious condominium? It was the Hebrew unity of opposites all over. Disruptive forces operated in both camps; the feudal world was powerfully drawn toward the Roman camp, and many clerics acted like the feudal lords and vassals, which, indeed, they were.

Rome won the fight and lost the world. How could the theorist of the elite explain that failure of a ruling class armed with the most majestic of all formulas? The customary answer is because the future lay in regional and national, not ecumenical articulation. But that explains nothing. We are still left with the questions: Why was that inevitable? Why could the one genuine ruling class not tame the war lords? It was not feudal interest that could destroy the hard-won unity of the triumphant church organization; feudalism was already on the wane. The papal empire broke apart because part of its intellectual elite began to doubt the magic formula. The accelerating process of urbanization no doubt helped to bring into existence an unfrocked intelligentsia which turned the rebellion against the One God of the One Church into the advocacy of a mighty king and, finally, of the strong nation-state. But to explain disintegration (of the Christian world republic) and reintegration (of the parts as so many new wholes) as an internal crisis of the ruling class, we need a theory more flexible and comprehensive than the rigid frame of the *Teorica* could make possible.

The Rise of Absolute Monarchy

The transformation of the ruling class in France from feudal looseness to a unified and centralized force in the service of the king took five hundred years more or less. Its first results became apparent with the reign of Louis XI; under Louis XIV the process was completed.[5] What social force represented monarchy initially? It was, of course, no other than the feudal class, on which the king depended for financial as well as for military help. What existed of a rudimentary royal bureaucracy was for the most part staffed by clergymen; this was an element that made for independence of the crown from feudal pressures, insofar and as far as the clerical advisers of the king would be his allies in the never-ending war against the forces of disunion. Then again, the first allegiance of the clergy to their greater Roman monarch would more often than not conflict with the interest of the French crown. So for a long period, the French monarchy was at the mercy of the ruling class (or the two ruling classes, if we care to stress the tensions between French lords temporal and spiritual), and not infrequently it was quite literally taken over by one of the independent border dynasties, or by a combination of those proud provincial families. To mention only one example, in the sixteenth century the Guise clan virtually established an *imperium in imperio* centered in Lorraine.[6]

How did the French kings free themselves from that dependency? First, in the cities they found an element of countervailing power in the nascent social force of the commercial class, which furnished them with the sinews of war. The second liberating factor was lay education. As it grew, the kings could recruit capable administrators and crown lawyers from a social group which, as a class, could not yet threaten the king's power. The times when the Third Estate would advance its own, revolutionary, "formula" were still far off. Meanwhile, the royal civil servants of ignoble blood could be relied upon to combine the best bourgeois virtues, thrift and industry, with a complete lack of bourgeois aspirations. No wonder they played an increasingly important role in government; this was a universal trend, but nowhere more impressive than in France.[7]

But that still did not make the king a "representative" of the new social force, a bourgeois king before the bourgeois age. For "even under Louis XI the nobles, though no longer the masters of France, still were a most important part of the ruling class." The wording of this statement indicates that Mosca viewed the ruling class of that time as a partnership of several important groups, two of which have already been identified as the crown lawyers and bureaucrats, the first forming the tight, hereditary bourgeois aristocracy of the *gens de la robe*, the latter, commoners of the *roture*.

Now, under Louis XIV the nobles can no longer be said to be "a most important part of the ruling class." After the last "semiserious" revolts of the feudal *Fronde* had been put down by Richelieu and Mazarin, the French lords lose control of military power.[8] Their political role becomes negligible, though their economic status remains unaffected. Who controls the government? Or, to ask Mosca's question: Which new social force controls the ruling class?

We have a problem on our hands. A ruling class in Mosca's terminology there obviously was, because France was governed as never before and, be it added, as long as fortune smiled upon Louis *Le Grand*, with popular approval. But if it was a ruling class that governed France, it was a very strange one—at least, so it should have looked to Mosca. For it was not representative of anything that deserved the name of a social force. The king was master of all, representative of none. In complete truth he could say: *L'état, c'est moi.* The state, arisen out of feudal anarchy, still made use of the old elites for decorative purposes, but otherwise they had lost their *raison d'être.*

Monarchy then filled a social vacuum between the old social forces and their obsolescent ruling classes on the one hand, and the as yet unborn forces on the other. It is, to borrow once more Schumpeter's phrase, "a most un-Marxian situation." But, alas!—it's a situation even more intolerable for a theorist of the elite. A Marxist would, of course, deny that absolute monarchy was above the classes, and Franz Mehring has put up a very potent argument to show that even the most absolute of all the Prussian monarchs was a mere, if refined, instrument of the aristocratic class.[9] And if you pushed him to the wall, a Marxist could always resort to still another weapon from his master's arsenal; he might explain the power of the fourteenth Louis the way that Karl Marx explained the success of the third Napoleon: as "Bonapartism," the parasitical rule of a man or a group of men who represent no class but manage to exploit the deadlock between classes to establish a tyranny over them. In the case of Louis Napoleon it was a "benevolent and popular" despotism, anticipating by more than seventy years some signal aspects of contemporary fascism.[10]

But such evasive action is not open to the theorist of the elite. Under no condition can he permit an elitist void. And so, forgetting what he had said only a few pages earlier, he succeeds in discovering a ruling class in the age of the *Roi Soleil*. It will be difficult to reconcile the following two statements, first:

> Under Louis XIV, when the nobility had reached the . . . end stage of political decay, it was completely separated from the people, known to its own peasants only by the ruthlessness with which it exacted feudal rights long since converted into payments of rent. [These nobles] hardly performed any function of importance, and their very lack of training had made them incapable of managing public affairs . . . [11]

Translated into Mosca's technical vocabulary, the aristocracy of France no longer represented any social force; it was completely alienated from its economic base, the agricultural class; it no longer managed government. Contrast with these conclusions Mosca's next:

> The organs through which the royal power made itself felt and understood throughout the whole of France were the court, the aristocracy, and the bureaucracy; those three together formed the ruling class and governed the country effectively, taking shelter behind the authority of the sovereign on whom, in all appearance, they depended.[12]

So now we know by whom the French were ruled. Not by the king, but by the court, that is, the immense royal family together with their hangers-on, by the nobility, no longer decadent and ineffective, and by the bureaucrats. Together, those three groups compose the ruling class. But if we ask what social forces they represent, we get no answer. All we hear is that the rulers act in the king's name. But since the king himself is a mere name, for whom, we repeat, do the three groups act? Obviously for themselves, since we hear of no other interest. But surely ruling classes do not operate in a political and social void?

Perhaps the "formula," if we can find it, will enlighten us. For if the three groups mentioned are a ruling class, they must have a political formula, which may, in turn, direct us to the social forces it speaks for. Can Mosca find that formula? He can indeed: "The political center of France, the political formula that justified the exercise of all power during the *ancien régime*, was the king..." [13]

We are back where we started. The old feudal France had found her symbol in the king. The feudal class had lost political control (according to Mosca's first interpretation) or else it was now sharing power with two other groups (according to his second interpretation) to form the ruling class. And that class still used the same hallowed symbol of the king to justify its power. The same formula, then, served a primitive society that hardly knew of statehood, and one organized in a state the like of which the Western world had not seen since the days of Diocletian.

Now, we have been instructed by our author that political formulas follow the changing needs and interests of their society as new demands and forces supplant older ones. But in France, we have seen, the formula had not been changed, although the social situation had changed very much indeed. And the French monarch, like his predecessor in the feudal age, is still only a front man! Somewhere lies the truly formidable power of that state, and it is formulated in terms of an institution which, we are asked to believe, signifies nothing, being a mere pretext of the ruling groups. Something, or somebody, must be absurdly wrong. But everything would be right, if only the French king could be restored to true significance. Suppose we say that he was a focal point, the point in which the total force of French society had found its integration and its fulcrum. Once that much is granted, there is little harm in granting the name of a ruling class to Mosca's bureaucrats, aristocrats, and courtiers; but it would be Mosca's second stratum, necessarily small, since it was lacking the broad base of modern mass society. And it would definitely not manipulate the sovereign, except in the sense in which the servant may manipulate his master. Furthermore, the faster we discard the notion that a ruling class must under all conditions rest upon a major social force, the better will we understand a past in which the state, within the technological and economic limitations of the time, was really supreme—not the "executive committee" of a class, but using and exploiting all the classes, and not for the sake of some mysterious interest of the whole either. It was Mosca's background which prevented him from facing that historical fact so distasteful to nineteenth-century liberalism.

The Bourgeois Revolution

How does elitist theory explain the downfall of the old regime? The task looks simple, and important spadework had already been done by two French historians. One of them was Taine who, Mosca says, had deeply influenced his thinking; Tocqueville was the other.[14] From these two, our author took over the notion of a decadent elite that lacked "the indispensable prerequisites for the successful use of any weapon, including that of power ... firmness and energy." A class that does possess those qualities may yield ground, make concessions, and yet retain its position.[15] Unfortunately, the French ruling class was both stubborn and weak. Above all, it was eminently stupid. No sufficient effort was made by the aristocracy to absorb the new, upcoming elite of the middle class:

> The means for a renewal of the political class were not missing. Throughout the entire eighteenth century the bourgeoisie had been acquiring the two major assets which one had to have in order to "belong": money and knowledge. As tax collectors, merchants, and industrialists, as lawyers and physicians, they were men of substance, even of wealth, who were able to buy the estates which bankrupt noblemen were forced to sell. Enjoying the same living standard, the bourgeois lived in the same style as the aristocrat: he was admitted to the best salons where by dint of *esprit* and erudition he was second to none ... [16]

In short, the French bourgeois had arrived in every sense but politically; the one touch still missing was the legal recognition of his social and political importance. One fact emerges clearly from the picture: what sapped the strength of the old dominant minority was not the absence of class circulation; the old aristocracy continuously, if grudgingly, renewed itself. But that is not quite what our author intends to convey. He makes much of the reluctance shown by the *new* aristocracy of rich bourgeois to share their privileges with their lesser fellows: "Those who had arrived . . . went to great length in placing obstacles in the path of others who desired to join them . . ." [17] Thus it was not so much the old aristocracy, but the rich section of the middle class itself which slammed shut the doors of status and thereby reduced the mobility of their own social group to a mere crawl. The pent-up energies of the great bourgeois mass, deserted by its upper stratum, were bound to explode in a Jacobin radicalism which threw the revolution off its bourgeois tracks.

Mosca's appraisal of the prerevolutionary situation in no way conflicts with the conclusions of more recent probings into the causes of the great explosion. Without stressing them, he does describe the symptoms of the process by which the trend toward centralized control, virtually realized under Louis XIV, was reversed under his two successors. Why Mosca, who had registered the fact that much aristocratic property had been acquired by commoners, fails to discuss the widespread sale of royal offices is not easy to understand, for this malpractice was perhaps the major factor in that process of re-infeudation by which the work of the great administrators of the absolute state was undone. It was a posthumous and bloodless *Fronde* again, this time a bourgeois *Fronde*, a silent counterrevolution that took place before the revolution, paving the way for it.[18]

What happened then was a concurrence of two things: an old elite disintegrated, and a new elite, refusing to identify itself with its own class, intruded, without changing the old formula, with the result that it became involved in the disintegration of the old regime. It was a tragedy which not only *could* be foreseen—it *was* foreseen: the best minds of the time were conscious of the problem and of the only possible way in which the calamity could be averted. Nor did reform remain in the realm of mere speculation; it was tried by good men acting on behalf of the French government. Why, then, did they fail? Why could the monarchy not be transformed from a state already at the mercy of the bourgeoisie into a state belonging to that now mature class?

The reason is not difficult to find. The ruling class, or, rather, the three groups which Mosca chose to call the ruling class of France, obstructed the reforms which the French government attempted. But what exactly do we mean here by "French government"? It would have to be, if not the whole, then at least an important section of the bureaucratic group which made itself the spearhead of reform. Thus the French ruling class immediately before the revolution would appear to be a house divided against itself. Unfortunately, Mosca nowhere indicates that such a split occurred. Are we then to believe that the reform movement originated at some point outside the ruling class? To be sure, the massed criticisms of the bourgeois philosophers (of the physiocrats, to mention one group that had at some time an almost Fabian influence in bureaucratic circles) led the groundwork of reform. But the decrees that tried to implement it, the decrees of a Turgot or Necker had to be, and were, signed by the king himself.

If anything can convince the still unconvinced that Mosca was mistaken when he equated the ruling class with the French royal government, they ought to be undeceived by now. Monarchy, as long as it was strong, had kept that bureaucratic class in line as a mere adjunct of its supreme, royal power; the revolution from below became inevitable when the bureaucratic apparatus of a weakened monarchy could not impose its peaceful revolution from above upon the new *Fronde* of the upper classes.

Yet, is not that very failure, Mosca could retort, the best corroboration of my claim that the King reigned but did not rule?

If we grant Mosca that much for the sake of argument, it still remains to explain the fact that the political class, already bourgeois in part, retained its feudal solidarity in the face of reform. The explanation is again quite simple. State reform meant tax reform, and the new oligarchy of high finance was fighting for its tax immunity. In this fight they found allies not only in the *parlements*, the legal strongholds of their own class interest, but also in the old nobility to which they now felt tied by the affinities of status. The great revolution was precipitated by a double class defection: the old feudal class deserting their king, the new feudal class deserting its bourgeois base. Too late did the upper-class bourgeois rejoin his lesser brother in the solemn oath sworn in the *Jeu de Paume*, declaring that the Third Estate was one, and also the whole state. The middle stratum of the bourgeoisie was already in full motion, and behind it stirred the petty bourgeois masses of the Paris suburbs.

If this is the correct interpretation, then Taine's version of the suicide of the old ruling class, which Mosca basically makes his own, needs some elaboration. Once more, his dualistic scheme (the ruling class versus the ruled) breaks down; once more we find a trialistic tension between royal government, a disunited ruling class, and a new social force (deserted by its own elite) crowding the third corner. The king had to ascend the scaffold because he refused to become the king of the triumphant middle class. He left it to Napoleon to play that role with world-shaking if brief success.

Meanwhile a new political formula had replaced the old. Its success was more enduring, though the ghost of 1786 continued to haunt the modern democratic state. For that prerevolutionary breakaway of the bourgeois elite from its own social moorings only set a pattern which will be repeated in the nineteenth century and after: the class of the middle will continue to be torn by the conflicting wishes to attain to and to abolish privilege, torn between infeudation and equality.

Immortal Ideas, So-called

The formula of the victorious revolution had matured long before the Bastille was actually stormed. The buttresses of the old ideology had all been radically undermined when its whole structure was at last blown up. In the traditional manner Mosca credits the philosophers of the enlightenment with the essential spadework that prepared the final blow; Mornet had not yet written his seminal work showing that the propaganda against the old system prepared French public opinion for reform, not revolution, that it agitated for a better monarchy, not for the radical republic of Saint-Just and Robespierre.[19] There was, of course, Rousseau, but when he had to draw a constitution for the Corsicans or Poles, he too turned out to be a moderate. Yet even Mornet grants that by 1770 Voltaire's *infâme* was definitely *écrasé*, and with the respect for the Church went the belief in monarchy by divine right. With its religious plank removed, the whole of the old formula could be effectively demolished.

The same substitution took place in the field of law and civil rights, until, in the wake of the American model, the new trinity of liberty, equality, fraternity were written into the new Rights of Man and The Citizen. In speaking of "the so-called immortal principles of '89," Mosca in fairness points out that this bundle of "abstractions and a priori concepts" satisfied a real historical need. Unlike Edmund Burke, he felt that the demand for impersonal justice and equality of status was a natural reaction against the arbitrary power of a "ruling class formed not by all politically conscious elements but only by one part, a group excluding violently all the rest..." [20]

If Mosca's account of the revolutionary years exuded a coolness rare in one so young, this may be pardonable in his case. Living in the aftermath of the Italian *risorgimento*, his own personal experience was with a political regime which, emulating the French formula, seemed to display in a most drastic and distressing manner "the impossibility of its practical realization." Mosca's bitterness was that of the infuriated, disillusioned idealist. A certain amount of social fear creeps into the discussion when he treats of liberty, a grand idea as long as it includes notions of restraint, of obligation to state and society: "but for the most numerous class—we are thinking of the plebs—political liberty means just the absence or the weakness of authority;... more freedom becomes an equivalent for paying fewer taxes and for shorter military service..." In the popular mind, "the maximum of liberty would be achieved when there would be no government at all, 'each man being a law unto himself'..." [21]

In these passionate lines our author touches on the latent anarchism of the "little people" of most times and nations. He does not investigate the possibility that the dislike of government is the inevitable "natural reaction" against arbitrary government by ruling classes disregarding their own obligations toward the community—obligations which our author would be the first to insist upon. The argument against plebeian anarchism is an indication not so much of Mosca's social bias—to be sure, he was afraid of the contemporary masses—as of his aversion for "abstractions and a priori concepts," in this case, the attempt of a Spencer, Proudhon, or Kropotkin to transform one symptom of asocial character—or social unrest—into an abstract and all-exclusive principle: the anarchist ideal of society.

Coming from an enemy of mere abstractions, Mosca's statement that the mechanisms used by the French revolutionary constitution makers were "more imitative than inventive" would sound like approval. But it is meant to be a criticism. England was the model for the French regime of '91; the only blueprint demonstrating "some originality" was the proposal of Sieyès, "of which it can be said that it had never before been tried out." [22] This may indeed be said, because the constitution of both the directorate and consulate which the ingenious *Abbé* drafted, was in fact new as a practical experiment. But the model for his three-ring circus of assemblies based on labyrinthine indirect election methods can be found in Harrington's old *Oceana*, so that even Sieyès' singular originality would become questionable.

And now we should expect our author to unwrap the shiny instruments of his new method to perform an autopsy on revolution. To our great loss, the idea never once occurred to him, neither when he wrote the *Teorica*, nor later. He left it to Crane Brinton to apply the theory of the elite to revolutionary situations.[23] This is all the more regrettable as Mosca, speaking of those "ten to twelve years during which France was left without any regular government," discovers in the center of "unprecedented violence, bloodshed, and absolute disorder ... the audacious sect of Jacobins." It was a "tightly organized group behind a few leaders who carried doctrinairism to its extreme consequences, undisturbed by any scruples in the choice of means to achieve their ends. They knew how to stir up the brutal instincts of the masses and how to direct their movements, always, with fanatical effrontery, pretending to be the mere executors of the people's will. They played an important role throughout the revolution and even succeeded, for some time, in controlling and leading it." [24]

That is all. How Mosca could have failed to recognize in that "audacious sect" the perhaps purest type of a political elite that Europe had known since the Company of Jesus (which he will discover later), and was not to know again until in our time Lenin organized his Bolshevik conspiracy, is beyond understanding.[25] A study of the metropolitan organization of the Jacobin club with its provincial affiliations would have given us some insight into structure and stratification of a revolutionary group; the analysis of the control devices by which that elite manipulated the assemblies and executive committees of the revolutionary governments would have led to greater understanding of the mechanics of power; and finally, a study of the struggle for predominance within the dictatorial group, of the swings first from the center to the left, from the far left back to the center, and once more back to the left—that study would have revealed a great deal about the tendencies at work within elites, about the problems of internal circulation and eventual decomposition or "apparentation." [26]

Further, why do masses respond and then again fail to respond to one and the same stimulus? Was Robespierre's defeat due to a split in the elite or to a loss of "charisma"? To a failure of nerve, to use simpler words? Was he no longer listened to because his time was up, or was his time up because they refused to listen? Is there any iron law of Thermidor, or should perhaps Fortuna, Machiavelli's goddess, be restored to her vacated pedestal? Even the most thorough study of the Jacobin elite would still leave a vast area of chance unreconnoitered. Still, such a study would have been very much worth Mosca's while.

The Revolution Tamed

After Thermidor, "central authority grew weaker all the time, and perhaps only the restoration of the old regime could have prevented complete anarchy and brought about the fusion of old and new elements, had not the army, which had come out of the struggle of those years invigorated rather than enfeebled, taken over control of the country. It placed on the throne the luckiest, most energetic and ambitious among its commanders, a man of strength, will power, and ability to plan and carry out the complete reorganization of the nation." [27]

Napoleon's great achievement, the consolidation of the changes worked by the French Revolution, Mosca sees, almost exclusively, under the aspect of military power. Bonaparte becomes the French

Augustus. Through their general, the armies of the new Republic become the decisive social force. They impose peace and social order on the country, while at the same time defeating the concerted efforts of old Europe to defeat the revolution. Mosca almost revels in the contrast between the dispirited and tired Republic and its "youthful, bold, and disciplined" armed forces under their "young captain, whose ambition was matched only by his genius . . ." The paean of these same armies, fighting for, and carrying abroad, the revolution under other leaders than Napoleon, remains unsung. True, Mosca does not altogether overlook the democratic character of Bonaparte's armed rule; he even points out, in connection with the plebiscites to which the First Consul resorted twice, that the idea of popular sovereignty was the equivalent of the old formula of divine right. Nor does Mosca forget Napoleon the superb administrator and originator of the code named after him. But something is amiss. What is it? Political participation of the people, answers Mosca. He believes:

Had the Napoleonic Empire survived its founder, it would always have lacked those essential elements without which a government may be accepted momentarily as a bulwark against anarchy, but could never develop into a consolidated and enduring organism. It could become that only when all the political elements of the country, all the living values and social forces find recognition appropriate to their importance. But that was not the system which Napoleon Bonaparte inaugurated . . .[28]

The sentiment of these lines is as laudable as it is, shall we say, unrealistic. That the revolutionary tensions within French society had much abated when Napoleon won his victory of grapeshot in the Rue Saint-Roch, nobody will deny. But they persisted, and a liberal Napoleonic charter, granted, say, in 1803, would only have anticipated by twelve years the fate of the concessions to "all the political elements of the country" which the revenant from Elba granted on the *Champ de Mars* before he left for Waterloo.

Our author's grief over Napoleon's deplorable lack of liberal convictions could have found some solace in the fact that the imperial armies went on exporting the liberal ideas with their bayonets. Again, as in the case of the imperial Roman armies, the conception of the social force proves to be somewhat less than helpful; it traps Mosca into oversimplifying and rigidifying matters against his own better

knowledge. Insofar as the French army's military function is concerned, it has the aspect of a social force distinct from other social
forces dedicated to pursuits more peaceful. But what Mosca always
forgets: armies are people, and as such they carry the effects and
interests of the nonmilitary social forces in their knapsacks—especially when they serve only as draftees and not as professional men.
Like most of their officers, they remain uniformed civilians; they are
soldier citizens. As citizens of the new French Republic, and as subjects of Napoleon's Empire, the troops of the *Grande Armée* were a
political and social as well as a military force of the first order. The
impression they made upon conquered Europe could not be oblit-
erated by the national resentment that was, in the end, Napoleon's
undoing. No 1848, no national awakening in Belgium, Italy, and even
Germany without the memories of freedom trees and tricolors un-
furling the so-called immortal slogans of the democratic dream.

But Mosca's simple-mindedness in that respect has its rewards.
Without wasting a moment to consider Bonaparte's attempt to reconcile the old and new elites in his imperial hierarchy—surely a worth-
while undertaking from the viewpoint of elitist theory!—he hammers
away at Napoleon the statesman: "His political class consisted exclusively of the bureaucracy, . . . and all political activity of other social
classes showing indications of political maturity was savagely repressed. Such a system," Mosca goes on, using the particular case to
make what is possibly the clearest and most comprehensive statement
of his doctrine, "could not fail to produce the most ruinous effects,
inasmuch as it gradually separates the ruled from the rulers, instilling
in the former an indifference toward, and even hatred of, the latter.
In turn, the ruling class will contract into an oppressive caste which
even the most energetic sovereign cannot influence or modify." The
ultimate resort of such regimes is the police power. Its indeterminate
and willful use "was not the least cause of the revolutionary ferment
which, during the first part of the nineteenth century, spread throughout Europe." [29]

Thus, the failure of the Bourbon restoration to unite and reconcile
the social forces of the past and present would appear as a mere consequence of the Napoleonic sin. The result was that formulas as rigidly
opposed to one another as was Rousseau's to that of De Maistre con-

tinued to compete for the allegiance of the French. And in a way, they do so compete even in our day.

The post-Napoleonic ruling class of the French *ci-devants*, too narrow to encompass all the forces which it ought to have included, was pried open twice to admit, in 1830, the financial oligarchy, and in 1848, more elements of the advancing middle class. But by that time, the bourgeoisie had taken fright; between reaction and the proletarian class begotten by the new industrial revolution, it recoiled from the conclusions of the democratic gospel and threw itself at the mercy of the third Napoleon.

But long before that turning point in modern history is reached, Mosca takes his leave from France to give, at long last, full attention to his native Italy.

5

THE PARTY STATE

Gaetano Mosca has now reached the time when parliamentary democracy is accepted as the master institution by the greater part of Europe. It had spread from France, and France is still the country in which to observe the practical implementation of the system with the greatest profit, Mosca feels. But he corrects himself at once. For Italy too is a parliamentary democracy, and there is very little difference between it and the Gallic model. French parliamentary experience, to be true, is older; but it lacks the one thing without which tradition remains questionable: continuity. Between her First and Second Republics, France had been governed by an emperor and three kings; another empire intervened between the Second and the Third Republic. The last-named (born in 1875) was, at the time of Mosca's writing, less than ten years old, whereas the Italian regime, a constitutional monarchy, could look back upon an unbroken record of twenty-three years.[1]

Shall we inquire into the cultural credentials of the nation that gave to the world a Dante, Machiavelli, Michelangelo? But Mosca does not waste our time in listing the many splendid assets of his country. He prefers to state his real reasons for devoting the rest of his book to Italy with a disarming and quite moving candor: "My reason is quite personal: I write in Italy, she is my motherland, the country I know better and have studied more than others and love best of all." [2]

We gladly will accept his choice but in turn take the liberty of not accompanying him all the way on his detailed investigation. There will be better opportunities to test his judgment if we wait until a time when the Italian scene reflected the contemporary democratic situation much more closely than it did in 1884. We will have done our duty by referring to the aspect which seemed to be crucial to our author: parliamentary democracy is *government by parties*; hence the deputies of parliament "may be said to be the most important elements of our political class, the wheels that set the whole machinery of government in motion and give it direction." [3]

This being so, and keeping in mind that in a democracy the representative elected by the people is supposed to execute the will of the majority, Mosca at once proceeds to the attack. It is worthwhile to quote him on this point at length, for what he has to say anticipated the by now famous formulations of his *Ruling Class* almost verbatim:

> The legal assumption that the representative is chosen by the majority of voters forms the basis of our form of government. Many people blindly believe in its truth. Yet, the facts reveal something quite different. And these facts are available to anybody. Whoever took part in an election knows perfectly well that *the representative is not elected by the voters but, as a rule, has himself elected by them.* Or, if that sounds too unpleasant, we shall say instead: his friends have him elected. In any case, a candidacy is always the work of a group of people united for a common purpose, an organized minority which inevitably forces its will upon the disorganized majority. [4]

Compare with this the formulation of the later work:

> When we say that the voters "choose" their representative, we are using a language that is very inexact. The truth is that the representative *has himself elected* by the voters, and, if that phrase should seem too inflexible and too harsh to fit some cases, we might qualify it by saying that *his friends have him elected.* [5]

Now, there is nothing criminal about quoting oneself. The happy phrasing of the older version could not have been much improved upon; besides, the author had no reason to believe that it had received much publicity. Nor did he simply repeat his dictum and leave it at that. Lest the statement still seem "too inflexible and too harsh to fit some cases," Mosca added a significant qualification, in accordance with his greater understanding of the democratic process. The majority still does not rule, but through its representatives it enjoys a modicum of indirect control on governmental policy. "Whether their component personnels be good or bad," the coteries which "make" the candidates do "represent a considerable number of social values and forces." More important still, each representative will, in his own best interest, pay some attention to the wishes of his voters, and so "echoes of a widely disseminated opinion, of some serious discontent, will easily come to be heard in the highest spheres of government." [6]

Whether that is always a desirable result is quite another matter. Later, Mosca will be heard to say that catering to public pressures usually makes for bad, or in any case mediocre, government. But even then that government will still represent the social forces in the widest sense, reflecting the will of the great majority two steps removed. But this is no longer the Mosca who wrote the *Teorica*. There he is still adamant about the subject:

> When people feel very passionately about something, the majority might triumph at the polls; but under ordinary circumstances, when the choice at issue is a matter of cool judgment and deliberation, then the wills of the majority are most unlikely to agree . . . and the organized few, who can much more easily achieve agreement and change attitudes, will necessarily triumph.[7]

It is hard to believe that Italian elections, even in the comparatively peaceful times of Mosca's youth, were ever anything but very passionate affairs. Nor is it necessarily true that matters which seem more conducive to cool judgment such as public health or public highways, on the surface mere housekeeping problems, were ineligible topics for the rabble rouser. But in the end result we may agree with Mosca: There are public issues which inflame our passions more than others, and there are some which seem less intractable to reason, or what we think to be reason. The paradox is that agreement between humans is more difficult when we approach it as rational beings, easier when gushes of emotion drown our rational objections. Mosca only says what Aristotle said before him when he spoke of the individuating quality of "passive" human reason.[8]

The question of why majorities are bound to remain passive in the game of politics does not cause Mosca any trouble:

> Theoretically each voter has the greatest latitude of choice, but actually his choice is very limited. Unless he wants to waste his vote, he will give it to one of the two or three candidates, or to one of the two or three lists of candidates, who have a chance to win because they are backed by a group of friends and followers. Hence the isolated voters who make up the immense majority of the electorate have only two ways open: either to abstain, or to vote for one of the candidates who have a chance ... [9]

Young Mosca does not mince his words: "To say then that an election is tantamount to an expression of the will of the country or of the majority of the voters is in all ordinary cases to assert a falsehood. . . ." Only a falsehood? Worse is to come: "The legal or rational basis of any political system that admits the masses of the people to representation through elections is *a lie.*" The polite way would be to speak of a legal fiction.

If the voters do not matter, neither do, in the last sense, the representatives themselves. The real victory belongs "to the elements who know how to assert themselves in that special and often artificial *ambiente* created by the elective system." Name your friends, and I shall tell you who you are. The representative not only "has himself elected by his friends," he is the creature of those selfsame friends. They do not only elect but select him. It is they who are "the elements" that matter, influential personalities "who know how to assert themselves"—a negligible quantity as numbers go, yet an important, possibly the most important, group of the *pays légal.*[10]

The Kingmakers

Mosca divides the elements who "direct the elections and create the deputies" in Italy into three categories. The first is the government itself, manipulating the electoral process through its own provincial prefects by the methods too well known to need description here. What the big stick of authority does not accomplish is achieved by "distribution of the carrots," patronage, particularly in the southern part of Italy, where it has proved well-nigh irresistible.

More important for the purpose of this study is the second category of important individuals whom Mosca calls "the grand electors." They are "so to speak, the monads, the indivisible entities of the parliamentary system, in which they hold power without responsibility." Technically, the deputy ranks above the "grand elector"—on whom he in actuality depends. Still higher ranks the minister, who in turn is, officially at least, accountable to all the deputies, whereas "the grand elector is accountable to none, for the simple reason that the little people whose votes he controls, are, for economic and intellectual reasons, at his mercy."

We recognize the type: the man who can deliver votes, who is a power in his city, city district, club, or association, be it cultural, religious, or commercial. He may be a lawyer in politics, a wealthy landowner with many tenant farmers, a banker controlling small businessmen, or just a man of overwhelmingly strong personality who "tells them how to vote."

Mosca has no very high opinion of the morality which that group displays in its dealings with the rest of the community: "Naturally nobody desires evil for evil's sake, and *in abstracto* everybody wants the state to prosper and government to be conducted honestly. But in practice everybody is out for his own advantage; he wants to extort all he can from the public power, while contributing as little as possible. And that is only natural; only a few have the intellectual acumen necessary to understand that a seemingly innocent single act, when repeated many times, will turn into a general habit with ruinous consequences for the community . . ." The grand elector, though he may well realize the damage he inflicts, will still exploit his influence to the limit, and only external restraint will check him, some power or will that is stronger than his.[11]

This is almost a Hobbesian view of man; and who is bold enough to say that Mosca's picture of society is overdrawn? Political influence in our time may have evolved subtler, more impersonal means to assert itself, but Mosca has a premonition of more modern methods of manipulation when he mentions that in urban politics the grand elector as a rule is not an individual but a collective. He discusses the political societies and proletarian organizations which dominate the cities, and large cities in particular. His description sets the pattern for the "iron law of oligarchy" promulgated by his close disciple, Robert Michels.[12] The membership of all organizations is "invariably" composed of "those who command, the founders and directors of the association, and the rest: those who receive their impulse from the former and obey them blindly. The latter contribute nothing in terms of initiative and energy, and yet their usefulness is enormous: it lies in their number." Mosca clearly thought of Machiavelli in the following: "A compact block of a hundred voters represents a tremendous force as compared to, say, three to four thousand isolated voters who possess no means to get together and co-ordinate their action." Once more he returns to his initial point: if they want to accomplish anything at all, The Many must team up behind The Few.[13]

There exists then an electoral elite. But it is very uneven in quality. Mosca distinguishes sharply between the private and the public morality of the leaders. The grand elector will without compunction plunder the state, while in all other respects remaining an honorable man: his private dealings and his negotiations with officialdom take place, as it were, in two separate compartments. Not so the leaders of political organizations. Here the principle of negative selection is at work: ambition will win out over sincerity, the demagogue will silence the good citizen. In the end the bad money has driven out the good; the honest, the disinterested elements "either withdraw or remain inactive, leaving the field to the rascals and intriguers . . ." The result is the corruption of the whole, the triumph of the baser instincts in political and social action.

Mosca is at pains to add that, as all rules, this one has its exceptions too. Not all party leadership is bad, sometimes its record is above reproach. Turning to working class organizations Mosca has some interesting things to say. The impact of bourgeois society on the Italian proletariat was particularly great because, in contrast to most northern countries, residential class lines did not yet exist in most Italian cities. The rich lived among the poor, who fell under the spell of radical but bourgeois politics, and a specific proletarian consciousness had a hard time developing. Only in some larger cities, where masses of workers lived in districts apart from the rich, did the proletarian exodus from the camp of the bourgeoisie become a possibility. Those independent working class societies were frequently led by men of superior social background, men who were perfectly honest in their pursuit of naive and dangerous utopias, but even more frequently by swindlers devoid of all conscience, who were inciting their followers against the upper classes and against the government. "Today they organize the masses for the battle of the ballot boxes, and tomorrow they will lead them to the barricades." [14]

These remarks show, if no sympathy with the working-class movement, a remarkable insight into the proletarian leadership problem. Almost ten years earlier than Lenin, Gaetano Mosca clearly recognized the bourgeois character of the first working-class elite. There is no indication that he visualized, as did Sorel, the possibility of working-class elites arising from the working class itself.[15]

The Elite of Mediocrities

Parliament then would appear to be the creature of those not-always-so-grand electors, individual or collective. In Mosca's Italy "the deputies for the most part reflect the interests of landed property and capital ... and only to a very slight extent the aspirations of the laboring classes. Among these representatives are some whose names evoke lengthy memories of scandal and disgrace ..." But the —avowedly—few cases of rascality and outright criminality are not the cause of Mosca's worry. What perturbs him is the generally lowered level of performance which in turn, he thinks, is due to lower standards of selection: "The decisive element [in the assemblies] is of overpowering mediocrity: mediocrity of intellect, mediocrity of character ..."

Most deputies are leaders only in appearance, leaders of that bogus "loftiness" that overawes the common herd, and their morality will always closely conform to the line of least resistance. Not that there are no truly original, superior individuals among them, but their days are numbered: most of them belong to the first generation of parliamentarians, men not yet the product of the system. All the younger elements must either pass through the machines of the political societies, or they are forced to cater to the whims of groups controlled by grand electors. Few of them will survive with their moral and political integrity unscathed. In the long run, those who do not choose to conform, "a major part of the moral and intellectual forces, . . . will find the doors of parliament forever closed to them." As "an ever-increasing portion of vital forces, of potential leaders thus remains excluded," the Chamber of Deputies becomes increasingly unrepresentative of the whole country. Here, at last, the author resorts to the polite term: representation becomes more and more "fictitious."

Those who do get into parliament, are by no means all ill-intentioned men. If the public interest can be squared with their private convenience, they will do their level best to legislate accordingly. So not all legislation will be bad. But that fact does not, in Gaetano Mosca's view, "derogate one whit from the chief defect of the parliamentary system, which is not so much the lack of quality in the incumbents as their moral predicament; . . . given unlimited authority, with all the irresponsibility that goes with it, they are prone to abuse their power under the tremendous pressure of the multifarious private interests and greeds they are supposed to serve and satisfy . . ." [16]

We are now able to sum up the author's argument. It runs as follows:

> The deputies are the most important element of the political class. They are recruited by a system of negative selection.
> The truly valuable segment of the political class is being made inactive.
> The result is a regime of mediocrity.
> Absolute power makes for arbitrary power.
> Parliamentary government is the despotic rule of nonentities— an impossibility resulting in non-rule, the abdication of government in favor of private pressure groups.

Whether or not Mosca's judgment of modern representative democracy is correct need not concern us here. The author himself takes pains to warn readers of his first work that his own appraisal of the democratic system had become more favorable as the years went by.[17] But even so we are left with a serious problem.

The difficulty is how to reconcile his treatment of the modern type of party government (which even in the revised form remained basically negative) with his general theory of the political class. It is a task in which we receive hardly any help from Mosca who, in the *Teorica* but also later, remained curiously uninterested in the new phenomenon of large-scale party organization. When Robert Michels filled that gap along the lines sketched by the older master, Gaetano Mosca reviewed the resulting work benevolently in a scanty dozen pages and left it at that.[18] He never felt the need to relate his appraisal of party elites to his conception of the political class, that is, to the elites existing prior to, or outside the "new" democratic system of representation. Had he attempted to do so, Mosca might have found himself face to face with trouble in the form of the inconsistency, already referred to, which runs through his entire work; his use, in working out a value system for elites, of two distinct, conflicting methods.[19]

Mosca may have had a notion after all that parties did not merely usurp the position of the old elites but should be treated on an equal footing with, and judged by the same standards as, the ruling groups that had preceded them in history. But that was just what Mosca stubbornly refused to do. We know his reason: It is the mediocrity of the contemporary politician which disqualifies him from fulfilling the true task of an elite, which is to lead, not to be led. Somehow Mosca must have felt that parliament *ought to be* an outstanding body —otherwise it would be utterly impossible to comprehend why he should have devoted articles and speeches by the dozens to the task of reforming the representative institutions of his country. To be sure, he put his hopes primarily on the countervailing powers of the royal office and the upper house, rather than in the improvement of the quality of popular representation.[20] And the remedies which he proposed would at best have improved the government. The parties, in all likelihood, would have remained unchanged, and that means, in the author's view, unsatisfactory.

But by what standards should they have been better? What is Mosca's rationale for measuring the modern party system with a yardstick that he had not used on any of the older ruling classes? His warriors, merchants, bureaucrats had stood for some important social values, as the most successful elements of various social forces. They had formed the nucleus of the political class, exercising organized control over a unified society. In getting to the top, those elements established themselves as "superior" to the vast majority. To ascribe their success to superior qualities would be redundant, unless by superiority we mean the claim of an elite to rule by right of moral superiority. But that in turn would imply the existence of some normative standard, a belief in absolute values by which to judge the performance of elites. And that would be a lapse into idealism which the naturalist Mosca could not possibly permit himself.

On a remarkable page he asks Plato's question, what the perfect government would be like. His answer, given more in jest than sorrow, is that it would be the rule of "merit," to use Mosca's term for virtue. No privilege of birth or wealth would be permitted to exist. Such a society would, of course, still be under some sort of a ruling class. But being based on scientific methods of selection, it could easily dispense with all emotional justifications for its power: it would govern without any "formulas." Mosca concluded: "Unless events take an entirely unexpected turn, we may legitimately doubt that even the most distant century will ever witness such a state of things." [21]

If this is true—and with Plato concurring we may assume that it is—it becomes very difficult to understand why the class of politicians should be treated differently from all other elites. The party orators and organizers, too, base their claim to pre-eminence on certain assets which are being honored as superior. Deputies and bosses would not be where they are unless they were better at playing politics than the mass of their followers. The old elites were also a motley crowd; their prestige was based not primarily on ethical considerations (although it was enhanced by personal examples of superior moral conduct) but on the degree to which the ruling class *considered as a whole* fulfilled its social function satisfactorily in meeting the demands of communal utility. And if the "formula" used by a ruling class continues to exert its spell long after that class has outlived its usefulness, this merely means the transformation of a fact into a myth—a myth which takes the place of a social force no longer operating or of an equilibrium of social forces.

Now, the selection of the ruling class which dominated Mosca's Italy, the politicians, was conditioned by the character of the new all-important social force of our time, not identified by Mosca: the articulation of society in large-scale technological and human units. In the period of transition from incipient to mature industrial civilization, the first managers and verbalizers of mass integration met a need as real and essential as any which had faced the oligarchs of old. If the latter seem to have attained a higher level of efficiency, of virtuosity, of cultural refinement than can be said of our present Whigs and Tories, if these appear to be boors and intellectual dullards in comparison, might we suggest that the scope of contemporary government has infinitely broadened, raising questions unheard of a century or even thirty years ago?

Not the least of all the troubles haunting the post-liberal elites stems from the fact that they took over, virtually unchanged, the "formula" of preindustrial, bourgeois society. The myth of popular sovereignty, which had served well a middle class in its fight against feudal privilege, had now to be adapted to the fact of the new masses. In their service, it would give a moral seal even to activities directed against the very essence of the dogma, which, if anything, implied the prevalence of the collective over all particular class interests. What stumped our author was precisely this new use of the unitary principle in favor of what, to him, was a mere particular. Thus he could censure the discrepancy between creed and performance, the sharp contradiction between the proclaimed faith in strong central government and the disruptive impact on that government by party pluralism. Thus he could attribute to the democratic system itself all the failings of a transitory period which is always marked by crudity and fumbling. In the eyes of those who grew up in a stable society, the level of civilization appears dangerously lowered; they see everywhere "mediocrity." The future looks disreputable, as the present is fast wearing out the forms of yesterday. Things seem to move too rapidly nowhere. And so our author fails to recognize the parliamentary elite for what it actually was: expression, in the disguise of the liberal tradition, of new social values for which the appropriate forms had not yet been found. And since he could not see, and approve of, these novel values, he confused them with their necessarily imperfect articulation. These imperfections he absolutized and blamed upon democracy, confusing a mere symptom with the cause. In taking the low standards of emerging mass society to be definitive, he came close, more than close, to measuring them by the very standards which should have no place in his pragmatic survey of historical elites.

Not daring to go forward, Mosca of necessity turns back and takes what today would amount to the neo-conservative view. For a moment he becomes quite panicky and rejects his own theory, according to which the appearance of new social forces calls for a revision of the "formula." Since he refuses independent status to the working classes—to him they were only mobs misled by demagogues—he could see no need to change the sole formula his country had adopted as the seal of nationhood: hereditary monarchy. And so he proclaims on a note of frenzy: "First of all, the political formula now in force must not be tampered with. To advocate the abolition of our monarchy is to incite the masses to ... insubordination against the established order." [22]

Hardly did he then suspect that there would be a day when the Italian king would lend the formula of monarchy to the Caesarian leader of one party and thus sanction what to Mosca was the very contradiction of the ancient formula: the rule of the plebeian demagogue.

The Social Question

And yet, some deeper urge, some half-acknowledged doubt compels the author to lean over and to probe the lower depths of his society. Proposals for the cure of the political disease which he has diagnosed will always remain foremost in his mind, but he is equally convinced that the reform of politics must go together with a thorough study of the social question. Not himself a member of the wealthy classes, Mosca is acutely conscious of the misery in which large sections of his country live:

Our plebeians are among the poorest and most wretched of all Europe, in particular our rural population which lives in conditions of appalling squalor. In the twenty-three years since our nation achieved unity, their lot, far from improving, has to some extent grown worse.[23]

And so he turns, for the last fifteen pages of the work, his full attention to the various theories and programs of reform or revolution. Our author finds no merit in the radical proposals of the socialists and anarchists. Familiar only (at that time) with the more vulgar form of proletarian agitation promising equality for all, and unable to see how there could ever be, in this world, a society without some ruling class, Mosca rejects the notion of a classless future as an idle dream which is not even beautiful, for the awakening from it, if the experiment should ever be attempted, would be horrible and possibly "the end of civilization itself." [24]

He will never budge from that position; in his view the social revolutions of our time are merely reproductions of the pattern he discovered in the antique city. The upheaval of the poor against the rich can only lead to plunder and destruction, never to a reconstruction of society along new lines. Not for Gaetano Mosca the distinction which Max Weber draws between old-fashioned and modern industrial capitalism, nor that which Sorel makes between the revolts of the eternal poor and modern class warfare.[25] What he later heard of Russian Bolshevism only confirmed his worst fears about the negative, merely destructive character of revolutions and prevented him from studying the newly risen proletarian ruling class as a superb example of his own elitist theory.

Having turned down the two radical solutions, Mosca as emphatically rejects the proposal to do nothing. He has nothing but scorn for the advocates of laissez faire. The idea that, if only government would cease to interfere, "the economic order would ... lead automatically to fairest distribution of wealth among the various classes" —that idea is to Mosca's mind no less utopian than the proletarian panacea. Liberty indeed! He exclaims: "Yes, the kind of liberty such as the fish in the sea and the birds in the air enjoy, the big fish eating the small and the falcon pouncing on the sparrow ..." These diehards of liberalism are not even consistent, for they veto economic intervention even in a case where the old order would collapse "unless it is maintained by bayonets." [26]

Economic nonintervention is predicated on political and military intervention.

Having ruled out the suggestions of the extreme left and right, Mosca goes on to explore a third alternative. It is the one now more or less adopted in the West of moderate state intervention. The community is actively engaged in organizing the just distribution of wealth "in a calm and orderly but energetic fashion."

Mosca sees at once the cardinal objection to that method. Since the political class still represents, if not exclusively then in the main, the interests of property, "wealth, even though no longer a legal prerequisite of power, remains the *de facto* criterion." [27] The question then arises: can the ruling rich be expected to act against their own interest and to make concessions to the poor? The answer would have to be no, if the political class were indeed, as Marx held, nothing more than the "executive committee" of the wealthy bourgeoisie. However—and here Mosca can employ his study of elites to great advantage—the new element of "merit" has already greatly changed the composition of the ruling group. The educated of all classes and professions have been joining it in steadily increasing numbers. "They will become more and more important, and not merely in the legal but also in the material sense. In the end, no single office of significance will remain open to the ignoramus."

So there is hope that "the slow crisis of the present time" will bring about "a reconstruction of the ruling class on an improved foundation." We may see a new elite "accessible to those among the poorer classes who have demonstrated extraordinary qualities of character as well as talent." Not only has the modern tendency toward more and better education assumed the proportion of extreme "political importance ... the redistribution of public offices and intellectual services will make itself felt also economically: knowledge will be at a premium, and give its possessors affluence, prestige, and power."

This, then, would be the elite in which "superior culture will be obligatory and the influence of education decisive." No more the monopoly of wealth because, being "wide open to the sons of all social classes," the new ruling class "is not likely to set its sights so low ... as to subordinate the actions of the government to the interests of the great capitalists and landowners." How, Mosca asks, could the capitalist and landowner groups, never very large, "prevail over the vast majority of independent and high state officials of superior culture?" Being satisfied that culture would remain the winner in the contest, Mosca launches into a most eloquent and moving peroration, which reveals his final hope and with it, strength and weakness of a mind divided by conflicting aims:

> If there is any social class prepared to set aside, if only for a while, the private interest, and able to perceive the common good with the detachment needed, it is certainly the one which, thanks to its exacting intellectual training, has what should make for nobility of character, for broad horizons and for enlarged faculties . . . of foresight and prevention: that class, and that class alone will freely sacrifice a present good in order to avert a future evil.[28]

Pax Platonica?

At first sight, the case which the author makes for his elite of educated men seems plausible enough. In making his surprising plea for a Platonic social peace and thereby, in a complete about-face, his peace with Plato, Mosca does not just imagine things. The rule of the intelligentsia was distinctly "in the air" when the *Teorica* was being written. What he foresaw has since come true: the Platonic sage, in the disguise of the trained expert, has established himself, by a process of slow infiltration, as the type on whom executives as well as legislators have to lean and depend.

To the extent, then, that he posits a political class permeated by college-trained specialists, Mosca has identified a veritable trend. But he goes further.

The disturbing factor in the passage quoted is not its loud special pleading. Surely Mosca speaks for his own class, the *literati*. He, for one, was soon to enter government. From all we know, he served, within the limitations of his time and up-bringing, with exemplary statesmanship, the perfect model of his postulated cultured and disinterested ruling class.

But what made him believe that the educated, once arrived on the scene in full force, would really control the government? That he could only hope for but not prove. But even that hope is, unfortunately, inconsistent with his own assumptions as developed in the text of the *Teorica* and later.

Why should the wealthy oligarchs no longer be the dominating influence in Mosca's future ruling class? He answers that the educated elements would be in the majority. But since when are, in Mosca's book, majorities the masters, and minorities their servants? Does his First Law suddenly pertain to the relationship between elites and masses only, while inoperative within the elite itself? Have we not been instructed that the few can organize more easily than the majority?

To this our author could reply that the intelligentsia in the ruling class, though the majority, would still not be so numerous as to become unmanageable and unable to unite in action. He might add that even if wealth were to control the whole upper stratum of the ruling class, with the intelligentsia confined to the second layer, the rule would still hold good that the former utterly depends upon the latter.

This we may grant. But there remains a further difficulty to resolve.

Why should the educated leaders act in a disinterested manner, why should they be the impartial arbiters between the classes? Mosca's argument that they would acquire affluence because their talents would be at a premium may be turned against him at this point. For which is the more likely outcome: that the intellectuals, having added lucre to their luster, once in power will retain their previous social outlook, or that they will change it and adopt the attitudes and interests of the class to which they have graduated? All available evidence points to the second alternative.[29] To dismiss it or, as Mosca does, to ignore the whole problem of class assimilation, is to leave the world of probability and to enter utopia—the very utopia so firmly renounced by the scientist Mosca. Having started out with an analysis of social facts, he ends up as a moralist, appealing from an imperfect to a more perfect human race. The melioristic belief of the eighteenth century defeats the positivist of the nineteenth. We who have to face life in the twentieth will sympathize with the two Moscas, without being able to resolve the conflict. If the prophet of the truly disinterested ruling class should ever come

into his own, the theorist of the elite which rules for its own good
first and for the good of the people afterwards will stand corrected
—by his alter ego.

He must have had an inkling that the end of his work does not
bear out the beginning, for the tone of the last pages becomes almost
suppliant, even if we allow something for the natural dramatic elo-
quence of the Italian language. "If we wish reform to be successful,"
Mosca pleads, "we must now start in earnest." In his eagerness, he
even forgets his animadversions on democracy. If it had been a
"lie" to say that the majority could ever rule, how can he now accuse
the political class heatedly that, notwithstanding all its talk about
equality and liberty, it "still retains its exclusiveness in forms and
habits"? [30]

This is strange. For after all, the ruling class has done no more
than what a ruling class would do. It has been using the mechanics
of the democratic process in the interest of its own preservation.
Call this a perversion of democracy, it still would not be a perversion of the rules by which elites live and let live. The democratically
chosen leaders may be ineffective and mediocre, but it is precisely
that mediocrity and ineffectiveness which, so far, have prevented any
drastic change of the existing social order.

This would seem to be the logical conclusion from all Mosca has
been saying in his work—so far. But now he urges change, the leaders
ought to change, or else a revolution will sweep them aside. "We
play with fire," Mosca warns us; we can hear the masses stir uneasily,
but we continue to talk, talk about reform. Traditional society still
seems secure, the great explosion still far off. "But watch out, when
the time is ripe, a single match will light it!" [31]

Rereading these apocalyptic lines when he prepared a new edition
of the work two decades later, in the third year of the Fascist era,
Mosca felt the need for toning down the gloomy prophecy by adding
a short postscript saying that those lines had after all been written
long ago.[32] But actually, he did not take back anything. He still held
that the reformer ought to aim at "the true, real renewal of the whole
political class . . . in such a way as to eliminate, to the extent humanly
possible, all irresponsible and arbitrary kinds of action by one individual or groups of individuals." [33]

Did he think of Mussolini and his self-styled elite of plebeian bullies? In 1925, when he had already published the two volumes of his *Elementi,* Mosca could well say of the *Teorica* not only that it had been written long ago, but also that it had been written in another country.

Part Two: Maturity

6

A GOVERNMENT OF LAW

After the *Teorica*, Gaetano Mosca did not publish anything of the same scope or interest for the next dozen years. That is not to say that what he wrote during that period has no merit; one book which he began did in fact continue the line of investigation traced in 1884, but with the stress on constitutional and legal factors. The work, which remained a fragment, does, however, bear upon our study insofar as it foreshadows one of Mosca's later master concepts, the idea of "juridical defense." [1]

The work in which that notion was developed in its final version first appeared in 1896. It was not yet the book now known in English-speaking countries as *The Ruling Class*, for it included only eleven of the seventeen chapters well known to all students of recent political thought. The American editor, the late Arthur Livingston, merged into one volume two books published twenty-seven years apart. The work of 1896 was complete in itself; there is no evidence that Mosca at the time thought otherwise. The second volume, added to a new edition of the first in 1923, was, as the author states in the new preface, written "during the last two, three years," hence shortly after World War I. It reflects the need to bring a work which antedates

125

that cataclysm by twenty years in line with the new, radically altered situation. The choice before the author, then in his sixties, was to rewrite the old text completely or, at the risk of being repetitious, to incorporate his recent findings into a new, supplementary extension, leaving the first part intact. Mosca chose the second solution and published the work in two distinct volumes.[2]

To dwell on these details may be what Arthur Livingston, in his introduction, called "systematic literalism," and since his arrangement of the text was made with Mosca's full approval, there seems nothing left but to accept it as it stands. However, this being an essay in intellectual biography, we propose to keep apart what even Livingston's great editorial art could not make one. His annoyance with the Italian edition of 1923, which "shows two books moving side by side, one as text, the other as notes, with a third book added as a tail that is sometimes inclined to wag the dog" is understandable.[3] But his own version is no less confusing to the English or American reader. What shall we think of an author who, in Chapter XII, starts all over again, bringing up the subject matter of his Chapter I a second time? Surely a translation published in one volume but in two distinct parts might have done no harm to Gaetano Mosca's Anglo-Saxon reputation.

A word about the English title. Here the editor received little help from the author. Livingston refers to the original work as the "Elements." Clearly, "Elements of Political Science," as a faithful rendering of the original, would not have done. Besides, the English "elements" does not convey the sharper thrust of the Italian, *elementi*. "The Main Elements" or "Fundamentals" or "Essentials" might have come closer to expressing the sense of the original, at the price of sounding ponderous and colorless. "The Ruling Class" is, of course, the incomparably better title. It is also misleading.

It has caused many readers, this one not excluded, to examine the book in the light of the specific theory suggested by the English title, and to look for nothing else. When we discover that the work is many other things besides, that the analysis of the elite, far from being sustained systematically, is embedded in a treatise about politics in general (in the Aristotelian sense), the effect is one of baffled irritation. In our disappointment we are apt to blame the author, who, unfortunately, like so many authors, is not very helpful as a guide when questioned about the direction of his work. Thus, speaking of Rousseau in one of the first chapters, he states as his own major aim the refutation of democracy and not, as we would think, the demonstration of the ruling class.[4]

The first victim of his own brilliant misnomer was Arthur Livingston himself. He chose, of all places, his own essay introducing Gaetano Mosca to America to compare him, rather harshly, to another writer, also edited by Arthur Livingston, Pareto. Mosca receives credit for some brilliant hunches and approximations, but it is Pareto who transforms those hunches into a coherent system. What remains with Mosca, mere "shrewd intuition," blossoms into the Paretian "masterly" and "scientific study" of elites. Yet the same Livingston accuses the detractors of Pareto of "limiting the question of Pareto's indebtedness to Mosca to consideration of the concept of the ruling class. Really ... Pareto holds in view all the major positions of Mosca ..." In other words: Pareto's indebtedness to Mosca is not confined to the theory of the elite, but I heartily agree with Livingston when he says that the whole question of indebtedness is "irrelevant." And it is only fair to add that my remarks are in no way meant to detract from his great merit as the American discoverer and editor of Mosca's work.[5]

Comparison of *Elementi* and *Teorica*

If our contention is correct that the *Teorica* already contains all or most of the ideas which the author will develop, more elaborately and more elegantly, in *The Ruling Class*, then the comparatively briefer treatment of a book available to Anglo-Saxon readers requires no excuse. Still, a few words of orientation seem to be in order. Mosca, like his great competitor Pareto, was no systematic writer. The organization of *The Ruling Class* leaves much to be desired, and that is not merely true of the whole composition, as has been already noted, but of the constituent parts. There is hardly a chapter into which the multitude of associations and the wealth of Mosca's erudition do not crowd, and sometimes they overcrowd the major issues. Our attempt to hack a straight path through the thicket will mean sacrificing many a good tree and vista. If the result will make for greater clarity, it also will make the work appear much the poorer. And Gaetano Mosca is anything but an intellectual miser.

The first chapter, clearly introductory, establishes the method of procedure. Mosca does not even try to evoke the impression of an author in quest of the proper methodology; his mind is already made up: he sees no cause for changing the view already expressed in the *Teorica*. So his treatment of diverging theories emphasizing factors of environment or race instead of the historical approach preferred by him is more or less perfunctory, an act of duty rather than of intellectual curiosity. Some of his most important predecessors are not treated at all in the chapter but just hinted at and shunted into later chapters.[6] We shall meet them there. However, one remark critical of Darwin is worth quoting here. In one of his most memorable formulations, Mosca says:

> The struggle for *existence* has been confused with the struggle for *pre-eminence* which is ... far more conspicuous ... Competition between individuals of every social unit is focused upon higher position, wealth, authority, control ... Even in the lower classes every individual in the long run gets a loaf of bread and a mate, though the bread be more or less dark and hardened and the mate more or less unattractive and undesirable.[7]

This passage calls to mind another author. The name of Friedrich Nietzsche is not mentioned in the *Elementi* or in any other major work of Gaetano Mosca, with the exception of the very late *Storia delle dottrine politiche*, where Nietzsche is briefly discussed on pages 334-37. But in 1882 appeared that writer's *Fröhliche Wissenschaft*, in which we find the following remarks about Darwinism:

> To seek self-preservation merely, is the expression of a state of distress, or of limitation of the true, fundamental instinct of life, which aims at the *extension of power* ... The struggle for existence is only an *exception*, a temporary restriction of the will to live; the struggle, be it great or small, turns everywhere on predominance, on increase and expansion, on power, in conformity to the will to power, which is just the will to live.[8]

The similarity is striking but almost certainly a mere coincidence.

Ending his methodological *tour d'horizon*, the author comes to the conclusion that the historical approach is the only one to promise solid results. He briefly reviews some objections to it and finds them all wanting in merit. If Montesquieu fails to convince us altogether, it is not because his environmental historicism was essentially at fault, but because he did not have enough facts at his disposal.

But what about the reliability of those historic facts? Is not all tradition highly questionable? Not so. We must distinguish between gossip, anecdotes, and documented data. Scientific history is possible: "The real safeguard against . . . error lies in knowing how to lift one's judgment above the beliefs and opinions which are current in one's time or peculiar to the social or national type to which one belongs." [9] It is easy to see why the leading Italian philosopher of the period could not agree with a viewpoint so different from his own interpretation of history as an art, as the creative re-enactment of the past in the contemporary mind of the historian. If Benedetto Croce could still, on the whole, endorse the work of Gaetano Mosca, that was possible because he found "much sturdy common sense" in it, enough to overcome the drawbacks of a, in his own view, faulty methodology.[10] In writing these kind words, the great philosopher hardly expected that the older man would mend his ways. In that he was right: Mosca never reconsidered his positivistic method. As late as 1923, the same year in which Croce published his benevolent critique, our author wrote, in the first chapter of the second *Elementi*:

> It is a question, after all, of using the procedure that is so much used in the natural sciences . . . If it should be objected that it is difficult, and we might add, virtually impossible, to make experiments in cases where social phenomena are involved, one might answer that history, statistics, and economics have by now gathered such a great store of experimental data that enough are available to permit us to begin our search.[11]

If one considers certain recent tendencies in political science, it would seem not only that the old man is not out of date but that he is in the van of progress. According to the distinguished Italo-American scholar Renzo Sereno, one of the pioneers in our particular field of interest:

> Mosca was keenly interested in American political thought, much more so than most continental scholars of his time . . . He was greatly pleased with C. E. Merriam's *American Political Theories* and *American Political*

Ideas and was extremely interested in the approach of Harold Lasswell, which appealed to him because it involved social disciplines and points which he deemed most important to the development of a study of politics—psychology and positive scientific systems.[12]

The second chapter, which gave the translator the title to the book, in the original called "The Political Class," contains only ten pages, as against three times as many in the comparable Chapter I of the *Teorica*. Everything is carved to the bone now, but the splendid formulations of the older work appear again, as we already know, with hardly a word changed. Society is still divided between the organized minority, called the political class, and the majority of simple citizens. Within the dominant group we find, as before, two layers of authority, a small circle around the "head of the state" and, under it, the larger, second stratum without which no ordered government is possible. Even if that second group could be eliminated by the sovereign, "he would at once be forced to create another such class." Minority rule equally asserts itself if the old ruling class falls victim to a revolution of the discontented masses. In such case, "there would have to be another organized minority within the masses themselves to discharge the functions of a ruling class."[13] Political change thus may take the form of a renewal or of a displacement of elites, but the essential dualistic notion of society (the rulers versus the ruled) and the narrow definition of the political class as the group in actual charge of government are still maintained in their original rigidity.

The intimation, therefore, that two ruling classes might very well co-exist within one and the same society comes almost as a shock when it is made two chapters later in the *Elementi*. When the distance between ruled and rulers has become too great:

> As a consequence of their isolation, within the lower classes another ruling class, or directing minority, necessarily forms, and often this new class is antagonistic to the class that holds possession of the legal government. When this class of plebeian leaders is well organized it may seriously embarrass an official government.[14]

This is the first appearance of the counter-elite. To say, as Mosca does, that it must "necessarily" form is to assert the wisdom of hindsight. Rome had her plebeian elite; in other societies the plebeian classes were denied the chance of organizing their own aristocracies. But we must be grateful for this liberalization of the ruling class concept. It was a first step in the direction later taken so spectacularly by Pareto. Mosca needed twenty more years to broaden his view of the elite sufficiently to include both the "ins" and "outs." (See Chapter 8.)

When Mosca wrote the first part of the *Elementi*, it was the stability inherent in all ruling classes which struck him more forcibly than the factor of social mobility. And so he wrote: "all political forces seem to possess a quality that in physics used to be called the force of inertia."

Now the democratic principle seems, on the surface of it, to upset that principle of stasis. But it does so only in appearance; in reality there is something which may be called the parliamentary law of heredity: "In the English, French and Italian parliaments we frequently see the sons, grandsons, brothers, nephews and sons-in-law of members and deputies, exmembers and exdeputies." [15] In allowing for a parliamentary elite, the author here fails to mention its mediocrity, but he will return to the fray in later chapters.

The third chapter briefly states the concept of the "political formula" and at once turns for evidence to history, as Mosca had done once before in the *Teorica*. But here he soon deserts the beaten path to indulge in an argument with Ludwig Gumplowicz. Since the political formula is an expression of group consciousness, the question of how to explain the latter arises. Mosca has a set of answers ready, three in all.

First we are told that "individuals who belong to one . . . group are held together by a consciousness of common brotherhood and held apart from other groups by passions and tendencies that are more or less antagonistic and mutually repellent." [16] But to say that people cling together because they belong to one group and not to another explains only one of the two major tendencies which Mosca notes on the next page: "the tendency that every social type manifests to consolidate into a single political organism," and the tendency, characteristic of a later, more complex stage of civilization, "to divide into separate and almost always rival, political organisms." And even the first tendency toward close social integration "prevailed only sporadically" under conditions of primitive isolation which should have strengthened it. Mosca cites as proof Confucian feudal China and the frequent fragmentation of old Egypt into "individual nomes" and, occasionally, "separate kingdoms." [17]

Integration, then, would not be typical of early stages of civilization, and differentiation no prerogative of late, advanced societies. We still do not know what, according to the author, makes for group cohesion. It seems that he himself despaired of giving a convincing explanation. In a later chapter (VII), he is satisfied that men form into mutually exclusive groups because of a mysterious urge of human nature: "Buffon reports that if a certain number of stags are shut up in a park, they will inevitably divide into two herds which will always be in conflict with each other. An instinct of very much the same sort seems to make its influence felt among men." Man is by nature a pugnacious animal, but even as such "remains a social animal." It is precisely his agonistic instinct that will drive him "into groups, each group made up of leaders and followers" who will be "conscious of a special brotherhood . . ."

What have we here? A "law of human nature," the desire to quarrel and to fight, which in turn makes us look for allies, for protection. Hence the group; it is no longer an originally given datum but a consequence. But that would be sheer Hobbes, a mechanistic, individualistic explanation of society, which is repugnant to our author. So he hastens to pair off the agonistic with the opposed element: the social instinct. People fight in groups and live in peace—except "sporadically"—with the other members of their own group.[18] This view reduces war, all wars between groups, be they races, nations, or classes, to a simple emanation of the will to fight. The author does not ask himself what these fights are about. And that refusal to acknowledge that men may not simply war on one another for war's sake (which may be so), but that they may fight wars in pursuit of some definite objectives such as conquest of another group and its possessions—that reluctance on the part of Mosca to consider war as a means to something else besides the satisfaction of an instinct, rather than as an end, has its good reason. For the author's formulations merely paraphrase what Gumplowicz calls "syngenism." But the Austrian sociologist applies that term in a way unacceptable to Mosca: group cohesion and hostility between groups are seen as the *effect* of power conflicts; all phenomena of integration and differentiation, among states as well as classes, are based on the fact of conquest. And since Mosca, as we know, had decided long ago that ruling classes exist even where external conquest could not be asserted, Gumplowicz was of no use to him. He had to be rejected root and branch. Gumplowicz' emphasis on an initial racial conquest made Mosca's emancipation from the teacher (to whom he owed, after Saint-Simon, his own conception of the ruling class) relatively easy.

But our author made it too easy for himself when he represented Gumplowicz as a crude racialist. He knew that this characterization was unfair, and his short reference to the work of his predecessor fails to do him justice. Gumplowicz did not claim more than that the racial factor was a starting point, the first cementing influence which later on gives way to others, cultural and economic. The two races of the conquerors and conquered merge, become one nation with a common consciousness in which the memories of racial cleavage are transformed into, and absorbed by, the new rationale of class.[19] To Mosca this must have appeared as some sort of biological Marxism, the acceptance of which would have placed him ominously close to the very system he wanted to disprove. And so we end up with finding the erratic block of "syngenism" in Mosca's workshop; what had been a capstone in another structure has become mere ornament.

Social and National Type

The term, "social forces," so important in the parallel chapter of the *Teorica*, does not occur yet (it will be introduced rather late, in connection with the new, still more important concept of "juridical defense" in the fifth chapter of *The Ruling Class*). In its place, the author interjects another dualism; to the distinction between dominant minority and ruled majority is added that between the social and the national type. Historically, it appears with the three world religions, Buddhism, Christianity, and Islam. These engender supernational societies whose social boundaries cut across the existing class frontiers. Mosca describes the resulting dichotomy of the two types, the social and the national, in terms almost suggesting Toynbee's theory of the "internal and external proletariats." It is a fruitful notion which, for instance, helps to understand how Rome could Romanize the Mediterranean rim with such ease: with the exception of the Jews, the conquerors met no "resistance of hostile, exclusive and strongly organized religions." [20] The later conflict between God and Caesar is presented with a wealth of detail and insight that we did not find in the *Teorica*. The struggle between medieval church and state is brought into much sharper focus, though again without the slightest attempt to apply the theory of the elite to that great contest. Only indirectly does that theory assert itself when Mosca tries to size up the comparative strength of the national and social types of culture: "When there is a more or less masked antagonism between a doctrine, or a creed, that aspires to universality, and the sentiments and traditions that support the particularism of a state, what is really essential is that those sentiments and traditions should be really vigorous, that they should also be bound up with many material interests..." If a sufficiently strong part of the ruling class reflects those sentiments and interests and is, "in addition ... soundly organized, it can resist all the religious or doctrinary currents..." [21]

This is a most intriguing view, suggesting at once the successful defense which France, under Philip the Fair, put up against the imperial claims of the eighth Boniface. But it remains an oversimplified view, even if we disregard the fact that prior to that victory of "particularism" over universalism, the contest had been between two regimes aspiring to universality; the Holy Roman Empire no less than the Holy See stood for a supernational idea. More important, taken at his word, Mosca would seem to say that the French triumph over the *curia* showed the superiority of the "parochial," national type in a test of strength with the religious social type. But Philip won that test precisely because he had on his side at least a part of the French clergy. The split between the two camps went right through the Gallican church itself, just as the earlier war to the finish between papal centralism and the anarchy of the lords secular and their Germanic emperor had placed the issue squarely into the laps of the church nobility, which was materially as closely wedded to the feudal system as it was, in spiritual respect, bound to the monarch in the

Vatican. The same internal conflict rent of course the other camp; the vassals of the Emperor, too, were torn between their spiritual and secular allegiances, with the former still exerting the stronger pull. Mosca's second dualism is again too simple to account for the complexities of history.

More helpful is another typological distinction which the author introduces at this point. Rather suddenly, we are informed that there are "two types into which ... all political organisms may be classified." They are identical with the two struggling forces of our last example.

The Feudal and the Bureaucratic Type

A feudal organism is, of course, one in which power is widely scattered, and, more precisely, one "in which all the executive functions of society—the economic, the judicial, the administrative, the military—are exercised simultaneously by the same individuals," whereas the concentration of most but not necessarily all executive functions in a central government, with duties highly particularized, is one of the characteristics of the bureaucratic state. Even more important are the ways by which the central power utilizes the resources of society. There can be no bureaucratic government unless it can reach and tax all subjects directly, and that need makes the destruction of all intermediary, small sovereignties imperative. Once the power to tax has become the undisputed and effective weapon of the one and only sovereign, everything else follows as a matter of course: the creation of a large, directly controlled military force and a "more or less extensive" civil service. (The author does not put it quite that way because he is, at this point, interested in evolving a typology of the end product rather than in the historic evolution of the bureaucratic system.)

Mosca makes several important subdistinctions: in feudalism, sovereignty is dispersed among a plurality of persons, but each of those persons exercises all the functions of control. In the national state, sovereignty is concentrated in one point, but the control functions are dispersed among a plurality of officeholders. However, "bureaucratic organization need not necessarily be centralized"; it goes often hand in hand with decentralization and a "very liberal provincial autonomy."

Because in the feudal system control mechanisms are practically non-existent on a national level, the feudal state "demands much energy and a great sense of statemanship in the man, or men, who stand on the top rung of the social ladder." His or their death frequently means the lapse of the whole organism into anarchy. On the other hand, "the personal qualities of the supreme leader exert relatively little influence on the destinies of a bureaucratic state." The Italian original speaks more concisely of the *durata*, the duration, or stability of bureaucratic government (*Elementi*, 1st ed., p. 128). The latter has more staying power than its feudal counterpart.

At this point the author's argument takes a surprising and, be it added, highly convincing turn. We would expect him to dwell, as is popularly done, on the relative rigidity of bureaucratic organisms. Mosca on the contrary lays stress on their great flexibility:

A society that is bureaucratically organized may retain its freedom even if it repudiates an old political formula and adopts a new one, or even if it subjects its social type to very far-reaching modifications. This was the case with the Roman Empire. It survived the adoption of Christianity in the West for a century and a half, and in the East for more than eleven centuries. So our modern nations have nearly all shifted at one time or another from a divine-right formula to parliamentary systems of government.

Mosca does not pursue the thought any further; he is unquestionably right in crediting the bureaucratically organized state with flexibility as well as stability, but that is not the same as saying that the bureaucratic organs of that state themselves are flexible, in the operational sense. But even as it stands, his statement will have to be qualified; his examples from history could be matched by others telling a quite different story. Not all societies of the bureaucratic type accomplished the change-over from one political formula to another without violent upheavals. Only if we decide to dismiss the cataclysm of the great French Revolution as a mere episode will the historical development of France, from the *ancien régime* down to the present time, reveal a continuity of bureaucratization. The same can be said of the Russian "great October": it could be called a mere interlude between two bureaucratic eras of Eurasian Russia.

Mosca knows, of course, perfectly well that some illustrious societies were neither of the feudal nor of the bureaucratic variety: "the ancient Hellenic cities and the Italian [medieval] communes are examples that flock to mind." The Roman Republic would be an additional example. Why Mosca refused to introduce that type of government as a third category is not easy to understand. He will do so in a later work (see Chapter 11 below); here he insists on treating it as a subspecies of bureaucratic society, because in his language the term "bureaucratic" simply means that a state has a modicum of central control and public services staffed with salaried employees. What about governments that did not meet the latter requirement? Some of them "have accomplished miracles of energy in every branch of human activity with the barest rudiments of bureaucratic organization or with practically none at all." Mosca, one notices, cannot concede that bureaucratic elements might be totally absent in some state; they must at least potentially exist, for otherwise the twofold scheme would be in jeopardy. If there was "practically" no bureaucracy in the Italian and Greek city-states, that was possible only because they were such "very small political organisms." As the political community grows larger, the bureaucratic apparatus, too, must increase both in size and scope. Without that mechanism, the administration of "vast human organisms, spreading over huge territories and comprising millions and millions of individuals" would be impossible.

How far can bureaucratization go? It is not quite clear what the author has in mind when he declares that "history shows no instance of a great society in which all human activities have been completely bureaucratized." If by this is meant that there was no such society, then Mosca would be wrong. He could of course deny that state the attribute of greatness. He himself refers to "the maximum development of bureaucracy in ancient Egypt" and to Diocletian's Roman servile state, both ending in catastrophe. In contrast, Byzantine Rome, Mosca's earlier example of accomplished—and successful—hyperbureaucratization, did not so collapse. The author does not claim that the *durata* of the Eastern Empire was due to its bureaucratization. But neither does he suggest any other explanation. He might have suggested that Byzantium lasted in spite of its bureaucracy, lasted as long as the economic structure of its Anatolian heartland stood the weight of administrative exactions in goods and manpower.

States may become organizational leviathans, "but production itself we never see entirely bureaucratized," Mosca insists. Even a Diocletian only regulated the economy, he did not take it into state *régie.* The cited statement makes it clear that whenever Gaetano Mosca says "bureaucracy," he means "state bureaucracy." What we call the bureaucracy of private industry today was still beyond his ken. What worries him is the increasing role of the state as an owner and producer of public utilities and basic raw materials: "The extension of bureaucratic control to the production and distribution of wealth as a whole would be fatal." One wonders what would have been his reaction had he written his work in our day when the discussion is no longer confined to the bureaucratization of the state but has to encompass the bureaucratization of the whole society.[22]

Comte and Spencer

The question Mosca does face, or at least attempts to face at this specific juncture, is how far he is in agreement with those thinkers who preceded him in cataloguing history in terms of various "social types." At least that is what we find Mosca doing at the end of the third chapter of *The Ruling Class,* to which the editor saw fit to transfer those parts from the sixth chapter of the *Elementi* dealing with the schemes of Comte and Spencer. We are anxious to learn Mosca's views about the two. If our curiosity is greater with respect to Comte, that is becaue of the affinity of method which our author shares with the Pope of Positivism.

The pages in which Mosca deals with the two fathers of sociology are unsurpassed for brilliancy and wealth of critical detail by any other section of *The Ruling Class.* The student of the theory of the elite will be forgiven if he treats them only briefly, all the more as Mosca's answer to Comtism and Spencerism is a foregone conclusion.

Mosca has no use for Spencer, because the Englishman predicts that we no longer live in the coercive military phase but in the voluntary phase of industrial society. Just like the Marxian, the Spencerian state is a coercive residue, bound to dissolve into a voluntary association. This is, of course, unacceptable to Mosca who believes, citing Aristotle as his witness, that "any political organization is both voluntary and coercive at one and the same time..." Although Mosca does not say it in so many words, Spencer is wrong—he must be wrong because his law of evolution does, implicitly, deny the perpetuity of domination, Mosca's law of the perennial ruling class. State and society are not antinomies but complements; wherever they exist, there must be "a minority that rules and a majority that is ruled by the ruling minority." Mosca ascribes the fallacy of Spencer's theory to the "aprioristic" character of his "assumptions which do not stand the test of facts." [23] Yet Mosca's innate fairness reasserts itself when he concedes that Spencer had "glimpsed a great truth. ... If we follow not so much [his] criteria of classification as the mass of his incidental assertions, and especially the spirit that animates his work as a whole, we cannot fail to see that by a 'militant state' he means a state in which juridical defense has made little progress and by an 'industrial state' another type of society in which justice and social morality are much better safeguarded." [24] This is, incidentally, the first time that this important concept appears in *The Ruling Class*, to be explained only two chapters later.

Spencer is, then, not completely wrong, because he gave Mosca a chance to set him right. But about Spencer's main point our author remains unconvinced: the validity of "periodization," that is, the attempt to make civilization appear teleological by dividing history into succesive, mutually exclusive stages of progress, first used among moderns by the pious Vico and transmitted, in a secularized version, to the nineteenth century by Condorcet. As he declares in his polemic against Comte: all "periods coexist—not only in one historical epoch and in one people, but also in one individual." [25] It is not scientific to equate the "military," the "feudal," and the "industrial" periods with specific intellectual stages either. There is no truth in the Comtian sequence of the theological antiquity, the medieval metaphysics, and the scientific dawn of modern, positivist humanity.

"In Athens as in ancient Rome, in Paris as in Berlin, in London as
in New York, the majority of individuals were and are in the full
midst of the theological stage, or at best in the metaphysical
stage . . ." On the other hand—and here Mosca anticipates a serious
criticism against Pareto's concept of the logical—"the savage who
sees a fetish in a plant or a stone, or who believes that his tribe's
medicine man produces rain and makes the lightning, could not live
in this world if he did not possess a certain amount of soundly positive information." [26]

This is just good hard-headed common sense. Nobody will quarrel
with the author when he states that "man is an exceedingly complex
animal, full of contradictions." [27] But in accusing Comte of being
superlogical, Mosca forgets that he himself has sinned in that respect
in his *Teorica* where the "three stages" of the military, feudal, and
industrial type are very much in evidence. Nor can it be said that
they are absent from the scheme that underlies *The Ruling Class*. To
be sure, Mosca makes use of periodization with much greater subtlety
and flexibility than either Comte or Spencer, but his whole doctrine
of the ruling class assumes their third, industrial stage with all its
connotations of enlightened intellectualism, the existence of the
New Clerks, and the viability of scientific, "managerial" government.
The very doubt in Mosca's mind that scientific government is possible is not the skepticism of the unbeliever, but the disappointment
of the ex-believer. The defensive note in his dispute with Comte is
unmistakable. Here speaks not a calm critic from a distance, but the
former student eager to dissolve the bond which links him to the
teachers. He will go on moving in the medium of progressivism while
scorning progress, declaiming the rule of the political class, but without the missionary zeal and hope that had inspired the prophets of
the scientific age.

Relations Between Ruling Class and Social Type [28]

The fourth chapter of *The Ruling Class* reads like a companion
piece of the important second chapter. The main thesis is developed
further and again embroidered with historical examples that illustrate an important point but also give evidence of Mosca's strong

aversion for protracted abstract argument; it makes him feel like a
fish on dry land and at the first opportunity he will relapse into the
more familiar medium of political and social evidence, extracting
from it, as he moves along, food for his intermittent cogitation.

He starts out by remarking about the wont of each social type "to
concentrate into a single political organism" at the onset, and then
to expand and spread itself abroad.[29] Mosca does not, at this point,
concern himself with group aggression as a psychological phenomenon; he takes it as a fact and looks at the results. There are two possibilities: complete assimilation of the conquered by the conquerors,
or else some sort of symbiosis. When the ruling class of a state made
up of a mixture of two social types is not exclusively recruited from
the dominating group, "the country may be looked upon as a sick
country that stands on the brink of serious political upheavals."
(Example: Turkey in the nineteenth century.) However, various
social types may "coexist in guises more or less masked within a
single political organism . . . in countries that present all the appearances of strong social unity." That pseudo harmony exists where the
political class is either unwilling or unable to transmit its formula
to the ruled social type. (Examples of exclusion: the slaves of antiquity, the Indian pariahs.) The older the political formula, the more
likely is its chance to penetrate the lowest strata. Mosca echoes
Machiavelli when he stresses the great unifying force of the religious
sentiment. Whenever ruling classes could appeal to it, the moral
unity engendered in the people was a source of often unexpected
strength for regimes which, by all odds, should have disappeared.

Among the forces working in the opposite direction, away from
moral unity toward a more or less accentuated, often absolute disparity of social types, our author lists intellectual ferment in the
ruling group: "when rapid flows of ideas agitate the higher classes,
or the more active intellectual centers, . . . the lower classes . . . are
likely to be left behind, and differing social types tend to form inside
the society." Since it is in the urban centers that this intellectual
ferment as a rule develops, the rift between country and city tends
to deepen.[30]

As social stratification becomes more complex, "disparities in intellectual cultivation and differences in language, habits and family

customs" will become intensified. Growing bureaucratization has the effect of making relations between individuals or groups of individuals increasingly impersonal. That is what Mosca must mean when he says that "disparities in upbringing among the various social classes are likely to become more marked in bureaucratized societies." For he goes on to point out the advantages the feudal lords derived from their close integration into the small world controlled by them: "The baron knew his vassals personally. He thought and felt as they did . . ." For all his harsh and sometimes arbitrary rule, "he was a man whom they understood perfectly. . . . It requires utter ignorance of the psychology of the lower classes not to see at once how many things this real familiarity based on an identical education, or lack of education if one prefer, enables an inferior to endure and forgive . . ." [31]

Enough has been written about the growing anonymity of social relations in modern society, about the tendency, because of the frustrated urge for personalization, to create a magnified, symbolic image, and at last the superpower of the father-Fuehrer. But, even if depersonalization is a necessary complement of bureaucratization, that process does not necessarily lead, as Mosca suggests, to increased educational disparity among the various classes. Mosca's observation was more or less true of Europe with its older, deeper social furrows. In the United States the opposite development has taken place: as bureaucratization has become more marked, so has the classless uniformity of education. It has grown in width if not in depth. Social mobility, to be sure, has slowed down considerably even here; stratification has become more rigid than before. But though the Alger myth may no longer be potent, the American formula of social harmony is still an operative force, thanks mainly to the leveling and unifying influence of democratic education. By widening the channels of intelligent communication, education counteracts the tendencies toward exclusiveness in a society managed by "bureaucrats." One might go still further and say that the bureaucratic ordering of things *depends* on the existence of a universal educational regime and thrives on it. If that is true—and in this country it seems to be true that general literacy has helped rather than impeded the centralization (rationalization) process—then it may be said, *pace* Mosca, that parity in upbringing among the various social classes is likely to become more marked in bureaucratized societies. Bureaucracy and universal education go together.[32]

However, in the world that Mosca knew, the centrifugal trends in mass society affected the cohesion of the ruling class unfavorably. More important still, among groups left unrepresented in the ruling class, indigenous elites could now appear to make their bid for power. It is at this point that Mosca, as has been remarked before, begins to broaden his conception of the ruling class by pointing out that "as a consequence of their isolation, within the lower classes another ruling class, or directing minority, necessarily forms." [33] From this "discovery," the author goes on to develop his own law of elite circulation, almost but not quite anticipating the conclusions of Pareto: "Whenever and wherever a section of the ruling class tries to overthrow the legal government, whether because of conversion to a new political formula or for some other reason, it always seeks the support of the lower classes." Or else: "the portion of the ruling class that is holding power ... may find its main support in the lower classes, which still cling loyally to old ideas and to the old social type." [34]

In the first case, the rebellious opposition inside the official ruling class enlists the whole, or part of, the plebeian out-elite against the government, while in the second case the same rebellious in-elite will be defeated by a combination of the governing, conservative wing of the ruling class and all, or a part of, the out-elite. Mosca recognizes now, as he had not yet done in the *Teorica*, the triangular character of many class struggles. For if the masses are already organized by their own leaders in "widespread and fairly permanent associations, which levy assessments, administer a special justice of their own and have their own hierarchies of officials, their own recognized institutions," the two competing factions of the ruling class will not be able to decide the issue without turning to the masses. But in doing so they have to deal with the plebeian leadership; the price for the allegiance of the masses, cheap when they did not yet have organizations of their own, has gone up sharply.

There is no need to go any further to see that all the prerequisites for an elitist theory of "indirect democracy" are within Mosca's grasp: the struggle between dominant minorities inside and outside the political class proper has the incidental effect of promoting popular demands. The democratic conquest of rights by the people may be a chimera, but these rights are being conquered just the same, only as Mosca will say, they are won by and on behalf of the ruling class and only indirectly benefit the people.

He does not say it yet; for the time being he is merely anxious to resolve the question: Why do ruling classes lose control? Unfortunately Mosca adopts Taine's doctrine, attributing the downfall of the governing minority to "a decline in energy." The upper classes become "poorer in bold and aggressive characters" and "richer in 'soft,' remissive individuals." That change is "the most dangerous among the consequences that may result from differences in social type between the various social classes." [35] Mosca knew of course that the closed or the open character of the elite had something to do with that loss in energy: "A ruling class is the more prone to fall into errors . . . the more closed it is, actually if not legally, to elements rising from the lower classes." [36]

Precisely why the exclusion of new elements should cause the change from a "bold" into a "soft" ruling class the author does not say. For him the cleavage between the minority in power and the masses is essentially a difference of social types and not of psychologically distinct dispositions. The decline of the elite Mosca accredits to the absence, and not to the presence, of new elements in it. The ruling class degenerates, it loses character, but it is not basically altered. Yet, the terms "bold" and "soft" almost suggest Pareto's archetypes: the lion and the fox. But the traffic between the two genera is not yet spelled out in terms of elitist circulation.

Juridical Defense

This important concept has already made its brief and rather furtive entrance earlier (see p. 139). Developing it fully, Chapter Five becomes the core of the first *Elementi* and the author's most significant addition to the groundwork laid in the *Teorica*.

We know already that the dominant minority will always try to justify its rule by some attractive rationale. The "formula" will represent, or make a pretext of representing, the popular consensus about what is just. And that consensus will in turn reflect the level of morality as it exists in a particular community at any given time.

Mosca feels that "we might very well dispense with defining the moral sense. It is something we all feel and understand." [37] But his sense of duty prevails, so he reviews two contrasting schools of thought (the followers of Buckle, who denied all moral progress, are compared with the selectionists who held that evolution favored the most altruistically inclined individuals) and rejects them both. His own position Mosca states in these well-guarded terms:

> We have so far carefully avoided, it will be noted, any speculation as to the origins of the moral or altruistic instincts. For our purposes here, it is sufficient to observe that they are innate in man and necessary to social living. It will further be noted that our view is contrary to the doctrine of Rousseau, that man is good by nature but that society makes him wicked and perverse. We believe that social organization provides for the reciprocal restraint of human individuals by one another and so makes them better, not by destroying their wicked instincts, but by accustoming them to controlling their wicked instincts.[38]

One sees that the genealogy of morals is not Mosca's business. What matters to him are "the social mechanisms that regulate this disciplining of the moral sense." They "constitute what we call 'juridical defense.'" [39] The degree of its perfection is determined by "the organization that establishes the character of the relations between the governing class and the governed and between the various levels and various sections of the ruling class."

Juridical defense exists where there is "honest government . . . truly liberal in Guicciardini's sense of the term." And Mosca lovingly cites the Florentine's definition of political liberty as "a prevalence of law and public decrees over the appetites of particular men." His favorite writer also characterized honest government as one which guarantees "that property will be protected." [40]

Now, many writers, in the great tradition that originates with Aristotle and runs through Polybius and Cicero to Locke and Montesquieu have advocated, as the best protection of "life, liberty and estate" a mixed form of government—mostly in conjunction with a separation of powers. Mosca has no quarrel with that school, except that it has, in his view, placed an exaggerated trust in the mere mechanics of government and "often forgotten that if one political institution is to be an effective curb upon the activity of another it must represent a political force." Mosca is quite specific about the conditions which that force will have to meet in order to be an effective force: it must be "the organized expression of a social influence and a social authority that has some standing in the community, as against the forces that are expressed in the political institution that is to be controlled."

This is just a tiny bit confusing. On first reading, one has the impression that the force which is supposed to curb the "political institution" is to be some public body, parties, economic associations, churches, or the like—in brief, society, or part of it, versus the state. But that is not what Mosca means, at least not at this moment, for he speaks in the next breath of "certain parliamentary monarchies," where "in spite of the letter of constitutions and fundamental charters, we see heads of states . . . becoming powerless to counterbalance the influence of elective assemblies." How can this happen? Because these assemblies "actually comprise within themselves a considerable body of capacities, interests, ambitions and energies." They represent, in other words, the "social forces," and these forces are organized as an official branch of government. Mosca reiterates the same thing in reverse when he refers to "senates and upper houses . . . made up of pensioned officials, deputies and assemblymen . . . along with a few rich men whose vanities the ministries have found it expedient to flatter. Such bodies, therefore, do not offer adequate fields either for aggressive minds or for ambitious talents. They do not represent important social forces." But they are of no importance simply because mind and talent have found another place, within government. Therefore, those ceremonial upper houses "have easily been relegated to subordinate positions by lower houses that are functioning at their sides." [41]

Up to now it seems that the power equilibrium is achieved by forces legally entrenched within the government—a view slightly more realistic than, but not so drastically different from, the traditional interpretation of mixed government. Mosca only repeats in a more elaborate way Montesquieu's "Tout seroit perdu si le même homme, ou le même corps des principaux ou des nobles, ou du peuple, exercoient ces trois pouvoirs...," [42] when he declares:

The absolute preponderance of a single political force, the predomi- nance of any over-simplified concept in the organization of the state, the strictly logical application of any single principle in all public law are the essential elements in any type of despotism, whether it be a despotism based upon divine right or a despotism based ostensibly on popular sov- ereignty...[43]

The separation of powers in itself is no assurance against either menace unless each branch of the government is controlled by an- other social force. But Montesquieu, to quote the late Franz Neu- mann, "was not completely blind to this objection, because he, indeed, although inadequately, related the three powers to social groups. To him the monarch...represented social interests different from those of the legislature; the legislature, in turn, composed of two houses, was to represent the aristocracy and the bourgeoisie respectively; while the judiciary...was to represent everybody, and hence nobody..." [44]

But Mosca does not merely echo Montesquieu. Step by step, he now extends the concept of the separation of powers beyond the boundaries of governmental institutions. To ensure juridical defense, "the prime and most essential requisite is that the secular and ecclesi- astical powers shall be separated." For no system that admits only one truth can tolerate debate and moderation.[45]

We may pause for a moment to consider whether that is neces- sarily so. There is no logical necessity for equating philosophical with political absolutism. The two will more often than not concur, but that is not the same as saying that they are identical. A convic- tion, absolutely held, say, of the sanctity of human life may not indeed inevitably make us tolerant and understanding of our fellow man, but if it fails to have such an effect, the blame can certainly not be attributed to the intensity or absoluteness of the moral code enjoining tolerance, love, and humility. In the same way, philosophi- cal relativism is not necessarily conducive to behavior usually asso- ciated with the liberal or democratic way of life. You may be, or think of yourself as, a political relativist and yet be prone to invoking

the coercive power of the state whenever, say, your notion of toleration seems to be offended by the forces of intolerance. In that case,
philosophical relativism would tend to become indistinguishable
from political absolutism. One might go further and assert that a
society with an empiricist or relativist formula will be most sorely
tempted to invoke, in times of stress, the help of absolutist methods
precisely because social cohesion cannot, in a civilization believing
in tentative, experimental truths only, be taken for granted. On the
other hand, a social system based on absolutely held and promulgated
values may well afford tolerance in individual cases as long as the
general need for conformity remains unquestioned.[46]

The second and third most important requisites which guarantee
juridical defense "are to be found in the way in which wealth is distributed in a society and in the way in which military forces are
organized." When the monopoly of wealth is fused with the monopoly of arms, then "we get despotism in its worst form—namely a
barbarous and primitive system of government that has the instruments of an advanced civilization at its disposal, a yoke of iron ...
which is very hard to break ..." No matter whether the wealth of
the nation is still in the hands of a small plutocratic group or already
expropriated and administered by government officials, in each case
"political power and control of economic production and distribution
are irrevocably delegated to ... the same persons," who "become the
arbiters of the fortunes and welfare of all, and we get a more powerful oligarchy, a more all-embracing 'racket' [in the original: camorra],
than has ever been seen in a society of advanced civilization." [47]

Mosca and the U.S.A.

In a special note attached to the third edition of the Elementi,
published in 1939, Mosca refers to Russian Communism (but not
to Italian Fascism, for obvious reasons) as the classic example of his
prophecy of 1896 come true.[48]

But the same tyranny, Mosca believes, could have a democratic
origin: "One of the most important reasons for the decline of the
parliamentary system is the relatively huge number of offices, con-
tracts for public works and other favors ... which the governing class

is in a position to distribute . . ." [49] This way, the power concentration works through the corrupting influence of patronage. This may sound like a sly dig at the United States where the spoils system was after all still flourishing when Mosca wrote. But he shows more respect for this country than his strong bias against all things democratic would lead us to believe. He grants, for instance, that "as an organ of juridical defense the American presidency is far superior to the cabinets in the parliamentary countries of Europe," the reason being of course that the president has more security of tenure than any prime minister, in addition to having more power. Mosca adds that the same applies, to some extent, to the state governors.

But having said that much, he gets a firm grip on himself and states that "the formal perfection of mechanism in federal and state governments has only to an extent made up for a defect which is fundamental in the whole political and administrative system of the American Union . . ." Equal and universal suffrage is that evil thing. As a result, "a single class of electors now casts its votes in all elections . . . The same electoral clique chooses federal and local authorities . . . Under this system, in other words, all the powers that should balance and supplement each other emanate from a single caucus or electoral committee." Although he nowhere mentions him, our author might have endorsed, in a general way, the grand principles of John Calhoun. In the United States Mosca saw "the inability of a democracy to control and limit itself." [50] Mosca would apply to us his general remark:

> When a system of political organization is based upon a single absolute principle, so that the whole political class is organized after a single pattern, it is difficult for all social forces to participate in public life, and more difficult still for any one force to counterbalance another.

And likewise the following statement: "The checks which bureaucracy and democracy can enforce upon themselves and which are applied through the agency of other bureaucrats or elected officials are always inadequate." [51] He is very emphatic on this point; near the end of the first *Elementi*, he repeats:

> Because of a constant, flagrant and manufactured contradiction between the duty and the interest of the man who governs, and of the man

who should judge and limit governmental action, the bureaucracy and the elective elements, which should control and balance each other, end by corrupting and denaturing each other.[52]

The impression that the "early middle" Mosca of the first part of the *Elementi* would like to see the demise of this "corrupted" and "denatured" system is, however, incorrect. Contrary to what he had proclaimed in the *Teorica*, he now finds that representative democracy has something to recommend it after all. He has real praise for "the public discussion that takes place within representative assemblies" and calls it "the real juridical safeguard." The existence of "a small independent minority" among all the "disparate political forces and elements" that make their way into those assemblies happens "often enough to control the conduct of a large majority, and, especially, to prevent the bureaucratic organization from becoming omnipotent."

Again, the author feels that he has said too much, and adds: "But when, beyond being organs of discussing and publicizing, assemblies come to concentrate all the prestige and power of legitimate authority in their own hands, as regularly happens in parliamentary governments, then . . . the whole administrative and judiciary machine falls prey to the irresponsible and anonymous tyranny of those who win in the elections." [53]

This time the author indicates in a note that he has France in mind. Yet, he is for that reason not a Vichyite before Pétain. He knows that "under the conditions that prevail at present in society, the suppression of representative assemblies would inevitably be followed by a type of regime that is commonly called absolute." Since that remark occurs in a context free from any reference to socialism, it is difficult to see how the Italian reader of the second and third editions of the *Elementi* (1923 and 1939) could have thought of any other than the "absolute" regime to which he was subjected in those years, nor how he could have failed to miss the thrust of the remark "that the defects of parliamentary assemblies . . . are merest trifles as compared with the harm that would inevitably result from abolishing them or stripping them of their influence." [54]

Power Against Power?

Knowing what he wrote before, and how he still feels about parliaments and democratic demagogues, we follow the whole tortuous argument that takes place in the author's mind and soul with an ironic sadness not unmixed with admiration for his honesty, as when he writes, repeating over and over again the same phrases: "It cannot be denied that the representative system provides a way for many different social forces to participate in the political system and, therefore, to balance and limit the influence of other social forces and the influences of bureaucracy in particular." He is going to deny that possibility two pages later in a passage which we have already quoted. At this point, however, Mosca wavers. If the democratic process, and that process alone, gives the guarantee for a just balance of the social forces, then that ground alone might make acceptable the odious doctrine of popular sovereignty, "however clearly we might realize that [its ideas and sentiments] have a very slim basis in scientific fact." [55]

In the end, the consequences of democracy prove to be far too many for the author to accept, and on the second to the last page of the first edition of the *Elementi* Mosca once more reverts to his traditional hostility—perhaps because he once more eyes the dreaded "spectrum that haunts Europe": "In the world in which we are living, socialism will be arrested only if a realistic political science succeeds in demolishing the metaphysical and optimistic methods that prevail at present in social studies . . ." Socialism and democracy are children of the same nefarious spirit—an argument which would be heard more plangently outside the academic halls two decades later.

Inside those halls, "*a whole metaphysical system must be met with a whole scientific system,*" Mosca exclaims, and the italics are his own. The antiscientific influence of Marxism must be destroyed, and that is only possible if the critique is widened to include the suppositions of the democratic mother creed. Walter Lippmann and, with a strong reservation as to "metaphysical," Professor Eric Voegelin, who would substitute his own term, "gnostic," might give plaudits to Mosca's *pronunciamento*. We might follow suit, but not until we had a second look at Mosca's doctrine of juridical defense. As it stands in the first part of the *Elementi*, it is hardly the bold scientific break from the tradition which the author and some of his recent readers made it out to be.[56]

Our list of Mosca's passages relating to juridical defense may seem exaggeratedly redundant. However, there is purpose in the repetition. A plethora of evidence may provide some insurance against the temptation to read more into the text than is there.

As usual, we discover not one but two Moscas, one a pluralist, the other cherishing throughout his life a unitary notion of society. The pluralistic argument is summed up admirably in the final chapter of the first part of the *Elementi*. In the ideal case—and we know that, in Mosca's view, the liberal regimes of the past century came close to realizing the ideal—"the individual and collective will of the men who have held power in their hands has been curbed and balanced by other men, who have occupied positions of absolute independence and have had no common interests with those whom they have had to curb and balance."[57] As yet, those independent forces are not taken to be independent in the sense that they assert their counter-power, or to use David Riesman's happy phrase, their "veto power" against the encroachments of competitors acting either in isolation, or combining with some other groups, but themselves not necessarily represented in the actual government. This is a later phase in the slow evolution of our author's thinking. Mosca's final notion of the ruling class does include Riesman's "veto group" conception and thus would not seem to justify the general contempt with which that most inspiring writer treats the doctrine of the ruling class.[58]

"A multitude of political forces" is then the "necessary, nay indispensable"[59] condition for that equilibrium which is, in turn, conducive to juridical defense, due process of law, the enjoyment of full civil freedom. Taken at face value, this is political pluralism. "Only power can control power"—that is the scientific law, the Machiavellian message which Professor Burnham has discovered in the work of Gaetano Mosca.[60] And there is indeed much to make that reading a convincing one. Law, justice are no manna from heaven but the formal recognition and normalization of demands backed up by social power; governmental policy is the natural resultant of the compromise and tenuous reconciliation of conflicting interests. Seen in this light, the demarcation line of civil rights will sway with the increasing or decreasing strength of the contending groups. The gauge of what the author calls juridical defense, in other words, will be determined not by notions of morality endemic in a certain social system, but by power.

Clearly, Mosca was not satisfied with a doctrine of equilibrium depending on the constitutional mechanics only; hence his criticism of the separation-of-powers theory; hence his inclusion of all or most social forces into government, until he had discovered those "positions of absolute independence," from which alone, he thought, the battle of juridical defense could be fought adequately.

However, much as Mosca insists on the "multitude of political forces" to ensure variety, he always insists, and with equal if not greater emphasis, that the political class must stand for the principle of *social unity*. That class will be successful only and as long as it reflects such a principle. To some extent, homogeneity may be induced by social and political manipulation from above—but only to some extent. "If the dispassionate study of the past can tell us anything, it tells us ... that it is difficult to modify very appreciably the mean moral level of a whole people of long-standing civilization, and that the influence that one type of social organization or another can exert in that direction is certainly far less powerful than the radicals of our day imagine." [61]

An interpretation which would leave the state at the mercy of each power fluctuation, a theory of equilibrium which must be labeled mechanistic even though the framework has been widened to include all social forces of society—such a theory makes nonsense of all the assumptions on which Mosca based his other doctrine, that of the "political formula." For those who did forget what it implies, the basic unity of moral notions which all formulas must satisfy, the author restates his convictions in the very chapter in which he explains the meaning of juridical defense: "Now, public opinion, religion, law, and the whole social mechanism that enforces observance of the law, are expressions of the mass conscience ..." The Humean character of this statement becomes even clearer when we hear that generally mass conscience "is dispassionate and disinterested as against the one, or the few, whose perception of what is just and honest is clouded at the given moment by the violence of selfish impulses."

The notion of what is to be regarded as "just and honest" may be different in different civilizations, but there is no question in the author's mind that there is always some consensus about the proprieties of social and political morality. In a mature civilization, "moral instincts—and for that matter selfish passions—become more refined." It is on that basis that deliberate, directed moral progress becomes possible: "In a society in which political organization has made great progress, moral discipline is itself unquestionably greater . . ."[62]

We do not wish to stretch the point by saying that the author, unable to square his pluralistic with his unitary notions, tried to overcome the difficulty by subordinating the former to the latter. Rather he follows custom and assumes interdependence between the two principles. Pareto alone of his generation was consistently a pluralist when he declared that "human society is heterogeneous. The theology of equality denies that fact . . ."[63]

A pluralist and relativist could not have placed his hope in a disinterested class of people such as Mosca postulated. Public morality, the expression of mass conscience, calls for personalization in terms of the doctrine of the ruling class. So Mosca is only consistent when he says:

A society is best placed to develop a relatively perfect political organization when it contains a large class of people whose economic position is virtually independent . . . and who have sufficient means to be able to devote a portion of their time to perfecting their culture and acquiring that interest in the public weal—that aristocratic spirit, we are almost tempted to say—which alone can induce people to serve their country with no other satisfactions than those that come from individual pride and self respect.

Plato haunts these lines with their assumption of "the public weal," but otherwise Mosca's disinterested class reminds us very much of Aristotle's middle class. Our author nods agreement when he states that "in all countries that ever have been, or now are, in the lead as regards juridical defense—or liberty, as it is commonly called —such a class has been prominent." He provides a long list: there was, in Rome, the "teeming plebs of small property owners," there was "England's numerous gentry," once made up of "moderately rich landowners," and now of "moderately rich businessmen." The British ruling class derives from that group its "best elements." And Mosca does not forget the United States: here, too, there "has been, and there still is such a class." [64]

The disinterestedness of all those classes may be questioned, but not the fact that the economic climate of the middle class was favorable to the rise of that "aristocratic" public-mindedness that makes for civic greatness.

It was the tragedy of Gaetano Mosca that he lived to see the dissolution of that solid middle class in Europe. In a postscript added to the third edition of the *Elementi*, he states sadly that in the wake of the [First World] war, almost all the European middle classes were "if not destroyed, then decimated." The introduction of the general suffrage only hastened that development in his own Italy. Worse still, "the parties of the extreme left are led by members of the middle and lower middle classes." Part of the bourgeois elite, Mosca wants to say, deserted their own class, and hardly from a sense of public duty.[65]

At the end of the first *Elementi*, Mosca's hope for a disinterested class is nothing more than a nostalgic dream.

7

PROGRESS REPORT

For an intimate glimpse of the writer and man who was Gaetano Mosca, one has to turn to his minor writings. There can be seen the Ciceronian "force, clarity and elegance" that the American editor of *The Ruling Class* so justly praises.[1] Gone is the occasional self-consciousness of the main works, in which the scholar, plodding through huge masses of material, sometimes seems to frown on the impatient and bold other Mosca who is the originator of a new idea. It is as if his mind had rid itself of a great burden in those shorter pieces; he is frankly, unabashedly a journalist in the tradition of the Latin countries, a tradition that permits the scholar to debate the issues of the day without tarnishing his academic reputation in the least.

Mosca's output in that genre, editorials, reminiscences of public figures, book reviews, is a testimonial to the untiring creative urge which marked the—often lengthy—periods between major productions. He did not write these occasional pieces in order to relax, to let off steam, or to change the subject. Sooner or later in most of them he reverted somehow to *the* subject, the *idée fixe* of his scholarly existence: the problem of the ruling class. Some of his most felicitous clarifications of that subject can be found precisely in those writings ostensibly devoted to another topic, and some signal advances in the elaboration of the doctrine were accomplished here where he could, and was obliged to, speak his mind with the conciseness that goes with the journalistic limitations of space and time.

He is almost a different person in these concentrated exercises: his Southern vivacity sparkles with a sly, dry humor; one can almost see him twinkle after some particularly telling thrust of his foil-like pen. And in how many different ways could he wield it! Gaetano Mosca was a fighter, but also a wry diplomatist for whom war is a means and not an end; a man quite capable of making enemies, but somehow ending up by being friends with even the most sullen foe. Only once did Mosca battle in the real spirit of vendetta: that was when the Marquess Pareto crossed his path without saluting him. (See Chapter 8.)

The Liberals and The Vatican

It was in 1897 that another nobleman, the Prince di Belmonte Granito, raised a question which was heatedly debated among Italy's outstanding economic writers. Twenty-seven years had passed since the Savoyan king had taken the Holy City by force of arms, but the impasse between the two Romes was as severe as ever. The particular argument of the Prince was of a kind to create considerable embarrassment in the liberal camp. How, asked the Catholic gentleman of the scholars in the distinguished *Giornale degli economisti*, how can you attack the government for intervening in the economic affairs of the country? How can you Liberals declaim for laissez faire while at the same time praising the same government for intervening in the business of the Church? This is a Catholic nation, but you will not permit that education be administered by Catholics. The Church has large property interests, but so far not a single Liberal has been in favor of free enterprise whenever the Church wanted to dispose freely of its own holdings. Will you deny that you are inconsistent? [2]

No greater insult was imaginable, and the battle, at once joined by the editors of the journal, was a dubious one. The hard-pressed editor-in-chief no doubt accepted eagerly the helping hand of his old friend and academic colleague, Gaetano Mosca, and sent Mosca's long open letter to him to the printers. "My dear De Viti" the missile began, and the note of intimacy and cordiality is sustained throughout the text, which duly appeared in the journal, ostensibly a rebuttal of the clerical-minded Prince. But friend De Viti must have published Mosca's contribution with somewhat mixed feelings. For the author of the *Elementi*, which had barely hit the bookstalls, took from the first a strange, very strange, tack for an avowed Liberal. Even today's reader, hardly familiar with the atmospheric problems of *fin-de-siècle* Italy, cannot suppress his admiration for the nimbleness with which our author manages to straddle the issue without in the least appearing a trimmer. Having secured a sufficient freedom of maneuver, Mosca puts his forces through a series of gyrations until they are finally deployed in something like the oblique battle order of the second Frederick of Prussia. The effect is stunning: the free traders as well as the Papal Guards are nowhere to be seen; the field belongs exclusively to Gaetano Mosca. And when he is done, his flag, unfurled, displays the Liberal colors—with some shadings of his own, to be sure—but Liberal just the same. The trade winds still blow freely, and the lay state protects free thought by restraining the intolerant religions of the day, the old one of the Catholics as well as the new secular religion of the Marxists. These two have to be restrained, for everybody knows "that the great majority of teachers in Italian elementary schools are either socialists or priests." The small, frail flame of scientific truth must be carefully nursed by an impartial government, acting, it would seem, on behalf of an infinitely small minority of Mosca Liberals. The fear that knowledge might become subjected to regimentation is unwarranted: "we have state universities in Italy, but there exists no science of the state." [3] The author does not add "'unfortunately'"; but when all is said, when the new positive state is proclaimed, the state which has the duty to remove the obstacles to intellectual freedom, the new science of the state has been once more revealed to us. Behind the scaffold of classical liberalism appears, visible as never before, the state of Gaetano Mosca.

Once again "our Guicciardini" is invoked: political liberty is the prevalence of the law over the appetites of "particular people." Who are they?

They are the ruling class.

But this is obviously not the political class Mosca wants to see in power: "For my part I should add to Guicciardini's definition that, if there is to be liberty, not only must the will of governors and gov· erned—and that of the former in particular, since they have greatei opportunity to sin—be subject to the laws, but these laws themselves must not owe their existence to the powerful *appetites of particular* people . . ." As an example Mosca mentions "certain custom tariffs" representing special interests and not, as they should, the collective good. The latter is not to be understood as the result of any "felicific calculus," but rather as the sum of notions for which Mosca chooses the term "common sentiment." Social morality, in other words, is not the product of one class, the ruling class, but of all classes: of society. This definition reminds one of the late and no longer lamented Joseph Stalin's famous statement about language being the creation not of one class but of "all the classes," only applied, as he did not yet dare to apply it, to ethics, and to socio-political ethics in particular.[4]

As if this were not clear enough, our author adds explicitly that, in a liberal society at least, "law ought to be the emanation of the conscience of an epoch and a people; it ought to conform to those rules which all of us, as dispassionate, disinterested, well informed judges of the case in question, would consider just and equitable."

And there is much more in that vein: "those countries are considered to be the most liberal where there is public discussion of governmental policies, where representative organs of the people participate in the making of the laws and see to it, if not always efficiently, that these laws correspond to the general interests and sentiments and are not violated by those who stand at the apex of the power pyramid." And, we are told, "the freest country in that sense, is, as most people know, Great Britain."

All this will not cause any crowds to riot in the streets with joy. In fact, we would not bother quoting any of these passages from any other author, since they are the liberal clichés. But coming from

Mosca, these sentiments are eminently quotable. They do not at all sound like the tough-minded, "realistic" Mosca of some recent commentators. To them, Mosca's conclusion that political freedom, "according to Guicciardini and myself, means justice and morality in the relations between ruled and rulers" will be news, and unwelcome news at that.[5] This is not Mosca's fault. He had already in the *Elementi* stated his position rather clearly: all social morality conforms, in a broad sense, to the "calm passion" of Hume's sympathetic observer, who takes "the party of humankind against vice and disorder." [6] But that party by no means speaks with a "still, small voice," as Hume would have it. Our own earlier remark about "the infinitely small minority of Mosca Liberals" was rather rash, because in Mosca's view it is the great majority of people who "in the generality of cases are disinterested and, therefore, less likely to have their sense of equity and justice obscured by passion . . ." Apparently, they are not, after all, so likely to be misled by a Catholic or Socialist intelligentsia.

Mosca has some friendly words to say about the classical separation of powers: a well-thought-out system of checks and balances will, he believes, help to make government as a whole less oppressive. However, since "all state power is based on some directing force," the indispensable prerequisite of freedom, we are told once more, is "that there be in society a multiplicity of such directing forces . . . None of these hierarchies must be in a position of absolute superiority to any other," and for that end "they should all stand in a relationship of mutual independence . . . and be organized in such a way as to effectively control each other." Such a state of affairs will be possible only "where a society has reached a certain level of civilization." [7]

What all this amounts to is that the original clear-cut distinction between The Few and The Many, Rulers and Ruled, already toned down in the first *Elementi*, is progressively disintegrating. The dominant minority still performs an important function, but it no longer performs it exclusively. For, we are told, "the modern state is not, as some imagine, an entity removed from the rest of society, its friend and protector, according to one interpretation, its enemy, according to another . . . Rather the state is the organization of society proper, and of the various hierarchies regulating the various social activities." [8] As for those social forces not officially included in the govern-mental framework, "they too have a *raison d'être*, which is the great influence they do, or may, exert upon the state, since to them is en-trusted the control, the right to discuss and restrain those forces which do form part of the executive power." [9]

If we keep in mind that this free interplay of social forces takes its cues from a collectively accepted and *created* moral code, then it is rather difficult to see how this so strongly unitarian concept of society could ever lend itself to an interpretation in which law would merely follow the diurnal, ever-shifting boundary between conflicting power thrusts. If there is any reader left who still believes that Gaetano Mosca was a theorist of Machiavellian politics, he will have to find evidence which seems to have eluded me.

To sum up, Mosca's ruling class is, at this more advanced stage of his thinking, no longer identical with the minority that dominates the state machinery; it is now found both inside and outside the government—it is a house divided against itself. And that division is precisely what prevents the state from becoming more than "the organization of society proper"; as long as the state is not permitted to become the organizer of society, all will be well in Gaetano Mosca's world. Liberty depends on the frustration of the urge for total control by those who have power as well as by those to whom power, or a share in it, is still denied. The liberal "formula" thus understood would be the rationalization, in the minds of both the in- and out-elites, of that denial, a kind of self-denying ordinance whose more or less strict observation will depend on the degree to which the moral code of the community is still the undisputed standard of all social action. Those who interpret Mosca's theory of balance in a strictly mechanistic and pragmatic sense must necessarily start from the assumption that the basis for that communal agreement about values is no longer given in our modern liberal society.

The author, though refusing to concede that point, is very con-scious of the dangers threatening his freedom from three different directions in the shape of three "totalitarian," all-exclusive claims to domination. These are advanced by the Socialists, the Catholics, and by those heirs of bourgeois rationalism, the Freemasons. What eluded Mosca was the fact, now visible to us, that his three dangers were in turn only the symptoms, not the causes, of a far advanced decomposition. He was still to see the triumph of totalitarian force, the violent, but under the conditions natural, reaction of a sick society attempting to recover unity by swallowing an overdose of it.

Once more the forces necessary to arrest the fusion of all power in one group or movement are identified: "there must be a public opinion, a science, a press . . . capable of discussing freely the affairs of government and governors . . ." But this is not enough: those secular forces must be joined by the spiritual force of religion; the Church, too, must be free to play its part safe from the encroachments of the lay state. Not without reason did we say before that Mosca knows how to ingratiate himself with his adversaries without yielding any ground. The Prince di Belmonte Granito, while not making headway with our author in the question of material independence of the Vatican from government control, receives a free and unexpected gift in form of religious freedom. "And to hear this," Mosca sweetly remarks in parentheses, "will please the Prince . . ." [10]

The social forces listed by the author reflect an advanced type of civilization in which public, as distinct from official, opinion is articulated by the class of people who have "merit." They comprise the free professions, the skilled specialists in every way of life—in short, the educated class. The men of science would be part of it. But in choosing the abstract noun science, Mosca must have had in mind something besides the scientific personnel, namely science as the modern key to man's control not only over nature but over his fellow man. That power more than anything must be safeguarded against ever being turned into a government monopoly.

Social forces, we have learned, form their own leadership groups. So we should be able to spot the elites of the "free sectors" of society. And what do we, according to the author, find? Public opinion, virtually honeycombed with all kinds of organizations in charge of the mass communication media, exercising a controlling function of decidedly elitist character. But these communicational elites are by no means all free and independent agents. Some represent the interest of the governmental class proper; others, technically free, employ their influence with the electorate "not so much to control government as to buy its complicity." [11] This is not to say that public opinion is entirely "owned" by special interests; indeed some of the most important news purveyors do live up to their responsibilities as honest brokers of the public business. But even if they were to represent the rule instead of the exception, public opinion in our day would still lack the essential feature of a social force as understood by Mosca: the homogeneity of interests. Not really a social force in its own right, public opinion merely reflects other social forces, their inter-relations and antagonisms.

The same may be said of the other forces on the list. There is no scientific class, and if there were, it too would lack the group cohesion which is Mosca's mark of the elite. Nor is there a managerial class which could maintain its independence as a social force; it is split, as all classes are, into many segments, some of which will fuse with the political class, thereby refuting the myth of the managerial revolu-tion, while the rest, not able to identify themselves with any one class in particular, will gravitate toward a great variety of groups, thus leaving the political class free to practice the old maxim of divide and rule.

This brings us to the most important force, the economic interest. In the ideal liberal society, the government would merely be the arbiter, not interfering with the automatic functioning of the free market mechanism, except in cases of particularly gross abuse of social power. This is indeed what Mosca posits. In addition, he seems to expect that the great economic pressure groups would vir-tuously refrain from making full use of their power. Inside govern-ment, they would not dominate; outside the government, they would not try to bribe it.

But Mosca himself has been telling us that the great interests do govern or do bribe. Perhaps he meant to say that the part of the economic force which governs is checked by another part which re-mains "free" and uses its ability to bribe the government in order to achieve a balance of the economic forces, thereby minimizing the danger of totalitarian fusion. Such a situation did in fact exist in Germany both before World War I and afterwards, as long as the Republic lasted. The conflicting tariff interests of the export indus-tries on the one hand and of heavy industry on the other were reflected in the political alignment of the bourgeois parties.

Unfortunately but perhaps not accidentally, our author, in this contribution to the economic journal, has nothing to say about the role of large-scale industry inside and outside government. His very telling remark about "buying the complicity" of government does not, on the surface of it, refer to the industrial interests at all, but to "that part of the political class which controls the votes." [12] We know he has in mind the "grand electors" and the party leaders of his native Italy, which was not, as he wrote, too far advanced as an industrial country. But we also know that in his view, "the most important elements of our political class," the elected representatives, were in reality the creatures of those "irresponsible" and not at all disinterested vote collectors, who knew "how to extort as much as possible from the public power, while contributing as little as possible." So even in a preindustrial society the economic forces are already strong enough to control the electoral machinery, thereby dictating their wishes to the government though not *through* the government itself.[13]

What remains of the "independent" social forces (independent in a double sense, in that they neither bribe nor can themselves be bribed)? Little enough, and what remains is not too reassuring either. The freedom predicated on an equilibrium between many freedoms and on what amounts to a true split within the ruling class itself was at best a precarious thing in Mosca's Europe. But the fully clarified conception of a governing elite contained by its nongovernmental counterparts does represent a great advance over the previous notion of a single, firmly integrated dominant minority. It is a notion, incidentally, which applies less to the old parliamentary democracies of Europe than to the United States, where so far the fierce competition of the pressure groups has kept the struggle for predominance in a state of fluidity and has, as yet, not reached the stage at which it would be possible to speak of a consolidated ruling class.

"The Aristocratic and the Democratic Principle"

This is the title of another essay Mosca published during the first decade of this century. This time he addressed himself to an academic audience. The occasion, an inaugural lecture delivered at the

University of Turin, colored both style and content of the learned paper which had, after all, something in common with the letter to De Viti. Again Professor Mosca had to forgo the fine points of his argument; since he was talking to an audience largely composed of undergraduates, simplicity and brevity again were of the essence. And again necessity was turned into an asset. Much of what the author has to say is already known to us. But in the mind of a true master the old elements tend to develop a peculiar restlessness, they are not content to remain in the same molds. What Pareto was to call the "instinct of combinations" was surprisingly developed in our author who, with his strong conservative bent, should have shown a predilection for the "persistent aggregates," according to Pareto's scheme. But this conservative was always trying out new amalgams. The piece under discussion is a good example of that tendency. The Gaetano Mosca of the *Elementi* is still learning, still exploring ways to make his theory more solid, but also more flexible, and, thereby perhaps more acceptable to doubting minds.

Faced with a student audience, Mosca wisely resists the temptation to begin with the Egyptians and Sumerians and starts his account of social and political ideas with the Greeks. We had often been told that the "two cities" of the polis had been populated by the vast majority of the poor on the one hand, and by the minority of the rich on the other. Mosca taught us differently: both sides in that everlasting civil war were parts of the minority, the dominant minority of the free citizens, who were united against the majority of slaves and metics. It was "the coexistence within the ruling class of political equality and inequality of wealth and social status which caused those incessant struggles..." [14] The wealthy constituted a minority within the privileged minority of citizens, and the poor its majority, but if the entire polis is considered, they too still were a minority, though a much larger one. The fight between the "democratic" poor —frequently led by members of the wealthy class[15]—and the "aristocrats" took place within one and the same group: the political class of the city. The civil war between democracy and aristocracy was simply caused by the attempt of a new ruling class to join or to replace the older one.

This, says the author, is the gist of "the new doctrine ... in detail

expounded in a couple of volumes which have not yet been refuted." [16] Indeed, the line is still essentially the same. If there is any
change at all, it is in the direction of a further sharpening of Mosca's
main contention. The debunking, antidemocratic aspect of the doctrine is intensified to the point where a compromise seems utterly
impossible.

And yet, it is precisely the intransigence of Mosca's central argument that makes it possible for him to grant peripheral concessions.
"Very well!" he seems to mutter to himself, "I shall now yield some
ground. But mind you, Messieurs critics, it is ground I have completely occupied and conquered." Aloud he observes that we need
not be discouraged by his message. Full acceptance of the fact revealed by history that the majority can never rule and that all power
struggles are merely disputes within the ruling class does not exclude
"the possibility of gains for the majority or even the whole of society." In fact, whenever a minority in power grows in stature or is
replaced by another of superior quality, society makes progress.
When, on the contrary, the dominant class lapses into decadence
and no other minority stands ready with a better answer for the
questions of the time, then the result will be stagnation or slow disintegration.[17]

But all this is mere introduction to what Mosca calls "the most
serious problem posed by the new doctrine but as yet left unresolved." If we accept the doctrine's major premise, namely, that a
ruling class is both a fact and a necessity, what happens to that other,
older doctrine which is still dear to so many? The dogma of popular
sovereignty, the democratic gospel of majority rule—do these stand
irrevocably condemned?

That seems, at first sight, to be a foregone conclusion. "But we
must distinguish: if by democracy is meant, as Rousseau believed,
that the state must be governed by a majority of citizens, then let us
say at once that the new anti-Aristotelian doctrine does not find it
necessary to give battle—it simply denies the democratic principle
on the ground that it cannot be realized in practice." This is the
negative part of his statement. "However," he goes on, "if by democracy is understood *de jure* and *de facto* equal access for all to no
matter what position in society . . . then the anti-Aristotelians will say

neither yes nor no, but limit themselves to a study and discussion of the problem . . ." [18]

The proponent of a new idea is not likely to apologize for overstating it in the excitement of discovery; indeed our author retracts nothing. But he does make room for the admission of the democratic principle into his own elitist system. In the end, that move will serve him well, by giving the theory more subtlety and flexibility. For the time being, he is satisfied that the new formulation enlarges, without contradicting, his previous views.

His tentative solution tries to free the notion of the ruling class from its aristocratic connotation. Mosca does it by demoting the aristocratic as well as the democratic doctrines to verbalizations of two principles or tendencies (he does not yet, as in the second *Elementi*, make a sharp methodological distinction between the two terms) which are perennially at work in every society regardless of the constitutional arrangement. Both drives, the "aristocratic" and the "democratic," correspond to an innate demand of human nature. Man's desire to hold on to what he has made his own, his wish to pass on to his descendants the advantages he has enjoyed, his concomitant dislike of seeing these benefits and privileges cheapened by their being made accessible to outsiders—all these considerations enter the aristocratic tendency to limit, to exclude, to withdraw or, if necessary, to fight change with all means, fair or foul.

The other tendency is no less natural: man's urge to improve his condition, to find recognition and reward based upon merit and not on the accident of birth or unearned wealth—these are the main components of the democratic surge. Although Mosca does not make the point, both tendencies can be said to be coexistent in each individual and at war with one another within one and the same individual. What matters to the author is that the warring tendencies are equally essential to the healthy evolution of society. If only one would be at work, to the exclusion of the other, the result would be either unmitigated anarchy or *rigor mortis*. For once Mosca gives the enemy the full benefit of the doubt: "There still remains the future. As of now, it is impossible to tell whether it might not bring the final triumph of democracy." [19] Mosca adds hurriedly once more that democracy is not to be understood as government by the majority but as the end of privilege. And once all privileges are abolished, the most qualified to rule would in fact have a chance to rule: "a true democracy would also be true aristocracy."

But until such a time, a balance of the two conflicting tendencies remains the safest and hence most desirable solution—even if it should mean tolerating some degree of social inequality. The triumph of collectivism would not really abolish privilege; it would destroy inherited wealth only to replace it by the benefits which those in office could bestow upon their children. Nepotism is a power that defies all social change. "It may well have its *raison d'être* in the nature of things; in other words, it may be in the interest of the social organism." [20]

The vulgar-Hegelian character of this last statement may be open to attack ("what is, is rational"); it does not necessarily follow that the social interest must coincide with the "nature of things," that is, with all and any tendencies and wishes of the human ego. We will have less reason to dispute this statement:

As the democratic principle can never die, since it is indispensable to that continuous motion which spins human society toward its unknown destiny . . . so it likewise stands to reason that its great antagonist will not die either . . . [Aristocracy] too has a mission to fulfill in the life of the human race . . .[21]

On this impartial note the author rests his case. It would be premature to shout: "The case is altered!" But the tone has changed, and as the French say, "it's the tone that makes the music." As seen from our vantage point, the interim report on Gaetano Mosca's intellectual evolution between the first and second editions of *Elementi* is favorable.

8

RIVAL AND DISCIPLE

One of Gaetano Mosca's most attractive qualities is the unruffled dignity of his demeanor toward other minds, alive or dead. His discourse with them is occasionally flavored with wry humor. At one occasion, in the letter written to De Viti, we discovered, to our delight, a Mosca who was outright gay, gay to the point of provocation, of aggressiveness. But that aggressiveness was not offensive; Mosca's self-assurance is usually controlled by that characteristic diffidence of his which shuns all rigid dogmatism as much in his own work as in that of others. Where he does meet it, he feels ill at ease but, with two notable exceptions, never loses his detachment. His objections will take an ironic rather than an angry form.

One of the exceptions was Marx.[1] For Mosca, Communism was not just another doctrine in the grand tradition of European radicalism, but was a mortal threat to that tradition, the complete denial of the Graeco-Roman, Christian type of civilization. It was a matter that could not be settled by the methods of well-mannered scholarship. Accordingly, our author turned polemicist, using the long sword rather than the scientific foil. One of Mosca's Italian biographers, Mario delle Piane, has observed that he never showed the least inten-

169

tion of acknowledging the moral intent of the Marxist "religion." [2] Unlike Sorel, Mosca never treated Marx's work as a "myth" of liberation but confined himself to showing it up as a false utopia. Marxism was an evil thing because it was inspired by hatred, not by love. In one of his last meditations, Mosca compares doctrines which appeal to the benevolent instincts with those which cater to malevolence: "Typical of the former is Christianity, Marxism of the latter." To be sure, "Christianity too brought forth not only the martyr and the ascetic, but also the crusader and the inquisitor. Conversely, there are those who will believe that Marx's *Capital* represents the last word in science, and who at the same time abhor violence and bloodshed. Generally speaking, one may say however that the effects of a doctrine based on love are wholesome, and those of a doctrine based on hate, pernicious." [3]

Among his contemporaries was one author for whom Mosca must have felt something akin to hatred. His famous running feud with Vilfredo Pareto has already been referred to more than once. It involved a question of priority. Our author felt that he had been the first to give the doctrine of the dominant minority its modern form. He found that he was forming a school. But one of his disciples had assumed the role of master without giving his old teacher credit for the inspiration. That hurt. It would have hurt anybody, even one whose reputation was established beyond any doubt. But it so happened that Pareto's fame cast doubt on the importance of Mosca, for it was Pareto's version of the doctrine that became the celebrated theory of the elites, whereas comparatively few of the world fellowship of scholars had adopted Mosca's term of the "political class." To have one's key discovery accredited to someone else, to hear it called by a name not your own, is an experience that is more than just annoying—it may poison your whole life. No wonder Gaetano Mosca's dignity broke down to become indignation, some may even call it peevishness. For once he gave up his reserve and engaged in personal recrimination.

It all began with a short reference to the unpleasant subject which, since it occurred in the Inaugural Address of 1902, was widely noted.[4] Speaking of the new, anti-Aristotelian doctrine "proclaimed for the first time in Italy toward the end of 1883" (that is, in the *Teorica*),

Mosca lists some authors who had arrived at similar conclusions independently (Novikov, Ammon). He goes on: "Last year, another Italian writer, Rensi, based a work in which he criticized direct democracy and the whole system of political representation explicitly on the scientific conception already proclaimed in Italy" (meaning the one proclaimed by Mosca).[5] Pleased with this proof of unexceptional scholarship, our shock is all the greater as we learn that "the same theory has been adopted by Pareto in his recent work about *The Socialist Systems*, though, unlike Rensi, the illustrious professor of the University of Lausanne, with strange forgetfulness, failed to make mention of the Italian writer who has had the good fortune of being the first to enunciate the doctrine now so strenuously propagated by Pareto." [6]

Not content with this reprimand, our author follows it up with a lengthy note attached to a later page of the same paper. There Pareto is accused not only of having annexed the theory of the political class but also Mosca's argument against Marx's one-sided, economic interpretation of history. Pareto's version, reproduced by Mosca, runs as follows: "The economic conditions are supposed to determine all other social phenomena: but do the latter not react upon the former? By what cause are the economic conditions themselves determined? ... In reality, there is simply a state of mutual dependence between the economic and the other social factors ..." [7]

This sounds as if Pareto had been unaware of Engels' cautioning remark about the interaction between base and superstructure, allowing for the economic element to be decisive only "in the last end." But Pareto knew his Engels and tried to show that all qualifications do not save the theory from being meaningless.[8]

Mosca comments thus: "Unfortunately for the professor of the University of Lausanne, I have preceded him once more, because the same idea can be found, differently worded, to be sure, in a publication of mine dating back to 1897." [9]

Mosca had to wait four years for a reply. When it came, in 1906, he had good reason to be furious. For Pareto, in his scrappy way, had added insult to the injury. He chose to relegate his answer to this curious footnote: "Professor Mosca complains and worries very much if his name is not mentioned in connection with the fact that all societies are governed by a small minority; he seems to think that this is his discovery. To satisfy him, I shall list the titles of his works, of which I know only the last one." He lists the *Teorica*, the *Costituzioni moderne* of 1887, and the first edition of the *Elementi*, 1896. "But the principle that minorities rule," Pareto continues, "has been known for a long time, it is a commonplace assumption which occurs not merely in the works of scientists but also in writings of an exclusively literary character." Samples from Pareto's list: E. Fournier, *L'esprit des autres* (1856), Balzac, *Physiologie du mariage*, Sumner Maine, *Popular Government*. The last-named work Pareto cites from its prepublication in the *Quarterly Review*, April 1883–85. His intention is transparent: 1883 antedates Mosca's *Teorica*. And in conclusion, Gabriel Tarde is mentioned as the author of "volumes demonstrating that the civilizing process is exclusively the work of a few people." Again, much of Tarde's work had seen print before 1896, that is, before the publication of the *Elementi*, the only one of Mosca's works which Pareto acknowledged having read.[10]

Counterattack

The time had come to elevate the feud from the lowly status of annotations to official, large-type warfare. Mosca sat down and wrote a "Short Polemic" which he published in a well-known scholarly review. Quoting Pareto's grudging recognition of his own existence in full, Mosca has this to say:

The Marquess Pareto might have added that the fact of [minority control] has always been intuitively and implicitly known to the popular mind everywhere . . . But the Marquess is a scholar and cannot be unfamiliar with the fact that . . . political philosophy until now was either not aware of that popular intuition or else in complete disagreement with its findings. And this was so much the case that until recently, let us say ten years ago, we can discover even in the writings of the same Pareto, who as an educated man must then have already read Balzac, Fournier, and Sumner Maine, no disagreement with the current doctrine of popular sovereignty . . . and majority rule.[11]

It is a perfect tit for tat: the first part of of the *Elementi* had appeared exactly "ten years ago"—the very work that Pareto, on his own say, had been on familiar terms with; and its publication also marks the date before which he, Pareto, had still been expounding the traditional "majoritarian" doctrine.

Mosca does not claim to be the only one to represent the new approach to politics: "There is no lack of political scientists and sociologists who base their systems on the concept of a constant prevalence of an aristocratic, or political class, or an elite, as it has pleased Pareto to call it." [12] Mosca does not like that term. As he explains in the only substantive reference to the great rival which can be found in his major works, the ruling class simply included the elements most apt to govern, "which is not always the same as saying that these elements are also intellectually and, above all, morally superior to the rest." And in a note he adds: "That is why the term elite, adopted by Pareto to designate what many years earlier we have called the *political class*, seems inexact." [13]

This accusation against Pareto seems unjustified. In his definition of elite, Pareto clearly states that it possesses "certaines qualités, bonnes ou mauvaises d'ailleurs, qui assurent le pouvoir." [14] The qualities which assure the elite of power may be either good or bad, as long as they are qualities of *rulers*, says Pareto, and that is exactly what, in slightly different words, Mosca claims for his political class.

Once again our author renders homage to some of the older writers who preceded him in using the new method; this time he names Taine and Gumplowicz. As for his own contemporaries, Mosca grants that most of them hit on the same solution more or less spontaneously and without knowing of each other. "The only case in which I was not able to convince myself of that same spontaneity is that of Professor Pareto." And he does not stop at this insinuation, but cites the colleague for the vilest of all crimes, literary theft: "Plagiarism in the social sciences cannot be as easily established as in literary productions, because what matters most in the former is the concept, not the form, and it is always possible to repeat and to reproduce a concept by changing words around ... An educated and shrewd man may always introduce modifications and even add a little something of his own."

But there is one supreme test by which we may know whether or not an intellectual theft has been committed: "In the one case we can tell that a new system of ideas either has spontaneously originated or else germinated and developed by slow stages in the writer's mind. In the other case, the system will reveal the traces of a previous workout in another mind through which the [plagiarizer's] thought . . . has first traversed."

The scene is set for the great reckoning: "When I read for the first time Pareto's study published in the *Rivista italiana di sociologia* of August, 1900, entitled "An Application of Sociological Theories," and even more so when I read his *Socialist Systems*, I was convinced at once that the Marquess Pareto had arrived at his conception of aristocratic or elitist rule as a result of his acquaintance with my notion of the political class which I had not only proclaimed but elaborately developed in my *Elementi* as well as in earlier publications." Nor was he, Mosca adds, the only one to notice the coincidence. The similarity between political class and elite was too great to be a mere accident. It showed "that special, common bond which reveals the paternity." But even more conclusive was the fact that the "elite" came into being as the brain child of a mature father whose former intellectual conceptions would not bear out that particular daughter. "He must, therefore, have undergone some recent impression which resulted in a major change of mind, directing it toward a new set of ideas notably distinct from those which he had held before."

This discovery, Mosca believed, was justification enough to "expose, with sober moderation, once and for all the lack of, let us call it scientific courtesy on the part of Marquess Pareto . . ." This exposure Mosca made, as we already know, in his Inaugural Address, alluding "very briefly to the strange forgetfulness of the professor of the University of Lausanne." And what was the result? Pareto tried to confuse the issue and did so in an "insolent and rude manner. I take the liberty of telling him that he has not been too intelligent. For there will be but few who will go to the trouble of . . . comparing my *Elementi* with Pareto's prior and succeeding works, but rather many who will take delight in a polemic more personal than scientific in character. And those know well that in this genre of writing, haughtiness, acrimony, and gratuitous insinuations are almost invariably the boon companions of him who is in the wrong." [15]

Pareto never replied to that devastating challenge, unless the fact that he did not reply can be regarded as an answer. But Pareto must have been uneasy because he omitted the footnote which had provoked Mosca's wrath from subsequent editions of the work in which it had appeared, the *Manuale di economia politica*. In the index to Pareto's master work, *Mind and Society*, the name of Gaetano Mosca is conspicuously absent. But others did not remain silent, and the "Short Polemic" grew into an acrimonious and protracted controversy in which such an illustrious scholar as Luigi Einaudi, Mosca's colleague at the faculty of the University of Turin and, after World War II, second President of the Italian Republic, took a prominent part.[16] Other participants were De Viti de Marco, Robert Michels, Rodolfo de Mattei, G. H. Bousquet (who, although Pareto's French biographer, regretted his author's role in the quarrel), and Arthur Livingston, who, in his double role as the American editor of both Mosca and Pareto, found himself in a most delicate position.[17]

The debate was none too favorable for Pareto's moral reputation, but it could not change the main fact: fame continued to smile on Pareto, while the work of Gaetano Mosca remained the possession of a relatively small if more discerning group of scholarly admirers. How profoundly Mosca must have felt the injury may be guessed from a letter which he wrote as late as 1938 (July 5) to a friend, Renzo Sereno.[18] The recipient published it a couple of years ago, together with a lucid and emphatic commentary, under the too modest title "Note on Gaetano Mosca." [19] In the moving document, our author once more restates the old case against Pareto. He does it calmly, speaking of himself in the third person. But although the heat of the polemic had died long ago (Pareto, after all, had been dead since 1921), Mosca has forgotten nothing, and he even adds some touches which had previously been missing: "Pareto's first publications," he writes, "were limited to the field of economics." They reveal "a purely liberal and democractic orientation. His later views appear for the first time in August, 1900, in an article entitled '*Una applicazione di teorie sociologiche*' . . ." [20]

This is the same article he had already mentioned in his "Short Polemic" thirty-two years earlier. But the two statements are not quite identical. Previously Mosca had only remarked upon the fact of having read "for the first time Pareto's study" of the turn of the century; now he asserts unequivocally that the same study marks the beginning of Pareto's "new science." The date, 1900, is decisive for him and will also have some relevance for my own tentative conclusions. The letter continues: "In 1896 Mosca, at the behest of the economists Maffeo Pantaleoni and Enrico Baroni, had sent a copy of the *Elementi*, recently published, to Pareto. Pareto however wrote to Baroni, berating Mosca for his reactionary ideas. After a more careful examination Pareto found much to be praised in these reactionary ideas. He was enough impressed by them to change his point of view radically, as he showed in the above-mentioned article ... and his other successive publications in the field of sociology."

In a postscript Mosca tries to explain why Pareto's term "elite" has found so much wider acceptance than his own "political class." He offers two reasons. His own concept, when it first appeared, found the world still unready to accept the notion of minority rule. "The term elite came to the fore when minds were ripe ..." And by then "Pareto had already achieved an international reputation as an economist, while Mosca was little known outside Italy." [21]

The modesty and terseness of this record are most admirable. But it leaves us puzzled nonetheless. According to our author, the impression of his doctrine on Pareto becomes first apparent in the 1900 essay. But Pareto's theory of the elite makes in fact its first tentative appearance three years earlier, in the second volume of the *Cours d'économie politique* of 1897. The first volume, not concerned with politics, had appeared the preceding year, the year of the first *Elementi*. Theoretically, it is possible that the political considerations in Pareto's work which appear at the very end of the *Cours*, Volume II, do represent an afterthought inspired by Mosca's work. Arthur Livingston considers carefully that possibility and comes, for technical and other reasons, to the fair conclusion that Pareto's doctrine could not have been influenced by a book which preceded his own by a matter of a few months only.

It is curious that our author, in his letter to Sereno, does not mention the *Cours* with a single word, except for saying that "Pareto wrote his greatest works in French (particularly the *Cour d'économie politique*)." The work cannot well have escaped the close attention with which he had scrutinized all of Pareto's writings of that period.

And yet he insists that the first statement of Pareto's new elitist dispensation dates from 1900. Could it be that Mosca found no trace of the elite simply because that term does not yet occur in the *Cours?* The question bears investigation. A short summary of the politically relevant parts of that work seems justified, as long as it is not construed as an attempt to add new fuel to an ancient controversy which is only of peripheral importance to this study.

The First Appearance of Pareto's Elite

The conception of the dominant minority is introduced in a most casual manner, namely, not at all. Pareto seems to take the fact for granted that societies are ruled by "aristocracies"—he has not yet hit upon the term elite. But the important notion of the "circulation of elites" is already explicit in the very first remarks pertaining to the subject: "#624 ... The aristocracies maintain themselves only by constant renewal and absorption of the most distinguished individuals from the lower classes. As a rule, all closed aristocracies deteriorate sharply after a certain number of generations. That fact is of the greatest importance for the entire social evolution." [22]

Only twenty-seven pages later does Pareto treat of minority rule in a declaratory statement; it has nothing of the solemnity with which Mosca introduces his law of The Few and The Many, The Rulers and The Ruled. Important also is the qualification which Pareto at once adds to his announcement: "#659. The differentiation of human societies generally begins with the formation of an aristocratic class. But it constitutes only one phase of the evolution. When the differentiation continues, the aristocratic class loses power..."[23] This does not mean the end of minority rule, only that one aristocracy will be replaced, as we already heard, by elements from the lower classes. The latter are "the crucibles of the new aristocracies which replace the old, degenerated ones." This process is hastened by the fact that in the upper strata zoological selection is less actively at work, "while in the lower classes Malthus' 'positive checks' are most rigorous." [24]

The degree of social differentiation (Mosca's "level of civilization") is the sole criterion by which we should judge a social and political regime. All absolutes are to be avoided: "Despotism may be tantamount to progress if it results in differentiating an anarchically homogeneous society. The aristocratic regime represents in turn a new advance, and since that phase is rarely absent from evolution, one might say that, in a certain sense, the nations owe their freedom to their aristocracies." It seems that democracy is, in Pareto's view, an early form of differentiation, for he says: "The character of the Greek tyranny was essentially democratic; it was a case of decadence, a return to less heterogeneous forms of life." [25]

So far, we have agreement between Mosca and Pareto: aristocracy means freedom (relatively speaking). But now the ways part. "Societies," Pareto says, "are not homogeneous. They differ, first of all, among each other. Nor does any one society present a homogeneous whole; it is composed of heterogeneous individuals and classes of individuals." [26] That seems to be rather elementary, but it is nonetheless one of Pareto's fundamental premises: his pluralism stands, as has been noted once before, in vivid contrast to the basically unitarian attitude of Mosca, who starts with the group and ends up with almost a fusion of the social forces operating inside and outside the formal government. Hence Mosca's strong dislike of "intermediate sovereigns." [27] The function of his political class is precisely the amalgamation and disciplining of the originally autonomous group wills of society.

Compare with that the following quotation from Pareto's *Cours*: "Despotic governments show the right instinct when they outlaw all [independent] associations of their subjects. Those intermediate organisms standing between state and individual are in effect most powerful agents of social differentiation." In Pareto's terminology differentiation is equated with liberty, the intermediary associations are an essential element of "juridical defense"—a view utterly alien to Mosca, who saw in them the greatest threat to liberty. Mosca's "balance of the social forces" presupposes that there already exists a fully integrated Great Society. It is not the equilibrium of the social interests that brings that Great Society into existence; on the contrary, the Great Society makes possible the equilibrium and with it, freedom. Mosca never could have written, as Pareto did, that "whoever wants to arrest social progress must, above all, prohibit all kinds of societies, except those which are under the direct control of the government and form therefore part of a homogeneous whole." [28] Mosca would have said that government ought to outlaw those associations in the interest of social progress. As an economist, Pareto knew, of course, that intermediate associations have a tendency toward monopoly; apparently he saw in that no threat to freedom. In that respect he would agree with the late Joseph Schumpeter, and both would disagree with the American tradition.[29]

In sketching his elitist theory, Pareto is especially careful to avoid equivocation. Superiority in some respects must be distinguished properly from superiority in all respects, and both types again from the type of superiority that is characteristic of a ruling class: "...To say that some members of society possess certain qualities to a more eminent degree than others is not the same as saying that there is a class of people who are absolutely *better* than the rest of the population. And to go on from there to say that those 'better' people 'ought' to govern all the rest is to commit that most egregious fallacy: to make an illogical deduction from a dubious premise." [30]

Mosca himself found, as we know, the term elite equivocal, suggesting moral superiority. Pareto levels the same accusation against those who employ the term aristocracy without discrimination. "Sometimes they seem to use it in the customary sense, to indicate the top group of a social hierarchy; sometimes, when it is pointed out to them that their aristocrats may intellectually and morally be below the social average, our authors will reverse themselves and say that aristocracy means simply the 'well-born' [*eugéniques*]. That somewhat mysterious term ends up by playing the same role in the new doctrines which the 'vital force' had played in ancient medicine." [31]

Differentiation into various social classes is due "sometimes to birth, to true or assumed common origin, to certain religious practices, or to the fact that people are engaged in the same kind of work. But one of the main causes of differentiation is certainly wealth. The rich have a tendency to band together, and the same is true of the middle class and the poor. That grouping is to be found even in the Indian castes where the rich form a distinct caste within the caste. The power of the aristocracies of all types declines rapidly if it is not sustained by wealth."

Again, that is quite different from Mosca who, though recognizing that wealth, on the average, does make for social power, hesitates to say that this must always be the case; he insists that in many instances, in past societies at least, the process was reversed, with power (martial prowess) leading to positions of control where wealth was incidental. This attitude, expressed in the *Teorica*, is quite consistent with our author's general unwillingness to overemphasize the role of economics in the social process.

Not so Pareto. In his *Cours* at any rate, he still shows a marked sympathy with Marxist viewpoints. "The socialists," he says, "are entirely right to attribute great importance to the 'class struggle' and to call it the great factor dominating history. In that respect Karl Marx and A. Loria merit our utmost attention." Two forms of the class struggle must be distinguished. One is simply economic competition. The other operates through extra-economic channels, each class trying to secure control of the government to use it as "a machine of spoliation." Pareto is outmarxing Marx when he proclaims that "the struggle in the course of which some individuals appropriate the wealth produced by others is the great fact dominating all of human history. It is disguised and disappears behind the most various pretexts which have often misled the historians. One might even say that it is only in our time that the full truth has become known."

The recognition of the fact that at all times society is dominated by minorities had not made Mosca the uncritical admirer of aristocratic rule. We know his preference was for an aristocracy of educated wealth and merit, tempered by a suitable admixture of both democratic "principles" and "tendencies." He was sincerely critical of plutocratic oligarchy. But that criticism did not make him partial, as it did the author of the *Cours*, to the demands of democrats and socialists. To Mosca both these movements represented the worst threat to freedom. Compared with him, Pareto is almost a rabble rouser. He had gone on record that the nations owe their freedom to their aristocracies. But a few pages later he declares that "the ruling class not only causes distress to the classes it exploits but to the entire nation ... In that respect it does not matter whether the ruling class is an oligarchy, a plutocracy, or a democracy."

One sees that Pareto's disregard for the Aristotelian categories is as complete and radical as Mosca's. It may even have been inspired by Mosca. However, the next passage Mosca never could have written: "The more numerous that [ruling] class is, the greater the evils resulting from its domination, because a large class consumes a larger portion of wealth than does a class restricted in size. That is probably the reason why a demagogical regime will never last as long as a tyrannical or oligarchical one. This will also be most likely the great obstacle to the realization of a system of popular socialism." What Pareto understands by "popular socialism" becomes clear when he goes on to speak of "bourgeois socialism," his interesting term for the protectionist and interventionist state policies of democratic governments, another being "depreciation of the currency." That bourgeois type of socialism is, however, in Pareto's view, the lesser evil, since a bourgeois government is not obliged to satisfy as many appetites as would have to be satisfied by a regime of socialists: "it will be able to fill pockets without wrecking the entire economy." [32] A seductive argument which, alas, is somewhat at odds with what Pareto had said earlier about the distress which the ruling class is causing to the entire nation.

Do these passages reveal that "purely liberal and democratic orientation" which Mosca had found in all of Pareto's writings prior to 1900? It was hardly a democrat who could write in 1897:

Some authors are confusing two absolutely different questions, one being the existence of a ruling class, the other being the way in which that class is recruited. According to those men, the subject class, provided it has the right to choose its masters by some system of elections, must consider itself in a state of perfect bliss, with not a wish left unfulfilled ... The yoke of a class that is not elected but recruited on the basis of heredity or else by way of co-operation may appear more odious. But it does not follow that it is also the *heavier* of the two. It is by no means proven that an oligarchic government is more dishonest than the city council of New York elected by general suffrage.[33]

Between the oligarchic and the democratic yoke, what chance is left for modern man in search of freedom? Pareto's answer leaves some hope for him:

From time to time dissensions arise in the ruling class, or between it and other classes wanting to replace it. As long as these dissensions last, they tend to soften the yoke resting on the subjects, since the weaker of the two contestants will try to enroll them in his drive for power. But as soon as he has reached his goal, he will at once try to consolidate his domination by employing, possibly disguised under new names, the same old methods which he had denounced before.[34]

It is the answer which we found in Gaetano Mosca's writings, the same one which will be found in the work of Robert Michels. But the tenor of Pareto's argument is different. The man who wrote the last installments of the *Cours* was not, as was the author of the *Elementi*, bent upon announcing a new truth. Instead he took minority control for granted, as one among various elements to serve as the materials for a system as yet dimly seen. This was no last-minute adaptation of another man's idea, no mere verbal camouflage of alien property. Pareto is at once more passionately bitter and less morally engaged than Gaetano Mosca. He is not, as the latter, a crusader in the guise of the detached observer, but a one-man army fighting a two-front campaign against aristocraticism and socialism alike: "Often a one-sided theory gives birth to another which is equally exaggerated, only in the opposite direction. Certain socialists, preaching the gospel of complete equality, . . . have reached the point where they propose to waste the rare gifts of the greatest scholars in facile and unimportant manual tasks. The neo-aristocrats . . . have simply turned that doctrine upside down. According to them, the whole human race exists merely in order to produce a few superior men; it is only compost for some flowers." The reference to "neo-aristocrats" is no veiled attack on Mosca but a thrust directed against certain followers of Nietzsche whose "neo-aristocratic theories" are explicitly mentioned.[35]

This is a plague-on-both-your-houses attitude, very unlike anything we find in Mosca's *Ruling Class*. Pareto's later works have been accused of being violently biased, in clear violation of the professed scientific principles.[36] It must be said, however, that Pareto, again unlike Mosca, nowhere advocates any specific political philosophy of his own. The Paretian irony impartially X-rays all kinds of human self-deception. His theory of the elites was certified by Arthur Livingston as being similar to that of Mosca's but the product of an independent mind. We cannot prove the independence, but a careful reading of the *Cours* would seem to indicate at least dissimilarity.

The Sociology of Modern Parties

Once more the distasteful name of the Lausanne Professor turns up in an essay published by our author. This time the occasion is a pleasant one, and so the reference to the competitor is written without anger if not without thought. Something wonderful has happened: the philosopher of the political class has no longer any reason to feel lonely; he has acquired a disciple utterly his own. True, he had been head of a group before, to which he liked to refer as the New School. But as he knew, some of its members had reached their conclusions independently, or else were younger men who would not graduate to national importance until later.[37] Little wonder, therefore, that Mosca was delighted when in 1911 a scholar came into his ken who was both a disciple and an author in his own right, who not only had absorbed the master's teachings but had put them to the test in a new sociological environment.

When Mosca first wrote of the ruling class, he did so with the situation in mind as it existed in the last two decades of the nineteenth century in Europe. The phenomenon of mass organization was still in its infancy then. That was true particularly of the country in which and for which our author wrote: Italy. It was true of social life there in general, which was that of a country still preponderantly preindustrial and rural. These conditions help to make understandable the backward character of those political organizations in which Mosca was specifically interested. Mass parties in our sense could not yet exist. When Mosca writes of parties, he does not describe modern "machines," large-scale political bureaucracies manipulating the mass media of communication, but comparatively small groups formed around a "grand elector" or some fiery "tribune of the people," highly personal coteries without much stability or unity of purpose. The Socialists were the exception to this rule, but even they were far from forming a cohesive party: splits between reformists and the left were in the order of each day. The situation was the same in the trade union movement; here, too, the anarcho-syndicalist tendencies were militating against any real mass consolidation.

Such were the conditions which explain and excuse Mosca's failure to see the importance of the modern party system for his theory of the elites.

What the master lacked was, perhaps, the experience which had benefited so well the great Machiavelli, who, as an ambassador abroad, was able to observe what he could not find in his native land. Robert Michels, an Italian by choice but a German Jew by birth, had the advantage not available to Gaetano Mosca. He had studied modern mass organization in the country where that art had been perfected as nowhere else, long before World War I. Not without reason did the managers and organizers of all nations look upon Germany as their mecca, did a Russian or French socialist regard the German Social-Democratic party and *Gewerkschaftsbund* as the one model to be emulated. These organizations, formed and run as democratic counterparts of the Prussian war machine, became the objects of Michels' scrutiny.

He knew what he was looking for—perhaps too much so. Armed with Mosca's theory, he proposed to discover dominant minorities where they should *not* exist. A party dedicated to authoritarian principles could obviously not be expected to allow its rank and file the kind of influence in decision-making which is usually associated with the democratic concept. But to find the same authoritarian attitude in parties and organizations openly professing their allegiance to the democratic principle would be a shocking, unbelievable discovery. And that precisely is what Robert Michels claims to have done: discovered what he calls "the iron law of oligarchy," operative in all human associations, rendering all democratic aspirations illusory. Writing before Lenin's revolutionary coup and hence assuming that all socialists were also sincere democrats, Michels could write that "the socialists might conquer, but not socialism, which would perish in the moment of its adherents' triumph." [38]

Gaetano Mosca must have felt the greatest satisfaction when these lines first came to his attention, and he did not hesitate long to express it, with the dignified restraint so typical of him (except when he was engaging in polemics).[39]

The short article is something more than just a book review and is something less than equal to the subject. There are two distinct types of creativity. One is keenly aware of the work done by others, eager to absorb it and, occasionally, capable of judging it on its own ground. The other type views all things as reflections of the self; such authors study others only for the purpose of discovering themselves: the alien work is nothing but a mirror. Georges Sorel was such a critic. He was always ready to write introductions to books he found fascinating in the manuscript stage. But these introductions turned invariably into essays about Georges Sorel, shedding precious little light on the work he pretended to be analyzing.

It is the same with Mosca. One cocks an eager ear to his fanfare for Michels only to discover that one hears a variation on a theme by Mosca. The year is 1912. Democracy, that world force, has gained still another victory: Italy had just adopted general suffrage. "Today, no one active in politics dares to declare himself an outright antidemocrat." And yet, a small group dared to swim against the seemingly all-powerful current. For thirty years now, Mosca says, a new scientific school has been battling with democracy—"not with the customary arguments in favor of aristocracy or monarchy, but in a strictly negative way ruling out the possibility of a true democratic government. It is a school, if I may coin a new term, not so much antidemocratic as *ademocratic*. Its principles, well known to the Italian scientific world, have been popularized abroad, to some extent, by Professor Pareto, whose books written in French are more accessible to foreigners."

We know what the principles of the New School are, but there is no harm in restating them once more, if only for the reason that the earlier disclaimer of aristocratic bias need not be taken too literally. For the author ascribes to his school the notion that "all political regimes are of necessity ruled by an aristocracy or, rather, by an organized minority controlling a disorganized majority." [40] To state a fact is, of course, not the same as to approve it, but since Mosca is notoriously opposed to democratic government, the logical distinction would not seem to matter much. One might say that the author, cool as he may be toward the *old*, traditional aristocratic classes, favors the rule of another kind of aristocracy, one furnished by the educated middle class.

After that "summary of the fundamental concepts by which Michels' work has been inspired," we are presented with a factual account of Michels' argument. It is a fair account, not missing out on any of the points the younger writer makes to show why leadership is of the essence in all human associations, what the qualifications of the leader are, and how the leader manages to keep control. The critic notes "the natural conservatism" developing in all social movements as soon as they have reached the stage of institutionalization and have become subjected to the needs of bureaucratic routine. He might have quoted his own words: "Once the heroic period of a movement is over, once the stage of initial propaganda comes to an end, then reflection and self-interest claim their rights again." [41]

Have we been unfair to our author when we said Mosca was the only subject he was interested in while ostensibly reviewing Michels? What we had in mind was that the master, in the fullness of his praise for the disciple, nevertheless overlooked the one point in which Michels' work, not comparable in significance with Mosca's, represents a big advance beyond the *Elementi*. Mosca fails to see it because he treats Michels' book not as the study of a *new* phenomenon, but as a mere corroboration of his own elitist doctrine valid for all times and social systems. Thus he insists that Michels' findings are not only correct "with regard to modern revolutionary parties, but that somewhat similar results were typical in all human sodalities which [in the past] had tried to discipline and rally individual aspirations in pursuit of an ideal aim." To what extent he misses the historical uniqueness of contemporary mass organization may be seen from the example he is using to show that there is nothing new under the sun. The same "routinization of charisma," Mosca declares, took place in the Franciscan Order when the ardent idealism of the founder was toned down by his successors in accordance with the wishes of the Church.[42]

In another instance Mosca equates socialism with religious sectarianism by comparing it to the Mohammedan Senusi of North

Africa. In essence, it is the same line of thought which counters the contention of a Marx or Weber (that modern capitalism is something *sui generis*) with the view that capitalism is as old as ancient Babylon. This means overlooking, in favor of some superficial similarities, the fundamental differences which alone enable us to understand the nature and significance of all historic change. To lump together modern socialists, Franciscans, and Senusi makes it rather difficult to grasp the meaning of such modern institutions as the bureaucratic or the party state. To what extent our author is unable to do justice to his subject proves his statement: "Of the many great and complex questions which arise in connection with the theory of the political class, Michels sees and treats, though in a masterful way, only one." [43]

But the one aspect analyzed by Michels is precisely the changed character of social and political control. That this great fact should have escaped Mosca's attention is in some measure Michels' own fault. For he too, faithful to the master's teaching, weakens his own argument by generalization. Instead of stressing the new character and methods of mass manipulation as he found them in the parties and trade unions of his native country, Michels proclaims "iron laws" and thus it might be suspected that he only saw what it suited him to see. Georg Lukacs, who has his own Marxist ax to grind, may still be justified in charging Michels that "for the purpose of denigrating democracy, and working class democracy especially, he elevated those phenomena which were created by reformism ... into 'sociological laws.' From a specific phenomenon, valid for one part of the labor movement in the age of imperialism, he deduced the 'law' that the masses are constitutionally incapable of generating their own leadership." [44]

It is a daring feat for the Hungarian author to confound the Bernsteinite, reformist socialists of Germany whom Michels singled out for attention, with the example of the correct "democratic socialism" as practiced by the party favored by Georg Lukacs. But the Marxist camp has no monopoly on criticizing Michels; even better arguments have come from bourgeois quarters. In the words of a contemporary social scientist: "When ... Michels spoke of the 'iron law of oligarchy,' he attended solely to the ways in which organizational needs inhibit democratic possibilities. But ... if oligarchical waves repeatedly wash away the bridges of democracy, this eternal recurrence can happen only because men doggedly rebuild them after each inundation ... There cannot be an iron law of oligarchy ... unless there is an iron law of democracy." [45]

By proclaiming "timeless truths," Michels missed the opportunity of writing a book even more important than the one he actually wrote. He left it to his readers to discover the uniqueness of the Party State, the government controlled or even constituted by the new bureaucratized electoral organizations. For that is the fact which dominates our century in Europe (east and west of the dividing Iron Curtain); it is in the process of shaping the destinies of Asia (China, India); to a much lesser extent, but still prominently, parties do rule the United States.

The question, never tackled by the founder of the New School or by his disciple, was: To what extent do parties and related mass organizations change or deny the existence of traditional elite formations? And if they do interfere with the traditional way of selecting the political class, what happens to Mosca's general contention that the ruling class is formed by, and reflects the contest between, distinct social forces? How can this doctrine be reconciled with the new fact of mass organizations which tend to cut across the old demarcation lines? Or are the novel organs of mass management indicative of a new social force, replacing altogether or in part the older forces as a catalyst and clearing house of popular elites?

Mosca had an early premonition that his system was in trouble when he denounced the new party leaders in and out of parliament as mere "mediocrities." [46] But these misgivings never evolved into systematic insight. Robert Michels could have filled that gap but never did. One wonders whether Mosca was aware that something was amiss when he praised Michels' "notable contribution to the laborings of the school in which he had enrolled," adding that much remained to be done by the school "if it really intends to change the outlook of the world of politics." There remains to be studied "the great variety of attitudes, of the virtues and vices in which the ruling classes of the various countries differ from each other during various periods ..." The advantages and disadvantages of closed or open ruling classes are another vital subject for the social scientist. And finally, the question which reveals unerring instinct: "No less useful would be a minute examination of the various types of organizations to be found among the governing minorities . . ." [47]

Since Gaetano Mosca wrote those lines, much has been done that would have pleased him; in particular the great development of behavioral research has opened up new avenues not accessible to his own generation.[48] Robert Michels almost recognized the paramount significance of the organizational phenomenon, but since he concentrated his attention on the "governing minorities," the other aspect of organization, its mass character remained blurred in his important study. And that, too, may be attributed to Mosca's influence: to the old teacher's tendency to put organized minorities in opposition to the unorganized majority. The possibility that millions of men might be organized and be articulate, that they might be informed enough to exchange places with their leaders—such possibilities would have been utterly denied by our two authors. Mosca saw his "balance of the social forces" upset by the new, "plebeian" parties; Michels reassured him that they could not possibly succeed. The very notion that they would one day become the focus, the decisive factor in determining the character and range of the new social and political elites would have been incomprehensible to Gaetano Mosca and his alter ego.[49]

9

RE-ENTER ARISTOTLE

The interval of twenty-seven years between the publication of the first and second *Elementi* could not at all be called barren, even should we judge it by the number of full-length productions, which comprise a respectable list. There are four volumes: two of them deal with questions of constitutional law; one book (irrevocably lost) was about John Locke; the fourth is concerned with problems of Italian foreign, in particular colonial, policy.[1] True, the chronology of these reveals a major gap of ten years between 1898 and 1908, but it is filled by a whole spate of minor contributions to periodicals and dailies. Between 1900 and 1923, the author wrote no less than forty book reviews and essays for learned journals. In addition, eighty-seven of his articles appeared in various newspapers. This cannot be considered a mean output, in view of the fact that during that same period Mosca not only simultaneously taught important courses at the universities of Turin and Milan, but during this same time served his country as a deputy (from 1909) and senator (from 1919), not to mention his brief service as colonial undersecretary during World War I. In the Chamber he spoke seventy-four times, and forty-five times in the Senate.[2]

Only very little of that immense effort bears directly on the subject

closest to the author's heart: his still inconclusive doctrine of the ruling class. He deals with it in half a dozen essays altogether, two of
which I have already discussed. Now, the second volume of the
Elementi was not the result of many years of toil; the author himself
states, as we already know, that it was written in the last two years
before its publication.[3] Rather than re-edit or rewrite the twenty-
five-year-old work, he decided to let it stand as it was and to sum
up the conclusions of the intervening years in a new, second volume.
That volume, therefore, represents more than a supplement. It is
more than the mere attempt to bring the factual information contained in the first part up to date. The new text could stand by itself;
it would make complete sense if nothing else were known of Mosca's
writings. The organization of the subject matter is identical with that
of Volume I, a fact confusing to the reader of the English one-vol-
ume edition who may easily gain the impression that the author had
forgotten what went on before. In fact, the second part is virtually
a fresh beginning, on a higher level. Looking back on the completed
work, on the occasion of the third edition, published fifteen years
after the second, Gaetano Mosca, then past his eightieth year, observed: "The facts that have political importance reveal that mobility
is something natural, while immobility is artificial. So it need not
come as a surprise that the mind of the author too had to adapt itself
to the new times . . ." [4]

One cannot help remembering what Mosca had said about the
"natural" aristocratic tendency toward immobility, and feel the distance which the author has come since he wrote his essay on "The
Aristocratic and the Democratic Principle" thirty-seven years
earlier.[5]

The Ancestors

The first, brief chapter of the second *Elementi* has the Italian title,
"Origins of the Doctrine of the Ruling Class and Reasons Which
Obstructed Its Diffusion." In the English version this is the twelfth
chapter and the title, "Theory of the Ruling Class," simply echoes
that of Chapter II, "The Ruling Class." The author showed in this
case better editorial sense than his foreign adaptor.

Beginning with a terse reiteration of his central concept, Mosca turns to a discussion of his intellectual pedigree. He starts the list with Machiavelli, quoting his words that "in any city whatsoever, in whatsoever manner organized, never do more than forty or fifty persons attain positions of command." [6] But Mosca does not claim the Florentine as his true ancestor. "Ignoring such casual allusions," he finds the first distinct statement of his theory "in the writings of Saint-Simon." [7] The Saint-Simonian father of positivism, Auguste Comte, receives a dozen noncommittal lines, the coolness of which strongly contrasts with the praise bestowed upon Taine, who is in turn followed by Marx-Engels. Their philosophy is briefly stated, but the emphasis is on the fact that Taine developed his own notion of the ruling class before they did.[8]

Reaching the time when he began to formulate his own ideas, Mosca shows spectacular restraint. We know how deeply he felt about his claim to have been the first to state the modern doctrine of the ruling class and how much he had suffered from Pareto's callous disregard for his accomplishment. But not a word about this in the *Elementi*. On the other hand, his own indebtedness to Ludwig Gumplowicz, a considerable one, is not acknowledged either, except in the dry announcement: "... it will suffice to note, as a matter of record, that in 1881 Gumplowicz's *Der Rassenkampf* appeared." Mosca's outline of that work, a masterpiece of condensation (six lines), makes the intellectual affinity between our author and the Austrian appear to be rather close. But unlike Saint-Simon or Taine, the great eccentric among the sociologists receives no praise. We have had already several occasions to refer to that involved relationship and will have more; here it may be enough to mention that the date of publication given for *Der Rassenkampf*, 1881, is not correct. The work appeared in 1883, the same year in which the *Teorica* came from the press. However, Gumplowicz had already presented his whole doctrine in a book which had appeared in 1875.[9] It is most likely that this publication rather than *Der Rassenkampf* had been the work which impressed Mosca as he was conceiving the *Teorica*.

Speaking of his own contributions to the doctrine of the ruling class the author uses the same level tone of the reporter. For his seminal *Teorica* the outline is again of six lines, succeeded by the summary announcement: "In years following came the first edition of the present work . . . and, among others, works by Ammon, Novikov, Rensi, Pareto and Michels." [10] That is all.

The theory, Mosca continues, is today accepted by all thoughtful people, and "this is due to the influence of the writers mentioned." But lest we think he is blowing his own horn, he quickly asks us to attribute the *succès d'estime* of the new doctrine to "an automatic enrichment of collective experience in our world" rather than to the efforts of a small band of political philosophers.

However, Mosca never was content with being the observer and the scientific analyst; it seems he agreed with Marx's saying that "the philosophers have only *interpreted* the world in various ways; the point, however, is to *change* it." [11] And there was as yet no indication that the new philosophy had changed the pattern of political reality. Mosca attributes this "slight practical influence" of his method to a variety of causes. Some are of an "extrinsic" nature, the most important obstacle to change being mental sluggishness, the inability of most minds to shed those most powerful traditions leading back to Montesquieu and to Rousseau. There is another reason why "the democratic system probably has greater powers of self-preservation than all others." As nobody will ever openly come out for sin, so no political opponent of democracy will dare to attack openly the proposition that all men are born free and equal. "All those who, by wealth, education, intelligence, or guile, have an aptitude for leading a community of men, and a chance of doing so—in other words, all the cliques in the ruling class—have to bow to universal suffrage . . . and also, if occasion requires, cajole and fool it." [12] As a witness, Mosca cites his own disciple, Robert Michels, who wrote that "in countries which have representative governments, conservative parties are obliged to pay homage to democratic doctrines." [13] The democratic doctrine had been very useful to the bourgeoisie of the French revolution; being "hardly more than a century and a half old . . . it had not completed its historic task at the end of the nineteenth century . . ." [14]

Those are the extrinsic reasons for the failure of the new idea to make headway. More important still are the "intrinsic" factors. Here the author has some harsh words for those who would apply his method in a mechanical fashion and would forget that "merely to assert that ... power resides in a ruling minority is to dismiss the old guides without supplying new ones." The new theory remains a platitude as long as "we do not know the various ways in which ruling classes are formed and organized." At this point Mosca reasserts his confidence, already voiced in the *Teorica*, that "the procedure ... so much used in the natural sciences" can now rely on such a wealth of data, that the "analytic study" of the genealogy of ruling classes definitely has become a possibility.

The new historian will do well to focus his attention on the second stratum of the dominant minority: "We must, without denying the great importance of what has been done at the vertex and at the base of the pyramid, show that, except for the influence of the intermediate strata, neither of the others could have accomplished very much ... " [15] The middle-class character of Mosca's elite theory has never before emerged as clearly as in this statement. His political class is not actually the ruling class, but rather the class without which society could not be ruled. Again one feels reminded forcefully of David Riesman's concept of the "veto group." The ancient question: "where does sovereignty reside?" has become meaningless. If anything at all, the sovereign power has been reduced to that hovering, elusive entity which holds together a society articulated in the various social forces and agreed on one and the same moral code.

Once More: The Historical Test

Chapters II and III of the new *Elementi* (XIII and XIV of *The Ruling Class*) are almost replicas of Chapters II and III in the *Teorica*. The various types of social and political organization are traced through history, from the primitive oriental monarchies on to the democratic systems of today. The ancient city-state, Rome, medieval feudalism—they all pass in review for a second time. Not much has changed, the narrative shows the same virtues and the same lacunae as before. Documentation is this time more ample and more up to date; particularly, the account of early Roman institutions is enriched by much juridical detail derived from the works of De Sanctis and Ferrero.[16] Rewarding as these pages are, there is no need for us to go over that ground again. With one exception: What the author has to say about the problem of bureaucracy presents it in a new and interesting light.

This seems, at first sight, an exaggerated statement, for much of the information is already known to us, such as the wide interpretation of the concept of bureaucracy as comprising all developed forms of government, no matter whether they are representative or autocratic systems. Mosca is as unwilling as ever to admit that the democratic-liberal state, like the feudal and the bureaucratic, is a type in its own right. He does not just try to be ornery. His interest at this point is in setting up a purely administrative, and not a constitutional typology. From that viewpoint he is justified in disregarding the third form of social and political articulation in the Middle Ages: the commune, and its predecessor, the Greek polis. It is only in the work of his old age, the History of Political Doctrines, that the author relents and acknowledges the city-state as one of three types of organization.[17]

That was a belated recognition of the role which the Italian and transalpine cities played in the emergence of the great absolute monarchies and nation-states from feudal anarchy. In his brilliant "Analysis of Growth," Arnold Toynbee lists the three achievements of the medieval commune as "the substitution of a democratic for an aristocratic form of government; the substitution of a commercial and industrial for a purely agricultural economy; and the introduction of a new standard of businesslike efficiency into the conduct of both economics and politics." [18] Our author was, of course, aware of these accomplishments, although he does not go beyond some hints. But strangely enough, that awareness deserts him when he tries to explain just how and why feudalism changed into the bureaucratic state.

We are informed that "economic causes seem to have exercised very little influence on the transformation . . ." That remark is unmistakably directed against Marx, who held that nothing else but economic reasons is responsible for the development of bureaucratic monarchy. Marx would particularly scoff at Mosca's further allegation that the triumph of the king over the barons was due to "a far-reaching revolution . . . taking place in military art and organization." [19] Really, one does not have to be a Marxist to arrive at the conclusion that, before those royal weapons could be made and used, there had to be an urban bourgeoisie to provide king and emperor with the proverbial sinews of war. Mosca could not really disagree. He says the same thing himself when speaking of the medieval communes as supporters of the crown against feudalism, and again, when he says of the kings that "they . . . made shrewd use of the support of the communes . . ." He has a dim notion that the administrative and managerial know-how of the city-states was at least partly instrumental in making the transformation from the feudal to the modern era possible. While calling the French case of a slow evolution from a feudal monarchy to absolute bureaucracy the "typical or normal" one, Mosca allows for "other processes which led, or might have led, to the same results." It is here that he refers to Milan, a great commune, which "developed first into a signoria, or tyranny, and then into a duchy . . . It subjected many other communes and . . . might easily have become a modern national kingdom." [20] It was left to Toynbee to point out that "the new Italian principalities, large as they were by comparison with the former Italian city-states, were still not large enough to hold their own against the Transalpine Powers." In Italy as elsewhere, city-state democracy went into an eclipse before it re-emerged in the new large-scale nation-states which had absorbed the lessons of Italian city-state efficiency.[21] Only the British Parliament survived that general decline of representative institutions.

Discussing the relationship between bureaucracy and parliament, Mosca remarks that their "co-operation and reciprocal control are two of the outstanding characteristics of the modern representative state." That combination, we learn with amazement, makes it possible "to utilize almost all human values in the political and administrative departments of government, and the door has been left open to all elements in the governed classes to make their way into ruling classes."

We hardly dare to trust our eyes. But there is more in the same vein: "It may also be claimed that there is an almost perfect harmony between the present political system and the level of civilization that has been attained . . ." Our artistic culture, our morality may be inferior to those of a century ago, but twentieth-century society "has shown itself far superior . . . in its wise organization of economic and scientific production . . ." But surely these gains are exceeded by the losses, the waste and incompetence of democratic government? Not in the least! For "there can be no question that the political system now prevailing has won over the spontaneous energies and wills of individual human beings the same victory which the complex of institutions, instruments, knowledge and aptitudes that form the culture and the strength of our generation has won over the forces of nature." [22]

This is a far cry from the harsh judgment that "the checks which bureaucracy and democracy can enforce upon themselves . . . are always inadequate." [23] Mosca himself must have felt the great discrepancy, for he interpolated, in the third edition of the work, a lengthy footnote, not present in *The Ruling Class*, in which he explains his changed attitude toward the bête noire of his early years. The document follows here in full:

Some readers who may still remember how much I had to remark about parliamentary government in my *Teorica dei governi* may have noticed that I have considerably modified my views about that subject. It is not easy to imagine how that could have been avoided in the course of roughly half a century. The first signs of that change are already apparent in the first volume of this work . . . In substance, we still hold fast to the fundamental concept of the *Teorica dei governi* which asserts that all state structures are made up of organized minorities, and that therefore a system which affects to be based on the free expression of the will of the majority is perpetrating an unmitigated lie which in the long run must result in a catastrophe. I still believe that almost everything I once said about the parliamentary regime is based on solid fact. But a greater familiarity with history and the experience of a lifetime taught me to regard those weaknesses with more indulgence and to realize that there is no such thing as a political system which, in actual operation, would be free from the inevitable moral blemishes and intellectual shortcomings of human nature.[24]

Which is to say that the defects which Mosca had been blaming on the democratic system would not disappear with its removal but might become even worse. It means, to use the popular expression, that for fifty years he had been barking up the wrong tree. Or, in more dignified language, that the state with its "political classes" and "formulas" may not in itself be "an intelligible field of study." [25]

Principles and Tendencies

The thirty-five pages which make up the fourth chapter of the second *Elementi* (Chapter XV of *The Ruling Class*) are very likely the best Mosca ever wrote. Entitled "Various Principles and Tendencies Affecting the Formation and Organization of the Ruling Class," this section is the heart of Volume II, as the one on Juridical Defense is the core of the first. It is not so much the elaborate, yet at the same time lucid, pairing of two different classifications that impresses so much as the rich and variegated use to which the scheme is put. The chapter represents the author's answer to his own stern summons: if the doctrine of the ruling class is to be meaningful at all, "the comprehensive and generic demonstration" must be supplemented "with an analytic study." [26] Here is the proof of the pudding; the full potentialities of the new method are established beyond any reasonable doubt.

Plato—the Plato of *The Laws*—has the first as well as the last word of the chapter. His two-fold scheme, deriving all existent variants of government from the two archetypes, democracy and monarchy, serves Mosca as a starting point for an elaboration of his own Inaugural Address of twenty years before.[27] This time the author uses the term "principle" when he refers to *the direction of the power flow* in a political community. There are, of course, only two ways in which that flow could move: "authority is either transmitted from above downward . . . or from below upward." In the first case, Mosca says, "the autocratic principle" is at work. He might have called it "the monarchic principle," but autocratic won out, being more inclusive, since it could be applied to the nonmonarchic types of government as well.

Conversely, when authority is assumed to reside with all, or a part, of the people, Mosca chooses to speak of "the liberal principle," preferring the term "liberal" to Plato's "democratic," since democracy denotes the sovereignty of all the people, whereas "liberal" would also include all those systems which restrict the ballot, as in Rome and Athens, to a more or less large fraction of the total populace.

"Tendency," as distinct from "principle," is Mosca's label to identify the *source* from which the ruling classes are recruited. Here Plato's terminology is readopted by the author: the term "democratic" seems more suitable to indicate that an existing ruling class is open to the lower classes, or else that the ruling class ought to be open to the lower ranks.[28] This tendency "is constantly at work with greater or lesser intensity in all human societies." [29]

The same is true of "the aristocratic tendency" which is at cross-purposes with democratic methods of selection. It is the label for the human urge "to stabilize social control and political power in the descendants" of the ruling group.

Now all this is at first a bit confusing. Was it necessary to inflict upon the reader, at this advanced stage of the discussion, four new, complex, easily confounded terminologies all in one heap? From this objection one might easily proceed and try to simplify the matter. Could the four terms be reduced to two? Why not pair off "the autocratic principle" with "the aristocratic tendency" and "the democratic tendency" with "the liberal principle"?

But Mosca has been waiting for just that attempt, and he is quick to point out to us our mistake: "At first glance it might seem that the predominance of what we call the 'autocratic' principle should go with what we call the 'aristocratic' tendency; and that the opposite principle which we call 'liberal' should go with the tendency that we call 'democratic' . . . That, however, would be a rule that is subject to a great many exceptions." [30] Not a few autocracies recruited their officials from the lower classes, and elective systems could be mentioned in which the electors were identical with the political class in control. So intermixed are the two principles and the two tendencies that it is difficult to isolate them properly. But nothing less will do if we intend to understand which way society is moving.

Accordingly, the four components of the system are now taken up in sequence and the pluses and the minuses in each case toted up.

Much can be said in favor of the autocratic principle. "A political system that has been so widely recurring and so long enduring among peoples of the most widely various civilizations ... must somehow correspond to the political nature of man. The artificial or exceptional thing never shows such great tenacity." The political formulas of autocracy, based on a theocratic, charismatic, or dynastic principle of authority, are "simple, clear and readily comprehensible to everybody."

Against autocracy speaks the fact that "it does not allow the peoples that have adopted it, and especially their ruling classes, to attain all of the moral and intellectual development of which civilized mankind is capable." In some way, size and cultural accomplishment of a community seem to be correlated: thus, autocracy appears to be the system most congenial to large communities.[31] The glory that was Greece, or Florence, issued from parochial ground. Another correlation can be found between duration and intensity of cultural achievement: the actual flowering of Athens lasted only 150 years (479–323 B.C.), and Rome's greatness did not last much longer (203–31 B.C.). The United States and England are the modern nations which proclaim the triumph of the liberal principle. But English institutions deserve to be called free only after the Glorious Revolution (1688), when "the great North-American Republic" was not even born. The real greatness of both countries did not come until much later, Mosca says. In other words, it is too early to say whether Anglo-Saxon liberty is going to outlast the Graeco-Roman span of a hundred and fifty years. This is in any case what Mosca seems to think when he says that apparently the liberal principle tends "to prevail at those exceptional periods in the lives of the peoples when some of the noblest faculties of man are able to show themselves in all their intensity and energy." However, those enormous outbursts of creative force seem almost always to be followed by a kind of collective fatigue. It is then that "human societies feel, as it were, an overpowering need for a long sleep." That is the time when Rome submitted to the autocratic rule of the Augustus Caesar.[32]

This periodization, linking periods of historic creativity or barrenness with certain types of government, has a definite Spenglerian note, but possibly it was the secret, unacknowledged influence of Giambattista Vico's Corso and Ricorso that inspired our author at this point. It would not be too difficult to puncture his *ballon d'essai* —for the whole passage has decidedly the character of a brilliant "aside"—by simply pointing to the well-known fact that eras of political and social dynamism do not always coincide with those of cultural grandeur. But since the point is not of capital significance for Mosca's argument, it need not be pursued here any further.

Commenting on the wide application the aristocratic principle has found in the past, Mosca wisely leaves room for the human factor. His four tendencies and principles are not to be considered iron laws. One instance will suffice to demonstrate their flexibility: "In countries where the autocratic principle and the aristocratic tendency jointly prevail, the [ruling] group is usually made up of members of the highest nobility." That will be so in all those instances where the incumbent of the highest office is a man of only average ability. But when the monarch happens to be a great ruler, "he sometimes succeeds in breaking the ring of aristocratic cliques that serve him—or, more often rule him—and he snaps it by elevating to the highest positions persons ... of ordinary birth ..." In doing so, he brings about a change from the aristocratic to the democratic tendency, thereby not only not abandoning the autocratic principle but, in most cases, reinforcing it against the cabals of his court. But such a change, such reassertion would not correspond to any basic shift in the relationship of the great social forces. It would be exclusively the work of chance, although the author does not say so in so many words. But he makes plain that this is what he means by introducing us to Basil, Emperor of Byzantium (9th century A.D.), and Nadir, Shah of Persia (18th century), two autocrats of humble origin who rose to power on the strength of their own genius. Incidentally, they showed how flexible the autocratic principle may be in times of trouble.[33]

As the level of civilization rises and specialization becomes more and more important, autocratic aristocracies, that is, states in which the supreme authority is buttressed by a second stratum composed of the members of the noble families, will "almost always develop into more or less bureaucratic autocracies." [34] The type is so preponderant that Mosca virtually equates it with the autocratic principle and treats it as such at considerable length.

The Level of Bureaucracy

The systematic study of large-scale organization, the analysis of administrative techniques and structures which, one might say, are the essence of contemporary society, is of a relatively recent date. When Mosca wrote, Max Weber and his school had already begun their great investigations,[35] but with the exception of Michels' well-known work, they seem to have been unknown or neglected by our author. But then, his major interest went in a different direction. Still, although he never bothered to define bureaucracy, he had a pretty shrewd idea of its workings even when he started writing his *Teorica*. The *Elementi* only amplifies the information of a lifetime spent in research and in close personal contact with officialdom. When Mosca writes about bureaucracy we may be sure he writes as one who knows.

Once more he considers the conditions under which a bureaucratic order may emerge from feudal fragmentation: [36] "Before an autocracy can begin to bureaucratize a great state, the political organization must be so strong that it can regularly levy on the income of private citizens a portion that is large enough to pay the salaries of public officials and defray the expenses of a permanent armed force." Direct channels of revenue must connect the great mass of subjects with the sovereign. As long as the locks of these channels are manned not by the king's men, but by baronial interlopers who deflect the stream into their own domains, the monarch will depend, almost exclusively, on the financial resources of the free cities. It is only with their help that he will ultimately break through to the primary resources of the nation. He must have a nucleus of bureaucratic cadres able to extract state revenue, and once that nucleus exists and operates with some efficiency, a whole train of effects is set in motion: "Once bureaucratization is well advanced, it in turn enhances the coercive efficiency of the state machine and so enables the ruling class ... to exercise greater and greater influence over the governed masses ..." Bureaucracy snowballs into the magnitude of the mortal god leviathan. Or to use another simile: the instrument becomes the master which the sorcerer's apprentice—in our time, the ruling politician—is no longer able to control.

The bureaucratic type of government ("bureaucratic" always understood in the broad sense which Mosca gave to it) is treated with a certain sympathy which has its valid points. The reader is once more reminded that bureaucracy was "opening all doors to talents that are forging upward from the lower strata in society, and therefore ... making room for personal merit." [37] The last word in the sentence is the key: the bureaucratic order, by establishing the "democratic tendency," not only gives deserving individuals from all classes a fair break, it favors in particular one class of people *as a class*, namely the very educated bourgeoisie of which our author himself was unknowingly the spokesman: "Though a bureaucracy may be legally open to all social classes, in fact it will always be recruited from the middle class, in other words, from the second stratum of the ruling class." [38]

But if Mosca had a more than sneaking admiration for bureaucracy, that feeling did not obfuscate his critical intelligence. He cites the observation of Ferrero: "personal merit is one of the things that the passions and interests of men best manage to counterfeit." [39] Intrigue in a tightly knit autocracy, and flattery of the electors in a liberal society are frequent substitutes for real merit. In both systems, the superior officer who has to judge the aptitudes of his staff members "will in all good faith give a candidate a higher rating for ... qualities which he likes or happens to possess himself." Rare is the administrator—and, we may add, it would be a rare philosopher-king—who surrounds himself with rebels rather than with faithful human replicas of his own image. "Blind conservativism, the utter incapacity to correct one's faults and weaknesses" are the characteristics of "exclusively bureaucratic regimes." [40]

Another aspect of this "intractability of institutions," [41] in addition to its immobility, is the mediocrity of administrative performance in large-scale bureaucracy. This is, in Mosca's view, a product of what may be called bureaucratic equalitarianism. As the late Joseph Stalin loved to say: It could not be otherwise. The basic principle of bureaucratic action being the streamlining (rationalization) of procedure, the elimination of all arbitrary elements, the choice of personnel will of necessity rely on "automatic rules of advancement" rather than on personal decision with all its uncertainties and vagaries. "Such rules can be based only upon the principle of seniority. In this case, unfailingly, the lazy and the diligent, the intelligent and the stupid, get along equally well." [42] Ambition is discouraged; nobody will exert himself more than is necessary to "hold down the job." Thus the abodes of bureaucracy "become the refuge of the talentless . . ."

Surprisingly, another marked effect of bureaucratization does not come in for the systematic treatment it deserves: the tendency of the official to shun personal responsibility, to "pass the buck," an attitude which is so unavoidable in any system using long and interlocking chains of command that it could be deduced a priori even if we did not know the facts. Mosca is, of course, aware of it, without however seeing the connection with the central theme: that bureaucratic action is collective action, and so of necessity prone to reifying and depersonalizing any and all individual contribution to the total process of decision-making. Consequently, no official may move beyond strictly defined boundaries without imperiling the entire system.

Mosca takes a different approach. He does not explain bureaucratic behavior as the product of the bureaucratic process but, on the contrary, explains the bureaucratic process in terms of human behavior. A good bureaucracy is, in his view, one which would not encourage "base servility in subalterns." Lack of backbone and related failings of the bureaucrat would merely be a poor reflection on the class from which the civil servants are recruited: "The moral level of the bureaucracy is the moral level of the ruling class." Proceeding from there, Mosca tries to establish a "law of communicating moral levels." The bureaucracy will perform on a higher level when the ruling class "has been formed and disciplined over long periods of time, and has devoted itself for many generations to the service of the state . . ." In that case the bureaucracy, too, will have a tradition of high standards; it will have what the French call *esprit de corps*. Of course, its "level will be lower when the ruling class is of more recent date and stems either from rustling, bustling and lucky adventurers, or from families of peasants and shopkeepers who have acquired, at best, the first rudiments of manners and education."

This point seems to be well taken. The routinization to which human spontaneity must submit in discharging bureaucratic functions is a process which will not be rushed. The past experience of the Soviet regime would tend to bear out the observation of the author. He is less convincing in his final argument against bureaucracies which lack tradition: "Even if such people have developed a certain competence, they are still often without a spark of idealism and retain an inveterate and sordid greed for large, and even for petty gains." [43] This certainly is true in many instances, and perhaps the one Mosca had in mind was not too far removed from his particular point of observation. But why bureaucratic novices should be distinguished by an absence of idealism rather than by an excess of it is difficult to see. Not a few new bureaucracies made up for their lack of experience by a frightening abundance of administrative zeal. The Bolsheviks of the first generation and the agencies of the New Deal in its initial phase displayed that holy frenzy; the renowned administration of the first Napoleon drew much of its efficient personnel from the fresh cadres of the revolutionary element.

The same example of the French imperial civil service might have served our author to make a strong point in favor of his own class-biased view of bureaucratic levels. Had he laid less stress upon the moral aspect and more on the element of continuity, so necessary to maintain a modicum of administrative efficiency, he could have demonstrated to his and our satisfaction that the bureaucratic apparatus never has been seriously affected by triumphant revolutions. Where they did disrupt the mechanism, it had to be put in order quickly, at a heavy expense to the solvency of the new revolutionary government. Attention has been drawn by many writers to the fact that the bureaucracy of France only increased in strength after each revolutionary shock.[44]

Now, continuity strongly suggests stability, and from there it is merely one more step to the impression that bureaucracies, since they show so much staying power in the course of history, play an essentially conservative role in the social process. That is indeed often so, and Robert Michels has presented a strong argument in favor of such views.[45] In doing so, he assumed that what was true, in each and any case, of bureaucratic *structure* was a pertinent characteristic of the bureaucratic *policy*. But the former may be quite conservatively organized and yet be in the service of the wildest revolutionary schemes, such as five-year plans and the like.

However, Mosca's dislike for upstart bureaucracies is understandable as soon as we reverse the logical sequence of his argument. For unlike Michels, he did not start out from the essential immobility of bureaucratic bodies to explain the ultimate futility of all plebeian, democratic aspirations. Michels' ultimate conclusion is the proposition from which Mosca starts. *Because* democracy is, in his view, not viable as a device of social and political control, he turns for comfort to a type of bureaucratic order which would guarantee the continuity of his sort of society if not the domination of his own, the educated, class.

On Middle Ground

In Gaetano Mosca's nomenclature the old concepts have a way of taking on much broader meanings than we are accustomed to. The elasticity with which he handled the term "bureaucratic" is matched by the flexibility of his term "liberal," which is applied by him to all the cases where authority is nominally exercised by the community. A liberal system, in the author's parlance, is one in which "the law is based upon the consent of the majority of citizens, though only a small fraction of the inhabitants may be citizens..." [46] Normally, if the electorate comprises only a small portion of the people, we would call such a society an aristocracy or oligarchy. We would speak of democratic government if all the citizens or the majority of them possess the franchise. But in Mosca's view, democracy is merely liberalism on a rampage, "carried away," as he has said before, "by logic, its worst enemy." [47] Or in more sober words, democracy is an extension of the liberal principle which "varies from narrowly exclusive to broadly inclusive."

At its most exclusive, even "a large part of the ruling class, or of those who have the requisites for belonging to it, are kept out." In that case, one might speak of a "masked autocratic rule by a narrowly limited class of people." [48] The voters and the actual rulers are identical, or, in Rousseau's language, the citizens are both the sovereign and the magistrate. When, on the contrary, the franchise is all-inclusive, the autocratic principle, officially denied, may in a time of crisis still assert itself, this time disguised as "the will of the people." Then it would be a "new Caesarism" deriving its authority from a plebiscitarian mandate, "as the two Napoleonic Caesarisms did." Today, we would, in such a case, speak of "totalitarian democracy." [49]

In a normal democratic situation, "the various party organizations into which the ruling class is divided" are forced to compete for "the votes of the more numerous classes, which are necessarily the poorest and most ignorant." This sentence is important for more than one reason. The assumption that the ruling class is a composite of warring factions or cliques is already known to us; the author has discarded long ago the fiction of elite cohesiveness in favor of a pluralistic equilibrium of the leading social forces. But the recognition of the fact that ruling classes are divided into various party organizations might have prompted Mosca to discover the contemporary role of the mass party as a catalyst of leadership and to revise his theory of the elite accordingly. Unfortunately, Mosca never faced that issue.[50]

His low opinion of the democratic masses still comes rather as a shock to us, although we ought to be sufficiently prepared by now for his conviction that "these classes ordinarily live in submission to a government which often they do not care for ... Their most spontaneous desire is to be governed as little as possible, or to make as few sacrifices as possible for the state. Their second desire ... is to profit by government in order to better their economic situation ..." [51]

Whether or not this is a correct description of the "common man" will remain undebated here. One wonders only whether Mosca, in thus positing a maximum of political inertia at the base of the social pyramid, has remained faithful to his own assumptions. The dichotomy between the excellent Few and the *hoi polloi* seems to be once again restored in all its old severity. It is a view that no longer fits the conception of an advanced and articulate civilization such as Mosca had developed in the work of his maturity. It is no longer reconcilable with his portrait of a society in which one social force after the other rises to the fore to claim its share of power.

But a close reading of the text reveals that Mosca has not really retreated from his new, advanced position. We have only to remember that, according to his view, the leading elements of the social forces are, or ought to be, incorporated into the political class, now conceived as the totality of all elites, inside and outside government. It is, in Mosca's reading, the peculiar disability of democratic systems that in them the ruling class has to cater to the instincts of all those who have been left behind in the competitive race for pre-eminence. Add to that the condescending view which the well-educated class of Mosca's generation took of the illiterate majority of their Italian fellow countrymen, and the result smacks very much of social snobbery. In Mosca's case, however, it is more than that: here is a man sincerely frightened by the methods which all factions of the ruling class, including the conservatives, must use if they wish to survive the ordeal of the ballot box: "Often enough the parties against which this demagogic propaganda is directed use exactly the same means to combat it . . . A despicable competition, in which those who deliberately deceive lower their intellectual level to a par with those they deceive, while morally they stoop even lower!" [52]

Again the Mosca who describes what is finds himself at odds with the other Mosca who insists on certain standards of morality and intellectual excellence. The theorist of the political class which contains "the individuals who are best fit to govern" [53] secretly continues to hope against hope that these would also be "the best" in all respects.

How much popular participation in decision-making is the author ready to accept? He is quite frank about it: "All in all . . . the liberal principle finds conditions for its application most favorable when the electorate is made up in the majority of the second stratum of the ruling class, which forms the backbone of all great political organizations."

Aristotle, scornfully dismissed in the Teorica and in the first installment of the Elementi, is, without apologies, restored to honorable status. What is to happen to the democratic, universal franchise in Mosca's ideal state we are not told, but obviously it would have to

be limited to "the second stratum of the ruling class." We may derive some comfort from the likelihood that the size of the electorate
may still tax the imagination of a Palmerstonian liberal: "When it
is sufficiently large, no very great proportion of the voters can aspire
to candidacies, and the candidates therefore can find judges in them
and not rivals and accomplices." But our Palmerstonian will recover
his composure as he goes on reading: "At the same time, when the
electorate is fairly limited, success does not depend on paying homage
to the beliefs and sentiments of the more ignorant masses. Only
under such circumstances can one of the chief assumptions of the
liberal system be made, we do not say complete, but not wholly
illusory—namely, that those who represent shall be responsible to
the represented."

These lines have the authentic Aristotelian ring. Now, Mosca does
not say that he believes that the ancient polity could be resuscitated
in our time. Nor does he proclaim the desirability of such a hope.
Yet, the whole tenor of the passage has an unmistakably nostalgic
ring: if only we could somehow go back to that kind of liberal regime
which will forever be associated with the glory that was Europe in
the nineteenth century.

One final remark of the author should be noted: he acknowledges
that public discussion of all issues is one of the valuable assets of the
liberal regime. But, Mosca warns, if that debate is to have genuine
effect, "the newspapers must not be organs of political or financial
cliques nor blind instruments of faction. If they are, the public should
know about it . . ." [54]

But the newspapers are just that, and the public does know, and it
makes no difference. Still all this is no reason to treat Mosca's two
suggestions in a churlish manner. Naive as it sounds, the notion that
communication media are a public rather than a private matter can
no longer be dismissed as a mere phantasy.

The Circulation of Elites

This theory, which is Pareto's special claim to fame, is a more systematic and elaborate development of Mosca's democratic and aristocratic "tendencies." Both are constantly at work as the accelerating

and retarding factors in the shaping and reshaping of society. Rejuvenation from below will occur sometimes rapidly (in the event of some great upset of the social structure due to foreign conquest or internal revolution). "More often, in fact normally, it takes place through a slow and gradual infiltration of elements from the lower into the higher classes." Mosca was apparently not thinking of the present when he wrote the second *Elementi*, but of the preceding decades when violent alterations of the social pattern could still be "regarded as exceptional." The Russian revolution had registered as little then as the incipient Fascist turmoil that was to convulse the rest of Europe soon. But the historian Mosca was astute enough to see that such quick "overturns sometimes give a vigorous impetus to intellectual, moral, and material progress." His choice of words 's careful: he does not say that the violent acceleration of the democratic tendency is the sole cause of the material, intellectual, and moral "leap," because at other times it connotes "the beginnings, or else the results, of periods of decay and disintegration ..." [55] The democratic tendency, in that case, has a negative effect: it hastens the decline.

In normal times, "if it is confined within moderate limits, the democratic tendency is in a sense indispensable to what is called 'progress' in human societies. If all aristocracies had remained steadfastly closed and stationary, the world would never have changed." Notwithstanding the fact that he had just placed the word between inverted commas, Mosca now becomes almost poetic in his praise of progress: "The struggle between those who are at the top and those who are born at the bottom but aspire to climb has been, is, and will ever be the ferment that forces individuals and classes to widen their horizons and seek the new roads that have brought the world to the degree of civilization that it attained in the nineteenth century." Mosca here comes dangerously close to an acceptance of the class struggle idea in its gradualist version. He goes even further: when the democratic tendency is not too powerful and not exclusive, "it represents a conservative force," inasmuch as the slow influx of qualified elements from below does not endanger the stability of the regime; not only are they easily absorbed but they add to the power of the ruling class. That way, the level of civilization may be securely maintained or even raised still further. The belief, so powerful in our time, "that every advantage due to birth can . . . be eliminated" only harms the evolutionary process,[56] Mosca says, and in this context, he pays a rather left-handed compliment to Saint-Simon as the first modern to enunciate clearly the idea "that in an ideally organized state there would be absolute correspondence between the service rendered by an individual and the rank he comes to occupy . . ." And Mosca—it is the tough-minded Mosca who has here the upper hand—though agreeing in principle, is doubtful that the human race is ever likely to evolve an order in which "merit" would become the sole criterion of reward. The record shows that there is something in our nature that clings stubbornly to the belief in what we may call "biological merit." Nor are the apostles of equality themselves immune from that same tendency: "Every time the democratic movement has triumphed, in part or in full, we have invariably seen the aristocratic tendency come to life again through efforts of the very men who had fought it and sometimes had proclaimed its suppression." [57]

It is here that Mosca makes the harsh remark already quoted that "in order to abolish privileges of birth entirely, it would be necessary to . . . abolish the family, recognize a vagrant Venus and drop humanity to the level of the lowest animalism." [58] The sally is of course directed against Plato and such later Platonizing works as Campanella's *City of the Sun*. But, Mosca does not have to depend on that type of argument in order to defend the privilege of birth. In his discussion of the antidemocratic, or aristocratic tendency, he first presents a list of its demerits: the "sense of caste" which will develop in a narrowly defined aristocratic group; the superiority complex which makes the members of the caste oblivious of their duties to society and cuts them off from human contact with the lowly born. The self-imposed aloofness becomes ignorance of two kinds: one, a refusal to take notice of the sufferings and aspirations of the common lot of people, a lack of sympathy; the other a wrong notion of reality, a false benevolence indulging in romantic and utopian misconceptions about the "primitive simplicity and goodness of mankind." Such vagaries render "the ruling classes . . . unfit to exert any influence whatever on the mental and sentimental developments in the masses"—in short, they lose control.[59]

They may continue to retain their status for a while, as the French nobles did in the *ancien régime*, long after they have lost their social function, that is, when they had become a class of drones: "the most insidious enemy of all aristocracies of birth is, undoubtedly, idleness." There have been eulogists of noble idleness, and Mosca finds much merit in the theory of Miguel de Unamuno who in *En defensa de la harangeria* pointed out how much the world owes to the wealthy loafer. Without them and their "conspicuous consumption" no fine crafts, no science, no morality.[60] It is strange that our author gives no credit to de Mandeville who in his famous *Fable of the Bees* propounded the same theory two hundred years before the great philosopher of Spain.

But why give the name idleness, asks Mosca, to what "may be the noblest form of human labor"? What looks, to the superficial mind, like loafing may in truth be passion, "a disinterested passion" for pure knowledge, "labor that envisages no immediate utility" and yet may be the very effort which lifts us "above the status of animals." It is man's highest type according to the Stagirite, of whom the author speaks here. This kind of contemplative man has had "the best chance to develop in people who have belonged to ruling classes—classes which have been so firmly established in their rule that some of their members could be exempted from the material cares of life . . ."

This is one of those unquestionably true remarks which do not endear Mosca to the democratic reader. Sensing this, he quickly turns around to reassure us that "it would be untrue and unfair to maintain that a disinterested passion for knowledge is not to be found in individuals belonging to the lower strata of society." We are most gratified to hear also that "one of the happiest applications of the democratic tendency would lie in enabling such individuals to develop their superior qualities." But, alas, Mosca does "not believe that compulsory elementary education will alone be sufficient to accomplish it." [61] For unto everyone that hath shall be given, and he shall have abundance: not satisfied with their two privileges, birth and wealth, the dominant few arrogate to themselves genius too. At least they have a head start in the race for intellectual and moral superiority:

It is not far-fetched to imagine that in the beginning, the upper classes, on whatever basis they may have been constituted, attracted many of the more intelligent individuals ... and that when such classes are not hermetically sealed they are continuously replenished with intelligent elements deriving from the lower strata of society.

In stating that the average intelligence of the higher social classes "becomes higher and stays higher than that of the lower classes," Mosca gratefully acknowledges the influence of Otto Ammon. "The phenomenon of family inheritance is more striking still in the regard of moral qualities." [62] Self-restraint, honesty in dealings with subordinates, and courage are some of the virtues to be found in families which have "for long generations been able to maintain a high social position." Families short in these virtues will be weeded out by the selective process. If that process is to go on, "the ruling class must have a certain stability and not be renewed every generation." All this may be expressed in a "law":

Penetration into the upper classes by elements coming from the lower is helpful when it takes place in due proportion and under such conditions that the newcomers at once assimilate the best qualities of the old members. It is harmful when the old members are, so to say, absorbed and assimilated by the newcomers. In that event an aristocracy is not replenished. It turns plebs.[63]

The statement points up the apparent plausibility and the essential weakness of most social "laws": it is couched in such careful, reasonable terms that nobody would want to quarrel with it. The trouble begins as soon as we try to apply the "law" to any concrete situation. Then the statement reveals what might be called the "fallacy of misplaced absoluteness." Mosca assumes that the qualities which are essential to a ruling class are constant. So they are, but only in a very general way. Surely, all minorities that possess power must have courage, self-restraint, and intellectual capacity if they want to stay where they are. The question, however, is: Courage, restraint, and intelligence *concerning what?* We answer that the "what" is ever changing, as the author himself told us, in accordance with the changing needs of the communities articulating themselves as new social forces. So the constancy of the elitist attitudes will of necessity be relative to the particular *objectives* of the social interest or interests prevailing during any given period. If the interests undergo a metamorphosis, then "the best qualities" will be those of "the newcomers," and the old members of the ruling class will be the ones to do all the adapting to the changed requirements. That may indeed have the effect, as Mosca puts it, of transforming an aristocratic ruling class into a "plebs," but as he also says, that plebs will soon develop all the attitudes of aristocracy, that is, show constancy in the pursuit of the new variable.

With these qualifications, Mosca's "law" may stand.

Another point he makes concerns the relative "cost" of a dominant minority. He doubts that a new ruling class will be content with the same share of national wealth as had been its predecessor's. "That is another way of asking whether democracy is more economical for a society than aristocracy." It seems the author tries here to reach some *modus vivendi* with Pareto's theory, which had found its definitive shape prior to the writing of the second *Elementi*. Pareto's distinction between the foxes and the lions, symbols standing for the "residues of combination" and of the "persistent aggregates," respectively, may have had some slight influence on Mosca's democratic and aristocratic "tendencies," although our author had conceived his own scheme independently, if sketchily, in 1902, the same year in which the great rival published his first full-dress version of the theory of the elites (in his two-volume *Systèmes socialistes*). Not that it matters, but there is a certain amount of internal evidence suggesting that the traffic of ideas between Mosca and Pareto was not all one-way. Take the following assertion of the *Elementi*: "Ruling classes, whether democratic or aristocratic, which keep in power by systematically favoring the interests of private individuals or small organized minorities at the expense of the public are always the most costly." [64]

This reminds one at once of certain passages in which Pareto sizes up the policies of plutocratic governments:

The individual comes to prevail, and by far, over family, community, nation. Material interests and interests of the present or a near future come to prevail over the ideal interests of community or nation and interests of the distant future. [Such governments] are very expensive, since they must make up with chicanery, and with the money that that costs, for the force in which they are deficient.[65]

For once, Pareto was ahead of Mosca, his *Trattato*, published in 1915–16, antedating the second *Elementi* by seven years. But Mosca, if he knew those passages at all, adapted them characteristically to his proper purpose by both narrowing and broadening their meaning. For with him, the lions as well as the foxes may be spendthrifts: "there is little to choose between the tendencies in that regard." But simultaneously he qualifies that criticism: "The class that rules polit-ically ... must have a large enough share ... to spare it from show-ing too great an attachment to ... those economies which sometimes lower a man in the eyes of his fellows more than any amount of bad conduct." [66]

A certain opulence of spending thus may be a social asset, strength-ening, not weakening, the hold the rulers have upon the people. But this once the author thinks it "premature ... to formulate a law." In a particularly brilliant paragraph, he urges us to watch "for atmos-pheric changes in the times and in the peoples who live about us. When, for instance, a glacial calm prevails ... then we may rest as-sured that the autocratic principle is prevailing too strongly; ... when a wild wind of social equality is howling ... it is evident that the democratic tendency is ... approaching the danger point."

So Mosca reaches the conclusion:

The soundness of political institutions depends upon an appropriate fusing and balancing of the differing but constant principles and tend-encies which are at work in all political organisms ... Violent upheavals ... arise primarily from the virtually absolute predominance of one of the two principles, or one of the two tendencies ...

What else is this but "the old doctrine of the golden mean, which judged mixed governments best." Gaetano Mosca has made peace with Aristotle, although "there would still be the difficulty of deter-mining just where the golden mean lies." [67] All we can do is to watch for the atmospheric changes, or, in other words, rely on our political and social instinct rather than on Aristotle, Mosca, or Pareto.

10

CLARIFICATIONS

It is not easy to determine the main purpose of the chapter before the last of *The Ruling Class*. The subject of the one preceding it stood out in high relief: it was to give the doctrine of the balance of the social forces a still wider and, above all, a dynamic meaning which it did not have before. No such unifying theme could be ascribed to the fifth chapter of the second *Elementi*, characteristically called "Clarifications and Polemics." The corresponding English title, "Ruling Class and Individual" [1] does not do much justice to the vast scope of this chapter, ranging from the question of what are the qualifications of the leader to a discussion of Historical Materialism, from Plato's "rule of the best" to the possibilities of scientific politics in our own time. One is reminded of a classical overture in which the themes and melodies of the whole opera are joined toward the end in a grandiose if slightly hurly-burly stretta.

The beginning merely seems to carry on the argument of the preceding chapters. The problem of elite selection is still very much on Mosca's mind. He is particularly bothered by the question of the links between the various strata of the ruling class. How close is the connection? What precisely is the interlocking mechanism operating

216

between ruling class and masses? One should think enough has already been said—short of empirical investigation—to satisfy curiosity in these respects. Why is the author so intent on thrusting on us still more information, in the main historical, about the subject of elite formation? He does not disclose his reason in so many words; it must be looked for in the interstices of his argument, in what he fails or does not care to say. However, before arguing from Mosca's silence, we must first establish what he says.

Close intellectual and moral ties, we are informed, connect the first and second strata of the ruling class, the top group being "more or less imbued with the ideas, sentiments, passions, and, therefore, policies" of the secondary level. History knows of not a few cases where the head of a political organization was a mere nonentity or even quite insane (such as the Roman emperors Claudius and Nero, England's George III). Yet the political class carried on as if nothing had happened in the royal or imperial palace.

Now, to say that normally—unless the ruler is a genius—the level of the ruling class will be that of the second stratum is to state the obvious. Unless the top rulers have come from an alien race of conquerors, the upper stratum would quite naturally rise from the larger body (which unites in itself one or several of the indigenous social forces). They would rise the way a medieval king had to be first a *primus inter pares*, first among his peers, before he could become the absolute prince, *legibus solutus*.

What is true of the small inner circle applies equally to the secondary elite. Again, unless it came into existence through an act of conquest, it has to, and does, come from the ruled majority. To restate once more Mosca's general idea of the way civilizations grow: they crystallize out of a multitude of little power centers until some kind of unity has been achieved. (The unifying agent need not be a central government but could be, as was the case with feudalism, a cultural, religious bond and institution.)

That is integration in its horizontal aspect, centripetal. The same process takes also a vertical direction: power flows toward the apex of an ever higher-rising social pyramid. It is permissible to say that Mosca's law of social and political organization is identical with his law of the "democratic tendency." Nor is that an accident. Whether he likes it or not, his whole theory of the political class has a crypto-democratic character. It is one not concerned with conquerors, and only at the very outset with the men of military valor. The political class is not even any more exclusively the wealthy class. Professional skills, knowledge, training have become the indispensable tools of political control, and these tools are in the hands of the educated class—Mosca's class. This class is still, essentially, the middle class, but with education having become general, the flow of intellectual energies is no longer confined to it. The new elite comes from the masses.

Mosca is aware of it, and he calls the connection between masses and the second layer of the ruling class even "more certain and less varying than the other" (the connection between the two strata of the ruling class itself).[2] But having said that much, he becomes frightened. Being afraid of the "common man," Mosca veers and falls back on Taine, Renan, and even on the so severely censured Gumplowicz. The results of the selective process once more become questionable; the renewal of the ruling classes from the masses is not necessarily identical with their improvement. "It is easy for a man to preserve certain virtues when it is materially impossible for him to acquire certain vices," Mosca says, meaning that the vaunted moral superiority of the poor is nothing but lack of temptation. The real test comes when the poor rise high enough above their class to enter "good society." And Mosca's test is quite exacting. It is not enough for the plebeians to retain their moral stamina in their new class surroundings: "only if they and their children are really better than their new class associates, could one, with any assurance, claim moral superiority for the class that is ruled over the class that rules." The author tersely adds: "An investigation ... does not seem, on the whole, to yield results that are at all favorable to the new arrivals." [3]

Apparently the reservoir from which the ruling class draws its resources is polluted. Woe to the alien conquerors who intermarry with the native stock! "Not a few examples serve to show that as long as a dominant class of foreign origin keeps fairly pure in blood, the state retains its strength and the country its prosperity, but that, as the class begins to fuse and confuse with indigenous elements, the political structure weakens and the nation falls into anarchy or comes under a new foreign domination." And if that is the case not just once but frequently, we must conclude "that the indigenous elements . . . did not possess the aptitudes and virtues required for developing a native ruling class . . ." [4]

Now, that is an astounding passage. So far Mosca had not shown the slightest sympathy for any theories of racialism. He had rejected Gumplowicz because of that, although the Austrian's doctrine was not quite as crude as Mosca thought it was.[5] How shall we explain his sudden reversal? Does he seriously believe the fact of conquest proves that the conquered race could not develop its own ruling class?

The purpose of my argument is not to expose Mosca's inconsistency, for I believe that inconsistency is often the price of originality, the very birthmark of great minds. Only the second-rater will never be caught in any contradiction. Mosca's lapse into racialism is no contradiction of his basic faith; rather it is evidence that Mosca's central theoretical assumption itself is made up of elements so contradictory that their reconciliation seems impossible. And the explanation of that conflict cannot be found within the context of the author's doctrine—the dichotomy is the result of influences best studied by the method of the sociology of knowledge. Mosca's ambiguities must be seen in the context of his precarious middle-class position, between the old aristocracy of privilege which he admiringly combats, and the new elite of plebeians, in his terms a negative elite that threatens to replace both the old ruling class and his own kind, the men of cultured substance. His concern must border on despair indeed if he could disregard what he himself had written about ruling classes which refuse to open their gates to new social elements, and how society dies of attrition if those gates remain "steadfastly closed and stationary." [6]

Not only that, he also forgets the warning he uttered in this same chapter: "The history of human societies is very complicated, and very diverse are the material, moral, and intellectual factors that help to determine its development." [7] It is a view which should exclude the unicausal explanation of historical events, such as the absence of political capacity in conquered races. Many other factors may contribute to the fall of empire—technological discrepancy between the conquered and the conquerors for instance; the superiority in that respect, say, of the Mongol hordes would hardly qualify their rule as one of cultural and moral superiority.

Otherwise, the chapter is replete with very cogent observations. The greatness of a statesman may be measured, Mosca says, by his "success in transforming ruling classes by improving the methods by which they were recruited and by perfecting their organization." In that sense, Augustus was a man of greatness, for "he revived the old Roman ruling class, which had been decimated by almost a century of civil warfare, by introducing new elements into it." Vespasian, too, comes in for praise because he "raised representatives from many of the more illustrious families of Italy to senatorial rank." [8] Again, the author almost but not quite succeeds in reaping the full benefits of his own method. What Vespasian did was to broaden but also to *lower* the basis of the ruling class, by drawing the provincial notables into the second stratum, to which he had himself just barely belonged.[9]

In this connection Mosca shows that his lapse into unicausal explanation of historical events was only accidental, for he makes it very clear that even the most consummate practitioner of statecraft may be helpless if the situation is beyond repair. This time, he exploits the advantages of his own method to the full in using the example of Byzantium. As long as "its ruling classes still retained... considerable resources in intellectual power and patriotism, and the subject peoples were still able to supply large revenues to the public treasury and numerous soldiers to the army," the Empire could hold out. But when those classes were "run down," the end was only a matter of time.[10]

In other words, to spell out what the author fails to say, but clearly wishes to convey: The upper stratum of the ruling class depends upon the lower; both in turn depend upon the common people: if these are vigorous, the ruling class can perform wonders; if they are abused, *finis imperii.*

By implication Mosca says, although he would deny it fiercely and accuse us of indulging in polemics with him rather than of offering clarifications: The doctrine of the ruling class is a myth, in the sense that it directs attention to a single aspect of the social process which is slated to epitomize and symbolize the working of the whole. It is however not the whole but a mere part, although perhaps the most intelligible and enticing part. But taken by itself, the ruling elite is not an "intelligible field of study"; since it does not function in a void, we must be careful not to lose sight of the total context.

Different Standards, Different Elites

It is not only the aristocratic and the democratic tendencies that are at war in Mosca's mind; there are also (as the reader has already had more than one occasion to observe) the relativist and the absolutist Mosca. This time the relativist is in charge, as the discussion once more turns to the criteria for admission to the ruling class. The author calls essential "the capacity for hard work and a constant determination to rise in the world and to cling to one's place at the top when one gets there." [11] One might get the impression that Mosca took his cue from Robert Michels' very similar list of prerequisites for power, except that he had already, in the first *Elementi*, mentioned "certain intellectual qualities, such as readiness of perception and keenness of observation," and certain "other qualities ... tenacity of purpose, self-confidence and above all, *activity*." [12] Now he adds to his list still "other qualities, which vary greatly according to time and places ... " That is so because the requisites of leadership must vary in accordance with the "needs and natures" of the various epochs and societies. Again, the formula which sums up Mosca's viewpoint in this matter has the true Aristotelian ring: "In general, in every society, circumstances being equal, success is reserved for individuals who possess in eminent degree the endowments which, in that society at that particular time, are most widely diffused and most highly esteemed." [13]

The statement has that certain blandness of the answer which pretends to settle everything while in fact it only raises a new question. Why are the endowments which make for success "most highly esteemed"? Is it *because* they are "the most widely diffused" ones? But that does not automatically follow, unless there is a moral premium on success, no matter how achieved. That is, of course, not what the author has in mind. No less than Aristotle, he is conscious of the conflict between the "good man" and the "good citizen." [14] If the "most widely diffused" qualities are to be identical with the "most highly esteemed," a moral compromise is clearly indicated. Mosca has prepared for it by his remarkably suggestive simile of the "alloy." He used it first in his discussion of parties and religious sects. If they are to endure, he wrote in the first *Elementi*, "there must be a fusion, in certain amounts, of lofty sentiments and low passions, of precious metal and base metal—otherwise the alloy will not stand the wear and tear." This rule is generalized and applied to all political elites: "a ruling nucleus that is really well organized must find a place within itself for all sorts of characters . . ." [15]

The second *Elementi* carries that idea a step further. Our moral sense will most readily approve of qualities in others which are most akin to those we know to be our own. "It is not possible to grasp the noblest qualities of human intelligence and character if they are totally foreign to our natures." Such inability may lead to a complete reversal of conventions. In a passage very much reminiscent of a famous statement in *Mind and Society*, our author writes:

Where slyness, intrigue and charlatanry are the common rule and highly prized, the slyest man, the best intriguer, the most perfect char-latan, will, other things being equal, make a great success. If the majority believe that deceit is the royal road to fortune, those who excel in the art of deception will most often be the ones to make their mark.[16]

We know already that, in Mosca's book, democracy is so objectionable mainly because it seems to promote precisely that appeal to the base instincts which makes the good fortune of the demagogue.

But, fortunately, "there is and there will always be a relative justice in societies that are fairly well organized." [17] That justice will reflect the average morality of people bent upon a modicum of decency. The author explains this still further by employing one more simile. He speaks of "white" and "black magic" now, no longer of the "alloy," although his conclusion is the same. "We know that there is . . . a white magic that is based on the higher qualities of mind and character, and a black that is based on the lower." Agreeing with the Stagirite, he does not assume that the good man and the perfect citizen will often coincide in one and the same person: "Probably white magic has never really been very effective ... unless it has been mixed with a little of the black ..." But average morality will keep the dose of black magic at a minimum; when it "comes to be too much used ... public taste rebels and the individual who relies on the mixture is then disqualified, much as a gambler is disqualified when he cheats at cards." We must at least try to seem better than we are, adds Mosca, taking a leaf from *The Prince*, and he speaks seriously of "the arts of white magic" which bring luck to the practitioner.[18]

Mosca's relativistic detachment reaches its high point when he calmly contemplates a situation in which "the arts of black magic are more common and so more tolerated." [19] Again, he assumes absolute identity between private and public morality, and between the morals of the people and of the elite. The latter are no better and no worse than the majority of their ruled subjects. Mosca, at this particular point, is careful not to advance any claim of moral superiority for his elite.[20] He is, accordingly, forced to reject all hopes for a rule of the best as utterly utopian, whether these hopes remain sheer speculation, as with Plato, or are being taken seriously and made into the main objective of political reform or revolutionary schemes. "All that we can justly ask of our superiors is that they should not fall below the average moral level of the society they govern ..." The best thing is to translate the term "best" into "best fitted to govern," and in doing so, the author makes quite sure that the best in that sense are "by no means ... the 'best' individuals intellectually, much less the 'best' individuals morally." What distinguishes the born ruler is not so much a sense of justice, or altruism, or even "extent of knowledge or broadness of view" as certain other gifts, like "perspicacity, a ready intuition of individual and mass psychology, strength of will and, especially, confidence in oneself." Gaetano Mosca never was more close to Machiavelli than in this pronouncement which he caps by direct reference to the Florentine secretary who "with good reason ... put into the mouth of Cosimo dei Medici the much quoted remark, that states are not ruled with prayer-books." [21]

End of an Era

In 1928, six years after the March on Rome, the Committee for Political and Organization Questions of the Interparliamentary Union asked five European authorities in the field of "political economy" to write about the subject of "the crisis through which the parliamentary system is now passing in almost every country." The result of the inquiry was a slender volume comprising the contributions of one Englishman, Harold Laski, one Swiss, Charles Bourgeaud, M. F. Larnaude of Paris University, and M. J. Bonn speaking for Germany; Gaetano Mosca is the Italian representative in that distinguished company. The symposium was published that same year in Switzerland.[22]

An inspection reveals Mosca's contribution to be a facsimile of the last chapter of *The Ruling Class*. The differences between the two pieces are purely verbal. But it is that very fact that makes the 1928 pronouncement so remarkable. In 1923, when the second *Elementi* appeared, the future character of Mussolini's government, then barely one year old, could hardly be anticipated. That makes certain strictures against neo-absolutism and syndicalism in the final chapter of that volume all the more prophetic. But it took no courage yet to make those criticisms; Italy was then still a free country. To repeat the same indictments five years later was an altogether different affair. To be sure, the word Fascism is never mentioned, but no reader could have been in doubt as to the real target of the author's 1928 remarks. That took some courage in a man who was then, technically, still a member of the Senate and who could have used that pretext or pleaded his old age in order to avoid unpleasant controversy. But not only did he seek it then, in 1928, but three years earlier had given battle on the very Senate floor.

The grand occasion was the law proposed to strengthen the prerogatives of the prime minister, but actually to give the Duce dictatorial powers to wipe out the opposition stirred up by the outrage of the Matteotti murder. Mosca's speech rejecting the proposal was a masterpiece of dignity and firmness, made no less impressive by the fact that the address was the swan song of our author's parliamentary career. One more thing is remarkable about that senatorial peroration: in the teeth of the new tyrant, Gaetano Mosca took the opportunity to speak in defense of the very system which he had attacked throughout his life. He could have stood on his record as the Cassandra of democracy. Instead, he chose to follow in the way of the old prophet who had set out to pronounce a curse and instead was moved to utter a blessing.

The words pronounced by Gaetano Mosca on December 25, 1925, are memorable words. Nobody of his calibre rose in the German Reichstag to protest, in 1933, Adolf Hitler's similar *Ermächtigungsgesetz*.

No one, said Mosca, will object to a modification of the parliamentary regime. He had himself been advocating various measures designed to strengthen the executive power, to make it more independent of the vagaries of parliament. But now the tables were to be completely turned: the chamber was to lose its influence altogether. Its agenda was not only to be modified and limited by the new law, the chamber was to give up its right to initiate legislation. Another drastic change affected the position of the monarch. The new law made the prime minister all-powerful: he would no longer need the confidence of the king who appointed him.

Instead, the clearly stated intention is for the head of the state to leave [the premier] in charge of affairs as long as *the economic, political, and moral forces* which carried him to power do not desert him. As long as all those forces ... found expression in the votes of parliament, the situation was quite clear. But once those forces are no longer represented by parliament, then one would like to know: How are they represented? [23]

To a mind as much imbued with liberal ideas as that of our author the reply that social forces could express themselves outside the representative regime, in the mass organization of a revolutionary party, would have been incomprehensible. All he could see was that "the king was no longer to have the free choice of his government, which in turn would no longer depend on the votes of parliament."

Mosca speaks "with a certain emotion because, let us be frank, we take part in the funeral rites of a form of government. I should not have thought possible that I would be the one to deliver the funeral oration on the parliamentary regime . . . I, who have always taken a harsh attitude toward it, I am today obliged to lament its departure." [24]

But then he proceeds from lament to eulogy. His step is circumspect but firm as he approaches his antagonist. We may imagine at this point a tensing of atmosphere in the first chamber. The majority of his distinguished colleagues, Mosca knew well, had already made up their minds to vote for the insidious measure and thus to make true the Roman proverb: *ruere in servitutem,* to volunteer for slavery. A small band must have felt like Mosca, for the minutes note occasional approval of his speech, applause which scarcely could relieve the anguish of these men who knew the predetermined outcome of the session. As for the victors in the seats of government, they may have thought: let the oldtimer speak his piece, what do we care about mere words.

But the oldtimer did care, for with each of his words went a deeply meaningful part of his life. However, if his heart felt agony, his head remained as clear as ever. Gaetano Mosca spoke as if he were addressing his habitual academic audience, treating in judicious terms a remote problem of historical research. And how else could one understand the present, not to speak of future hopes, if not in terms of centuries! In this mind great political decisions were not a mere matter of the moment but the contribution to or wasting of a great inheritance.

"A form of government," he said, "can be judged only in one way: by comparing it with both its predecessor and successor. To speak of the latter would be premature. As to the predecessor, it was such that one may say in all sincerity: the parliamentary regime was better." [25]

Before advancing any further, Mosca once more makes certain of his ground. Nobody could accuse him of a change of mind toward the representative regime. He said that it had been operating well until the First World War; then it had "suffered a degeneration," partly caused by that great cataclysm which shook the political terrain to the foundations. But not to forget: human error played a major part too, because "two enormous blunders were committed, one immediately before, the second right after the war: I am referring to the introduction of universal suffrage and proportional representation."

Again the minutes register approval. Many liberals among the Senators may have used the opportunity to go on record as good patriots who condemned what they had adored for so long. By howling with the wolves, these men tried to establish a belated alibi. If so, their cheers were premature. For after saying that "the system of parliamentary representation neither must nor can remain impervious to change," the speaker added a great But. Changes, he said, can be radical and rapid, or they can be slow, deliberate. "That is a question of the utmost gravity which fills my soul with anguish and which, in my own opinion, the opinion of a lifelong adversary of the parliamentary regime, should be resolved in favor of judicious moderation." [26]

After having shot his bolt, Mosca becomes once more the historical observer. In the slightly mocking but benevolent tone of the elder statesman he addresses now the younger generation which "believes that it knows everything, can change everything, and has nothing to learn from the past..." As befits the learned man, he couches his last warning in a classical quotation. It is taken from the *Iliad*. Hector's farewell to his baby son Astyanax becomes the text of Gaetano Mosca's valedictory: "Then may men say of him, 'Far greater is he than his father'..."

Is he talking with his tongue in cheek? I doubt it. Gaetano Mosca was a good Italian who would not desire the ruin of his country just so he could say "I told you so." His own faith in liberty remained unshaken: "For my part, if I should approve the new law before us, I would act against my conscience, and therefore I cannot vote for it." [27]

Polite applause marks the end of a gallant speech commemorating the end of an era.

The Power of Illusion

In his contribution to the Interparliamentary Symposium Mosca twice refers the reader to his *Elementi*. It is indeed there that we will find the complete argument for and against the liberal regime. The period which saw it arise and flourish was, we are informed, in spite of all deficiencies, "one of the greatest and most magnificent of all the eras that humanity has traversed." [28] And that is true even though the democratic aspirations, "majority government and absolute political equality, two of the mottos that the century inscribed on its banners, were not achieved, because they could not be achieved..." Nor could it have come easy to our author "to admit the great benefits which constitute the undying glory of the nineteenth century as a result of the very illusions that guided it." But Mosca did admit those benefits unflinchingly: "The ranks of the ruling classes have been held open. The barriers that kept individuals of the lower class from entering the higher have been either removed or lowered." [29] The democratic dream did after all have practical results.

Under the new system, the political class was "divided...into two distinct branches, one issuing from popular suffrage, the other from bureaucratic appointment." One remembers Mosca's earlier disparagement of democratic check and balances. Now he has come around to the view that the democratic and the bureaucratic system of selecting leaders "has not only permitted a better utilization of individual capacities; it has also made it possible to distribute the sovereign functions, or powers, of the state, and that distribution...constitutes the chief virtue of representative systems."[30]

What about that state's effective range, what about its efficiency? According to the classical interpretation, the liberal state was a weak state, limited to the policing function—not to be compared in power with its autocratic counterpart. The strength was in the free, self-regulating forces of society.

That is not at all the view of the mature Mosca. Liberalism "has permitted the establishment of a strong state, which has been able to canalise immense sums of individual energies toward purposes related to the collective interest." In the original, that sentence is even more impressive, because Mosca speaks of *una forma di Stato fortissima*, a superlatively strong state, which, however, "has not trampled on those [individual] energies;...it has left them with sufficient vitality to achieve remarkable results in other fields, notably in the scientific, literary, and economic fields." [31] The emphasis on "the collective interest" is a significant, highly original interpretation of the liberal state by a liberal like Mosca. It antedates by several decades the interpretation which made a collectivist of Locke.[32]

All this sounds as if the magnificent achievements of "the age that is now closing" had been "due in large part to the beneficent effects of [its] political system." But this time Mosca avoids the monocausal trap and declares: "it might be more accurate to think of a number of different causes functioning simultaneously." Pareto and Max Weber, who both hold doctrines of interdependence, would have heartily agreed with Mosca's saying that "representative systems were able to function regularly ... because cultural and economic conditions ... were such as to enable them to function in that manner." They would likewise have agreed with his conclusion that the functioning of the political regime in turn enhanced the functioning of all the extragovernmental forces of society. For that is what our author must have had in mind when he suggests: "That would be another of the many cases where the effect becomes cause and the cause effect." [33]

Next, Mosca tries to find an explanation for the rapid decline of a system that had such outstanding merits. He blames it on what Daniel Halévy has called the "acceleration of the historic process" in our time.[34] We have been traveling too slowly in some countries but too rapidly in most. In Mosca's words: "Only by slow and continuous transformations of their political systems can peoples avoid periods of rapid disintegration accompanied by violent crises that bring untold suffering to the generations that have to undergo them ..." [35] Contemporary Russia would be the outstanding instance of a country whose political organization broke down catastrophically because it had not passed through the necessary stage of a "slow and continuous transformation." Everywhere else, Mosca would say, the democratic process went too far too fast. And that was, to a great extent, due to the perverse softness and short-sightedness of those in power. Thus "the ruling classes in a number of European countries were stupid enough and cowardly enough to accept the eight-hour day after the World War, when the nations had been terribly impoverished and it was urgent to intensify labor and production." The obvious retort that the ruling classes had to yield to the demands of the well-organized big unions, if not to the sentiment of a war-weary population, would not satisfy the author. Not proletarian strength but their own flirting with the postulates of the class enemy was the undoing of the ruling classes. Asking in vain for an explanation of the puzzling question, why "the European bourgeoisie should have offered such feeble and spasmodic resistance to the spread of socialist doctrines," Mosca here sounds like a man for whom he had little liking: Georges Sorel.[36]

And like Sorel in his post-syndicalist period, Mosca realized that there was, outside the Catholic Church, only one force left in Europe which could possibly restore cohesion to the fast disintegrating body politic. Mosca calls that force "patriotism." When he wrote, it was still "hazardous, and perhaps inconsistent with the facts, to assert that the middle classes in Europe have had any clear or definite awareness of the great moral obstacle that patriotism offers to the progress of socialism." But he remembers well "that, beginning with the early years of the twentieth century, a powerful awakening of patriotic feeling was observable in the educated youth of almost all the European countries." [37]

That revival was particularly vigorous in Italy, where it was centered in small literary elites grouped around reviews like *Leonardo* and *La Voce*, edited by Prezzolini and Papini. That current, which became a major movement under the distinguished leadership of Corradini, was well known to Gaetano Mosca, for his works, with those of Pareto and Sorel, were first presented to a nonacademic public by Giovanni Prezzolini in *La Voce*.[38] It seems strange that Mosca, with his dislike of democracy and socialism, did not greet the patriotic renaissance with more enthusiasm. The answer is that Gaetano Mosca was a patriot but not a nationalist: "Unfortunately, love of country . . . often goes hand in hand with diffidence toward other countries and sometimes with hatred of them." Mosca does not claim that this exaggerated patriotism caused World War I, but "the overexcitation of these patriotic sentiments undoubtedly helped to create the moral and intellectual atmosphere that brought on the World War." [39]

Three Evils

There may, however, be another reason why our author refused to identify himself with the unique cohesive force of patriotic sentiment. One may suspect it had something to do with the mass movement which had conquered Italy just before publication of the second *Elementi*. That mass movement, never once called by its name by Mosca, had incorporated into its own cadres most of the nationalistic groups of postwar Italy; it had annexed their gestures and their slogans, leaving their inventor, Gabriele D'Annunzio, to his memories of Fiume. But the new alloy, Fascism, contained, in addition to the national ingredient, still another element. Without it, the blend might have been less unacceptable to Mosca; like other famous Europeans, he might have looked upon Fascism as the "lesser evil" in comparison with communism.

This brings us to his theory of "the three evils." Surveying the European situation of World War I, Mosca finds:

> ... but three possible solutions of a radical nature for the present political crisis. One ... has already been resorted to in Russia—the "dictatorship of the proletariat," so-called ... The second would be a return to old-fashioned bureaucratic absolutism. The third would be syndicalism, in other words, a replacement of individual representation by class representation in legislative assemblies.[40]

Now, of these solutions, Fascism accepted numbers two and three, combining them and the old nationalist element into one system, with the Fascist party acting in lieu of the regimented social forces as the new Italian ruling class.

Mosca's reaction to the new regime is as complex as its own character. He is an anti-Fascist, because he rejects authoritarianism. But his distaste of the authoritarian element cannot compare in vigor with his antisyndicalist bias. How could one trust men who posed as anti-Marxists while at the same time endorsing syndicalist principles? The Mussolini who made war on socialists had Mosca's plaudits, but his schemes of corporate representation threw our author into a confusion which he was not able to resolve. One reason was that he had, like many of his time, including Georges Sorel, the wrong idea about the true nature of the Bolshevik regime; misled by such manifestations as workers' control, he took for syndicalism what was only early anarchy, soon to be extirpated by the Communist dictatorship. A note which Mosca added to the third edition of the *Elementi* (1939) and which is, unfortunately, missing in the English version, reflects Mosca's doubts about the "anti-Bolshevism" of the new, fascist dictatorships: "In Europe," he says, "those regimes which are in fact authoritarian gain ground steadily [because] they know better how to combat Bolshevism, the prime danger for modern European civilization." But he adds that those regimes, in order to combat the enemy, "had to adopt some of his very methods." [41]

These methods, call them bolshevist or syndicalist, are essentially of a plebeian nature. In the last resort, they all go back to democratic misconceptions of man and society. "The bureaucratic and military dictatorship...," Mosca predicts, "would not be like any of the various forms of representative government...It would be a sort of 'Caesarism,' such as prevailed in France during the First Empire, and, in more moderate form, during the Second Empire down to 1868...This new Caesarism...might even try to find a legal basis for itself in a popular referendum, or plebiscite, as the two Napoleonic Caesarisms did." The words which Mosca will speak in the Senate two years later are anticipated, almost literally, when he writes that "under those forms of government parliament had purely decorative functions...Liberty becomes a mere word devoid of any practical significance." The fascist doctrine is exposed as an attempt to hitch dictatorship to the old trusted chariot of democracy: "In such a case we would be going back to the old absolutist system, perhaps under a mask of popular sovereignty." [42]

Fascism is the daughter—or is it the son?—of mass democracy.

The mass base of the new regime was clear to Mosca even before Mussolini showed his hand. Speculating about what might happen in the event of a further decline of the middle class, the author writes: "We would have either a plutocratic dictatorship, or else a bureaucratic-military dictatorship, or else a demagogic dictatorship by a few experts in mob leadership...Worse still, there might be a combination of two of these dictatorships, or indeed of all three." [43]

When Mosca wrote these lines he could not yet be sure how closely he had hit home, and therefore he refrained from calling Fascism by its name. Afterwards that would have meant incurring martyrdom. Those who have never lived under totalitarian thought control may well afford heroic postures. Those of us who have know that mere silence also has its agonies.

The Legacy

Firmly believing in the superiority of the political and territorial system of representation over one employing economic, functional criteria, Gaetano Mosca ponders finally the question of how the ailing liberal regime could be restored to its old influence. That quest involves a diagnosis of the causes for so many people having lost faith in liberal institutions. "The war did not create the germs of dissolution from which the representative system is now suffering. Like any other system it contained those germs within itself . . . The war simply rendered them more virulent." [44]

The task of reconstruction is, as Mosca knows well, "not an easy one." The middle class, without which, he thinks, no political class could be formed, was decimated by the war and the inflation following it. Hence a general revival of the European economy would be imperative, in order to make possible the economic rehabilitation of the middle class. Otherwise, the representative regime could not survive. But if it was not merely to survive but also to improve, certain reforms were mandatory. Mosca has a small list of proposals ready which he offers with a certain diffidence. They are quite modest, more so than the urgency of the case would suggest. The freedom of the press must be preserved, but the press must be held strictly responsible for libel. The right of free assembly must be so defined as to prevent well-organized offenders of the law from terrorizing society and intimidating the government.

Remembering that Mosca used to "regard the granting of universal suffrage as a mistake," the reader will be gratified to learn that "one could not go back on it without committing a second mistake which might have unforeseeable consequences . . ." [45]

A temporary remedy for the crisis may be found in the return, for a brief period, of "strong government" which would help "to restore or provide conditions that will enable the representative system to function normally in a near future."

Did Mosca, for a fleeting moment, see the new Prime Minister, Benito Mussolini, preside over a "caretaker government" entrusted with the mandate to restore the representative regime "in a near future"? It almost seems that way, for Mosca makes a reference to Rome, where "in the best days of the republic, brief periods of dictatorship were not infrequent."

But he knew that no reform of the political machinery, no dictator, old or new style, could revive the liberal regime if the political class did not respond to the call of history. And so, having reached the end of the long trail, the author, on the page before the last of his monumental work, addresses himself to *his* ruling class—the one which knows, or *ought* to know its duty. Mosca the relativist steps aside and lets the absolutist Mosca have the floor for the great peroration.

Some critics of *The Prince* have said that Machiavelli's final appeal to his fellow countrymen was out of tune with the rest of the work. The same might be said of the final exhortation of *The Ruling Class*. But that fine piece of writing will seem inconsistent with the whole only to those who see in Gaetano Mosca a philosopher of power rather than a moralist. He may, at times, have flirted with the hard, pragmatic view of Machiavelli's politics. But when he finally came face to face with naked power in the years of red- and black-shirt terror, he recoiled in horror and became the moralist again, who cannot help but believe in a normative regime of values.

It is the moralist who never had been doubting that:

> ... the ruling class must rid itself of many of its prejudices and change its psychological attitude. It must ... gain a clear conception of its rights and duties. It will never be able to do that unless it can raise the level of its political competence and understanding ... It must be able to see a little beyond its immediate interests ...

Did Mosca actually believe that these were realistic expectations? Apparently he did. "Every generation produces a certain number of generous spirits ... Such individuals make up a small moral and intellectual aristocracy, which keeps humanity from rotting ... Rarely do members of such aristocracies attain the outstanding positions in political life, but they render a perhaps more effective service in the world by molding the minds ... of their contemporaries, so that in the end they succeed in forcing their programs upon those who rule the state." [46]

One sees that the author is no longer talking to and of the ruling class. He speaks, like E. M. Forster, of another aristocracy, which has no power, but whose "members are to be found in all nations and classes, and all through the ages, and there is a secret understanding between them when they meet. They represent the true human tradition, the one permanent victory of our queer race over cruelty and chaos ... On they go—an invincible army, yet not a victorious one ... Their kingdom, though they never possess it, is the wide-open world." [47]

The real ruling class of Gaetano Mosca is the class that never actually rules. But it will rule, eventually, vicariously. That is their faith, or at least, Gaetano Mosca's faith, which cannot be refuted by pedestrian argument.

Once more the doctrine of the ruling class becomes a myth.

Part Three: Old Age

11

THE GREAT COMPANIONS

Dramatic as his senatorial valedictory to liberty had been, the year 1927, not 1925, was the one in which the long, distinguished parliamentary career of Gaetano Mosca finally came to an end. Why did he stay at his post during those two years? He must have hoped to be of some use to his nation even after freedom had been lost. By 1927 these hopes had patently worn threadbare, and the elder statesman—then almost seventy—retired to spend all the rest of his time and energy in teaching and writing. One major work and several long essays testify to his unbroken intellectual vigor and curiosity. Unencumbered by civic responsibilities, the author undertook to fill a gap in his impressive list of publications. So far, they had been mainly concerned with the elaboration of his own political philosophy— always projected, to be sure, upon the background of a thorough institutional analysis. Now for the first time, Mosca turns to writing a condensed but systematic survey of the doctrines that preceded his.

Two practical considerations may have prompted him to execute the project. First, as he had been teaching a course in the history of political ideas, an introductory text, written for the benefit of his own undergraduates, grew naturally out of class notes taken by assistants.[1] Second, preoccupation with the past was the characteristic answer of the intellectual to dictatorial censorship. There seemed to be so little scope for heresy in a discussion of such remote subjects as, say, Plato or Rousseau. But on the other hand, there remained just a chance to illustrate some pressing problem of the present, without naming it outright, in terms of Plato or Rousseau. It must be said that, unlike the regimes of Hitler or Stalin, Mussolini's either was more liberal in intellectual matters, or possibly the Fascist masterminds were simply shrewder than their Communist and Nazi colleagues in permitting a restricted sphere to exist within which "objective" research of a strictly apolitical nature was still possible.

The *History of Political Doctrines* posed no problems for the censor. It was no clandestine anti-Fascist tract. But if our author scorned the use of the Aesopian language, neither did he change his well-known colors. The old liberal wrote not a single word to irk the Duce, as Benedetto Croce did so often in *La Critica*. On the other hand, he did not take back anything he had professed before. The work shows marks of great restraint; it hardly ever goes beyond a factual account of what his predecessors thought. The brevity of these portrayals sometimes borders upon the perfunctory. But then, the work did not claim to make any novel contributions to political philosophy. It was a précis meant for student consumption and no more.[2] For our own purpose the book retains its importance because Gaetano Mosca wrote it; the greatness of an author may be studied with great profit even in his more ephemeral productions. We know Mosca's mind by now, we know his style sufficiently well to guess what is in his mind even though he may refrain from any comment; his very silence will be eloquent. The impression of a certain aridity will soon yield to respect for the calm, self-effacing attitude that persists throughout. Or so we think as we approach the work which ends with a synopsis of the author's own political philosophy. It is his last word in the matter, and he never spoke his mind more lucidly.[3]

The book is organized in forty chapters, some only three pages long, and none running over eighteen. That gives an idea how compressed the subject matter is. The longest chapters are, significantly, those devoted to the subjects about which the author was particularly anxious and which he had been examining in special studies: Machiavelli, Thomas Morus, Marx, and modern racist theories.[4]

Two more characteristics of the work ought to be mentioned: unlike so many political theorists, our author pays the closest attention to the history of *institutions*. He does what Bertrand Russell, in his own comparative work, promises to do but does not quite accomplish.[5] The two works belong not only topically but also in terms of their specific weight to the same class. What Mosca does not know about philosophy, he makes up for by his greater knowledge of political and social data. He neither overrates nor underrates the power of ideas; what matters to him is the interplay of intellectual and moral forces on the one hand, and material forces on the other. The proper balance of the two assures "cohesion" in society.[6]

The study of that interpenetration is, in a way, influenced by Marx and his exaggerated emphasis on the economic "variable"; Mosca was only one of a great host of bourgeois scholars like Max Weber and Pareto who took up the Marxian challenge and tried to restore the nonmaterial factors to their role as equal codeterminants of the political and social process. With Mosca, the result of that attempt was not, as in the case of Weber and Pareto, an elaborated system; to the end he "played it by ear," falling back, if necessary, on his early positivist self-assurance rather than getting involved in problems of epistemology and method. This refusal, which may have been due to a subconscious recognition of his limitations, gives the work of Gaetano Mosca its peculiar note of diffidence and even truculence— but it is diffidence toward pontification, and the truculence is that of a man who refuses to be taken in. The heritage of the enlightenment, the sublime confidence in human reason and perfectibility has given way to scepticism. But it is a scepticism in turn blended with a moral heritage which, somehow, did survive the acid test of nineteenth-century materialism. What unifies all these potentially conflicting elements is difficult to say. Words easily suggest themselves. We might say that Gaetano Mosca's strength lies in his humanism, but that would explain very little. He has been praised for his common sense and for his relaxed, humorous indulgence of the human animal. But under the calm serene surface of *The Ruling Class*, as well as of the smaller work under discussion, we can sense great passions at work, pain, and much frustration. There is no one single formula that would fit Gaetano Mosca.

Not with the Greeks . . .

The other thing to be said in praise of the *History* is its insistence that the study of Western civilization does not and must not start with the Greeks. Since Arnold Toynbee that view has become a commonplace, but one could mention many renowned works of political theory written after Mosca which still date the beginning of our world from Socrates and Plato. In contrast to them, Mosca goes into prehistory [7] and then devotes two chapters to the great oriental monarchies and their class organization, as he had done in the *Teorica* and in both volumes of the *Elementi*. He does not make the cheap excuse that those civilizations had not left a written record of political philosophy. Like Vico, but availing himself of the evidence not yet accessible to the Neapolitan, he reconstructs the social and political development of early cultures from their legal and religious institutions.[8]

Turning to Greek history, he pays a great deal of attention to its preclassic, archaic periods down to the great economic revolution of the seventh century B.C.[9]

Approaching the mysterious figure of Socrates, the author wisely refrains from joining in the popular debate as to which Socrates is the authentic one, Plato's or Xenophon's. Mosca confines himself to saying that the Socrates whom Xenophon knew "expressed neither democratic nor aristocratic sentiments" and that he went on record against the system of electing magistrates by lot.[10]

His discussion of Plato and Aristotle as political philosophers is curiously reticent. The analysis is reduced to a brief if lucid capsule-form account of the Platonic argument, without the slightest indication of the problems that would easily occur to any sophomore. What criticisms are presented are put into Aristotle's mouth. In Mosca's view, the Stagirite, not Plato, was the greatest Greek philosopher.[11] His *Politics* are given much more space than *The Republic*, and hardly a trace is left of the old anti-Aristotelianism of our author. In fact, his sole, polite objection is to Aristotle's ethical criterion by which "normal" and "degenerated" constitutions may be told apart according as the rulers have the general or their own private interest at heart. Mosca objects: "a clear-cut distinction between the interest of the rulers and that of the ruled is difficult to make; in addition, those in power may be honestly convinced of their own excellence, although the facts would prove them to be wrong." [12]

Among the writers of the Hellenistic period, it is above all Polybius, with his doctrine of mixed government, who attracts Mosca's interest. Here the respect with which he had just treated Aristotle is less marked, and his own theory of the political class rears its head for a few seconds:

> We who were born twenty centuries after Polybius have no trouble seeing that the coexistence of those three elements, monarchy, aristocracy, and democracy, is a fact which can be ascertained in all political regimes. For everywhere one man or a small number of men are at the head of the political hierarchy. Everywhere we find a ruling class existing and by the same token governments which have to take into consideration the consent or discontent of the plain people.[13]

Mosca's account of Roman institutions and their evolution is, as one would expect from past performances, substantial. Being thoroughly at home with constitutional and administrative law, he does this part always more than creditably well. In this connection, it is much to be regretted that we do not have, from Gaetano Mosca's pen, a comprehensive manual of administrative techniques and principles as they have been developed through the centuries. Such a work would have closed a gap in our bibliographies which corresponds to a gap, still wide open, in the average political science curriculum. As it is, the student is taught a great deal about contemporary constitutional and administrative arrangements in this country and abroad, but hardly anything about their origin and evolution—that is a subject left to the history departments where it is, more often than not, fragmentized into its English, French, or other European components.

It is greatly to the credit of our author that the patriot in him did not prevent him from confessing that "the political doctrines of the Roman writers are not too original." [14] Accordingly, he devotes only a few lines each to Lucretius and Sallust, a mere two paragraphs to

Cicero, *Jus naturale* and *jus gentium* are atrociously neglected, Seneca is barely mentioned. Mosca's interest grows keener again as his narrative approaches the end of the Roman Empire. The perennial debate about the reasons that caused the Decline and Fall exerts its strong attraction on the author, an attentive reader of Ferrero.[15]

Unlike Arnold Toynbee, for whom Roman history is only an extension of an already decaying "Hellenistic" civilization, Mosca dates the decadence of Rome from the third century B.C.[16] The barbarian invasions are effect rather than cause of a disintegration brought about by many factors. The unsuccessful solution of the problem of imperial succession is one of them.[17] No less important were: the population decrease, the destruction of the middle class by excessive taxation, depreciation of the currency, and widespread brigandage. The author fails to realize that these, too, are mere symptoms of the malady and not its "causes." He is on much safer ground when he lists the excessive bureaucratization of the Empire as a further "aggravating factor." [18] Even that development could be explained as an effect of a still deeper trouble. That is what the author tries to do. We noted that there is, in all his writings, something like a latent "iron law of bureaucratization," although Mosca shies away from enunciating it explicitly. He is not, as is his best pupil, Robert Michels, a determinist. Therefore, bureaucracy in its excessive forms—as any other institutional defect—is for him something that it is in man's power to avoid, an aberration that can be reduced to sound proportion by timely reforms. Like Marx, Mosca believes that men make their own history, but unlike Marx, he is unwilling to define the limitations within which human volition has to operate, lest he become encased in a nonscientific system of new absolutes. For this freedom Mosca gladly pays the price of frequent vagueness and even superficiality. Thus the bureaucratic decline of Rome becomes a contingency rather than a necessity, something caused by man's foolishness rather than exemplifying the inexorable fate of empire.

From St. Paul to John XXII in Twenty Pages

There is no point in cataloguing all that Mosca has to say about the well-known figures of political philosophy unless he noticeably deviates from the conventional interpretation. In the following, there-fore, we shall confine ourselves to stressing those infrequent cases. In addition, we shall note quite a few authors in whom Mosca, as a Continental and Italian writer, takes a greater interest than would his Anglo-Saxon colleagues.

To the Middle Ages Mosca, again like Bertrand Russell, gives short shrift. It is impossible to say much in eight pages about "The Politi-cal Thought of the Middle Ages up to the Eleventh Century," but in those pages Mosca manages to cover the important points and even has some room left for the relevant quotations. We are intro-duced to one of the more seldom mentioned pamphleteers of the imperial, antipapal faction, Waltram of Naumburg.[19] Another eight pages deal with the second phase of the investiture struggle: the revival of Roman law, the imperial program of Innocent III, the influence of Arabian Aristotelianism on the West, the great Thomis-tic synthesis, the duel between Philip of France and Boniface VIII, seconded by Egidio Colonna, the rise of the North Italian com-munes.[20] The chapter is a masterpiece of condensed information. The two imperialist Aristotelians, Dante and Marsiglio, are the subjects, in four pages, of Chapter 14. Mosca, very much in contrast to James Burnham, his American disciple, has no grudge against the author of De Monarchia; his account of that work is objective and attempts no remark upon the fact that Dante's vision of world monarchy was utterly impracticable at the time of publication.

Marsiglio's doctrine receives all the praise it so richly deserves. His theory of government is seen as a reflection upon the political devel-opment and, in particular the anticlerical trend, in the writer's native commune, Padua. The famous pars valentior has for Mosca a de-cidedly elitist meaning: "the will of the people in the Middle Ages was expressed through its natural chiefs (barons, clergy, corpora-tion heads, the learned doctors)." The will of Marsiglio's commune was identical with the will of its notables.[21]

Among the luminaries of the fourteenth and fifteen centuries men-tioned by Mosca we note the Italian jurist Bartolo da Sassoferrato (1313–58) with his treatise, De regimine civitatis, and the French-man, Nicole Oresme, who argued against the encroachments of the royal power and against the customary debasement of the currency.[22]

Our author also credits Oresme—as we believe, erroneously—with having first established the distinction between lawful king and tyrant. But that notion was already known to John of Salisbury, if not before.

Now, Bartolo da Sassoferrato is of course identical with the great Bartolus, familiar to most of our students. But do we inform them about Mosca's other fellow countryman, Antonio Beccadelli called Il Panormita? Half a century before *The Prince* was written, "he exhorted the princes to emulate the example of King Alfonso of Aragon who had taken possession of the kingdom of Naples." And do we instruct about Platina? He was the author of *De Principe* and *De Optimo Cive*, the latter being dedicated to Lorenzo de' Medici. The author's list continues with Diomede Caraffa and Francesco Patrizi. All these writers addressed themselves to the virtuous prince in the manner of Petrarch, and "it is to them that Machiavelli probably alluded when he wrote that the maxims of certain authors would be excellent if one would live as one ought to live, but that they are in fact inept, considering the manner in which one does live in real life." [23]

Machiavelli, Pro and Contra

The new mentality which we associate with the term of Renaissance was, Mosca saw clearly, not as radical a breakaway from the tradition as tradition has it. "One cannot yet declare the Middle Ages terminated, because medieval notions and beliefs were still alive as well as its barbarian passions, now no longer kept in check by the much weakened religious sentiment." [24] The Renaissance was the beginning of the end and the transition to modernity, not yet modernity itself. The author then describes in vivid if brief passages the economic, military, and political aspects of the historic change, preparatory to his long discussion of the times and works of Machiavelli. The particular role which the Florentine plays in the intellectual evolution of our author justifies a special treatment of the subject.[25] That an Italian scholar should devote two entire chapters out of forty, twenty-five out of three hundred and sixty pages, to the writer of *The Prince* and *The Discourses* is as little astonishing as that he should use ten more pages to do justice to the authors whose fame was obscured by that of Machiavelli.

Foremost among these is Francesco Guicciardini, Machiavelli's fellow countryman, friend, and opponent. Mosca's preference for him has never flagged. Comparing him to Machiavelli, he says: "Guicciardini had more exact information about the political conditions of his epoch and his country," and he cites, with obvious approval, Guicciardini's comment on *The Discourses*: "How mistaken are those who in every sentence quote the Romans, for in order to govern as they did, one would first need to have a city organized after their manner." [26] How closely Mosca's definition of political liberty is patterned after that of Guicciardini has already been remarked upon.[27] His characterization of the man bespeaks a *Wahlverwandtschaft*, a more than instinctive recognition of affinity:

> Like many who have played an active part in public life, our author tends to be a pessimist. Indeed, he says repeatedly of those who plead their love of liberty: if they should find a city where they could get power, almost all of them would "make a dash for it." But his pessimism is not absolute, for he believes that "most men will desire the good and just as long as their own interests and those of their kin or the fear of being hurt by others do not lead astray their good intentions." [28]

J. W. Allen, commenting on the same passage, says that Guicciardini's "writings show that he saw, in the political world at least, very few signs of that natural inclination." [29] Mosca conceded that Guicciardini's reputation as a moralist was generally bad in his own time and after. "The truth is, he desired the good, although within the limitations of what he considered possible." He would have been shocked by Professor Allen's brutal judgment of his favorite: "we shall, I think, find that the term 'unmoral' applies to him far better than to Machiavelli." [30]

Mosca's list of anti-Machiavellian writers contains names not frequently encountered in a survey of this character. A sixteenth-century French critic, Gentillet, a Calvinist, blamed Machiavelli for the St. Bartholomew massacre. Among the Catholic polemicists, Mosca mentions the two Jesuits, Possevino and Ribadaneira, and as "even better known, a little treatise of Father Lucchesini, entitled 'Essay on the Foolishness of Machiavelli,' which the booksellers called

'The Foolishness of Father Lucchesini.' " As "prudent defenders" of the Florentine are named two Flemish writers, Justus Lipsius and Placidus Schouppe. Ernst Cassirer, in his brilliant study of "The Machiavellian Legend," mentions none of all these writers except Lipsius.[31]

More important to our author is the fellow Sicilian, Scipione di Castro who, when Mosca wrote, had just been rediscovered by the two Italian scholars, Giuseppe Ferrari and Camillo Giardina.[32] Mosca calls him "an observer of remarkable qualities." In di Castro's *Admonition to Don Marcantonio Colonna*, "undoubtedly his best work," the performance of the Spanish viceroys in charge of Sicily is analyzed with great acuteness, and the new incumbent of the office receives a great deal of "Machiavellian" advice, for instance, as to how to "manage" parliament by bribery and subtle deception.[33] That writer's "elegant cynicism" is surpassed by the "exaggerated amorality" of Gabriel Naudé, a Frenchman who "tried to impress his readers with his paradoxes." In his *Considérations politiques sur les coups d'état*, published in 1639, almost three centuries before Malaparte's similarly entitled work, he calls the St. Bartholomew massacre a blunder—but only because not all Huguenots had perished in it.[34]

Next Mosca takes up the anonymous Venetian writer whom he tentatively identifies as the monk, Paolo Sarpi. This was a man more after Mosca's heart, because in his main work he touched upon the problem of the ruling class. How to ensure perpetual domination—that was Sarpi's query, and his work purported to show how that could be done. But, Mosca comments, "he forgot to add that, due to the 'natural instability of all things human,' no government can last forever, and that its life cannot be prolonged, once ruling classes lose their energies. That was what Venice was to find out as the eighteenth century came to a close." [35]

Religious Revolutionaries

Mosca's interest in early modern communism was not confined to Thomas Morus; he pays much attention to the Anabaptist movement and discusses its outstanding leaders, Nicholas Stork, the "founding father," Thomas Münzer, and that famous rebel and dictator, John of Leiden, who tried to transform the city of Münster into a new *Civitas Dei*.[36]

The next chapter deals with the monarchomachists of France (Hotman's *Franco-Gallia*, the *Vindiciae Contra Tyrannos* which, in Mosca's view, were written not by Hubert Languet, but by Duplessis-Mornay) and Scotland (George Buchanan).[37] Their German spokesman was Althusius who, says Mosca, should not be called a precursor of Rousseau, since for him as for all late medieval writers, popular sovereignty meant the domination of the ruling classes. Not until the eighteenth century was the term "people" understood as the majority of all the citizens.[38]

Suarez and Mariana as the Spanish critics of rising absolutism receive one paragraph each. The "father of the modern concept of sovereignty," Jean Bodin, Mosca considers worthy of an entire page. The treatment of that author is, however, not very exacting. Not the same can be said of Giovanni Botero. As a native of Piedmont, which had become our author's second homeland, he attracts his fond solicitude. Botero's main work, *Della Ragion di Stato*, published in 1589, was translated into Latin, French, German, and Spanish. He was, like the Venetian, Sarpi, a conservative seeking the answers to the question of how to preserve that which exists. What endears him more than anything to Mosca is his insight into "the instability of human institutions which makes it more difficult to retain supreme power than to conquer it." Our author finds that "this thought does not lack profundity and has a great deal of truth." [39] We may add it is a truth which Mosca never tired of stating in his own works, along with, of all people, Georges Sorel, the last man Mosca would have cared to greet as a fellow conservative. "Our nature," Sorel wrote, "always tries to escape into decadence." [40]

In his thoroughly realistic approach to politics, Botero followed Machiavelli—except in one point: as a man of the Church (he served for a time as secretary to the great Archbishop of Milan who is now worshipped as St. Carlo Borromeo), Botero tried to reconcile the "reason of the state" with faith. His greatest strength, however, was in the department in which Machiavelli's weakness is conspicuous: in economics. His ideas on that subject "demonstrate an insight far in advance of his time." J. W. Allen suggests that Botero's economic theory was influenced by Jean Bodin, as was his doctrine that "the character of a people's mentality is determined by permanent 'climatic' conditions." Botero also was a physiocrat before the time in holding that the wealth of nations is what they produce, not the amount of gold and valuables, as the mercantilist credo of the age insisted.[41]

In the next chapter (23), Mosca lumps together such incongruous figures as the communist utopian, Tommaso Campanella, the Venetian Machiavellian, Paolo Paruta, his contemporary Traiano Boccalini, and, last, Hugo Grotius, who gets half a page. With obvious gusto, Mosca retails the romance of Campanella's tragic life, discusses briefly his anti-Aristotelianism (which he ascribes to the commanding influence of Campanella's Calabrian fellow countryman, Bernardino Telesio) and ends with a sober précis of *The City of the Sun*.[42] Paruta is brushed off—too lightly, I believe—as an inferior writer, and one wonders why he should have been included at all. His contemporary, Boccalini, also a Venetian, finds more favor with our author, who relates some of his satires on contemporary statesmen. In one scene of his *Raggugli di Parnasso*, Boccalini has these statesmen question Aristotle about his description of the Tyrant, which fits them too closely for comfort. But their peace of mind is finally restored by the forced recantation of the Stagirite, who fends them off with the tale that the Tyrant was a prehistoric monster, long extinct.

This is the only instance where one might suspect that Mosca intended an allusion to the jittery, guilt-ridden tyrants of his own time. If so, he could rely on his sharp-witted Italians, who would not be slow in getting the hint.[43]

In Grotius, Mosca once more could have faced the problem which he had so far avoided: natural law. But again he shuns it and has, therefore, not too much to say about the great Arminian. One has the impression Mosca planned to make this an exclusively Italian chapter and discovered suddenly that this was his last chance to tuck in the author of *De Jure Belli ac Pacis* before turning his attention to the, until now, neglected English scene.

1066 to 1928

At first sight this section is impressive: no less than five chapters, fifty pages, are devoted to political philosophy and constitutional development in England. Close inspection, however, reveals a startling incongruity of treatment: only one of the five chapters deals with doctrine—all the rest is institutional and social history. That is not quite what Anglo-Saxon readers would expect to find, but it shows Mosca in secure control of the main facts. It is the field in which he had done most of his research, and if its result is still disappointing, that is probably due to the character of Mosca's early training. Constitutional law was apparently in his youth taught with a supreme disdain for anything that could not be expressed in precise legal terms. By following that method, we will get all the details of, say, the struggle between crown and parliament under the Stuarts in their true juridical significance, and still not have more than an inkling of what went on in reality. We will not know what living forces, economic and religious, were at work to produce, in the end, the Great Rebellion. And that is a pity because Mosca might have found the real story in the great works of Guizot and Gardiner, with which he must have been familiar.[44] Again we must renew, in all respect, our old complaint that Gaetano Mosca's mind apparently worked in compartments; here was a last opportunity to rewrite history in terms of his elitist doctrine, and he did not use it.

That deficiency might still not have been too injurious had our author treated the political philosophers of England in a less cavalier fashion. His list begins with John Fortescue and goes on with Francis Bacon, Filmer, Milton, Hobbes, and Locke. The Levellers are mentioned in one sentence; Burke has his one paragraph. For Harrington, John Stuart Mill, and Bentham one will search in vain. To be sure, in such a survey one cannot expect completeness. But a certain balance is in order: why Boccalini and not Bolingbroke? Why not assign five lines to Winstanley, or Shaftesbury, Sidney or Halifax?

But even their omission would not count too heavily if only the few authors who are mentioned had received the thorough treatment they deserve. Alas! the best that could be said of Mosca's Hobbes is that the précis of *Leviathan* takes up two entire pages.[45] But the revolutionary character of that disturbing work could not be guessed from the account which carefully abstains from any criticism. There is, however, some oblique evidence to show that Mosca did not care for Hobbes; Spinoza who took, after all, his cue from Hobbes is treated much more gently.[46]

From Mosca's recapitulation of Locke's *Second Treatise* one would never divine the interesting fact that he had once devoted to that author a whole monograph. No copy of that work survived (not even in the author's private library), and I can conceive of only one way to explain the mystery: the manuscript of Mosca's *Locke* must have been ready for the press, the publication announced, but, for some reason or other, it did not materialize. If the two pages in the *History* are any indication, Locke's political philosophy cannot have played too great a role in the whole scheme of the lost work, of which perhaps the above-mentioned chapters on the constitutional development of England are more representative. One comes, regretfully, to the conclusion that the contractarian school of modern natural law simply did not register with Gaetano Mosca.

The Age of Light

It is with unmistakable relief that Mosca returns to the Continent. One feels at once how much more Mosca is at home in France. Accordingly, what he says about her great writers of the eighteenth century is interesting as well as informative. We hear about Bossuet, the great defender of the Divine Right tradition. We are told about the fiscal theories of the great engineer, Vauban, and we are introduced to the opinions of the men who represent what might be called the "abortive liberalism" of the Regency following the death of Louis XIV: the Bishop Fénelon, the Marquis d'Argenson and Bernardin de Saint-Pierre. We expect to find the Count Boulainvilliers in that illustrious company and are not disappointed. Mosca gives the representative of the aristocratic, antiabsolutist school his due and calls this writer who proclaimed the feudal and Germanic basis of French monarchy "De Gobineau's precursor." The Abbé Dubos, defender of the absolutist, "Roman" *thèse royale* is absent from this list.[47]

The author makes it easy for his readers to find their way through the maze of philosophic currents by distinguishing the negative, destructive thinkers from the positive, constructive ones. To the first school belong, in his view, all Encyclopedists and Voltaire. Their influence was great but in the main corrosive: it helped to destroy traditions without putting anything new in their place. Politically, those men put their faith in an enlightened despotism rather than in constitutional reform and representative devices. Two writers alone, both most intriguing personalities, played a constructive role: Rousseau and Montesquieu.

The latter is not merely treated as the author of *The Spirit of the Laws*, but rightly praised for his less well-known essay on *The Causes of the Grandeur and Decadence of the Romans*. The main work is diligently analyzed. Forgetting previous criticisms, Mosca calls the theory of the division of powers "without any doubt the most solid part of Montesquieu's work." As for the rest, his famous classification of governments is still unacceptable to Mosca, but less so than in the *Elementi*. Like Aristotle, Charles de Secondat, Baron de La Brède, has long lost his function as a whipping boy.[48]

Before turning to Rousseau, the author inserts a few pages about Vico. Perhaps stung by Croce's criticism, he tries to make good an old neglect. We are presented with a thumbnail sketch of Vico's *Scienza Nuova* and told that "his system needs modification and completion. For those uniform movements which he thought he could discover in the political life of the nations do not always exist, or, if they do exist, the uniformity is very relative. The causes of the progress or regress of . . . different civilizations are both multiple and varied; they do not operate in any uniform or constant fashion at all times and among all the nations."

Having placed himself on record as a pluralist and relativist (for the time ignoring any other leanings), Mosca can afford to recognize the greatness of the man who was the first, among the moderns, to apply the historic method—Mosca's method—to the study of political and social institutions. It is the only one apt to yield "truly scientific results." Of course, Vico was less fortunate than his successors, lacking as he did the scientific data which are nowadays available.[49] Old Mosca still stands on his two positivistic feet: a fact is a fact; if you have enough of them assembled, the result must equate "scientific truth," in politics exactly as in physics. It is one of the ironies of history that Mosca's faith in data begins to gain ground among the social scientists as many physicists begin to have severe misgivings about the reliability of their own observations and assumptions.

The chapter on Rousseau, it must be flatly stated, disappoints. Half of the space is given over to the story of his life, while the analysis of the works never penetrates the surface. Only once our author really "strikes pay dirt"—or so it seems when he discovers the one passage in the Social Contract "which stands in perfect contradiction to the rest . . ." Then Mosca quotes the well-known statement which is to be found in the fourth chapter of the third book, entitled "Of Government in General": "If we take the term in its strict meaning, no true democracy has ever existed, or ever will. It is against the natural order that a large number should rule and a small number be ruled." Mosca might also have quoted the concluding lines of the same chapter: "Were there such a thing as a nation of Gods, it would be a democracy. So perfect a form of government is not suited to mere men." [50]

Quelle trouvaille! Jean Jacques accidentally stumbling across the doctrine of the ruling class and contradicting his own democratic theory! But did he really? The scientific method saddles us with certain obligations. One of them demands of us to verify quotations. So we turn to the text of the Social Contract and discover, with a blush, that the respected author Gaetano Mosca has committed the most common sin of quoting out of context. For had he cared to read on, he would have found the following: "It is inconceivable that the People should be in permanent session for the administration of public affairs . . ." [51]

Now, the distinction between the sovereign who rules (infrequently, when laying down the fundamental law) and the government administering the law is central to Rousseau's whole argument. In the chapter from which Mosca quotes, Rousseau makes it quite clear that government by all would be as much against "the natural order" (since the result would be anarchy) as would be *sovereignty* (which is and remains inalienable) if possessed by less than all the people. If a lesser author would withhold such a decisive piece of information from his trusting readers, we should sternly charge him with deficient scholarship, if nothing more. In Gaetano Mosca's case we are inclined to think that it was merely a Homeric nod. Much more disturbing is his failure, in the case of Rousseau more conspicuously than elsewhere, to say what he really thinks of his subject. Granted that the limitations of space did not permit much analysis, we would have been content to get the author's "off-the-cuff" opinion. We feel frustrated by a dry, noncommittal attitude which, after all, may only reflect Mosca's customary self-restraint. And at that we shall leave the issue. For the rest of the work, we are going to confine ourselves to topics which the author treats with somewhat more than dutiful attention; in other words, we shall be using, more or less, a sampling method.

Technocrats and Positivists

For instance, we are curious to get a round picture, Mosca's picture, of the author whom he could have called his intellectual father (or, perhaps grandfather, since the father role might have to be reserved to Gumplowicz), Henri de Saint-Simon. So potent was the Frenchman's influence that it became a family trait of which Gaetano Mosca, with paternal pride, gives notice in the *Elementi*.[52] How indebted he was to the ancestor becomes most glaringly apparent in Chapter 32 of the *History* where Mosca states the Saint-Simonian version of his own *idée maîtresse*: "According to Saint-Simon, power in all organized societies is split between two orders: one controls the intellectual and moral, the other the material forces. These two powers are exercised by two organized minorities which together form the ruling class."

This formulation is identical with the one which appears, as Mosca's own, in the first chapter of the *History*.[53] In the succinct form in which it is here presented, it cannot be found in Mosca's previous writings, but its essence permeates them all.

For once, the author does not withhold his own judgment. Summing up the work of Saint-Simon, he calls it "a mixture, on the one hand, of the most original ideas and the deepest insights into the conditions of European society at the beginning of the nineteenth century, and on the other hand, of notions which were more or less absurd and sometimes outright infantile. He lacked that mental equilibrium and moderation necessary to prevent the partial truth he had discovered from degenerating into paradox." Yet his ideas did make a school, and such illustrious men as Auguste Comte, Herbert Spencer, and Karl Marx were his disciples. "It is remarkable that the idea which caught on least . . . was his notion of the ruling class and of the qualities which it ought to possess." [54]

This statement which seems to deny the paramount importance of the class concept in the works of Spencer, Comte and, last but not least, Karl Marx, is hard to understand unless we go back to the *Elementi*. There we may find the decisive clue to Mosca's strange ambivalence toward the teacher.

What strikes one first is the relatively small role accorded to Saint-Simon in a work expounding the theory of the ruling class. The first chapters mention Comte and Spencer but not Saint-Simon. His name appears for the first time in the eleventh chapter, and there in conjunction with that of the revolutionary, Buonarroti who, in Mosca's view, was influenced by Saint-Simon. Now, Buonarroti was a socialist, and Saint-Simon, too, "came in his last publication . . . pretty close to socialism on the sentimental side, and the Saint-Simonianism that flourished after 1830 . . . actually anticipated many of the views which later were adopted by socialism." The publication referred to was the *Nouveau Christianisme*.[55]

It is, of course, embarrassing in the extreme for Mosca to trace his own doctrine back to Saint-Simon the socialist, and therefore he adds quickly: "All the same, the thought that Saint-Simon develops in his early publications is too vast, too profound, and too original to allow him to be mentioned outright as merely one of the many writers who heralded the rise of social democracy as we know it." [56] This attempt to sever Saint-Simon the youthful genius from the old man who came under the spell of Bazard and Enfantin is taken up once more in the second *Elementi*, where Mosca says that the Saint-Simonian school in some respects "ranged far afield from the master's teachings." [57]

But Mosca realizes that a fringe attack will not accomplish much. And so he finally directs his fire against the core of Saint-Simon's new teachings: "To each according to his ability, to each ability according to its results." What Mosca tries to show is that a social system based exclusively on merit could not work: "To establish an exact and unerring relationship between merit and success, between the works of each individual and the reward or punishment that is due him, would be a superhuman task within the competence only of an omniscient and omnipotent being . . ." [58]

This is what Mosca had been saying all along. But as it happened, his own doctrine was the rationale, the "formula" precisely of that educated middle class which owed its fast ascendancy in recent times to intellectual or technical achievement. So one wonders whether Mosca's hesitation to identify himself completely with that formula was not due to the fact that the idea of a government by merit had been taken over by the socialists. If so, then not the Saint-Simonians only, but Saint-Simon himself had to be exorcized. Hard as he tried, however, Gaetano Mosca never quite succeeded in that task; the master's ghost returned to haunt our pluralistic-absolutist Hamlet to the end, when the "disinterested elements" are once more given their idealistic head.

With Comte and Spencer Mosca never had much trouble: both served him well to demonstrate his own superior insight into the complexities of social evolution.[59] But both men are treated with consideration in the *History* and Comte particularly is defended against those who charged him with having plagiarized Saint-Simon without naming him. Mosca conceded that "the fundamental conceptions of the philosopher of Montpellier presented a close parallel to the ideas of the man who was for seven years his master." [60] But, adds our author with his innate sense of fair play, "one must recognize that as to breadth of culture, method, and style, the disciple was by far superior to his master. He gave to Saint-Simon's ideas a development and a cohesion of which Saint-Simon would never have been capable." This is a handsome compliment very reminiscent of what the editor of

Mosca's *Ruling Class* said on behalf of a man whom our author had accused of plagiarism.[61]

Less comprehensible is Mosca's neglect of another author to whom he is heavily indebted. Taine is mentioned in the *History*, but merely in one line as a disciple of de Tocqueville, who is treated at considerable length.[62]

The *Risorgimento*—Henry George

Since his treatment of Vico, with the exception of Vincente Cuoco, an Italian ultra-democrat and communist, born 1770,[63] our author's *italianità* has been without a single worthy subject. Now at last he can devote an entire chapter (34) to the patriotic writers of the nine-teenth-century *risorgimento*. Of the four authors discussed, two, Vincenzo Gioberti and Cesare Balbo, are not germane to the pur-pose of this study, and the most important figure of that period, Giuseppe Mazzini, nationalist, democrat, republican, does not fully come to life in Mosca's portrayal—possibly because "he replaced the divine right of kings with the divine right of the people." [64]

Mosca's real interest is for another "ancestor": Domenico Roma-gnosi (1761–1835) whose career as a professor of constitutional and civil law, and as a state official dismissed for his liberal convictions, may have struck a sympathetic chord in ex-Senator Mosca. His ac-count of Romagnosi's work (which fills nineteen volumes) makes of him a Saint-Simonian and a Mosca before Mosca: "The author shows his preference for a limited monarchy based on a balance of the ruling forces which prevail in society. These forces are on the one hand material, on the other intellectual and moral." [65] Mosca missed a splendid opportunity when he forgot to mention that Romagnosi's starting point was Vico's *Scienza Nuova*, which he subjected to a trenchant criticism before launching upon his own enterprise, which was to give Vico's "fantastic presentment of the science he proposed" a truly scientific foundation.[66]

The problem of selection is, of course, most difficult in a work such as Mosca's *History*. The need for condensation has its odd re-sults too; one might say that it makes strange bed-fellows, such as

Chapter 38 which joins together two men as dissimilar as Henry George and Georges Sorel. Both, Mosca argues, differed with Karl Marx: *Progress and Poverty*, unlike *Das Kapital*, was not inspired by "violent hatred of the wealthy classes," and Sorel was no determinist; "in that respect he is in open conflict with his master..." *Ergo*: Henry George and Georges Sorel, since they do not agree with Marx, must agree with each other.[67]

The Racial Gospel

Before concluding his book with an exposition of his own political philosophy, the author devotes his most thoroughly researched and longest chapter to a refutation of the various racialist creeds of the last one hundred years.[68] Though Italy did not surrender to that doctrine until 1938 and under severe Nazi pressure, to reject it with the firm determination Mosca displayed in this chapter and in the long essay mentioned earlier was a courageous act. We would admire it even more had Mosca not, in his zest to *écraser l'infâme*, included Nietzsche, Hegel, and Carlyle in his stern, antiracialist indictment. The two last-named after all shared his own antidemocratic and aristocratic bias. To be sure, neither Carlyle nor Hegel was a liberal, but their elitist preference was for a ruling class of culture, not of race. To say of Hegel nothing else but that in his *Philosophy of History* he "dignified the German people with the mission to lead the world toward its third phase when freedom would no longer be the privilege of one, or of a few, but the possession of all" is merely to confuse the uninstructed reader,[69] who may get the wrong impression, namely that the author has been trying to praise Hegel with faint damns. And what idea will he get of Nietzsche, who is summed up as one who "proposed a cult of force and disapproved of the existing laws because they hampered the development and power of the supermen." [70]

Now, Mosca knew better than that. What prompted him to impose this strange censorship upon his public? Before we condemn him for it, we may do well to remember that the Fascists had adopted Nietzsche—a cut-rate Nietzsche to be sure—as one of their patron saints, together with Sorel. Rather than with the creator of the *Uebermensch* Mosca's mind was at odds with Nietzsche's apes, the Fascist supermen.

Heinrich von Treitschke comes in for a few appropriate remarks. He is followed by another German, Julius Langbehn, whose anonymously published work called *Rembrandt als Erzieher* enjoyed an enormous popularity before and after 1914. Idealization of the master race was not the only purpose of that work; it also gave expression to the growing discontent of the intelligentsia with the coarse materialism of the Wilhelminian Reich. The *Rembrandtdeutsche*, as Langbehn was called, merely popularized sentiments which on a higher level were expressed by Paul de Lagarde (whom Mosca does not name) and Jacob Burckhardt.[71]

Mosca makes it clear that in the field of modern racial theory the Germans could claim no monopoly. He credits Count de Boulainvilliers whom we have already met with having first enunciated the idea that the upper classes of a nation belong to a race different from that of the mass of their subjects. In other words, the French state, any state was the result of conquest. (Mosca might have found an earlier expression of the same view in Bodin's *Six livres de la république*.) The genealogy of racialism is continued with de Gobineau and Houston Stewart Chamberlain,[72] the son-in-law of Richard Wagner, who should also have been mentioned as a very influential preacher of the racial gospel.

Sandwiched in between the Frenchman and the Englishman-turned-German is "the Polish Israelite" Gumplowicz. From Mosca's account of *Der Rassenkampf* no reader of the *History* could possibly suspect the anguished protestations of the *Elementi*. Once more Mosca stops short of presenting the work's argument in its entirety. Instead, he tries to explain the theory as a reflection of the author's personal experience as a subject of the multinational Habsburgian Empire.[73]

In contrast, the précis of Oswald Spengler's work as well as the long refutation of Hans Günther, Hitler's favorite professor, are proof that our author, entering his ninth decade, had not lost one whit of his intellectual vigor. Spengler he treats with indulgence, and with reason: *The Decline of the West* pays obeisance to the theory of the elite, although Mosca makes astonishingly little of the fact. Nor does he notice that the prophet of the technocratic Caesars only echoed, on a lower level, Friedrich Nietzsche's Zarathustrian chants. Spengler's pessimism is too much for Mosca who, God knows, was not an optimist himself. But he could not help smiling wryly about the intensely serious Teuton; Mosca's Latin sanity remained immune to global gloom. He becomes almost jocular when he records Spengler's prediction about the near end of Germany's millennium (two hundred years from now), to be succeeded by the Slavic cycle. It is strange, Mosca dryly adds, but when it comes to saying something definite about the part to be played by the Europe now controlled by Russian bolshevism, Spengler suddenly adopts an unaccustomed caution.[74]

Günther's pseudo science furnishes the pretext for rejecting once more theories which Mosca had disposed of long ago. He patiently lists all the reasons against the contemporary racial myth which, however, like other myths, remains impervious to all reason. Mosca is ready to concede that race may be a factor of importance. But no single factor can determine all the changes in the social organism, "which is as complex as the organism of the human individual." [75]

It is what he has been saying, with occasional important lapses, all his life. Only the tone has changed. The fight is over. An old man looks at mankind, still with curiosity, but calmly, without the great expectations but, then, also without the exasperation of his younger days.

12

MACHIAVELLI AND THE MACHIAVELLIANS

What shall we make of Mosca's *History?* The inescapable conclusion seems to be the paradoxical one that the author of *The Ruling Class* was no political theorist in the accepted sense.[1] Not for him the methodic inquiry into the philosophic suppositions of an author, not for him the question of internal, logical consistency. His mind lacks analytical curiosity in the extreme. But then, we may be judging him unfairly. Obviously, the *History* stands no comparison with that of George H. Sabine, a philosopher by training. Indeed, we may be swayed by the fact that, until rather recently, political philosophy had been the province of the philosophic specialist: Cassirer, Collingwood, Joad, Russell, Murray, Kaplan—the list could be easily extended.[2]

Lately, the philosophers have had to share control of the field with political psychologists, political sociologists, and anthropologists. For that development, philosophy itself must in part take the blame, if blame is the right word. Political theory had been an ancillary science, a mere subdivision of the chapter on ethics in the philosophic systems of the Greeks. And there the matter had remained until, in modern times when "politics" became an integral part of "po-

262

litical economy," the emphasis seemed to be shifting from moral to economic man. Actually, the old relationship between moral and political philosophy remained unbroken: the new social theories could not deny their common origin from ethical and, finally, metaphysical traditions. Even the empiricist revolt never severed the link with ethics: in Hume social and moral philosophy are still identical, and the great author of the *Wealth of Nations* held the chair of moral philosophy at the University of Edinburgh.

Only in our own time has that old connection become more and more enfeebled, to the same extent that the professional philosopher has ceased to be a system builder, anxious to evolve "a working view of the universe and of man's place in it . . ." Instead, there has been underway a forceful movement which "tends to dissociate philosophy not merely from ethics and theology, but also from the *content* of the special sciences . . ." What remains is "a modest special science, dealing with definite problems and giving definite answers . . ." [3] It is this self-limitation of philosophy to problems of epistemology and logic which in part explains the present "twilight" that surrounds political philosophy. Its crisis is as much the result of the philosophic specialist's retreat from ethical concerns as of the inroads made by the new social science disciplines. What they are occupying is evacuated territory.

Where does that leave the typical political historian such as Mosca? He may be, and is in most cases, blind to such problems of ratiocination as, for example, can be found in Hobbes and as are the fascination of a Leo Strauss or D. G. James,[4] but he should still be able to show that the mechanistic, contractarian system of *Leviathan* was of the very essence of its age and even, in a qualified sense, valid for today. He need not be familiar with the intricacies of Platonic metaphysics, but the task of comprehending *The Republic* as the first great study and pathology of power should not be beyond him.

But that is precisely the task in which Gaetano Mosca fails. He hardly ever tries to judge a complex of political ideas on the author's terms or to explain it within the historic context. He would rather treat the past as a huge balance sheet of truth and error, mostly error. But that would, of course, not be "objective"; it would be "unscientific." And so between Scylla and Charybdis, between placing without judging and dispensing judgment without placement, Mosca plunges into the worst of both worlds; he refrains, in the majority of cases, from evaluating *and* reliving past experience and confines himself to "factual" reporting. There are some exceptions, duly noted, which reveal another Mosca, one who does speak out and lets his author speak so that we understand that author in the language of his time as well as of our own. And among those exceptions one would expect to find the most controversial figure of political philosophy, the name whose fame crowds Plato and outshines in popularity both Hobbes and—at least in the West—Karl Marx. What is more likely than that the Italian Mosca should pay special homage to his celebrated fellow countryman? He indeed did so in two chapters of the *History* and earlier, in a long essay.[5] Sufficient reason for us to reserve a special chapter for the purpose of discovering what Gaetano Mosca thought of Niccolò Machiavelli.

But not the only reason. Mosca has been called a Machiavellian, a representative, with Pareto and Sorel, of a new view of politics inspired by Machiavelli's scientific method and his hard-faced realism. Specifically, that new school is said to have derived from Machiavelli the doctrine of the ruling class and the idea that political rights, democratic institutions, depend on the brutal facts of power and not on the legal fictions in which they are clothed. Hence not the followers of Rousseau but the Machiavellians are the only true "defenders of freedom." [6]

Leaving Pareto and Sorel aside, the question of whether Mosca is a Machiavellian in the sense in which Professor Burnham has employed the word is an important one. So far, the evidence has yielded little to support the claim. But that may be due to a lack of perspicacity on the part of the present writer. The fact that Mosca wrote at length on his supposed preceptor is, if nothing else, an indication that he took the subject seriously. His findings may provide us with the answer for which we are looking. They may not bear out Mr. Burnham's thesis. Even that, however, would not prove that Burnham was wrong. Our author, after all, may be a Machiavellian without knowing it. But, I submit, the theory would be more plausible if Mosca should concur, less plausible if his and Burnham's Machiavelli were at odds with one another.

Now, the first thing that strikes one is the fact that Professor Burnham's Machiavelli is the freedom-loving Florentine republican who wrote the *Discourses*, while Mosca is exclusively concerned with Machiavelli's *Prince*. Still, even that need not preclude agreement. For *The Prince*, too, has some passages—not mentioned by Professor Burnham—which permit us to infer that Machiavelli had a high opinion of the limited, "mixed" type of government which, to use Mosca's term, reflects the balance of the social forces.[7]

Unfortunately, Mosca, always eager to discover intimations of his own ideas in the writings of his predecessors, does not seem to recognize them in this case. The reason may be that he is not looking for the things which are of paramount importance to Professor Burnham. Fortunately, that is not quite true: both men, for instance, discuss Machiavelli as a *scientist*. In the interest of readers not familiar with the thesis of *The Machiavellians*, it seems proper to develop it in some detail before proceeding with our main objective, the analysis of Mosca's reading of *The Prince*.

The Science of Power

Professor Burnham begins his investigation with a violent attack on Dante: the great poet's tract *De Monarchia* is a typical example of mere wishful thinking, utterly unscientific. In contrast, Machiavelli's aim is "the accurate and systematic description of public facts . . ." He tries "to correlate sets of these facts into laws" and "to predict, with some degree of probability, future facts." He is, in short, a scientist. If, as a scientist, he pursues any goals, these goals "must be nontranscendental" and "they must have at least a minimum probability of realization." However honorable, they must not affect, "the logic of the scientific inquiry." [8]

In Burnham's view, to say that Machiavelli divorced politics from ethics is to confuse issues. Machiavelli did so "only in the same sense that every science must divorce itself from ethics . . . This very refusal however [to pervert science], this allegiance to objective truth, is itself a moral ideal . . . Machiavelli divorced politics from a certain kind of ethics—namely from a transcendental, otherworldly, and, it may be added, very rotten ethics. But he did so in order to bring politics and ethics more closely in line . . ." [9]

Machiavelli's practical goal was the unification of Italy: "compared to Dante's glittering ideals, this goal is doubtless humble, almost sordid." But it was an ethical goal nonetheless, and "there was no reason to think it too improbable of accomplishment in Italy." [10] The very careful formulation of this sentence will be noticed; to have said that, at the time when Machiavelli wrote, unification was extremely difficult if not unlikely would have hurt his reputation as a scientist.

Does Machiavelli actually live up to Burnham's scientific principles? In answering that question, Burnham shows himself more generous than Mosca. He grants that "Machiavelli's conceptions often seem to us somewhat immature." But then, we must remember that "in those days, scientific method in our sense . . . was only beginning." On the whole, however, Burnham thinks that Machiavelli is on the right track. He "uses language in a cognitive, scientific manner." More important, he "delineates with sufficient clarity the field of politics." He understands it "as primarily the study of the struggles for power among men." [11]

What follows sounds familiar. Burnham's Machiavelli "implies everywhere a rather sharp distinction between two types of political man: a 'ruler-type,' we might call one, and a 'ruled type,' the other." That is indeed straight Mosca, but it may be noted that the terminology of the two "types" is not officially ascribed to Machiavelli—it is Mosca's language used by Burnham to describe what Machiavelli is supposed to have had in mind. That is not necessarily the effect the passage will have on a not too careful reader. However, careful or not, he will still expect proof of the claim that Machiavelli had, no matter in what terms, a theory of the elite.

Professor Burnham's evidence is compiled mostly from the Discourses. But first we hear that "the outstanding characteristic of the majority is . . . its political passivity . . . Under normal conditions, the ruled are not interested in power." That statement is based on well-known lines from Chapters XVII and XIX of The Prince.[12] Next, the need for authority is emphasized. This time the evidence comes from three places in *The Discourses*, all showing how, without firm leadership, the masses tend to be amorphous, or, in Machiavelli's words: "how useless a thing the multitude is without a head..." [13] However, when the masses "choose themselves a Head... as the Romans did when... they created tribunes from among themselves...," then Machiavelli says with Livy that "nothing is more courageous than the multitude united..." [14] The rulers and the ruled are made of the same moral stuff; the record shows "how many Princes there have been, and how few of them good... I conclude, therefore, against the common opinion, that the people are no more light, ungrateful, nor changeable than Princes..." [15]

The ruler-type has Machiavelli's *virtù*, which is Will To Power; in addition it is the ability to rule. "Strength, especially martial strength," is an important quality, but even more important is deception: "people rise rather by fraud, than by force." [16] The combination lion-fox makes the ideal ruler, as described in one of the most famous passages of Machiavelli's *Prince*, which Burnham reproduces *in extenso*. The same work stresses the importance of adaptability to changed conditions.[17] For "political life, according to Machiavelli, is never static... The process of change is repetitive, and roughly cyclical." This is of course a reference to Machiavelli's formulation, before Vico, of the law of *corso* and *ricorso*: civilizations rise and fall, as it were, by a law of nature; the same force that makes a nation great is also cause of its decline, and vice versa. In Machiavelli's unforgettable words, "virtue begets peace, peace begets idleness; idleness, mutiny; and mutiny, destruction," but also "ruin begets laws; those laws, virtue; and virtue begets honor and good success." [18]

Up to this point, we have not yet heard anything that would suggest Mosca's particular conception of society. To be sure, what Machiavelli says about the necessary qualities of leadership reminds us of related observations in the *Elementi*. But the lion-fox comparison has been more of an inspiration to Pareto than to Mosca. Likewise, Machiavelli's cyclical view of history has been developed by Pareto, not by Mosca. But these are not the important points. Essential is: can we distill from Machiavelli's text, as cited by Professor Burnham, Mosca's doctrine of the ruling class? So far, we have only heard of multitudes, ruled or unruly on the one hand, and outstanding individuals, leaders, princes on the other—never of the struggle, or the combination, of two or more organized minorities, and not a word of "social forces" either. One quotation referring to the Roman tribunes of the people is the closest approach yet to Mosca's own example of an elite rising from the plebs. But a re-reading of the sentence will not bear out that affinity. "The Romans," Machiavelli says, "created twenty tribunes from among themselves." [19] That is the customary democratic view of the elective process, without any inkling that the tribunes *had* themselves elected. Without better evidence, we shall declare ourselves unable to detect any elitist elements in Machiavelli's rudimentary analysis of class relations—at any rate not the conception of elitist *groups* as understood by Mosca, and Pareto, for that matter. If anywhere, these elements might be found in Machiavelli's theory of government, to which Professor Burnham turns toward the very end of his investigation.

He has no doubt that Machiavelli preferred the republican type of government to any other, and most writers will agree with Burnham. But even in *The Discourses* where Machiavelli's preference is most apparent, he "paints no utopia . . . It is true, moreover, that he does not attach quite the ultimate importance to the choice of form of government." What matters to him is the extent to which "liberty" is realized. He understands that word in an external sense, as independence from foreign domination: "arms are the first foundation of liberty." In the internal sense freedom is civil liberty. But, and this is, according to Professor Burnham, Machiavelli's great discovery, "internally, also, liberty rests on force." [20] As little as Hobbes, does Machiavelli rely on mere good intentions for the preservation of freedom. Good laws alone mean nothing, for:

> . . . the law is founded upon force, but the force in turn will destroy the law unless it is also bridled; but force can be bridled only by opposing force. Sociologically, therefore, the foundation of liberty is a balancing of forces, what Machiavelli calls a "mixed" government . . . Only out of the continuing clash of opposing groups can liberty flow.[21]

So far Professor Burnham. And one must concede that this time his proof, although still not ample, is impressive. The key passage occurs in the first book of *The Discourses*, where Machiavelli says that "there are two opposite humors, one of the people, the other of the Noblesse; and that all Laws which are made in favor of liberty, proceed from the differences betwixt them..." The meaning becomes even clearer in a different translation, reading thus: "In every republic there are two parties, that of the nobles and that of the people; and all the laws that are favorable to liberty result from the opposition of these parties to each other, as may easily be seen from the events that occurred in Rome." [22] Professor Allen goes still further in remarking about the same passage: "When [Machiavelli] declares that laws favorable to freedom in a republic originate in conflict between the faction of the nobles and the faction of the populace, he seems even to suggest that the more democratic the constitution the greater the liberty." The author of *The Machiavellians* might have referred to the even stronger statement that appears in the same chapter of *The Discourses*: "I maintain that those who blame the quarrels of the Senate and the people of Rome condemn that which was the very origin of liberty." [23] And Burnham might have found equally strong backing for his thesis in *The Prince*, where Machiavelli praises the "well ordered and governed" French monarchy with its parliament protecting the people against "the ambition and insolence of the great nobles," while at the same time relieving the king "of the dissatisfaction that he might incur among the nobles by favoring the people, and among the people by favoring the nobles." [24]

But even without these additional endorsements the draft presented by Professor Burnham must be honored. He has made his point that Machiavelli had a notion akin to our author's "balance of the social forces." As for his "juridical defense," we are reminded of it when:

... in chapter after chapter, Machiavelli insists that if liberty is to be preserved: no person and no magistrate may be permitted to be above the law; there must be legal means for any citizen to bring accusations against any other citizen or any official ... The ambition of citizens must never be allowed to build up private power, but must be directed into public channels.

No reference is given where these statements may be found in Machiavelli's *Discourses*, but they occur, if not exactly "chapter after chapter," then still in sufficient numbers.[25] As another author, the Italian communist Antonio Gramsci, puts it: "In Machiavelli one can already discover, in capsule form, the ideas of the separation of powers and parliamentarianism (representative government)." [26]

But does that make Gaetano Mosca a Machiavellian? Could not Machiavelli, with equal right, be called, the same as Mosca, a Polybian and a Ciceronian—even an Aristotelian?

When there is mutual fear, man fearing man and class fearing class, then, because no one is confident of his own strength, a sort of bargain is made between the common people and the mighty; this results in the mixed form of government which Scipio has been recommending.[27]

Scipio's mentor was Polybius; through him runs the great tradition which has been received and modernized—sociologized—by Mosca. Machiavelli is a milestone on that road, not its beginning. As for Professor Burnham's highly stimulating thesis, his elitist Machiavelli very much gives the impression of an *ex post facto* adaptation: he has read the moderns, Mosca and Pareto, into Machiavelli and then, with considerable ingenuity, reversed the process, ending up with the new school of Machiavellians. We had reason to believe that Mosca's work does not reveal a theory of power against power; we could find no evidence that Mosca wished to sever politics from ethics. In that sense, too, Mosca was no Machiavellian. Burnham's Machiavelli makes, however, a great deal of sense once he is understood as a *contemporary myth*, just as, according to Antonio Gramsci, "Machiavelli's *Prince* might well be studied as a specimen of the Sorelian myth—that is, as an ideology which is not offered as a cold utopia or a dry ratiocination, but as a creative image held up to a disunited, humiliated people to help it regain and assert its collective will." [28]

The modern Machiavelli would not conjure up a savior Prince to restore unity to a disjointed world—he would address himself to a whole group of men, exhorting them to become conscious of their mission as an international elite: an elite of Communists, as Mussolini's prisoner believed, of the New Middle Class in the myth of the Managerial Revolution.[29]

"Encore quelques mots . . ."

The image Gaetano Mosca paints of Machiavelli has not much in common with the visions of Antonio Gramsci and James Burnham.

"Scholarship," Max Lerner wrote, "has not done well by *The Discourses*. The scholars pay lip service to it as the larger frame of reference within which *The Prince* can be understood. But having done so, they go on to talk of *The Prince*." [30] To that accusation Gaetano Mosca may plead innocent because he never did talk about anything besides *The Prince*. There are two pages about that work in the *Elementi*.[31] The index of *The Ruling Class* lists Machiavelli sixteen times, but only one of all these references pertains to *The Discourses*, another to the *History of Florence*; the rest are to *The Prince*. The same is true of the two chapters in the author's *History of Doctrines*, of the lengthy study which appeared in a French journal, and of the short article on Machiavelli written for the *Encyclopaedia of Social Sciences*.

"Encore quelques mots sur le 'Prince' de Machiavelli" was published one year before the fourth centennial of Machiavelli's death.[32] It is a thorough study running to over fifty large pages, of which twenty deal with the historic background; seventeen are taken up by a chapter-by-chapter synopsis of *The Prince*, which leaves less than one-third of the total (fifteen pages) for analysis and critical evaluation.

The historical part is based mainly on the findings of two men, Italians both: one, Ferrari, writing in the 1860's, the other a contemporary, Alfredo Oriani.[33] Both represent the negative minority opinion among recent Machiavelli scholars. Mosca declares that he has been influenced by this opinion, which may explain the clipped tone of deliberate restraint that marks the essay. Behind the façade of objectivity one can hear faint polemic rumblings.

The sorry state of Italy in Machiavelli's time is described in detail by Mosca and summed up as territorial fragmentation, governmental instability, and military disorganization. Machiavelli was not alone in perceiving and lamenting all those ills. But most Italian patriots just threw up their hands in despair. Machiavelli, on the contrary, was confident that the three problems which bedeviled Italy could all be solved, and solved not in a distant future but in the immediate present. "It is this confidence which makes him so superior as a theorist and, be it added, so inferior as political practitioner." [34]

Machiavelli dedicated his tract on the times to first one, then another member of the family which had destroyed his Florentine Republic and had control of the Papacy. Was he, in flattering the Medici, betraying his past as a servant of the free Republic? Mosca does not think so. The very content of *The Prince* refutes the charge. "A vulgar but adept intriguer, instead of writing a treatise on practical politics, would have used much more direct and more effective means to get into the good graces of the Medici . . . Instead of speaking his own mind, he could have written things agreeable to those whose favor he was currying." By not doing so, he proved himself a man of courage and integrity.[35]

Why did Mosca himself write his *Prince?* Could he expect to add something new to the old, interminable argument? He thought so, and he said so right at the beginning. The discussion as to whether Machiavelli was a noble patriot or an arch-villain does not evoke his interest. The only question that seems still important to him has to do with the claim, made for Machiavelli, that he introduced the scientific method into the investigation of political phenomena. In anticipation, I shall say that Mosca does not recognize that claim. But there is, perhaps, still another, simpler reason why the article had to be written: Mosca plainly did not like most of the literature about Machiavelli. This is not the same as saying that he disliked Machiavelli himself, although it may be as simple as all that. But he was definitely annoyed with the commentators: "A great deal has been written about *The Prince.* And that is why so relatively few people have read that work or remember what it really says. As so often happens with books that are very famous and much quoted, many people rely on writers who exalted or condemned the author." That is particularly dangerous in the case of a writer as violently controversial as Machiavelli. For the fact that he provoked so much white heat was not conducive to much accuracy on the part of his admirers and detractors. Therefore, "at the risk of being . . . taxed with partiality," Mosca proposes to go back to the original. Accordingly, he does the humble thing and gives an ostentatiously dry résumé, from Chapter I to Chapter XXVI. In passing, he notes with considerable irony that one of Machiavelli's critics (whom he fails to name) spoke of those chapters as so many "books," which "seems to prove that the man never read the work." [36]

We shall not follow Mosca on his slow trek through the text, except for mentioning that Chapter XIX does not have for him the magic which it ought to possess if he were in truth a Machiavellian in Professor Burnham's sense. Not only does he fail to notice the elitist possibilities of Machiavelli's reference to the "well-ordered kingdom of the French," with its embryonic premonition of the balance-of-the-social-forces concept, Mosca does not even bother to discuss the passage in which Machiavelli treats of the French version of "mixed" government. The chapter most important to our author is the celebrated twenty-sixth, the call to liberation and unification by the savior-prince. Was the entire book written for the sake of that impassioned last appeal? If so, "that chapter sheds a bright light on the tragic situation in which Machiavelli found himself on account of the flagrant contradiction between the nobleness of his aims and the shabbiness of the means which he advocates..." No man could have such high ideals and then stoop to the low level on which Machiavelli's Prince was to pursue them; nor was the Italian nation ready to make the great effort necessary to achieve the goal. Three hundred years more were to pass before the cultural and moral climate had sufficiently improved to make it possible for the right leaders to arise and find a nation that would follow them.[37]

Before advancing further criticisms, Mosca quickly removes a few arguments from the discussion which, in his opinion, are irrelevant. He is not going to take seriously the theory, held by such luminaries as the famous Albericus Gentilis (who anticipated some of Hugo Grotius' thoughts), Rousseau, and the Italian poet, Ugo Foscolo, that Machiavelli's Prince was a veiled attack upon the princes of the time. An equal waste of intellectual energy, in Mosca's view, is the whole argument about the immorality of Machiavelli. "It is almost universally agreed upon today that... The Prince is not a treatise about morals but on politics, meaning the art of getting power and of keeping it as long as possible; and it is known that in no country, at no time, has it been possible to make that art conform to the accepted tenets of Christian, or just plain human, morality." [38] If Machiavelli can at all be criticized in that respect, it is for his exaggerations:

If it is true that the precepts of a most rigid morality cannot be observed in politics, it is no less true that politics is an art in which the sense of limits and proportion is of the greatest importance. It is for this reason that lies and disloyalty to achieve their purpose must be employed with great caution and parsimony. One discovered to be a habitual liar and a breaker of sworn agreements is not trusted. Elementary as these considerations are, they seem to have escaped Machiavelli's attention, a fact all the more strange since they were certainly not neglected by other Italian writers, such as Guicciardini and Scipio di Castro.[39]

The absence of that "sense of limits and proportion" is most glaringly "in evidence in Machiavelli's admiration for Caesar Borgia." As will be seen, our author did not think much of the vaunted statesmanship of Alexander Borgia's son.

What are, then, the essential Machiavellian problems which are still worth thinking about? In Mosca's view, the only question worth while asking is: "Did Machiavelli in his work . . . lay the foundations of a real science of politics, or did he at least come forth with recommendations which could be accepted as a canon of the art of politics?"

Our author tries hard to be generous. He credits Machiavelli with "two happy intuitions, indeed, strokes of genius, considering the time in which he lived: first, Machiavelli realized that the prosperity and decadence of social organisms can be explained only by . . . a study of their history; and furthermore he understood that there are, in all nations which have reached a certain level of civilization, general and constant tendencies at work, which is to say, in other terms, that the nature of political man is everywhere and at all times the same."

With these two propositions Mosca is completely in agreement. If Machiavelli had lived up to his own precepts, Gaetano Mosca would have gladly called himself a Machiavellian, for those principles are, as we know, his own. "One has to recognize that it is impossible to build a real science of politics on any other basis . . ." [40]

That new scientific method was within Machiavelli's reach but not yet in his grasp. For when he wrote his works, "historical research and criticism were still in their infancy—or rather, were not even born. His sole materials, in addition to some medieval chronicles, were the works of Sallust, Livy, Tacitus, and other writers of classical antiquity." Those men, to be sure, were great artists and psychologists, "but like all artists, they were sometimes carried away by the love of art." Worse, they only knew their own civilizations, and of them too little about the more distant past to understand the origins and the conditions under which political and social institutions had developed. Even about their own period they were not sufficiently informative. The reason is that common failing of historians: to take many things for granted which are known to their contemporaries but completely unintelligible to posterity.[41]

Machiavelli then has no claim to being called the founder of the science of politics. "All he could do was to trace lines from which the edifice could rise, and to lay the first stone." Had Machiavelli been born four hundred years later, "he probably would have put up some of the heavy walls." He had, to use a popular phrase, "what it takes." "Whenever he is in possession of the necessary information, he is able to discern and indicate with utmost clarity why one political organization is superior to another. For instance, since he knows how soldiers were recruited in republican Rome, he can tell it was a better way than to rely on hired adventurers, as was the custom in his Italy." When the Roman government had grown so weak that it could not suppress the custom which permitted private citizens to keep their own armed retinues, then, Machiavelli knew, the end of the Republic had arrived.

Denying him the title of a scientist, our author then proceeds to question Machiavelli's second claim to fame. Shall we consider his *Prince* as a handbook, a "guide" to ambitious men who wish to learn the art of how to acquire, and remain in, power? Most students of the work have answered that question in the affirmative; "others, among them the Frenchman Gentillet and the Italians Giuseppe Ferrari and Alfredo Oriani, were more negative, and we agree with them." [42] Mosca would have read with great displeasure J. W. Allen's comment: "Few or none of those who, in the sixteenth century, denounced him, had read his works or had read any of them but the misleading *Principe* ... Gentillet's *Antimachiavel* (1576) is little better informed." Even harsher is Max Lerner's judgment: "Gentillet gave just enough of Machiavelli to distort him, and not enough to make him either comprehensible or human." [43]

Another Antimachiavel

Mosca tries to prove his case by subjecting Machiavelli to a psychological analysis which is decidedly original. The "Secretary of The Ten" of the Republic on the Arno may not have been a successful statesman, but few writers ever went so far as to deny that Machiavelli was a keen observer of reality. "He obtained a wide experience of political affairs and how things were done administratively and diplomatically. He was not very highly educated in a wide sense. His serious training was that of the practical politician and man of affairs; and a politician he remained to the end of his days, in office or out of office. His experience went far to determine his views about politics, but it did not and could not make of him a political philosopher," wrote J. W. Allen.[44] "With his genius for political observation," writes Arnold Toynbee, "he studied and apprehended and recorded exactly those features in the political structure of the new transalpine nation-states which were of practical interest and importance for Italian statesmanship. After fourteen years of this experience, Machiavelli had become perhaps better qualified than any other living Italian for taking in hand the urgent tasks of helping Italy work out her political salvation, when a turn in the wheel of Florentine domestic politics suddenly expelled him from his whole field of 'practical' activity." [45]

This is the man who our author insists was a bookworm. Most writers and almost all educated people can be said to form their minds in part through reading books (and newspapers today, adds Mosca) and in part by drawing upon their experience. "Now with Machiavelli the first element, it seems to us, rules absolute, for otherwise it would be difficult to understand his boundless veneration for the classics, or his deep conviction of the superiority of the Greeks and, above all, the Romans over the people of his own time . . . He certainly was wrong in thinking that to imitate the ancients was sufficient to obtain identical results. This is an error into which he often lapses in *The Prince* and still more in *The Discourses* where he, almost continuously, draws parallels between old Rome and modern Florence . . . without realizing the great difference of circumstances and conditions separating the two cities." [46]

Not everyone will agree with that opinion. Ernst Cassirer for one, who may be called an authority on Machiavelli, says of him: "Unlike many other thinkers of the Renaissance he did not cherish the hope of restoring the life of the ancients. The Roman Republic was founded upon the Roman *virtù*—and this *virtù* is lost, once for all. The attempts to resuscitate ancient political life appeared to Machiavelli as idle dreams." [47]

But Brutus was an honorable man, and Mosca's Machiavelli was "above all a theoretician and idealist." As if these two epithets were not insulting enough, our author adds: "Like all idealists pursuing a noble dream, he is sometimes, in spite of all the pessimism he affects, naive." It seems that Mosca himself felt that the term called for some explaining, for he goes on: "That is a daring statement about one whose name has become synonymous with slyness and duplicity." But Mosca is quite confident that he can prove his case. He tries to do it by examining a few examples from the early chapters of *The Prince*.

The first illustration occurs in Chapter III where Machiavelli attempts to explain why Louis XII lost Milan. Mosca speaks of four mistakes to which the author of *The Prince* attributes the discomfiture of the French king, but only two of them are actually discussed by Mosca: Louis did not make Milan his residence and he did not colonize the conquered land with Frenchmen. How absurd of Machiavelli! "There is nobody who will not see at once," exclaims our author, "that it was impossible for a French king to shift his capital to Milan and to dispatch colonists into a country as overpopulated as Lombardy." [48]

It seems to me that Mosca took "the risk of being taxed with partiality" and lost. For what does Machiavelli really say in the chapter? He observes that, first:

Those states which on annexation are united to a previously existing state may or may not be of the same nationality and language. If they are, it is very easy to hold them, especially if they are not accustomed to freedom; and to possess them securely it suffices [to] bear in mind two things: the one, that the blood of the old rulers be extinct; the other, to make no alteration either in their laws or in their taxes . . .

Second:

But when dominions are acquired in a province differing in language, laws, and customs, the difficulties to overcome are great . . . One of the best and most certain means of doing so would be for the new ruler to take up his residence there. This . . . is what the Turk has done in Greece.

Third:

The other and better remedy is to plant colonies in one or two of those places which form as it were the keys of the land, for it is necessary to do this or to maintain a large force of armed men.

And fourth:

Further, the ruler of a foreign province . . . should make himself the leader and defender of his less powerful neighbors, and endeavor to weaken the stronger ones, and take care that they are not invaded by some foreigner not less powerful than himself.[49]

Now, the first thing to be noticed is that nowhere in the chapter does Machiavelli imply that these four rules constitute a "package." The first solution stands clearly by itself. Of the three others, any one may meet the need of the particular historic situation. Thus the second method was employed by the Turks when they transferred their capital from Asia Minor to Byzantium; the third represents the Roman answer to their problem. Louis XII, who, in Mosca's reading, figures as the violator of both the second and third precepts, does not at all appear to be involved in either case. The only crime for which he is arraigned by Machiavelli concerns the fourth principle —*which Mosca does not even mention.* It was the policy of trusting the wrong allies and antagonizing the potential friends which, Machiavelli says, brought about the collapse of the Italian empire of the French, and that is certainly a point which was worth raising. Mosca's strange omission is, of course, a minor matter, but it may serve as a good example of the subtle ways in which the wind of argument blows where it listeth.

Mosca's main attack is focused upon Machiavelli's idol, Caesar Borgia. At great length our author shows, I believe conclusively, that Caesar was not much more than a pawn of French diplomacy; his greatness lasted only as long as he could rely on the king's military help; each time it was withdrawn, his little robber empire collapsed like a house of cards. At Sinigaglia he succeeded in suppressing the conspiracy of his own condottieri not because he was a genius, but because they were such cowards. In addition they were stupid enough to confide in the most treacherous man of the century.[50]

Agreed. But what does it prove against Machiavelli? We must remember Mosca's reason for discussing Louis XII and the Duca Valentino at such length. They were to be his proof that Machiavelli was the naive, bookish type—not an empiricist. He never saw the real Caesar Borgia; he was dreaming up a myth.

Precisely, Machiavelli's Caesar was, as Gramsci recognized, a myth. A myth may fail us momentarily, as the Borgia failed his Florentine admirer, and yet contain elements of future victory. It is from the defeated pawn of the French king that Machiavelli appeals to his Medicean Prince to chase the French king and all other foreigners from the Italian soil. He was not interested in the man but in the method of the prophet armed, and if the prophet was a bandit, as long as he made an end of all the other bandits that was quite all right with Machiavelli.

But it is at this point that our author moves up his most formidable guns. A myth, as any creed, is made of that stuff which appeals to the generic and not the particular in man. But human action, in particular the kind of action which we call historic, is compounded of a mass of individual and often strictly accidental elements which defy the generic rule. This "factor X" is recognized by Machiavelli when he introduces into his work the old notion of Fortuna. It seems to ill fit his scheme of rational, pragmatic action. Many writers pounced on that concession to contingency as the weak point in Machiavelli's so-called system. Gaetano Mosca does not take that line; his argument is different: "From books one may derive generic knowledge of the human soul, but it is only through experience that we learn . . . something about particular man." The second kind of knowledge is more difficult, "because each human being constitutes a small world of its own, an ensemble of often mutually exclusive elements. Now, Machiavelli excels precisely in the general knowledge of man, while, as we have seen, erring frequently in individual judgment, and his precepts are, therefore, of little practical value."

The range has been found, and the barrage can now begin in earnest: "There is a great deal of truth in his opinions about people, but it is not the entire truth, because he looks only at one aspect of the very complicated passions and manifestations of the human soul. But in practical life, particularly in political life, a partial truth is frequently more dangerous than complete ignorance..." [51]

The gunsights are now trained on special targets: One will readily agree with Machiavelli when he says that one ought to make friends of those whom one cannot destroy. But how, asks Mosca, favor one without being unfair to others who are coveting the same reward? Besides, it is not always possible to reduce to complete impotence those whom we have to disappoint; it takes a great deal of astuteness to discover, among all the discontented elements, the one whom we must fear the most. Machiavelli was right when he said "of men in general that they are ungrateful, voluble dissemblers, anxious to avoid danger, and covetous of gain." [52] But he himself admits that this cannot be said of all men. Also, he forgets to add that even those who more or less match his description are occasionally capable of generous and altruistic gestures. Nor does Machiavelli show us how to recognize those who are morally superior and how to put to good use the small amount of loyalty and decency found even in those who are morally inferior. [53]

Machiavelli, Mosca goes on, expects the impossible of his new Prince when he endows him with both noble and base qualities, when he insists that he seem rather than be good and merciful, that he should inspire confidence and yet break his own word the moment keeping it would be against his proper interest. For Machiavelli "does not tell us how one could attain these contradictory objectives at one and the same time..." [54]

He does not. Indeed, there is a passage in *The Discourses* which Mosca could have quoted, indicating that those precepts represent a counsel of despair, an outburst of impatience rather than the author's most considered judgment:

It will ... be exceedingly rare that a good man should be willing to employ wicked means to become prince, even though his final object be good; or that a bad man, after having become prince, should be willing to labor for good ends, and that it should enter his mind to use for good purposes that authority which he has acquired by evil means.[55]

So Machiavelli knew that he was asking for the moon, but that was what *The Prince* amounted to: a challenge to accomplish the impossible. No work of scholarly sobriety, it was a call to action, to heroic action, an attempt to utilize the force of "splendid wickedness" at work in the new principalities for nobler ends. Was it because, after many centuries of normalcy, brute force had been unleashed again that Mosca was so cool toward the author and discoverer of the new Prince?

Having exposed the impracticability of Machiavelli's rules, Mosca attempts to improve on them. He writes, as it were, a postscript to *The Prince*: "The Secretary of the Florentine Republic might have added that it is one thing to tell lies and another to deceive, and that the first rule in the art of cheating is to use lies sparingly and cautiously." Echoing proverbial wisdom, Mosca declares that "he who lies often is never believed." As he wrote these lines, another writer proclaimed the exactly opposite philosophy, to wit, that any lie will ultimately be believed if only it is long enough repeated; and the bigger the lie, the better. Unlike Hitler's, Mosca's credence is the cultured one of Guicciardini who, "better advised than Machiavelli, recommends to act sincerely as a rule and to employ lies only in important circumstances, which occur but rarely." [56] Not to lie at all may be the most efficient way of telling lies. The author quotes one modern diplomat complaining of a colleague: "That man scares me. He could have confused me easily, if he had wanted to—he told me nothing but the truth." Bismarck, we may add, had used the same technique, when, as a young ambassador to Paris, he told the French Emperor, Napoleon III, quite bluntly what he had in store for him. He was, of course, not taken seriously, which was precisely what he wanted. Bismarck knew that one way to hide your thoughts, not the least effective one, is to reveal them candidly.

So if a lie has to be told at all, it should have an admixture of truth —"just enough to make it difficult to tell the two apart." [57]

So much for the fictitious Machiavelli. His advice, brought up to date by Mosca, may be summarized in a few phrases. The essentials include: a quick, precise insight into the thought processes, the character of other people, the ability to gauge correctly their intentions and their potentialities; to retain self-control at any time and under any pressure; to keep in check passions such as hatred, love, ambition, greed; and to control fear—"above all, we must not know fear." All this has been expressed by Horace in one memorable line which Mosca quotes: "*Aequam memento rebus in arduis servare mentem.*" [58]

Summing Up

If Machiavelli's work were as defective scientifically as it was, in Mosca's view, naive in its psychology, how are we to explain its lasting fame? Some of the Machiavellian influence must be ascribed to "temporary," distinct from the "permanent," components. Of the first type is the figure of religious controversy, the "old Nick" of Protestant and Catholic polemicists accusing one another for two centuries of practicing the evil precepts of *The Prince*. Our author does not tell the story of the Machiavelli legend in detail, remarking only that the erstwhile villain had become a hero to the Italy of the *risorgimento*, the great prophet of her tardy unity.[59]

Both as a villain and a prophet Machiavelli is a figure that exists in time; his reputation, good or bad, can and must be explained from the historic context. The perennial Machiavelli is much more elusive. But exist he did; he or some aspect of him has exerted a timeless fascination on all minds. There are so many Machiavellis that not even a Cassirer could keep track of all, and yet, there is one Machiavelli about whom Cassirer, Burnham, Foscolo, and Mosca all agree. But who can tell him? Who has self-control enough to keep in check his love and hatred when confronted by this most ambiguous, most tantalizing of all authors? Mosca tried, he tried sincerely to remain objective. But the spirit of partiality was stronger, to his great embarrassment. One senses it in his conclusion, which is highly laudatory. But the very fact that Mosca praises not the thinker but the writer Machiavelli is revealing; not what Machiavelli said but how he said it explains his success: the "icy calm" with which he describes what is human, all-too-human; the courageous candor with which he lays bare the faults of the great and lowly alike—these faculties could not but thrill a public tired of the conventional circumlocutions. Here was a man at last who called a spade a spade and who "portrayed humanity exactly as he saw it . . ."

Frequently he only saw one side of it, but that side he revealed with an incisivenes that struck the reader as a truth already dimly felt and now held up to him, a naked thing that made him feel and resent his own nakedness. No wonder people hated Machiavelli, but they loved to hate him, for he dared to speak out their most secret fears and longings.[60]

Machiavelli's very style has that same naked quality: "he does not waste his time with polishing his periods; . . . his supreme concern is clarity; form hardly seems to bother him at all . . ." He sets his thoughts down without worrying about the likes or dislikes of his readers. "Never does he try to sugarcoat the pill." The cynical would-be counselor of princes turns out to be a fanatic of the truth: "The same man who professed to teach his like the art of fraud, who tried to demonstrate that lying was not only profitable but an absolute necessity—that man was, as a writer, one of the most honest of all times." Had Machiavelli been less honest, "he would have done anything but write The Prince, for the true hypocrites of all times and all countries know quite well that their first rule forbids them to reveal their trade secrets to others." [61]

One is not quite sure whether to call all this a tribute or a consolation prize. There is no question about Mosca's absolute sincerity. This study revelled in the demonstration of his own honesty by showing how it often contradicted his own logic and how he refused to compromise where a less honest man would have glossed over difficulties with some facile formula. It is the same bewildered rectitude that makes him praise as well as condemn Machiavelli—praise his honesty, yet, in the end revert to the original position that the author of The Prince is a poor teacher.

Mosca is of course right: Machiavelli cannot tell us how to become good political psychologists and strategists. There is a story claiming that another Secretary, the late Joseph Stalin, kept the little tract for princes by his bed, consulting it before each major move. Poor

Machiavelli! You could not teach the great practitioners of statecraft anything.

But did he really intend to teach them? Mosca assumes that he did. But all depends on how one wishes to interpret one word that occurs so often in *The Prince*. The word is "rule," as it is used, for instance, in the sentence: "It now remains to be seen what are the methods and rules for a prince as regards his subjects and friends." [62] That sounds indeed deceptively like an attempt to define those norms by which princes *ought* to act. But "rule" not only may mean "precept" but also "law" in the scientific sense, description of some regularity observed in natural events. Suppose that Machiavelli had intended to discover the same regularity in human events, that he had tried to do for politics what Socrates had tried to do for ethics. How would he have gone about it? One way for him would have been to limit himself to descriptive statements such as "there are two methods of fighting, the one by law, the other by force." [63] This sentence states a fact and nothing else. But a whole book composed of nothing but such factual statements would have missed its purpose altogether. It would still have shocked the great majority of peaceful, law-abiding readers, but it was not for them that the book was written. If it were to reach the right, the princely address, its language had to be "splendidly wicked." Its brashness, its brutality were all parts of a literary stratagem. For merely to inform the rulers that they did what they were doing would indeed have been "naive" in the extreme. But once we take the view that Machiavelli's purpose was not to teach the past masters of hypocrisy the "rules" of power politics, but, under the pretense of talking out of turn, to reassure them of the soundness of their policy, then Machiavelli's work at once assumes a different dimension.

To let the cat out of the bag would in that case no longer be an act of "indecent exposure" but, quite on the contrary, an act of liberation, not to say of absolution. The new men are given a clean bill of health, they are presented with the gift of a good conscience. By imparting to them their stern duties, Machiavelli is, by implication, stating their new *rights* as well. By brushing aside the objections of the old morality, he clears the ground on which the modern state, conceived in illegality, could grow to be legitimate. *The Prince* was to encourage the spread of an intellectual climate which would make that new legality acceptable.[64]

Thus understood, the novelty and the importance of the Machiavellian work is not its content, not its "revelation" but the very *fact* of it, the act of revelation proper. Mosca almost saw that when he praised the "honesty" of Machiavelli, only to relapse into his old interpretation of *The Prince* as a political set of do-it-yourself instructions. How really "naive" *that* view is—shared by many others besides Mosca—can be seen by a short glance at Mosca's own work. If Mosca's *Ruling Class* were to impart no other mesage except the one that democracy is wrong because you find in all societies a dominant minority and a ruled mass—if that were all that Mosca had to say, his book could be dismissed in a short paragraph. As Mosca says himself, the facts of rule are known, and always have been known, by all.[65] What gives his work its *practical* significance is that it restates these obvious facts, at a critical juncture of history, for the benefit of an emerging elite to whom their own role is still far from obvious. For them *The Ruling Class* could be no more a handbook of political instruction than *The Prince* could have been to Medici and Borgia. What the book could do was to give the new elites not advice, but respectability.

If anything, the work of the man who was called a Machiavellian but who did not himself take to Machiavelli may have helped to formulate, if not to generate, the twentieth-century myth of the ruling class.

13

MORUS TO MARX

The long study of Niccolò Machiavelli was, a few years later, followed by a briefer piece on his contemporary, Thomas More.[1] Though adding little to the immense controversy grown up around the *Utopia,* Mosca's slender opus was not just a casual improvisation. To the author, it looked good enough to be incorporated, with some minor textual changes, into the various chapters of the *History* concerned with socialism.[2] Mosca's essay is a study of the genealogy of socialist ideas.

It is difficult to say which problem was the more important one to Gaetano Mosca: the new pseudo science, Marxist communism, or the "democratic fallacy." In the last analysis, the two problems were but one. In the first *Elementi* Mosca says: "The real parent of the sentiments, the passions, the manner of looking at social life and appraising it that resulted practically in the birth and growth of social democracy was Jean Jacques Rousseau." The same idea recurs in the second *Elementi*: "Communistic ideas ... were, after all, only natural corollaries to the democratic ideas that had already been formulated by Rousseau." [3]

But it is the contemporary, Marxist version of the democratic heresy that seems to present such a threat to Mosca's way of life that in comparison with it Rousseau and his mass-democratic consequences become minor evils. Consequently, references to Marx and his followers abound in Mosca's works; more than one-tenth of the entire text of The Ruling Class is taken up by criticisms of collectivist and other theories of socialism. The theme is literally the "red thread" that runs through Mosca's entire literary life; pronouncements about Marx and Marxism alone would easily fill a whole volume. The title of such volume would have to be "Mosca versus Marx" rather than "Mosca about Marx," for it would tell us more about our author and his animosities than about dialectics and historical materialism.

The reasons for this failure—if it must be called that—of the critic Mosca bear investigation; that it is not due to any lack of effort on his part requires no proof: the fact alone that he devoted a new study to the subject at the age of seventy, with his main work behind him, is sufficient evidence of his sincerity and scholarly persistence.

It is too bad that Mosca did not think of utilizing his resources to make a comparison between the two contemporaries, More and Machiavelli, the great moralist and the great realist. The result might have been a fascinating study in both contrasts and affinities, such as was the recent work by the German, Gerhard Ritter.[4] Mosca almost sees the point of contact between the two authors when he analyzes the third book of the Utopia with its implied message of imperialism: "The modern reader will be surprised by the norms which guided the foreign policy of the Utopians, because it is the foreign policy of England from the time of Queen Elizabeth down to the nineteenth century and perhaps even, with modifications, in the twentieth." [5] The description of the policy of economic penetration and alliances follows, as outlined by More. From there it was not far to seeing in his foreign policy the Machiavellian elements. But Ritter recognized what Mosca failed to see: "Having his Utopians live under a free constitution, More felt certain that their foreign policy too would always be rational and moral...But on closer consideration, even their pacific welfare state reveals its genuine imperialistic character (erweist sich als ein echter Macht- und Herrschaftsstaat); all the daemonic forces which our humanist had tried to banish from the rational construction of his state erupt again in its external policy." [6] In politics, too, the old Roman proverb holds good: *Naturam expellas furca, tamen usque recurret.*

But Mosca is more interested in the genealogy of More's work and in tracing its influence on later communistic system builders. The *Utopia* was, of course, informed by the *Republic*, but More, unlike Plato, retained the family as the basic unit of his social order. A strain of quasi-communistic asceticism runs through the history of primitive Christianity and reappears in the heretical extremism of the Cathari and Albigenses, of the poor men of Lyon, and among some of the followers of Wyclif and John Hus, although none of these movements can be said to have officially endorsed a communist program.

Turning to the period following the publication of *Utopia*, Mosca does not rule out the possibility that the German and Dutch Anabaptists were already influenced by More, because their leaders, Thomas Münzer and John of Leiden, were both "not without some education." But in the main they differed from More in that they rejected all political rule and in social matters appealed to the Bible. The same religious motivation Mosca finds characteristic of the British Levellers. His reference to that important faction in the Great Rebellion is not clear, for on the one hand he does not claim that they were in any way "utopians," on the other hand he seems to think that they were communists, asserting that "their aim, as their name indicates, was the equalization of all wealth." Our author obviously was not familiar with the modern literature which leaves no doubt that the Levellers, in contrast to the Diggers, were not communists but democrats.

What separates More's work from the utopianism of the Anabaptists and the Levellers as Mosca saw them is its consistent secularism. Indeed, in Mosca's view, *Utopia* was the first attempt made after Plato's "to construct a communistic system rationally, without a religious basis." [7] It is for this reason that for a hundred and fifty years More's work remained an isolated feat, until religious passion had burned itself out. In the pale, soft glow of eighteenth-century deism, the religious scepticism and tolerance of the *Utopia* at last came into their own. Whether the Rousseau who wrote the *Discourse on the Origin of Inequality* in 1753 was influenced by Thomas More must remain doubtful, but "without any question Rousseau's fundamental maxim, the preponderant motive of his entire political philosophy, namely, that man is good by nature but becomes corrupted by society—that motive is implicitly contained in Morus' famous book." [8]

In the same year as Rousseau's *Discourse*, appeared the *Basileade* of Morelly, to be followed by his *Code de la nature* in 1755. Both works develop a plan for a communistically organized society. In 1768, the Abbé Mably proposed a kindred program in his *Doutes proposées aux philosophes*. The Jacobins of the French revolution put down the conspiracy of "Gracchus" Babeuf and his fellow communists, among whom the Italian Buonarroti, their biographer, knew the *Utopia* "almost certainly." At least, the work in which he told the story of the movement (published in 1828) described the program of the Equals very much along Utopian lines.

In the case of Saint-Simon our author still maintains his previous reservations. He does not consider him among the ancestors of modern communism and denies that More had any influence on him. "We must," Mosca insists, "distinguish sharply between the more radical ideas of his followers and the authentic teachings of their master." Saint-Simon "was not on principle opposed to private property; his aim was to place the means of production in the hands of those who knew best how to use them, and political control was to be given to the economic and scientific leaders of society." [9]

But in spite of Mosca's conclusion, Saint-Simon will probably continue to be counted among the "utopian socialists"; that is in any case his role in Marx and Engels' *Manifesto*, and most bourgeois writers do agree with them. Schumpeter speaks of "the genuine brand of utopian socialism which St. Simon's ... writings display at its best." [10]

Mosca's catalogue of nineteenth-century utopians included Fourier, Louis Blanc, Leroux, Cabet, and Bellamy. Cabet is branded as "a virtual plagiarist" of More, and Bellamy in turn, according to our author, stole from Cabet, with the greatest of success. "Which goes to show that the efficacy of a book is determined not by its originality or its intrinsic merit but by the degree of intellectual and moral preparation of the public." [11]

Why Mosca failed to mention Robert Owen, probably the most successful of the practicing utopians, is a mystery. Schumpeter, who links the Englishman's experiments with More's *Utopia*, has this to remark about New Lanark: "It might seem that the plan was more operational than More's: there was not only an ideal but also a bridge leading to it." However, Schumpeter then qualifies his praise: "Both government action and individual efforts are introduced as *dei ex machina* . . . No soil was provided for the rose trees—they were left to feed on beauty." [12]

Did the *Utopia* influence Karl Marx? The very question would infuriate the orthodox among the Marxists. Even Mosca hesitates to answer it in the affirmative. He does not go beyond asserting that More's book unquestionably was among the intellectual influences which engendered, in the educated classes, the mentality which regards private property as incompatible with human justice. "But when Marx wrote his *Kapital*, socialist thought had been nourished from many other sources." One of them was, of course, Hegel, and Ricardo's economic theory another. The belief that capitalist competition will abolish competition was already held by Louis Blanc and Ferdinand Lassalle, who also conceived, before Marx, the "law of increasing proletarian misery." But none of the utopians, with the one exception of Leroux who had an obscure notion of it, came to Marx's conclusion that the coming of collectivism was inevitable. This conception, "which contributed so much to the diffusion of Marxism, is certainly not to be found in More or Campanella, nor in Morelly and Buonarroti." (Neither, let us add, can it be found in Marx—at any rate not in the apodictic form in which it is attributed to him by Mosca.) Yet, *Das Kapital* does, in Mosca's view, show traces of More's influence: "I have in mind that part . . . in which Marx tries to trace the origin of capitalistic accumulation in England to the substitution for pasture of grain cultivation in the sixteenth century, a process coupled with the usurpation of the commons by the great proprietors, which caused great masses of now unemployed farm laborers to migrate to the cities and to sell their brawn for hunger wages." It is the same story which More, three hundred and fifty years before Karl Marx, had told in the first book of the *Utopia*.

In the conclusion of his survey, Mosca asks himself the question: Did More take his own Utopia seriously, did he believe it could be put to work, or was it only meant to be a piece of social criticism? Was it just a tract against the new, capitalistic forces unleashed by the Tudor revolution from above? Our author sides with "the majority opinion," which holds that More's purpose was to draw public attention to the grave political and social crisis which convulsed his England. His work was a broadside aimed at the people who thought that those conditions were inevitable. In addition there was, Mosca felt, a streak of literary vanity in Thomas More, a confidence that he could conjure up a state even more logical than Plato's, more in tune with the new age than was *The Republic*.[13]

Without comment but with obvious approval Mosca cites More's own objections to Utopia: it must be the poorest of all countries, since nobody will work very hard—the communality of goods cannot replace private incentives; and how will government be possible under conditions of complete equality? Our author is convinced that these opinions are More's own—he would not otherwise have ended his work by first granting that much good might come from copying Utopian institutions, but then adding wistfully: "this I may rather wish for than hope after." [14]

In a way this is not what our author said before, when he interpreted More's book as an attempt to "stem the tide." The pessimistic end would rather indicate that he had, like some other leading writers of his period, given up all hope in the realization of the perfect commonwealth. His work was an ironic counsel of despair.[15]

The Utopia of Karl Marx

Though Mosca does not claim that Marx owed much to More, it is quite evident that he thought of him very much as a utopian in the wider sense, as postulating something that cannot be realized because it goes against the grain of human nature. When he cites More's doubts as to the viability of an economy without incentives and of a society of equals, he has obviously in mind the Marxian prophecy of the "free associations of producers," each of whom will get a share "according to his needs." Our author is, however, conscious of the fact that such predictions are not simply reckless fantasies of a great demagogue but tuned to several deep-seated human inclinations:

We believe that social democracy threatens the future of modern civilization, yet we are obliged to recognize that it is based on the sentiment of justice, on envy and on the craving for pleasures; and those qualities are so widespread among men, especially in our day, that it would be a great mistake to deny that socialist doctrines have very great powers of self-propagation.[16]

The middle class itself helped to unleash those powers. It was perhaps more than a mere accident that "the publication of 'Capital' coincided with the beginning of a series of extensions of the suffrage . . . Perhaps the bourgeoisie hoped that it would not be difficult to attract the new electors into the lists of the old parties . . ." But the masses understood soon that "political equality did not give them any concrete advantage unless it was accompanied by economic equality, and that the former was only of value to them if it served as an instrument for arriving at the latter, or at least for obtaining some material advantage."

Mosca could have cited Lenin when he wrote that the political class of the proletarian movement was either bourgeois in origin or made up of "self-taught workers who had more or less acquired a culture analogous to that of the bourgeois." The first of these "apostles" were sincere enthusiasts, but to them "were added afterwards, as always happens, the scoundrels, who saw in the new doctrine an easy means of getting on, of becoming conspicuous and of entering parliament. Thanks to the works of both, one arrived at the mixture of noble and ignoble passions, of the spirit of sacrifice and of cruel desire for domination . . . which has always formed the strongest cement of those great human organizations which have succeeded in modifying the history of the world." [17]

Like Marx before him, Mosca knew that many of those "doctors without patients and attorneys without clients" who deserted from the bourgeoisie were, in the main, the victims of the economic process. The pauperization of the middle classes in the wake of World War I accelerated that defection. Although Mosca does not say so explicitly, the meaning of his sociological analysis is clear: "In many countries the middle classes can hardly maintain the margin of economic well-being which is indispensable if one is to acquire a higher education . . ." A diploma from an institute of higher learning was "required for following the so-called liberal professions"; today Mosca would say that one had to look hard for professions which did not demand some sort of a diploma for even the lowliest job. "If that were all, the social harm would perhaps be endurable; but the worst of it is that those professions soon become overcrowded. Middle class elements, therefore, turn more and more to a panting search for public office . . ." [18]

The obvious inference is that the applicant who cannot be accommodated by the ruling class will seek employment with the multiplying party and trade-union secretariats of the growing proletarian (fascist) counter-state. Utopia, in our time, has become organized, large-scale, self-perpetuating operation and manipulation. The manipulated masses are taught, as they always were, to take the masters' words on faith: "The working man in Paris, Barcelona, Milan, the farm laborer in Romagna, the shopkeeper in Berlin, are at bottom no more emancipated from the ipse dixit than they would be if they went to mass, to a Protestant service, or to the synagogue. Instead of believing blindly in the priest they believe blindly in the revolutionary agitator." [19] The organized utopian movement is, in Sorel's terminology, inspired by a myth. Only it is a myth that, to quote Ernst Cassirer, "can be manufactured in the same sense and according to the same methods as other modern weapons—like machine-guns or airplanes." [20]

Unlike Sorel, Mosca sees no reason why a myth could not be analyzed and, if found wanting, be rejected by those who "set above every creed and every interest of party the dispassionate search for a social adjustment that shall represent the greatest good that is within the power of our poor humanity to attain." Believing only in "relative justice," Mosca feels:

. . . it is our right and duty to ask whether, with the realization of the communist system, justice, truth, love, and reciprocal toleration among men, will hold a larger place in the world than they now occupy; whether the strong, who will always be on top, will be less overbearing; whether the weak, who will always be at the bottom, will be less overborne. That question we now answer decidedly with the word "no." [21]

Now, this is indeed a crucial question, equally important to the Marxist and to the "dispassionate" seeker for truth. Our author already assumes what his opponent will most bitterly deny, namely, that the strong will always be on top and the weak always at the bottom of the social pyramid. The Marxist will suggest that many of the strong are, under bourgeois auspices, kept at the bottom and that they should be provided a better chance to reach the top. However, if one disregards that point, there still remains the problem of whether Mosca's question is directed to the right address. For surely Marx did not base his main argument on moral grounds: his ambition was precisely to advance a set of *scientific* propositions showing why the capitalistic system could not last. To talk of "justice, truth, love, and reciprocal toleration" was in his view both "utopian" and "reactionary," an attempt to dodge the real issue. To be sure, the critic has a perfect right to inquire into the utopian elements that one may easily discover in the Marxian doctrine—always provided he considers also, as objectively as possible, its scientific claims. For Mosca, the proud scientist, to treat the theory behind the propaganda talk as a negligible quantity is to underrate the formidable, if one-sided and therefore mistaken, logic of the Marxian system.

With that caveat, the strictures of our author, although not original, make perfectly good sense. His arguments against a future communist society anticipate the kindred views of his disciple, Robert Michels, by fifteen years. The theory of the political class is, in Mosca's view, as applicable to a communist state as to any other type of rule, and therefore what is true of class societies will equally apply to the so-called classless society of Marx and Engels. "Communist and collectivist societies would beyond any doubt be managed by officials." Mosca assumes, as does Michels, "that in accord with the norms of social democracy, they would be elected exclusively by universal suffrage." Knowing that "the selection of candidates is itself almost always the work of organized minorities," we will not doubt the outcome: a small bureaucratic oligarchy ruling in the name of the majority.

The communist objection that the theory of Gaetano Mosca would apply only to class societies controlled by influential capitalists finds him ready:

Those who argue in that manner forget . . . that even in societies organized as they propose there would still be those who would manage the public wealth and then the great mass of those who are managed . . . The administrators of the social republic would also be its political heads, and they would undoubtedly be far more powerful than the ministers and millionaires we know today.[22]

Written twenty years before the Bolshevik October, this prediction is not unimpressive. Later writers could do little but elaborate the argument with the wisdom of hindsight.[23]

Returning from the future to his present, Mosca states that "the strength of the socialist and anarchist doctrines lies not so much in their positive as in their negative aspects—in their minute, pointed, merciless criticism of our present organization of society." And Mosca, as we know, is no defender of the status quo: "Between the service that an individual renders to society and the reward that he receives there is almost always a wide, and often a glaring, discrepancy. To fight socialism by trying to deny, or merely to extenuate, that fact is to take one's stand on a terrain on which defeat is certain." [24] Mosca, therefore, picks a different terrain to make his stand. His answer to the critics of the left, the only one "that can be offered," is as elementary as it is, let us say, disarming:

No social organization can be based exclusively upon the sentiment of justice . . . It is natural that things should be that way . . . Human sentiments being what they are, to set out to erect a type of political organization that will correspond in all respects to the ideal of justice . . . is a utopia, and the utopia becomes frankly dangerous when it succeeds in bringing a large mass of intellectual and moral energies to bear upon the achievement of an end that will never be achieved and that, on the day of its purported achievement, can mean nothing more than triumph for the worst people and distress and disappointment for the good.

In support of this our author quotes Burke, Albert Schäffle, the Italian, Icilio Vanni, and the Frenchman, Maurice Block.[25]

Once more we must remind ourselves that Mosca is speaking here not of More or Fourier or Cabet, but of Karl Marx, the Marx who wrote the *Manifesto* and the *Kapital*—whose interest was not in changing human nature but in showing that political and social institutions change with the productive forces of society, sometimes in a slow, evolutionary fashion, sometimes in a revolutionary leap. But all these changes are not viewed as *caused* by man's insatiable demands for more material power (not to mention social justice); rather his activities both in the moral and material field will be *conditioned* by the social function which he and his class have to fulfill in the collective process. It is this Marx with whom we must come to grips; here is the real challenge for a theorist of Gaetano Mosca's rank. It must be said that he takes his own good time in meeting it.

Marxism As a Science

The section in which Mosca finally gets around to talking about Marxist theory will disappoint the reader waiting for a competent analysis of dialectical materialism or Marxian economics. There are, to be sure, extenuating circumstances to explain the all too obvious fact that Mosca was not well acquainted with his subject. When he wrote the first part of the *Elementi*, the authentic Marx was hardly known in Latin Europe. Georges Sorel, for instance, certainly an avid student of Marxism, for the most part got his information second-hand. In Italy the situation was a little better; there men like Napoleone Colajanni, Benedetto Croce, Antonio Labriola, and Achille Loria knew their Marx *kat'exochen*. But the majority of authors eager to discuss the fearful Lion from the North had to rely on a few fragments translated, more or less faithfully, from the original in some reviews; for the most part they had to take the word of the few experts, or, worse, of the journalists and social-democratic agitators whose Karl Marx was of the bargain-counter variety rather than the truthful image of the ponderous yet subtle scholar of *Das Kapital*. Among those who received their Marx by proxy must be counted our own author. His main source is Loria; in addition he seems to have studied Colajanni. Croce's seminal study appeared too late to benefit the first part of the *Elementi*.[26] And when Mosca wrote the second part, it was too late for him to shed the very strong impressions of his younger years and to begin to really read Marx. In all the

476 pages of *The Ruling Class* one finds not more than one direct quotation from Marx—a fact which would hardly merit notice if the subject matter did not play such a great role in Mosca's mind.

Writing in 1895, he limits his analysis to a discussion of the theory of the class struggle which, according to him, "is based on an incomplete, one-sided and biased examination of history." Our author has no trouble naming instances in which the struggle between classes played no role at all, such as the wars "of Greece against Persia and of Rome against Carthage, the rapid and tremendous growth of Christianity and Mohammedanism, the Crusades and even the revival of Italian nationality called the Risorgimento, which, as Angelo Messedaglia, a witty and learned economist, used to say, was much more due to the influence of poets and novelists than to economic factors."

Although a whole flock of comments may already at this point rush to the reader's mind, I shall ask him to be patient. Let us hear the author's argument in full before submitting a few critical remarks.

After having expressed his agreement with the witty Signor Messedaglia, Mosca goes on to expose the fallacy of the class struggle doctrine by relating how, in the Second Punic War, "the masses in many Italian cities" went over to Hannibal, "whereas the patricians for the most part remained loyal to Rome." Now this would indicate that the class factor, though it may not have caused that great war itself, was not completely absent from it either. But that is not the conclusion of the author. To him, "such a fact is easily understandable. The poor are always more desirous of change, and they also have less political intuition than ruling classes." (We could ask, why did the poor of Naples, why did the great mass of lazzaroni fight to a man for their royal tyrant against the French revolutionary armies? But we promised not to interrupt.) "In the Crusades, too," Mosca goes on, "love of gain was mixed with religious fanaticism. But the presence of an economic factor in a social phenomenon does not mean that it is necessarily the main factor, much less that it actually caused the phenomenon."

So much about foreign wars and their relation to the theory of class struggles. But when we turn to civil wars, "which should be espe-

cially likely to reflect class struggles," Mosca finds the socialist analysis
equally "incomplete and therefore mistaken." History is replete with
proletarian or plebeian uprisings, and "such outbreaks have sometimes been occasioned by unusual and truly unbearable oppression."
But, says Mosca, even more frequently those rebellions came in the
wake of "governmental disturbances, with the beginnings of which
the insurgents had nothing to do, but which offered them a chance
to get arms . . ." What Mosca understands by "governmental disturbances" becomes clear when he declares that those rebellions of
the masses either were suppressed "with relative ease and sometimes
with brutality," or else did not appreciably improve social conditions
for the rebels:

> The only social conflicts, bloody or bloodless, that have resulted in
> actually modifying the organization of society and the composition of the
> ruling classes, have been started by new influential elements, new social
> forces, rising within governed classes (but representing very small factions
> of them numerically) . . . [27]

Examples: the rise to power of the Roman plebs in the fifth and
fourth centuries B.C.; the triumph of the already strong bourgeoisie
in the French revolution. In both cases, the broad masses benefited
from the victory of the "new forces," but, as Mosca insists with
vehemence, "that does not mean . . . that the entire mass of the governed has in fact—whatever the law—supplanted the governing minority or stood so nearly on a par with it that the distinction between
the two has come to an end. Nor will this ever happen." [28]

Next Mosca tries to show at length that Marx has no right to accuse the entire bourgeoisie of parasitism, and he devotes many pages
to prove that superior skill in managing large capitals and labor forces
ought to be rewarded. Thus the Marxist notion of a "continuous and
sinister conspiracy of the rich against the poor . . . seems to be a sort
of persecution mania, to use very charitable terms." [29] Nor should
such statutes as the one passed by the English Parliament in 1339 in
order to keep wages down be taken as an indication of deliberate
wrong-doing (it is in this connection that the single quotation from
Das Kapital appears). Mosca wants us to be charitable toward the
rulers: "What they were thinking *in their ignorance* was that by passing the apposite laws they could either mitigate or prevent the serious

economic disturbances that resulted from sudden and excessive rises in the prices of all sorts of commodities, including the prices of labor." [30]

This will be enough to give the reader an idea of Mosca's approach. We said before that he confines himself, at least in the first *Elementi*, to one aspect of the Marxian system. There is basically nothing wrong with that, as long as nobody is left in doubt about the limited scope of the inquiry. The reader is entitled to that information. If he is denied it, the result is likely to be one of stark confusion or, as in the case at hand, of amused incredulity. Well might that reader ask: "If this is all there is to it, how in the world could anybody take Marx seriously?"

That is, unfortunately, the impression Mosca gives. There are two ways of criticism by reduction. One is to slim down a theory to manageable size, where it becomes innocuous, "safe." This is accomplished by elimination of all marginal claims of the doctrine not essential to the basic proposition. But the whittling process must stop somewhere if the critic wants to use the theory for his own purposes. Otherwise it would become too narrow to have general significance.

The other way is to refute one or some of the marginal claims of the theory and to take this to mean that the whole proposition is untenable.

The second way is Mosca's. He tries to show that the class struggle doctrine cannot be correct because, for one, it does not explain foreign wars. Now the relationship between external and domestic (civil) wars is indeed in need of much more explorative attention than it has received so far. However, this much can be said: no serious Marxist ever claimed that history is *nothing but* the history of class struggles. What he will say is that, if we are to make sense out of the general phenomenon of war, each particular war must be analyzed in terms of the socio-economic structure of the warring systems. He will not be satisfied with general pronouncements about war, such as that men have always fought and will always fight, slaveholders, feudal lords, bourgeois, or communists. The Marxist will insist that each of these wars had and has a different significance. He will inquire why the Athenians sent an expedition against Syracuse and will discover, as quite a few non-Marxists have also found, that Athens had to seek control of Sicily in order to protect a vital supply line of her far-flung economic interests; he will find that she was fighting an imperialist war, and that this imperialism was in turn conditioned by the need to satisfy the demands of the pauperized free citizens at home.[31] The Second Punic War mentioned by Mosca was a traders' war, fought in the interest of the equestrian class in Rome against the strong resistance of the landed aristocracy. The mass desertion of the lower-class Italic allies indicates the crisis caused by the change-over from rural self-sufficiency to a commercial slave economy, the change which soon leads to the Gracchian troubles, and on to the civil wars.

There is undoubtedly a much closer connection between wars and revolutions than our author seems to take for granted. The French and Russian revolutions both came after foreign wars which had exhausted the resources and demolished the prestige of both the French and Russian monarchies. That does not mean their defeats were caused by a social struggle in their countries—the class struggle was still dormant under Louis XV, and no self-respecting Marxist will have the temerity to assert that the underground activities of Lenin's party were responsible for the catastrophe which overtook the Romanoffs. But that is not the point at all. What matters is that Russia was a backward country, totally incapable of fighting the industrial war machine of Germany. Hence, the defeat of Russia was, the Marxist would say, economically predetermined, or, to express it differently: her class structure did not correspond to her industrial needs intensified by war. (The reader is reminded of the fact that the majority of Russian socialists, *including Lenin*, assumed up to 1917 that the collapse of Tsarism would usher in a bourgeois capitalist era. Lenin merely differed with the Mensheviks in planning for his party to administer a capitalist Russia in lieu of a bourgeoisie too weak to do the job). It might not even be impossible to locate a connection between the Cromwellian revolution, whose class character nobody will deny, and the great Continental war that raged for thirty years while King and Parliament engaged in a pre-civil war over the question, among others, of armed intervention. The half-hearted attempts that were made in that direction (La Rochelle) only intensified the feud between the Protestant and patriotic Parliament and the pro-Catholic, neutralist dynasty. A war not fought recoiled to become civil war. The temptation to pursue this line is great, but it will have to be resisted.

The relationship between religion and the economic factor is another difficulty for the Marxist to which Mosca rightly draws attention. But again he underrates the enemy in arguing, more or less like Max Weber, that religion may cause people to act in a way which will be economically relevant without, however, permitting us to say that it is caused by economic reasons.[32] But Marx knew that. So did Engels when he wrote that religion "stands furthest away from material life and seems most alien to it." He explains its origin, of course, "from erroneous, primitive conceptions of men about their own nature and external nature," but continues: "Every ideology, however, once it has arisen, develops in connection with the given concept-material, and develops this material further." Thus medieval Christianity "attached to theology all the other forms of ideology—philosophy, politics, jurisprudence—and . . . thereby constrained every social and political movement to take a theological form." [33]

To say that ideologies are very powerful tools of the ruling class is not the same as charging the rich with a "sinister conspiracy . . . against the poor." Marx never did so charge them consciously: "To prevent possible misunderstanding, a word. I paint the capitalist and the landlord in no sense couleur de rose. But here individuals are dealt with only in so far as they are the personifications of economic categories . . . and class-interests. My stand-point . . . can less than any other make the individual responsible for relations whose creature he socially remains, however much he may subjectively raise himself above them." Thus Marx in the Preface to Das Kapital.[34] And Nikolai Bukharin who, when this appears in print, may very well be re-admitted to the Moscow pantheon of honored dead, has this to say: "The fact that the class psychology is determined by the totality of the conditions of the class life, based on the general economic situation, should not lead us to ascribe the class psychology to selfish interest, which is a very frequent error . . . Class psychology includes many other elements." The pessimistic preachings of the late Roman philosophers, for instance, represented "a psychology of repletion, satiety, of disgust with life" which had "its roots in the parasitic role of the ruling class ... Yet we may not say that Seneca, when he preached suicide, was expressing the interests of his class." [35]

These few examples may suffice to show that, from the time when Engels was forced to explain that there is between economic base and superstructure "interaction on the basis of economic necessity, which *ultimately* always asserts itself," down to Stalin's 1950 *ukase* on linguistics, the whole subject has remained one that caused Marxists a great deal of anguish.[36] Mosca does not seem to be aware of that. Nor does he ever feel the need to understand what made Marx isolate the economic factor in the first place. Neither was he ready to concede that economics (in the broad sense in which Marx employs the term) while not directly causing any culture or religion to come into being, may still influence if not determine its acceptance, as Professor Hook suggests.[37]

Up to this point it is quite possible, although occasionally difficult, to follow Mosca. But when he attempts to prove that class actions of masses simply do not happen, or, if they do happen, lack historical significance, the argument becomes involved. He starts by saying that the masses never stage successful revolutions by themselves, and the historic record would appear to bear him out. There were many peasant revolts in the Middle Ages; they all ended badly, after their first impetus was spent. Matters were different where urban masses rose against their masters. But they were not the true actors either, just the chorus in the revolutionary tragedy. They were the poor who benefited from those "governmental disturbances" caused by "new influential elements." Where did those influences come from? Mosca answers: they were "rising within governed classes," representing only "very small fractions of them." [38]

In Mosca's terms, which are in this connection very carefully avoided by the author: the class struggle does not take place between rulers and ruled but between minorities within the "political class" in the widest sense (comprising all elites, within and without government). The masses never rule. "Nor will this ever happen."

The trouble with this attempt to refute Marx is that it equates the struggle of the classes with the struggle between rich and poor. Now Marx is not concerned with poverty as such but only insofar as it reflects a class relation. Surely the rebellion of the eighteenth-century French middle class against the semi-feudal Old Regime was no revolt of poverty against great wealth. And surely Marx was not naive enough to overlook the elemental fact that people follow leaders, and that masses, classes have their "vanguards."

On the other hand, this is the only instance in his work where Mosca makes that sharp disjunction between masses and minorities. He taught us to think of society as an array of "social forces"—the important interests: war, agriculture, commerce, industry, and science. Translated into human terms, these social forces easily remind us of Marx's classes, as their "ideologies" recall our author's "formulas." And like the Marxian classes, Mosca's social forces closely reflect all the changes, economic, social, cultural, of an evolving civilization. With every new need, new social forces rise to meet the challenge and to ask their share of power of the old established interests. They are spearheaded by the out-elite of the "political class," which is no other than "the most advanced and resolute section" of the Marxian revolutionary class.[39] The struggle between in- and out-elites ends either in a peaceful merger or in a "change of the guard." It is a struggle which goes on forever—or, in any case, as long as the particular civilization lasts (the proletariat is, according to Marx, the last class). That conflict is, according to our author, wholesome if it results in the "balance of the social forces" which is possible only when all the major interests either are represented in the government or, if kept out, are in a position to assert a countervailing power from without. But never are the "dominant minorities" in that scheme divorced from the masses; there is a continuous upward flow of new demands, new talent, new elites.

If that is so, and I believe this summary correctly reflects Mosca's thought, then the distinction between the class struggle and the struggles of the political class becomes rather labored.

Did Mosca draw the line so sharply because he was so uncomfortably close to Marx? It would not be the first time that a work meant as a counter-doctrine should show birthmarks of its origin. As Marx could never cast out Hegel, so perhaps our author was much more indebted to Marx than he cared to know.

The Monism of Marx

"To have pointed out the intimate relationship between political and social structure, between social and political control, is the outstanding contribution of various socialist writers, in particular of Marx and Engels..."

Mosca said this only one year after publication of the first part of the *Elementi*.[40] Had he changed his mind about Karl Marx? Far from it. The quoted praise is followed by a new attack upon the "unilateral" reduction, by Marx, of all social action to mere economics. Engels' famous definition of the superstructure-base relationship is incompletely cited, then rejected in these words:

In my view, the fundamental error of the system consists in establishing a single chain of cause and effect between social phenomena [instead of recognizing that] they form a complex of effects and causes influencing one another. Two equal weights put on a pair of scales will stay in equilibrium without our being able to declare that one upholds the other ... Likewise, a society is an organic whole in which the legal, military, scientific elements are in harmony with the economic system. None of these activities can be said to control and dominate the rest.[41]

With equal right, Mosca continues, one could make a case for half a dozen other explanations and "prove" that the military or the bureaucratic or the scientific or religious type of organization forms the base of the entire society. "But I know better than to do that, since I would arrive at a conclusion similar to that of the physician sold on the idea that his patient's health depends exclusively upon the functioning of his lungs, or his stomach or his nervous system..."[42]

Instead of losing ourselves in such speculations, Mosca says, we should investigate the ways in which, as a civilization grows, the various forms of social life develop and evolve their special organs, classes, hierarchies. By following that method we would find that in each case the ruling class, which always fulfills an essential function, in exchange receives a reasonable portion of the economic yield while at the same time leaving control over the productive process to a separate, distinct group of society.[43]

One more aspect of historical materialism fills our author with "astonishment." That is its assumption that "human events have been controlled, through centuries, by a tenacious, constant will which knew where it was going and prepared the means for the envisioned end..."[44]

That sounds like a summary rejection of Marxist determinism, but then it turns out to be merely one more irritated reference to the assumption that there is something like "a continuous, sinister conspiracy of the rich against the poor, of the leaders against the followers." Such a hypothesis makes Mosca "smile with faint compassion," because every historian worth his salt knows that "the social acts that matter are determined in part by unconscious passions, instincts, prejudices which care little about practical results, in part by interests which ordinarily have an immediate objective, and finally by what we call good fortune."[45]

This is as far as Mosca's Marx critique will go in 1897. While distinguished by the verve and confidence that pervades the whole open letter to De Viti, the analysis itself has not gained much in substance since the *Elementi*. But then the international debate between the orthodox defenders of Marx and his critics had not advanced either; Bernstein's heresy was at that time not yet transformed by Lenin into an explosive issue. Mosca would have found much to delight him in the book of Engels' renegade disciple. As we know, he was intensely proud of having "scooped" Pareto in rejecting all monistic, monocausal explanations of societal phenomena and in proclaiming instead, as his guiding principle, interdependence. But that notion was not his monopoly; it was at that time in the air, and was shared by most middle-class historians and sociologists. Max Weber was to make interdependence one of his methodological assumptions. It was Weber who also ventured forth where Mosca feared to tread and stressed religion as another "independent variable," equally influential and, in some societies and periods, even more important than the economic factor.[46]

In two instances our author's otherwise well-taken criticism must be called distinctly superficial and beside the point. One has already been referred to: Marx did not attach to economic exploitation any moral stigma: Capitalists act as they must. They could not, even if they wanted to, escape the dictates governing them *as a class*.[47] And to accuse Marx, as our author does, of underestimating the irrationality of most if not all human actions is quite a daring feat in view of the great role which ideology, "false consciousness," plays in the Marxian scheme of things. If Mosca could, in 1897 talk in terms of logical and nonlogical action, a distinction later systematized by Pareto, certainly Marx, if not already Hobbes and Hume, had preceded him in that respect.[48]

In the Inaugural Address delivered five years later, Gaetano Mosca, although still not recognizing his indebtedness to Marx, concedes the fact of affiliation while asserting at the same time with considerable pride that his own theory transcends the Marxian system: "The so-called materialistic interpretation of history has been noticeably modified by [my] new doctrine of the forms of government and, I should add, has been enlarged and transformed to such an extent that it has lost its characteristic physiognomy." [49]

This is an adequate description of the critical procedure mentioned earlier, by which an irksome doctrine is reduced to safe proportions. Mosca, it seems, honestly believed that he had penetrated to the core of Karl Marx's system. He feels ready to apply the *coup de grâce*. According to Marx, control over the means of production meant control over the state and cultural predominance as well. But is it really true, Mosca asks, that wealth, property determine all? No, declare "the men who recently investigated the historical development and found out how the various classes came into existence." One wonders whether Mosca was here thinking, *inter alios*, of himself. For those investigators came to the conclusion that wealth helps to make the grade, at least the lower grades, in army, church, and science. They concede that "wealth frequently placed at the disposal of some energetic individuals the forces that make the political decisions, or the means of social action and control; but very frequently it was possession of those means that led to, or made easier, the acquisition of great wealth." The record shows that the capacity to lead in war and peace was "the most indispensable prerequisite for the possession and, above all, the secure possession of all landed property. And for the longest time in many countries the ability to safeguard the material goods essential for human existence, to protect them from rapacious bands, was thought of as a more important task ... than the production of those goods themselves." [50]

But that was in the past. Is this still true today? Or true again? Is force, or, to use Spengler's phrase, is "blood" (or politics) in the ascendancy over the money power (economics)? [51] Mosca is no prophet of imperialism or—at least not consciously—of "Caesarism." But there is definitely a strong antiplutocratic streak in his middle-class mentality. Money, he cannot deny it, calls the tune in modern politics, "but many were the generations in which only the strong became rich and were able to retain their wealth." And in our own time, there is certainly no lack of "intellectual and, even more important, moral forces which have become powerful in politics and which are quite prepared to hold their own against those who control the riches and the armies ..." History repeats itself: "Those propagandists of collectivism who today treat on an equal footing with the great industrialists, with the provincial prefects and, occasionally, even with the central government, they were preceded by those martyrs and apostles who persuaded Constantine to recognize the Christian Church ... and also by those medieval monks before whom feudal lords and sovereigns inclined their knees."

An astonishing comparison! What an astounding author! Between Mosca the engaged and enraged citizen in hot pursuit of the collectivist chimera and the tough-minded historian Mosca, it is usually the former who wins out. Once in a while, however, the detached observer of events prevails, and then we will be treated to an observation like the one just quoted, and trade union leaders will be likened to the martyrs and apostles of Christianity. It is such a complete reversal of accustomed notions, Mosca's notions in particular, that we should not be too surprised if the "collectivists" among his readers did not take too kindly to the beatification of their bureaucrats. They may have felt, in this case, that our author threw the lions to the Christians (or the foxes, as the case may be).

The recognition of the Christian Church by Constantine starts Mosca on another trend of thought: "It could be said and has indeed been said that, once it had established itself as the moral government, the Church put money and the sword into the service of the Cross. That is unquestionably true, and let me add, that it cannot be otherwise: a moral force will always aim to secure for itself all the advantages of physical coercion; the contemporary socialists who strive for the collectivization of production . . . certainly make no bones about their intentions in that respect." [52]

Mosca has returned from his historical excursion to conclude that the road which the social and religious leaders travel starts from faith, from moral prestige, and ends with material power, not the other way around. "And if it is true that the edifice of faith is buttressed and cemented by material interests, it remains no less true that without the sincere enthusiasm and relative disinterestedness of the first dwellers there would have been no edifice at all."

Once more our author has, to his own satisfaction, demonstrated why historical materialism was mistaken: "because it establishes a constant and invariable relationship of cause and effect between wealth and the other means of social influence, whereas the evidence shows a more complicated and reciprocal relationship from cause to effect, and from effect to cause. Thus understood, historical materialism simply becomes a realistic historiography, as it is being practiced, if not elevated into an official theory, by all respectable historians." This is the "modification" of which Mosca had been talking earlier. In its new form, the method of Marx has become "the study of the rapports which exist between the personal qualifications and the moral and material means determining the role of single individuals in a given society, the form of government, the type of the political organization which prevails in it." [53]

There is only one task more thankless and more boring than to demonstrate, at this late date, the fallacies and ambiguities of the nineteenth-century bourgeois philosopher Karl Marx, and that is to expose the fallacies and ambiguities of his critics. In our case that need would never have arisen had our author clearly stated his objective, which was to combat social democracy as a widespread movement representing, in his view, a mortal threat to his kind of society (which also happens to be the society to which the present writer feels attached). Had Mosca limited himself to pillorying the bargain-counter Marx, all would be well. But he extended his analysis to what he thought was the authentic Marx himself. In other words, he engaged in an academic exercise, and that calls for the proper academic treatment on our part. And in accordance with the academic rules it must be said that Mosca's Marx critique is sadly off the mark. He never penetrated beyond the impressions evoked by the propaganda of the Marxist demagogues themselves. The Marxian notion of "wealth" (and its opposite) as capital (or lack of it), and social power as a class phenomenon, remained incomprehensible to Mosca from beginning to end. He rightly sensed that something was amiss with Marxian socialism, that the emphasis on economics was exaggerated, but his way of proving the materialistic fallacy cannot be called convincing.

Believing as he did that "wealth" was simply "having more than others" and not, as Marx saw it, the sum total of the social product, controlled and distributed according to the class relations in force at the various stages of civilization, Mosca thought he could disprove the law "from wealth to power" by referring to the men of war who, with their swords, won power and, with power, riches. Mosca might as well have said that the laws of capitalist enterprise in the United States have ceased to operate because some individuals acquire their dark dominions by the unorthodox method of the numbers racket (to omit the rest). The element of acquisition by force was not unknown to Marx when he wrote of "primitive accumulation," but his major interest was elsewhere. He was studying the normal processes by which goods are produced by the collective laborer; certainly the fact that the great condottiere, Francesco Sforza, made himself the master of Milan by force of arms did not affect the way in which his newly born wealth produced, and it is that way, the organization of the economic order which concerned Marx, not the rise and fall of individuals within that order.

We once before had occasion to point out that Mosca does not always remain loyal to the concept of the group—the only one consistent with his doctrine of the ruling class.[54] Sometimes he argues like a Lockean à la Hayek or von Mises, who regards society as the mere aggregate of human atoms. Once more one may wonder whether it is not his loathing of Marx that makes Mosca define, as the purpose of his own post-Marxian "realistic historiography," the role of "single individuals," and only in the second and third places, of "the form of government, the type of the political organization," without mentioning the word "class" once. And how far the confusion of polemics may go Mosca shows when he accuses "the collectivists" of lacking idealism. Surely, Marx was a confusing as well as confused philosopher, and his mistakes were of the magnitude of his gigantic generalizations. But to accuse the economic and historical materialist of postulating a materialistic view of life is like objecting to a shotgun being used for shooting.

Summary

The second volume of the *Elementi* represents, as far as Marx is concerned, some advance beyond the first part, published twenty-seven years earlier, but it does not add anything substantial to the findings of the "Program of the Liberals" or of the Inaugural Address. Again the impression is that Mosca's superb common sense was hampered by an insufficient theoretical equipment. Otherwise his onslaught upon Marx as historian might have been more effective.

According to the latter, "any change in the system of economic production should necessarily bring on a change in the form of government, in the legislation regulating relations between individuals and between individuals and the state, and even in those religious and political concepts which constitute the moral foundations of the state organization ..." [55] But Mosca is prepared to show that "very important [political] changes have occurred in human societies ... without any simultaneous or approximately simultaneous modifications in systems of economic production ..."

The evidence for this contention looks impressive. Mosca's first example is from Roman history. The change-over from the republican to the imperial form of government took place "without the slightest change in systems of production and without any alteration in the laws regulating the ownership ... of wealth. The only change that did take place, and it was certainly not a general one, was a change in the persons who owned the property." The last remark refers to the great confiscations of the civil wars. [56]

The triumph of Christianity may be called the next turning point in Roman history. That event "wrought a great intellectual and moral revolution in the ancient world ... But it does not appear, indeed it may positively be denied, that any particular changes occurred in the fourth and fifth centuries A.D. in the relations between manual labor and those who possessed the tools of economic production—chief among them at that time was land."

Last, the fall of the Roman Empire in the West, a major catastrophe in the history of civilization, was likewise unaccompanied by any signal changes in the "economic base." It "remained identical before and after the barbarian invasions. Rural serfdom was not brought about by the barbarian invasions. It was already a generalized institution under the Low Empire." The economic exhaustion of Roman society was "a consequence, rather than a cause, of the political decline..." [57] Incidentally, our author compares that event with the collapse of Tsarist Russia but adds that "the Russian disaster will almost certainly have less abiding and less far-reaching effects" than the collapse of Rome. He cites Ferrero's saying that Russia completed in four years a process of social disintegration for which ancient civilization required four centuries.[58] When Mosca wrote those lines, the Communist reintegration of the Russian orbit was still in the future, and although he lived to see it work, he never changed his mind about the matter. Toynbee's view of Lenin-Stalin as the modernizers of a backward outpost of industrial society would not have been acceptable to Gaetano Mosca.[59]

In the Middle Ages, Mosca likewise finds proof for his argument. The city-states of Italy "quite generally developed into tyrannies without any appreciable modifications in systems of production..." In the more recent past, "the modern absolute state was established in France and a middle class began to form, without any important change taking place simultaneously in systems of production... Nor can we believe that there has been any perfect synchronism between the rise of modern large-scale industry and the adoption of systems of representative government, with a consequent spread of liberal, democratic, and socialistic ideas." [60] Parliamentary government in England preceded the industrial revolution. All Mosca is ready to grant is that the economic element represents "*one of the factors* that most largely influence changes in the political organization of society..." And amplifying what he had already said in his Inaugural Address, Mosca explains:

Every great manifestation of human activity in the social field is at the same time both cause and effect of the changes that occur in manifestations of the same activity—cause, because every modification in it influences other manifestations, and effect, because it feels the influence of modifications in them.[61]

This sums up Mosca's case against the Marxist "single-track doctrine." [62] In reviewing it, I feel obliged to point out his occasional forensic aberrations along with the solid points he makes. Assuredly, Rome changed from a republican to an imperial form of government without a noticeable change in the "relations of production." What change there was had taken place before. Had Mosca chosen as his checking point the Gracchian "time of troubles," he might have discovered, with Ferrero's help, how to apply to a specific situation Marx's historic method which, however, was not meant by him to help explain minute variations and modifications of the social system.[63]

Marx never claimed that the rise of Christianity was caused by changes in the economic order. What he could have said was that the ultimate decomposition of the old religious (pagan) "superstructure" mirrored faithfully the economic retrogression of the Roman state. Engels said it for him, and Bukharin after him, in passages already quoted here.[64] Rome's conversion to Christianity was, in their view, only the final chapter in the history of a stagnating slave society, the institutionalization of the *taedium vitae* that tried to escape from an "impossible" reality. Nor would the ultimate collapse of Rome embarrass the historical materialist as much as Mosca thinks. The fact that the barbarization of the West was not accompanied, much less preceded, by an economic change would, to the Marxist, simply mean that Rome had been barbarian all along, and that the Middle Ages did not start with Odoacer or with Alaric. Non-Marxist scholars would agree that a new economic order, feudalism, had already come into being before the political catastrophe showed up the impotence of the imperial bureaucratic system.[65]

Again, the origin of modern absolutism in the sixteenth century and after may not be attributable to a revolutionary change in economic method, but it would be awkward to deny that Machiavelli's

Stato came into its own when feudalism gave way to the early forms of capitalist enterprise. Nor can we follow Mosca when he casually refers to the formation of a middle class without connecting that new class, and the new monarchy, with the new economics—already bourgeois in essence if not yet, for some centuries, in form. At one point Mosca comes close to agreeing with Marx's thesis that the movement in the "superstructure" trails behind the economic process when he says that "beginnings of large-scale industry appear in England during the second half of the eighteenth century, when parliamentary government had been functioning for about half a century; but the ruling class still rested on its old, aristocratic foundations." [66] It is not easy to see exactly what Mosca wants to prove here. First he says that the great economic revolution did not cause the representative regime to come into existence, for it was already functioning. But then he goes on to remark that the old ruling class remained unchanged. And so it did—until 1832, thus, we say with regret, completely vindicating Marx and his law of the "cultural lag."

I have tried to report what Mosca thought of Marx and Marxism —not relishing my role as the occasional defender of a monumental fallacy against a not so monumental criticism. In conclusion, we may ask, what did the Marxists in turn think of Gaetano Mosca? The answer is not difficult to guess. In the Red index his name is anathema, although attacks on the elitist school are mostly aimed against Pareto rather than our author. Nikolai Bukharin formulates the general line when he writes:

The ideologies of the bourgeoisie, insofar as they are compelled to recognize scraps of the "Machttheorie" [the theory of social force, of rule, subjection, etc.] generally extract the revolutionary sting from the Marxian theory, extinguishing the idea of class ... reducing the exploiting and oppressor role of the state to its historical sources and treating contemporary manifestations of this type only as "excesses" and "abuses." [67]

More specifically: "The minority [that is, the bourgeois minority] is that famous elite which representatives of positivist tendencies advanced and will continue to advance as the agent of every intellectual and cultural progress ..." Thus the Soviet academician Tiumeniev. And quite definitely Mosca is a co-defendant when the same

Red critic puts Max Weber in the dock for his "retreat from Marx." For Weber de-economizes history; like Mosca he believes in reciprocity, interdependence of a multiplicity of factors rather than in the unique importance of the economic element. He "slips into the most ordinary pluralism." [68]

The Hungarian Marxist pundit, Georg Lukacs, parlays the same argument into a general indictment of "pre-war imperialist sociology." Its central problem, he declares, was to make capitalism plausible and to make nonsense of historical materialism. Weber did this by "equating technique and economy"; in Weber's redefinition, modern capitalism is "sublimated" as technology and rationalization, while the socio-economic aspects like class and class relations are glossed over. From there Weber went on to sketch a world history of religions, "in order to show that only Protestantism (mainly in its sects) possessed an ideology congenial to that rationalization and distinct from all the Eastern and antique religious ideologies which did raise ethical objections to the rationalization process." Thus Max Weber's economic history became religious history: "he stubbornly refused to let social ethics be conditioned by the economic structure." [69]

To have denied so strongly "the priority of social being, the decisive role of the productive forces" would already be enough to condemn Weber (and Mosca) in the eyes of Marxist orthodoxy as "irrationalist" and "subjectivist." But Lukacs is not satisfied with merely hurling epithets at his opponents. He attempts to show that Weber saw the death trap of irrationality and tried to dodge it, unsuccessfully. His very attempt to escape subjectivism led him into it. Sociology, he held, could be a science only if it shunned all value judgments, limiting itself to "technical critique," that is, to pointing out, together with the means conducive to a postulated end, their incidental but expected consequences. Everything else is, in the view of Weber, outside science, in the realm of faith and hence irrational. And thus "what was intended to be a purge of sociology of all irrational components only serves to point up the irrationality of the historical and social process." It is, therefore, no accident that the problem of leadership was raised precisely by sociologists of countries where a genuine bourgeois democracy had not developed (Max Weber: Germany; Pareto: Italy). No wonder that Max Weber ended up with his philosophy of charisma, in which "the undefinable, irrationalist character of *Fuehrertum* is already in evidence." [70]

Carl J. Friedrich, not suspect of Marxist sympathies, agrees with Lukacs. The elitists "are all offspring of a society containing as yet many feudal remnants," Friedrich writes, and he refers specifically to "the deferential peasants on estates of large landowners in Sicily where Mosca's cradle stood." [71]

It is only fitting that a fellow countryman of Gaetano Mosca should have the last word. Once more the prisoner of Fascism is passing judgment in his saucy manner. Like some other critics, he, Antonio Gramsci, feels that Mosca's main sin is conceptual vagueness:

His political class . . . is a puzzle. [*Puzzle* in the original Italian.] One does not exactly understand what Mosca means, so undulating and elastic is the notion. Sometimes he seems to think of the middle class, sometimes of men of property in general, and then again of those who call themselves "the educated." But at different occasions, Mosca has apparently the "political personnel" in mind [the parliament]. In various instances he seems to exclude the bureaucracy, even its higher stratum, from the ruling class which is assumed to control all appointments and all policy.

Antonio Gramsci does not think much of our author as a Marx expert. Mosca, he says, talks about historical materialism "like a provincial who has vaguely heard of the discussions that are taking place in the capital, without being able to get hold of the essential documents and proofs. In Mosca's case this inability . . . is typical of the academician who will make a great display of scholarship when the subject is a third-rate medieval publicist; but when it comes to studying historical materialism, he will be content to leaf through a few newspapers and pamphlets meant for popular consumption." [72]

Some years later, Gramsci thought that he had solved the "puzzle" and noted in his diary: "Mosca's so-called 'political class' is nothing but the intellectual section of the ruling group. Mosca's term approximates Pareto's *elite* concept—another attempt to interpret the historical phenomenon of the intelligentsia and its function in political and social life. Mosca's book is a gigantic sociological, positivistic farrago, full of an up-to-date tendentiousness which makes the work less tedious and more lively, from a literary viewpoint." [73]

Coming from a Marxist, this is almost a declaration of love. But then, Antonio Gramsci was a most unusual Marxist. His allegiance was for him no obstacle to know a good foe when he saw one and to greet him with a bashfully left-handed compliment.

14

FUNCTIONAL FEUDALISM

Mosca and Rousseau

If the Marxist order of society looked like the nightmare of tomorrow (Lenin's Russia of the day was barely visible yet through the Nordic mist)—syndicalism was, in Gaetano Mosca's view, the clear and present danger which had to be combatted without respite. One glance at the literary record of our author shows that his preoccupation with that movement was persistent through the years; after the advent of Fascism it became almost frantic. "The syndicalist peril"[1] had, by 1923, become a matter of state policy. The corporative tendencies of the new masters looked to Mosca much more dangerous than their authoritarian, dictatorial acts. The syndicalist Mussolini was the real threat, because the functionalization of the social order flatly contradicted Mosca's doctrine of the function of the ruling class.

His syndicalist worries will not seem intelligible to the Anglo-Saxon reader unless he appreciates the importance that particular form of the proletarian movement had in Italy in Gaetano Mosca's time. The heyday of French revolutionary syndicalism had been in the decade prior to World War I. By 1908, when Georges Sorel made his main intellectual contribution to the movement, its momentum in France was already slackening.[2] Not so in Italy where it continued to gain ground among the working class. When "workers' control" was already a thing of the past in revolutionary Russia, factories were taken over and run, for a short time, by their workmen in excited postwar Italy.

There is nothing in *The Ruling Class* to indicate that Mosca actually foresaw a successful syndicalist revolution à la Lenin. His obsession with the syndicalist doctrine was so great precisely because it was, in his view, such an insidious threat. The functionalization of society was, theoretically, not irreconcilable with the old capitalist order. But if it were not a violent reversal of the social system, it would be its radical perversion. For in the disguise of parliamentary forms, syndicalization would perpetuate the domination of society by special economic interests—different, to be sure, from the interests prevailing in a liberal society, but still ensuring the supremacy of the part over the whole. That institutionalization had to be fought because, as Mosca says, "it is necessary to prevent, at all costs, the rise of new sovereignties intermediate between the individual and the state ... Devotion to the national interests must always be stronger than devotion to the class interests." [3]

That is a statement strangely reminiscent of a theorist with whom our author had been at drawn daggers all his life: Giangiacomo Rousseau. The Genevan—almost as distasteful to Professor Mosca as was the colleague and contemporary in Lausanne, Pareto—had expressed his similar aversion to the "intermediate" groups as follows: "It is essential that there be no subsidiary groups within the State." When Mosca comes to the conclusion that "the organization of sovereignty intermediate between the individual and the state ... is perhaps the most serious threat to society that we confront at the present moment in our political life," he merely echoes Rousseau's warning: "When intriguing groups and partial associations are formed to the disadvantage of the whole, then the will of each of such groups is general only in respect of its own members, but partial in respect of the State ..." [4]

At first sight, this agreement with Rousseau seems to make nonsense of elitist notions. The "collectivism" of the *Social Contract* is consistent with its author's individualistic starting point. A government that is to dispense equal justice to all must remove all obstacles which special privilege may raise against the "general will" of society. The result is a polarization process: the emerging individual becomes the isolated individual confronted by a gradually emerging superpower; the removal of the little intermediate sovereigns assures the liberation of the citizens but also, at the other end, the liberation of the state from the traditional restraints. At last, the individual has become a social atom, he and his like are a "lonely crowd," in David Riesman's term, that longs for a new integration. It can be had, at a price. The modern crowd state is the answer, with its artificial associations, now manipulated and directed from above. In Hegel's time, the growing freedom of the people and the growing power of the state would seem not only not to contradict each other but to be two aspects of one great historic movement. It took only slightly more than a hundred years to reach the stage at which the tendencies of force and freedom, have, in all appearance, become opposites.

Now, Mosca, with a very few exceptions, does not begin with the individual. Nor does he ever end with the supremacy of the collective. If "the national interest must always be stronger than . . . class interests," it is, at the same time, based on the recognition of the social *group* as the constituent factor in society. Mosca holds halfway between collectivism and individualism. His "balance of the social forces" is unthinkable unless the nation is conceived of as a plurality of minor aggregations. Thus the power of the liberal state may be, as he tells us, "formidable," but that state will never have the power of Leviathan. The "independent" social forces see to that.[5]

Yet unity there is or ought to be. The crucial task of the "political class" consists in bringing about that cohesion without which civilization cannot grow. Consolidation of the most important social forces in the dominant minority, however, must not lead to a strict separation between ruled and rulers; if there is "conspiracy" among the leading elements, it had better be an open one, excluding nobody who qualifies from joining it.

Understood in this sense, Mosca's "lapse" into Rousseauism is not altogether the apostasy from his own doctrine which it seemed to be at first. But it makes nonsense of the Burnhamite interpretation of society as an arena in which power fights with power for supremacy. Mosca's sharp injunction against intermediate sovereignties would be an oddity if "balance of the social forces" were but a neat phrase to describe the mechanical and ever-shifting equilibrium between hostile power drives. His view of social unity ("the national interest") was predicated on a broad agreement among all about the moral law.

Mosca and Sorel

No wonder Mosca was not fond of Georges Sorel, the one-time syndicalist and all-time pluralist. As elitists, the two men certainly had enough in common. But Sorel had chosen to discover *his* elite outside the middle class. Nor did the friendship between Sorel and Pareto (the two liked to cite each other frequently in their respective works) help to endear the author of *Reflections on Violence* to the author of *The Ruling Class*.[6] The latter work refers persistently to theories with which Sorel is usually associated, without ever mentioning his name. The only mention of the *Reflections* occurs in the *History*, where two chilly pages are devoted to the Frenchman. It is a rather strange Sorel who is presented to the Italian public— all the stranger as Sorel was quite well known to it, much better known, in fact, than in his own country. This is what Mosca has to say about the subject:

Unlike the evolutionary socialists, he sometimes manifested sympathies for the men of the extreme right . . . Sorel does not believe that history is predetermined (on that point he is in open disagreement with his teacher, Marx); in his view, revolutionary violence is necessary to achieve collectivism. For that reason he attacks persistently the socialist reformists who, to be sure, cater to the proletarian vote but, when elected, think that they have paid their debt by some minute reform in social legislation just so they can keep the masses quiet . . . [Georges Sorel was for boycotting parliament]: Instead, the proletariat ought to organize in syndicates and to wear down the ruling bourgeoisie by a series of strikes culminating in the general strike. Once the bourgeoisie was overthrown, Sorel wished to see it replaced by a regime that would be syndicalist and collectivist as well, but the details of the new system do not emerge clearly from his work. As for religion, it must be acknowledged that Sorel speaks of Christianity respectfully, but at the same time he maintains that it is out of date and no longer satisfies modern needs. Christian morality, therefore, must make room for the new morality of the workers.[7]

What Mosca thinks of Georges Sorel will be reported presently, but before doing so I feel the obligation to inform the reader not familiar with the subject that this Sorel of Mosca's is not the Sorel of the *Reflections*. First, a general and brief account of his philosophy ought not to start with the remark that Sorel was in sympathy with "the extreme right." That is less than fair to a man who began and ended his career as a defender of the proletarian cause. It is true that there was a time when Sorel, disappointed in the Left, became for a few months, the patron saint of a small coterie of intellectuals who attempted, in the name of his great love, Proudhon, to fuse the nationalist with the syndicalist tendency (ten years before the Mussolinian amalgam of nationalist socialism reached the market). But Sorel was not for long deceived about the true intentions of the group which, in the main, came from the *Camelots du Roi*— French royalists in search of a mass basis. The old man knew how to separate lost causes with a future in which he believed (such as Vladimir Lenin's) from romantic dreams, such as the highly literary monarchism of Barrès and Maurras and their *Action Française*. In Mosca's Italy the fusion of the extreme left and right turned out to be much more than just an intellectual fad, and that explains perhaps the undue emphasis on what, in Sorel's long career, was a mere episode.

One need not quarrel with a highly simplified account of the Sorelian doctrine as long as the reporter gets the main points right. It is a minor matter that our author should have had Georges Sorel advising the proletariat to form unions. That is to ignore the fact that he existed at the fringe of a vast movement which hardly had to wait for him to tell them to act. The militants not only turned a deaf ear to their self-appointed mentor when he tried to intellectualize their intents—they had their own theorists who were more closely tuned to proletarian needs than was Sorel.[8] Unfortunately, Mosca also fails to grasp the real intent of Sorel's plea: that the workers should withdraw from politics and limit themselves to *action directe*. He does not see the signal difference between Marx and Sorel: the latter wants the proletariat to remain the proletariat, while Marx's working class will cease to be a proletarian class once it has overthrown the bourgeoisie. The defensive character of Sorel's violence as a device to draw the class lines sharper so as to protect the proletariat's class identity—that aspect is as little understood by Mosca as Sorel's conception of the general strike as a "myth." Mosca does not even mention it, although his own "political formula" approaches it quite closely. But perhaps that very closeness was the reason that prevented Mosca from discovering Sorel the moralist. For the *Reflections* make it more than clear that the new proletarian ethics was the one which the bourgeois had lost: frugality, thrift, honesty. Sorel's dislike of representative democracy—compared with which our author's kindred bias is a tame affair—reveals a man essentially no less conservative than Gaetano Mosca, another minor prophet crying in the wilderness of modern decadence and drift.

A Moment of Discouragement

Mosca had warned his compatriots against the drift toward a syndicalist order as early as 1907, when he coined the phrase which gave this chapter its title.[9] He continued to speak out against the danger even after Mussolini had made clear that he intended to incorporate some syndicalist features into his new state. That was an act of courage on the part of Mosca that deserves our admiration. His critique of corporate ideas in turn made it necessary to stress the advantages of the regime which would have to be abolished before those new ideas could succeed. Our author never spoke in more respectful, almost glowing terms of representative democracy than he did after Mussolini came to power. That, too, took some courage, because to defend the "rotten past" was almost as offensive to the Fascist censor as an open criticism of the Duce's blueprint for the future. Wisely, Mosca focussed his attack on that part of the Fascist program which, although he could not know it, never was meant to be more than window dressing. Still, that part was high on the agenda of the ruling party; to lambaste it was a sure way to incur the wrath of the dictator. It cannot have been just accidental that the publication of two forthright denunciations of the syndicalist threat by Gaetano Mosca coincided with his virtual retirement from high office.[10]

Mosca's definition of syndicalism is much narrower than that of Sorel. To Mosca, it did not mean the control and management of industry by the "producers," if that meant the workers. The term had lost all its revolutionary connotations. What was left was the mere principle of parliamentary representation, now no longer on a geographical and individual basis but informed by functional, professional considerations. Represented were not citizens but interests. The deputies would be the messengers of the professions. Such a system would, in Mosca's view, destroy all liberty, or as much of it as the nineteenth century had realized.

The year is 1925 again. Once more Mosca returns to his old hunting grounds. It was still the same place, teeming with a great variety of feral beasts of prey—equalitarians, democrats, and hordes of socialists of motley colors. In the prevading gloom the hunter barely can make out the two lead animals, Jean Jacques and Karl; sometimes they seem to be one and the same most terrible scourge of mankind. The hunter raises his good gun, his hand is as firm as that of a man of thirty, his aim as secure as ever.

But suddenly the gun is dropped. What is the use of fighting, at this late hour, the old battles, what the use of laying low democracy? Democracy is dead already. It has died in Italy; soon it may be extinguished the world over. Gaetano Mosca feels incomprehensibly sad. He had been such a great killer of democracy in his own time. Should he have acted otherwise, should he have kept away from the big hunt? But then, in his time, there had been no mob—in fact, he had been quite a lonely hunter.

Now, as an old man, he was once more a lonely figure. That was because he refused to go on playing the old game. He could not help it: the thrill was no longer there.

All this of course cannot be said aloud. But this much can be said:

It is now useless to debate whether the elected deputies do represent and really can represent the thoughts and aspirations of the voting majority. Its freedom to select the candidates has been usurped by parties and electoral committees. Yet those candidates, if they know what is good for them, will keep those thoughts and interests of the electorate in mind. Parliament may or may not be truly representative of the popular will—the fact remains that it is made up of the majority of the controlling forces of the country. It is today the sole organ which can keep in check the government and its bureaucracy. The latter has increased its powers as the state has taken on new duties, and it would rule uncontested if not for the daily press and the existence of elective bodies outside the great bureaucratic class.

No, Gaetano Mosca has not changed at all—the times have changed, and what had once looked quite sinister now seems to be comparatively harmless. In fact:

Although the representative regime is not, as the official dogma has it, the rule of the popular majority, yet of all types of government it is the one in which the rulers on the whole will be affected by the sentiments of the majority, the one which furnished the best means of judging and debating governmental acts. In other words, it is a rule of freedom, to the extent in which that term can still have real meaning in our time of super-states with their immensely complicated structures.[11]

This resounding vindication of free institutions does not have the ring of a post-mortem. Representative democracy, for sure, "has lost a great amount of its prestige." [12] But of the dangers that confront it, only one is really a subject of concern to Mosca.

What are the alternatives to liberal democracy? They are three in number, the "three perils" of the second *Elementi*.[13] One answer may be "bureaucratic absolutism." But it is the form "less likely" to prevail, for "a society hardly ever reverts to an outworn type of government." If it does so, then it would be only for a little while, in order to cope with a serious crisis. In that case, bureaucratic absolutism would be a stop-gap solution leading to still other forms of government, or else to a revival of the liberal state. Democracy, it seems, does not belong to the outworn forms of government to which society is little likely to return, for Mosca says that it may "come out of the momentary crisis with invigorated strength." His good friend, Benedetto Croce, has voiced the identical conviction in words of great power: "The liberal state alone seems to rise again time after time, always with the vigor of youth. It seems so, but in reality it does not rise time after time; rather, it never dies. It is the only type of state capable of 'restorations'..." [14]

In Mosca's Italy the "momentary crisis" lasted more than twenty years, and Mosca did not live to see its end. But he was right, as Croce was right, insofar as Italy has in fact returned to liberal democracy. But whether the regime has gained in vigor remains to be seen. Its renaissance in any case explains the renewed interest in Mosca's work. A—regrettably anonymous—reviewer states the reasons well enough to justify our quoting him at length:

> The restoration of democracy in Italy and the subsequent development of a political situation increasingly dominated by two powerful tendencies, the clerical and the revolutionary, present so striking and close a repetition of the pattern of political evolution in that country before the introduction of fascism that Italians sometimes feel they have been allowed to put the clock back and are now living through the alternative to their experiment in dictatorship. The politics, the doctrines, and even the polemics of the generations between 1870 and 1914 have become the focus of attention both for the student and for the general public, and appear at times not only to fascinate the imagination but actually to influence the conduct of the protagonists in the present political scene. It is not surprising, therefore, that the more serious publishing houses should vie with one another in producing or re-editing the works of the men who originally set that scene or first began to analyze the weaknesses of the Italian parliamentary system.[15]

Most Likely to Succeed . . .

As early as 1897 Mosca had singled out the two powerful tendencies, the clerical and the revolutionary.[16] In 1925, only the latter seems important enough to hold his attention. And of the revolutionary currents it is syndicalism which has Mosca worried most, because, unlike that Russian attempt "against human nature," it seems to be based on some incontrovertible facts of industrial society as it had evolved during the past century:

> I recognize at once that the [syndicalist] solution is the one most likely to succeed because the other two are founded on ideas and sentiments which in a not too distant future can be modified since they are the results of variable or, as one says today, contingent social factors. In

contrast, syndicalism is the result of stable conditions which have been maturing during the second half of the nineteenth and in the first few decades of the twentieth century—conditions which are unlikely to change for a long time to come.[17]

What Mosca has in mind is the extreme specialization of production and exchange, with the concomitant extreme dependence of the many (as consumers) on the services of relatively few but powerful monopolies. Our author is particularly worried by the growing social influence of Labor; he points out that a few strategically placed trade unions could acquire a real strangle hold on the entire economy.[18] It is, of course, perfectly clear to him that the increased significance of Labor follows from the structural and technological mutations which have taken place in modern industry. As Bernard Shaw says, the trade unions are the capitalism of the working class.[19]

Now, Mosca is aware of the strongly plutocratic nature of contemporary democratic society; he is quite vocal about war profiteers and the new rich of postwar Europe.[20] But the political role of industrial and commercial wealth is quietly accepted by him, if for no other reason than that it had played the same role in the past. With Labor it was different. The nation- and world-wide organization of trade unions, affiliated with large, proletarian parties was a new phenomenon in Mosca's life. He was quick to enlist it for his theory. It was only consistent that Big Labor should wish to translate its economic influence into political terms, that it should ask for admission to the ruling class: "Since there is no social force which would not simultaneously aspire to becoming a political force, one of the elements politically in control of society, it is not surprising if the proletarian syndicates today want to send their own representatives into the sovereign national assemblies." [21]

If not surprising, it was nevertheless shocking. For from entering the national assemblies it was one mere step to the demand to do away with the traditional organization of the franchise and to substitute for it the principle of functional representation. Mosca could not know that Mussolini's corporative parliament would include both entrepreneurs and workers, nor that both would in fact be the appointees and stooges of the ruling party. In his book, the syndicalization of the legislature could mean one thing only: proletarian victory. Achieved by strictly legal means, it would nevertheless be no less revolutionary than the Bolshevik October.

Mosca somberly proceeds to sketch in the details of his own 1984: syndicate membership would be mandatory; the trade union bureaucrats would have the power to admit or to exclude the rank and file at their discretion. At the same time, unions would be recognized as the exclusive bargaining agents in their dealings with the other side. In short, they would have full-fledged sovereignty internally, and quasi-sovereign status in their diplomatic negotiations with the representatives of Capital. "It would be the revival of all that was destestable and harmful to the public interest in the organization of the medieval guilds." No longer are the labor leaders the successors of the Christian martyrs and apostles; rather we would have "the restoration of those intermediate sovereignties that stood between the individual and the State, so typical of feudalism and other badly organized regimes, some of them primitive and some degenerate . . ."

A premature Westbrook Pegler, Gaetano Mosca is disturbed by the despotic aspects of the new monopoly. The little fellow, "expelled from, or not admitted to, the syndicate, would have no way of exercising his profession. Faced by the prospect of starvation, he would have no choice but to put the demands and regulations of the union above the prescriptions and laws of the public power." Once the right to work was done away with, there could be no limit to the arrogance of the New Feudalists. "Just as the medieval barons had been on an equal footing with their kings, so the big union leaders, in particular if they should band together, would treat with the government as independent powers do . . ."

In parliament itself the influence of the trade unions would be overwhelming. They would have their proper representatives, and these would necessarily represent the interests of their organization rather than the public interest. Worse, the trade unions, besides having their own spokesmen, would most likely have the last word in the choice of candidates, to be elected on the basis of the present, individual system of representation (Mosca has in mind a period of transition to a fully functionalized parliament). The rule that the elected of the people should vote in accordance with their own best judgment would become a mere pretense, and deputies would simply act as messenger boys carrying the orders of their labor bosses. Nor is there any reason to expect that the trade unions of the intellectual classes could exert an efficacious counterinfluence against, say, railwaymen or longshoremen. They would not, because "the political force of a class is proportionate to numerical strength, to the indispensability and urgency of a specific function rather than to intellectual training or acumen. A strike of railwaymen or longshoremen has more severe reverberations than a strike of lawyers or schoolteachers—the only intellectual group in a position to stage an effective strike being the one which, for humanitarian reasons, never could refuse to serve: the medical profession." [22]

What a far cry this is from the "disinterested" cultural elite which Gaetano Mosca had extolled in both parts of the *Elementi*. Now he knows, and the experience of the British Labour Party bears him out. The power of its intellectual wing is negligible in comparison with that of the large unions. Their numerical preponderance, together with their control of the purse strings, is enough to keep the Labourite intelligentsia at bay. The only flaw in this example is that Mosca apparently did expect the educated members of the syndicates to act as a conservative, restraining element. But the majority of intellectuals in the British Labour Party are far to the left of the half-dozen key trade unions which control the votes in the Executive.

Tomorrow Is Today

Most writers of contemporary "negative utopias" will project their social criticism into a safe, remote future, while of course portraying, or purporting to portray, the ugly face of present-day society. In Mosca's case, the process seems reversed. His picture of a syndicalist future appears to be free of all suspicion that some of the fancied vices of tomorrow's neo-feudalism might be those of his own liberal society. Thus, when he voices fears that the professionalization of the representative regime would leave the public interest unrepresented, Mosca takes for granted that it can be and, in fact, still is determined, by discussion in and out of parliaments in the meandering way of the liberal tradition, wherever it is permitted to exist. But the very fact that Mosca wrote *The Ruling Class* would indicate that this consensus was no longer to be had in Italy, or even that it never had existed. It is highly doubtful whether it exists today in Italy or France, although both countries are in fact democracies. We keep our fingers crossed when we think of the resurrected Germany. The public interest, so we believe, is still articulate in these United States and also in Great Britain, not to mention some of the small democratic countries. But the influence of pressure groups, such as Big Labor or Big Industry, on the representative assemblies had been a decisive factor long before *Il Duce* thought of substituting corporate organizations for the older type of parliament. The problem, then, would seem to be not, as our author puts it, whether or not we "ought to hand over the sovereign organs of the liberal State to the syndicates," [23] because vast economic interests, comparative if not superior in strength to the syndicates, already occupied informally the sovereign's seat of power. Mosca knew that this was so: "Yes, the power of the syndicates is a true danger, but it is a danger *in re ipso*: it lies in the very economic constitution of our present-day society." [24]

The real question, therefore, was what could be gained by formalizing those great, already existent 'dangers": whether the legalization of the new *de facto* sovereignties, created by the only real, the industrial revolution of our age, would reinvigorate the representative regime and give all elements of the new mass society a sense of being truly represented.

It is not up to us to offer an opinion on this subject which is still undecided. Our author has no faith that anything would be gained through the syndicalization of the democratic order. No use getting panicked into radical decisions which, once made, cannot be easily undone. Our present system, he says, like all forms of government, is bound to change, as the conditions, economic, intellectual, and moral, out of which it was born change. And before we can think of changing anything, let us restore the bulwark of free institutions:

Ten years of peace, external and internal peace, will almost certainly heal the wounds of that middle class, which forms the indispensable substratum of the representative regime; to work for that recovery, or at least not to hinder it, is the most urgent task of European statesmanship.[25]

If in the past our author had occasionally shown a tendency to rely on small, technical improvements of the governmental apparatus (a penchant of which very little was made in this study), he now no longer takes the gadgeteer's approach. Not changes in the administrative or constitutional mechanics, but the restoration of prosperity in general, and of the middle classes in particular, is the first article of Mosca's faith. That faith is based on the experience of a lifetime showing that "the present organization of society has immense powers of resistance." [26]

Mosca's confidence in the resilience of the European middle class was not unjustified. Had he lived longer, the amazing comeback of the German bourgeoisie after the last destructive war might have served him as an excellent example. And is not the bourgeois way of life asserting itself even in the Soviet Union?

But granting him that much, one would have to point out to Mosca that the middle class of the mid-century is no longer the middle class he knew. And that is true not only of the European bourgeoisie. The literature about the new American middle class is ample evidence that it is a world-wide phenomenon. The economically independent but comparatively small class which was able to assert its independence against the encroachments of the state bureaucracy has given way to a new stratum which is broader than its predecessor but no longer independent. Only it is not so much the bureaucratization of our public life (the only one which Mosca knew) that is responsible for the dependence of the modern middle class as the bureaucratization of our private lives, the rapid growth of large-scale business enterprise with their innumerable "service industries." [27]

The implications of this signal change are serious for the validity of Mosca's theory. The new middle class—will it be the same mainstay of free government as had been the old middle class of Gaetano Mosca's youth? We can here only raise the question and refer the reader to those writers who suggest that there may be an intimate connection between the phenomenon of the New Clerks and the phenomenon of fascism. If Mosca's elite was the educated section of an economically healthy middle class, the fascist elite that succeeded it came from an economically sick, disgruntled bourgeoisie fused with plebeian elements likewise disgruntled: disappointed revolutionaries like Benito Mussolini, or displaced asocial elements like Adolf Hitler.

Fascist tendencies, however, are not limited to economically insecure societies: the combination of dependence and security may prove to have an equally corrosive although not quite so overt effect. It may not show at all in the political domain; in fact, that may be its most damning feature. If it is true that our malaise, our growing sense of insecurity is due to technological rather than economic factors, then the Moscas of tomorrow had better be industrial therapists and mass psychologists instead of students bent on the unraveling of politics.

But if this is beyond the scope of Gaetano Mosca, his intense hostility to the proposals of industrial government remains a puzzle. For that system had been advocated by the thinker he admired above all others, Saint-Simon. The only reason we can think of to explain our author's apostatic lack of faith in technocratic government is his known, constitutional aversion for, and disbelief in, all attempts to interfere with human fate as it unfolds in the mysterious course of history.

15

LESSONS OF HISTORY

A very old man sits behind his desk and meditates. He has much time, too much time on his hands. His political career ended long ago, and now he is not even teaching any more, because of age. That is a shame because his mind is as alert as ever. If anything, his interests have become broader. Politics has lost much of its fascination. The noise of world affairs just barely penetrates the ancient's consciousness; it is a rare day that makes him take notice of such an ephemeral event as a Romanian plebiscite. The date is February 6, 1938; the great crisis leading to World War II is already in full progress. Gaetano Mosca briefly comments: "I remember that I wrote and published, back in 1921, an article entitled '*I fattori della nationalità*' in the *Rivista Europea*, where I said that plebiscites are only good to sanction an accomplished fact but never to accomplish something new."

This possible allusion to the technique so dear to all Fascist rulers is the final entry in a notebook posthumously published after the war.[1] It shows how little Gaetano Mosca, almost eighty at the time of writing, bothered about the slight matter of chronology. For his essay on "The Elements of Nationality" had seen print not in 1921 but in 1882; in fact, it had been the first publication of our author,

332

then aged 24. A difference of forty years—but what are forty years to one whose mind was roaming across five millennia of the human race, a mind at home in Plutarch's rather than in Mussolini's Rome. The Duce is not even mentioned in these notes, which were not meant for publication, unless this remark refers to him: "We have a characteristic case of the Living Lie when a statesman pretends to feelings which he does not have, for instance, when a man of authoritarian disposition, who would instinctively despise the humble folk, is member of a democratic party and as such is forced to profess adulation for the very people he despises from the bottom of his heart."

Immediately below appears another, even more suggestive reference to the forbidden topic: "I read somewhere that Clemenceau once defined as a symbol (I would have said a myth) the statesman to whom the great public ascribes qualities which he does not possess. I have been sufficiently familiar with Italian politics to testify that they abounded with such myths or symbols. I should like to add that the best instrument for their creation is the daily press." [2]

But these quips are the only ones that bear upon the Fascist present in which Mosca lived, and they are carefully embedded in a lengthy disquisition on the art of deceit. Fifteen years earlier, when writing about Machiavelli, Mosca had suggested the same "most important topic" as a subject for a book. "It is not likely to teach the successful liar anything he did not know before, but it might be of some slight profit to his victims." [3] The same notion recurs in the diary, the wording is identical and followed by this postscript: "A book of that sort would assuredly be a most moral book ..."

Did Gaetano Mosca plan to write it? One section of the notes is headed "Lying and Deceiving," another treats of "Hatred and Revenge"—"the political philosopher yields to the moralist," observes the editor, Donato, in his commentary.[4] Mosca's pithy maxims sometimes sound like saws out of a copybook:

He who wants to deceive must use lies very parsimoniously and with great caution. Parsimoniously, because the frequent liar will not be believed; with caution, because it is very dangerous ... to be caught *in flagranti* ... Very clever people know how to deceive without telling outright lies: they merely twist the truth, they color it and thus create the intended impression in the other person's mind . . . A lie has over a truth the great advantage that it can accommodate itself to the tastes of the audience, something which the truth, given its inflexible and rigid character, can never do . . . I read once in a book whose author and title I forgot, that in an argument you can tell the truth only once but an infinite number . . . of lies.[5]

These perceptions are probably the leavings from a draft which Mosca had used for his study of *The Prince,* and a direct quotation from the Secretary speaks for that assumption. But one remains curious. Why was Mosca so infatuated with the problem of deception? Would it be far-fetched to say that he considered it the problem of his time? Was he perhaps attracted, if that is the word, by the phenomenon of the totalitarian lie; was Mosca fascinated by its evil power?

Seen in that light, the ramblings of an ancient man take on a different, much deeper meaning, and those excerpts jotted down at random become the deliberate attempts at reinforcing long-held, sacred certainties against the nagging doubts that come with the oppressive isolation of defeat. From a French text of Stubbs' *Constitutional History of England* Mosca culls these bitter lines: "Political freedom is nothing natural. Natural are violence, oppression, and the will to power. Liberty can be achieved only by a refined civilization. In its infancy, civilization needs the inspiration of an ethical ideal which is slow in forming. The control of savage instincts assumes a degree of reasoning of which the people of the Middle Ages were incapable." [6]

In copying these lines did Mosca see the writing on the wall? Did he intend to say that the new Middle Ages are approaching? That ours is a century of new barbarians? Possibly. To anyone born in the nineteenth century (which ended in 1914), the *ricorso* following World War I must have come as a most surprising shock. But it is also possible that Mosca copied those lines from Stubbs precisely because they confirmed a truth which he had always known: that liberty is the last flower of civilization. What else had he done but to embroider that old thought of the precariousness of freedom? What else was the meaning of his "balance of the social forces," predicated on acceptance, by the rulers as well as the ruled, of common standards of morality, suggested by a telling "formula"?

That communal acceptance, Mosca notes, is slow in forming, and it is at all times threatened by eruptions of new forces, new demands. If they remain unchecked, if the "political class," which is, or ought to be, reason holding back the savage instincts, should permit *imperia in imperio*, there would be a sharp acceleration in the rate of social growth, but at the cost of social unity. Only societies which manage to retard the upthrust of new social elements and to assimilate them in an orderly and gradual manner have a reasonable chance of survival. But if the rate of absorption is too slow, the pressure of new forces may become too great to be resisted.

In either case the blood transfusion by which the political class keeps alive, Pareto's circulation of elites, is no automatic process. It requires what Stubbs called the degree of reasoning which can be found only in a mature society. The question is, can that maturity be achieved by a conscious intellectual effort, or must it remain a happy gift, a wisdom which relies on instinct and good luck, but cannot be expressed in any rules which the political and social scientist may try to foster in the public mind. In Mosca's words:

Will progress in political science some day enable mankind to elimi-nate, or even to attenuate or make rarer, those great catastrophes which, from time to time, interrupt the course of civilization and thrust peoples that have won glorious places in history back into barbarism, be it a rela-tive and temporary barbarism? That is a most important question. From the practical standpoint it may be the most important of all the questions with which political science is called upon to deal.[7]

The section in *The Ruling Class* which deals with this "important question" might have been entitled, after one of Lenin's revolu-tionary pamphlets, "The Threatening Catastrophe and How to Fight It." A slightly different version of the answer appeared as a contribution to a scholarly symposium in the thirties.[8] The quest for salvation, the search for a truth revealed by history continues unabated in the last notes left by Gaetano Mosca.

Something else, of slightly lesser relevance than the salvation of society but still important, depends on the answer: the validity of Gaetano Mosca's doctrine of the ruling class. For what he likes to call "the level of civilization," the degree of social evolution, is the factor which, finally, determines also the political and moral level of the ruling class. And vice versa: the "political class" shapes, or is supposed to shape, the character of the society which it controls. It will receive the grade of good, or excellent, or merely fair according to its aptitude, or lack of it, to meet the problems of its day and generation. The "virtue" of the ruling class, then, is a variable. How do we measure it? How are we going to determine whether a particular regime is equal to its tasks? The only yardstick recognized by Mosca is the one which also takes the measure of the "level of civilization." If it is high, the level of the ruling class is also likely to be high. But when *is* the level of civilization high? Must we assume that higher stages are reached as civilization becomes more complex? It looks that way, for Mosca tells us, via Stubbs, that only "refined" civilizations achieve "liberty." And liberty is Mosca's *summum bonum*. Now, assuming that we could agree in that respect, all would be well. But if we should discover some societies in history which had refinement without freedom, and then others which were free but not refined, what then? For if we are deprived of the criterion of liberty, the only one suggested by our author, what is left? All we can say is that the level of civilization is reflected in the character and composition of the ruling class which is, in turn, conditioned by the level of civilization reached by the particular society. We are moving in a circle.

Iron Laws and Constant Tendencies

These are some of the problems, difficulties, ambiguities which puzzle Mosca. Knowing what he thinks of Vico, Comte, and Marx, we should expect him to be chary of proclaiming any Iron Laws of history. The following is fairly representative of his approach:

We are inclined to think that just as human beings, or at least the great human races, have a constant tendency toward social grouping, so too they have equally constant and powerful psychological tendencies which impel them onward toward ever higher levels of culture and social progress. Such tendencies, however, operate with more or less vigor, or may even be stifled, according as they find physical environments— complexes of circumstances that might be called "chance"—which are more or less favorable, and according also as they are more or less hampered by social environments, in other words by psychological tendencies equally universal and constant.

"Chance" is explained as "a chain of circumstances that escape human control and foresight." The outcome of a single battle, Mosca says, has in the past decided the fate of a nation. His examples are Plataea, Zama, Jerez de la Frontera, Poitiers, and Hastings.[9] But they are not too convincing. Was the outcome of Plataea or of Zama really an accident? Was not the fate of Carthage as good as decided at the time when Hannibal had to withdraw from Italy? Was Visigothic Spain or Saxon England not ripe for the conqueror? Poitiers may be a better case in point, but who can tell today whether an Arab victory would have decided Europe's fate for good? Would it not be more profitable to treat the "decisive" victories of history as consequences rather than as causes?

There is no thinking possible without some generalizations, and so Mosca's "constant, universal tendencies" will not unduly shock us, as long as he recognizes enough countertendencies which may, and do, as he asserts, deflect the course of history from any predetermined and "inexorable" end. We willingly grant that the human race has "a constant tendency toward social grouping." Nor are we likely to balk at the statement that unfavorable physical and social factors often thwart the group instinct. Montesquieu, whose theory of the milieu had been so critically treated by our author, had already said as much, anticipating Toynbee's theory of "challenge and response." But how are we to measure the success of the historic tendency toward more complete integration, not to mention again that most bothersome word, quality? Merely to speak of "psychological tendencies" impelling mankind "onward toward ever higher levels of culture and social progress" not only reminds one of the unilinear theory of history so dear to the positivist mind, but it lays Mosca open to the same objection which has been raised against Friedrich Engels' saying that "a perfect society, a perfect state are things which can only exist in the imagination. On the contrary, all successive historical situations are only transitory stages in the endless course of development of human society from the lower to the higher." The first sentence with its curt dismissal of progressivist idealism is an insufficient alibi for Engels' fervent, if relativistic, faith in progress.

How, asks one of many critics, "can he speak of historical evolution from the 'lower' to the 'higher' without some criterion that is outside historical development, i.e., an absolute existing 'only in the imagination'? How can we test this alleged progression if we have no definition of 'higher' that is independent of the process itself?" [10]

Mosca, too, was found by us in the same hesitation between absolute and relative standards; we found also that he was quite unaware of it. Sometimes he seems to sense that something must be done. Then the result may be a compromise, as in the case where he divides all states into two types, the feudal and the bureaucratic, cautioning the reader:

> This classification, it should be noted, is not based upon essential, unchanging criteria. It is not our view that there is any psychological law peculiar to either one of the two types and therefore alien to the other. It seems to us, rather, that the two types are just different manifestations, different phases, of a single constant tendency whereby human societies become less simple, or, if one will, more complicated in political organization, as they grow in size and are perfected in civilization. Level of civilization is, on the whole, more important in this regard than size . . .[11]

The denial of "unchanging criteria" by which feudalism and bureaucracy may be distinguished ends with the establishment of one essential, unchanging criterion which they share. It is the tendency of growth in size as well as in perfection. What is the criterion for perfection? We are told that perfection is another word for "level of civilization." We are back at the beginning.

But we must not quibble. It is perfectly clear what the author has in mind; he never doubted that the highest level of civilization was reached a hundred years ago under the rule of liberal democracy. This is the standard absolute which can be realized because "in large, highly civilized societies, which are held together not only by moral and intellectual affinities but also by strong and complicated political organizations, a much greater speculative and affective freedom is possible than in small and loosely organized societies."

The emphasis on unity is again undeniable. Society is not a mechanistic aggregation of wills; free thought and choice are predicated upon the fact of political and moral integration. But as there is freedom within unity, so unity in turn depends on freedom. The political organization reflects the complexity of underlying healthy tensions; it comprises a "large number of currents of ideas, beliefs, and attachments that succeed in asserting themselves—by the formation of different intellectual and moral crucibles within which the convictions and sentiments of single individuals are variously fused and alloyed." [12]

These conflicts, however, between the ideological and social groups might easily lead to disintegration, if not for another "constant tendency" of human nature which makes for cohesion and allegiance:

There can be no human organization without rankings and subordinations. Any sort of hierarchy necessarily requires that some should command and others obey. And since it is in the nature of the human being that many men should love to command and that almost all men can be brought to obey, an institution that gives those who are at the top a way of justifying their authority and at the same time helps them to persuade those who are at the bottom to submit is likely to be a useful institution. [13]

The din of Iron Laws has by now grown to such proportions that it takes some effort to distinguish the two voices with which Gaetano Mosca speaks in the above quotation. The beginning (all societies are hierarchically organized) may be accepted as a statement of fact, although, strictly speaking, it is more than that, the implication being that "the useful institution" will tend to remain the property of a small group of power-wielders, whereas one might point out to the contrary that power in advanced societies tends to become more widely scattered than it is in relatively small and uncomplex societies, and that it tends to be more functional as it becomes less personal.

But, for the moment, Mosca's theory may be accepted as a true description of existing facts. These facts, according to him, are inherent in the nature of organization. Rule and subjection are explained by the necessities of social structure, a collective need. However, the utility of the arrangement, of obedience and command, is then explained, not as one would expect in terms of communal needs and advantages, but along lines of individual psychology. It is, we are informed, a fact of human nature that "many men" are motivated by the will to power, and that "almost all men" can be conditioned to accept control. This is, unless I am mistaken, the only time that Mosca makes use of the psychological argument in favor of his theory, the only time also that the elitist urge, the will to dominate, is claimed for "many men" and not only for a minority. However, since it is a fact that only a minority of those aspiring to command are able to achieve their aim, one should assume that the majority, in fact the great majority of all the many would-be rulers, being frustrated in their ambition, would be the "unruly" elements, the backers of the various out-elites of their society. But that is not at all what Mosca says. According to him, the frustrated power lovers (of whom there are many) are identical with the habitually obedient (almost all). Most people have both dispositions in their make-up and are capable of reconciling what is, theoretically, contradictory. It stands to reason that society would be in an eternal uproar if that were not so.

This is, in my opinion, a most fruitful insight by the author, which, unfortunately, stops short of what seems to be the inescapable conclusion. But since that conclusion probably would wreck the main assumptions on which Mosca's theory is based, it would be too much to expect of him that he draw it. Before I attempt to indicate its outlines,[14] Mosca's own conclusions ought to be considered.

What We Can Learn from History

The importance of the means by which "those who are at the top" are "justifying their authority" and "persuade those who are at the bottom to submit" grows as society becomes more complicated. One might say that, other things being equal, a ruling class will be as strong as its political formula. Remembering that the myth which persuades and justifies is not the product of elitist ingenuity but the creation of all classes, the collective property of the entire society, we will not for a moment expect Mosca to assume that ruling classes are responsible for that decline of social and political morality (the weakening of the prevailing "formula") which usually accompanies the end of a civilization. It is true that we did find our author on occasion charging the ruling class with that responsibility, exhorting it to raise its sights and to fulfill its duty as "disinterested" guardians of the people. But that view is the exception, not the rule. For the political class is not a free agent who could choose its destiny; it rules but is in turn ruled by the forces which determine growth and decay of the body politic. That is not necessarily fatalism. Mosca says explicitly: "I do not hold with those fatalistic interpretations of history." [15] But he comes dangerously close to a Spenglerian view of cultures going through a cycle of youth, maturity, old age, ending with death; and the older Mosca grows, the more does he seems tempted to adopt that view. Much less so in *The Ruling Class*. There he takes a position much akin to Toynbee's: great civilizations must not die like individuals—they are sometimes able to preserve their physical identity under the domination of another race and culture. "History," says Mosca, "is full of such transformations and survivals." [16]

However, he concedes that "there is still a sense in which a people that has been able to create a civilization of its own and to maintain it through long centuries can be said to have died." That death may be attributed to two causes which are "inevitably" related: "Nations die when their ruling classes are incapable of reorganizing in such a way as to meet the needs of changing times by drawing from the lower and deeper strata of society new elements..." Or death is caused by "a dwindling of those moral forces which ... make it possible for a considerable mass of individual efforts to be concentrated, disciplined, and directed toward purposes related to the collective interest. In a word, old age, the forerunner of death, comes upon political organisms when the ideas and sentiments which make then capable of the collective effort ... lose influence and prestige without being replaced by others." [17]

Civilization lives in and through its controlling moral force and dies with it. The great importance of the ruling classes is not minimized: they are the catalysts of the collective effort. But they seem to be the agents rather than the prime movers of the "collective effort," less determining of, and more determined by, the "sentiments" which make that effort possible.

If moral sentiment is the decisive factor, then it seems almost pointless to expect that the appeal to reason, in a word, science, may have a therapeutic influence on moribund societies. Indeed, in the first part of the *Elementi* Mosca shows himself to be quite sceptical in that respect. Even in the first chapter he voices his doubt about the political scientist's ability "to modify the political conduct of the great human societies. What happens in economics is instructive. Free trade is unanimously regarded by unprejudiced experts in that science as a good thing, yet the most highly civilized nations are today turning to the fiercest protectionism." [18]

That was in 1896. In 1923 our author is somewhat more optimistic:

> An exact knowledge of the laws that regulate the social nature of man ... if it does nothing else, will at least help people to distinguish between things that may happen and things that cannot happen and never will happen, and so it may help to keep many generous intentions and much good will from being unprofitably and even perniciously wasted ... [19]

Strange as it seems, as the political horizon darkens, Mosca's faith in the eventual triumph of man's reason becomes brighter. In 1936, the year Mussolini conquered Abyssinia, Mosca asks himself the question: "What could history teach us?" And he answers: "History is not made only by the men whose names have been remembered..." The great historical accomplishments are "the fruits of the collective laboring of the entire society, or at least of its highest strata, of the most dynamic and most useful individuals who are the leaven of the social dough. That labor is continuous, for immobility is not a natural condition of society." We must remember that, in Mosca's view, the bureaucratic absolutism of Mussolini's government was a regression and, at best, a temporary expedient. Then we shall appreciate his pronouncement that "societies which tried to arrest their development have never quite succeeded and have been defeated by those which did not commit that error." [20]

That optimistic note is not consistently maintained. Mosca was no progressivist. Gradual or sudden relapses into barbarism are not at all improbable. "The chief task of the historian would be to establish the causes of such gradual decays and acute crises." But he could not do much better, Mosca thinks, than to repeat what "I wrote forty years ago." And Mosca cites the lines which we have quoted about the dispassionate observer who will find that human beings are determined partly by their passions, instincts, and subconscious prejudices, partly by their interests, and for the rest, depending on what we call chance. [21] Yet he concludes on the faint note of hope that "the immense amount of information gathered in the nineteenth century and in the first decades of the twentieth will make possible a real science of politics. It would enable the statesmen and the ruling classes to avert those periods of decay and above all the sudden crises...which caused, even if they were of short duration, untold sufferings for the unhappy generation which had to endure them." [22]

A few years later, around 1938, the author copies down a passage from a French book he is reading: "A civilization is an organism which has its youth, its maturity, and its old age. No organism is immortal, and the more complex they are, the more vulnerable and the least resistant. If we should have any illusions that our own civilization is immortal, time will disabuse us of that notion." Mosca comments. "This contains a great deal of truth, but not the whole truth. In the first place, even though the human individual will never achieve immortality, the progress made in hygiene, medicine, and surgery has notably increased the length of human life. And what is true for individuals may well come true for the social organism too, once the laws regulating its life are better known. Second...as I have demonstrated in my *Elementi*, every civilization which decays or dies bequeathes to those that succeed it an artistic, moral, scientific heritage which will not be entirely lost." [23] Indeed, more than forty years earlier, Mosca had written: "A whole society can hardly grow old in the same sense in which an individual grows old when his powers begin to fail." Like Toynbee, he believed in cultural "apparentation": "The descendants of a civilized people may stagnate or may even relapse into barbarism, but the learning of their fathers may fertilize the nascent civilization of uncouth hordes that happen to find themselves favorably placed for receiving such beneficent germs." [24]

Will we end the same way, leaving it to other races to pick up the pieces of our heritage? The author greatly fears that this will happen: "If European civilization is forced to keep long and incessantly on the defensive against the tendencies of the various socialist schools," he wrote in 1896, "it will be forced by that very fact into a decline, and the decline will come whether our civilization tries to compromise, make concessions and come to terms, or adopts a policy of absolute coercion and resistance." Anticipating many recent writers, Mosca knew already that, in fighting the totalitarian enemy, we may unwittingly have to adopt his very methods: "In order to maintain [resistance], our civilization will have to abandon most of its idealism, restrict liberty of thought and adopt new types of government which will represent a real retrogression in the safeguarding of justice . . ." [25]

Is there no way out? The faith in scientific statesmanship which will enable us to make the necessary changes gradually is strongly reaffirmed in Mosca's "Ultimate Reflections." But significantly, other entries sound another note. Quoting again from his French source, Mosca notes: "It seems that without the cement of a metaphysical faith a human group cannot preserve that simple peace of mind that makes us accept life and practice all those daily virtues of self-denial and submission without which society could not endure." And he adds: "This is also my belief. The waning of faith is the greatest weakness of our present European civilization." [26] Like Toynbee, Mosca in his last years seemed to feel that the history of world civilizations is the history of world religions.[27]

This is no longer the impassioned anticlerical of certain youthful essays. In the *Elementi* Mosca had already taken a more sympathetic attitude toward Christianity, if not toward the Church. Then he had written:

It has often been remarked that Christianity is the religion of hard times . . . It is not at all unlikely that the luxury and waste that was characteristic of the first three decades of the twentieth century will be followed by an era of depression and comparative poverty, during which Christian doctrines will again find the terrain propitious for recapturing the hearts of the masses.

This sounds as if it had been written, at the earliest, in the fourth decade of this century. But actually it was a prophecy pronounced in 1896, brought up to date in the American edition of *The Ruling Class*.[28] The "Ultimate Reflections" of the 1930's give no indication that the hope in a revival of Christianity among the masses, now that Europe was no longer prosperous, was coming true. How the old man could endure life without that hope I do not know. The rest is silence.

CONCLUSIONS

When Gaetano Mosca wrote, the bureaucratization of political and economic life as we know it today was still undreamed of. When he spoke of mass organizations, he meant state bureaucracies and modern, "democratic" parties, nothing else. These frightened him all right, but how much more terrified he would be today. In his time, the mass managers and bureaucrats looked like a serious threat to liberal society; toward the end of his career, they had become conterminous with government in many countries, and thus, due to the much enlarged possibilities of social and political direction, with society itself. When Robert Michels studied the sociology of modern parties, he saw them as one of various crucibles from which political elites arose. Enough other channels were still open through which the social forces could assert themselves. Two generations later bureaucratization had become the fate of all organized activity, and the term "bureaucratic" simply meant the way in which all large-scale business had to be transacted, whether it was public and "political," or private enterprise.

To spot today's elites should be a much more arduous job than it had been in Mosca's lifetime. One might go still further and decide, with Karl Mannheim, that our supremely diffuse and mobile type of society makes the formation of elites enormously difficult, if not impossible.[1] But that is not at all the view of the more orthodox elitist writers. Lawrence Dennis and James Burnham—to name two American examples—will agree on one thing if on nothing else: the field belongs to three groups, state administrators, party managers, and businessmen (the representatives of Capital and Labor). On a second thought, James Burnham added, during the last war, the military.[2] If we add the last-named to the bureaucrats, we get a triangular situation in which the modern, centralized mass parties would appear to be the apex.

To begin with Europe: in some, technically democratic, countries we will find the power contest polarized between two massive party blocks. In Mosca's Italy, for instance, the "machine" of the now ruling Demo-Christian coalition fulfills the same function for the bourgeois camp which the *Partito Communista* led by Ercole-Togliatti (seconded by Nenni's socialists) performs as the co-ordinating agency of proletarian protest. Mosca, if he were alive, would worry about the identity of mass appeal techniques used by both sides, and about the destructive impact that the inherently totalitarian character of these techniques, with their regimentation of opinion, might have on his "balance of the social forces." But, then, Mosca might relax again on finding out that behind the monolithic façade, regimentation is far from complete. The Demo-Christian Party, he would find, is actually a loose confederation of three far from agreed groups, reflecting right-wing, moderate, and left-wing tendencies. What Stalin's posthumous disgrace will do to the Communist-controlled plebeian coalition of workers, field hands, and depressed groups of the petty bourgeosie still remains to be seen.

Whatever happens, it is likely that one fact will remain unchanged: the major dislocation which the modern party system has effected in the methods of selecting the elites. The French example may serve as an illustration. There we found, after the liberation, a succession of weak governments controlled by shifting coalitions between more or less antagonistic parties. Through them and their appointees in the great nationalized industries as well as in the state bureaucracies, the social forces—or, to be precise, the interests—controlled the distribution of the meager social product. Every demand, in order to be heard, had to be channeled through the parties. What had been a slack electoral organization once, making demands upon the sovereign community, had now, in grim collusion with like-minded partners, usurped the position of the sovereign community: it was the sovereign in all but in legality. The part had made itself the whole, the party had become the state.

At this point our imaginary Mosca might consider toning down his statement, lest it seem "too harsh to fit some cases," [3] and reformulate the statement about the party become state to say this: A rearticulation of the sovereign will has taken place or is in progress in most countries, or at any rate in those which have, or else pretend to, democratic institutions. What the change amounts to is a shift of the decision-making function away from the constitutionally designated agents to new "intermediate sovereigns," irresponsible yet public powers: the great party, business, labor, pressure group bureaucracies with their central committees and executive boards.[4] If they are not actually the state, united they could easily absorb it and make it over in their own image. The balance of the social forces hangs on their disunion, a frail thread. Where the dislocation of the sovereign will took on a revolutionary character, such as in Russia, Germany, and Italy, the framework of the state was left standing as an empty shell, while total power accrued to the vast parallel bureaucracy of the triumphant party. The retention (or, as in France, restoration) of the democratic mechanism could only mask but not offset a world trend which is no respecter of national or ideological boundaries.

The effect of that displacement has two aspects that affect the old elites. The new bureaucracies tend to attract and absorb what is left of independent hierarchies. In the extreme case of the Soviet Union, the one ruling party has, so far, succeeded in containing the ambitions of all other (managerial, army) groups. Their social power, influential as it may be within the controlling party, is unable to by-pass it. A plurality of Soviet elites granted, they must gravitate around and merge with the elite of party bosses. Human engineering is still more important than mechanical and technical manipulation.

Elsewhere the mass parties must share the monopoly of power with competing bureaucratic bodies, such as civil service, army, business-labor. But there too we will find that in many cases power is acquired by entering the party lists (the many lawyers in the U.S. Congress).

Secondly, the mass-ive character of modern institutions not only means that elite selection becomes more and more monopolistic; it also affects the very type of leadership. A Mosca redivivus would find little reason to revise his views about the lower level of contemporary "aristocracies." For this he mainly blamed the democratic parties;[5] today, Mosca would extend his censure to all leader groups. Not only, he would say, are they now *operating* on a lower level— they *are* themselves downgraded, mediocre. To quote a critic native to this country: "By the middle of the twentieth century, the American elite have become an entirely different breed of men from those who could on any reasonable grounds be considered a cultural elite ... Knowledge and power are not truly united inside the ruling circles; and when men of knowledge do come to a point of contact with the circles of powerful men, they come not as peers but as hired men."[6]

Mosca himself was still content if the elite of knowledge would retain its independence; only in rare moments did he hope "knowledge and power" could be fused within the ruling class. In our time, if C. Wright Mills is correct, the independence of the cultural elite is a thing of the past; the man of knowledge has become the well-paid expert, the mere tool of power.

Democratic Revisionism: Duverger and Schumpeter

Four decades after Robert Michels, a French scholar who had obviously learned a great deal from him and from Mosca wrote another book about political parties. In it, he analyzed the evolution which his masters had anticipated in a sketchy way. He follows them—up to a certain point. It is instructive to observe that Maurice Duverger, while quite agreeing with his predecessors on the facts, comes nonetheless to very different conclusions.

"The organization of political parties," we read, "is certainly not in conformity with orthodox notions of democracy. Their internal structure is essentially autocratic and oligarchic: their leaders ... tend to form a ruling class ... a caste that is more or less exclusive."

This is rather elementary, and Duverger himself feels that "the argument must be carried further: even supposing that parties were ruled by parliamentary representatives, it would be an illusion to think them democratic. For elections themselves ill interpret the true state of opinion. Parties create opinion as much as they represent it . . . Growing centralization is increasingly diminishing the influence of members over leaders . . . Parliamentary representatives themselves are compelled to an obedience which transforms them into voting machines controlled by the leaders of the party. Thus there arise closed, disciplined, mechanized bodies . . . parties become totalitarian." [7]

This is straight Mosca—nothing that would shock the younger generation of American political and social scientists. They might point out to Duverger that, in this country, parties are decentralized (a fact of which he is aware [8]) and hence not likely to become "totalitarian." But they would accept with calm his main contention, expressed still more brutally by Schumpeter: "Democracy is the rule of the politician." [9]

Bleak as this picture may look to the faithful of the classical tradition, Duverger does not, as Michels did, end on a note of near despair: "The system makes it possible to form a ruling class, sprung from the people, to replace the old . . . The deepest significance of political parties is that they tend to the creation of new elites, and this restores to the notion of representation its true meaning, the only real one." A la bonheur! Nor is Professor Duverger much worried by the New Mediocrity; he obviously prefers it to the old . . . The modern party, in his view, provides "the necessary framework enabling the masses to recruit from among themselves their own elites."

This would be utter heresy to Mosca, who thought of the masses as mere objects, never as the subjects of political decision. But he need not worry too much because Duverger does not consistently maintain the notion of the mass elite; we will find him back on the old Mosca track in just a moment. He reverts to it already when he says that, with respect to *government*, the parties are a socializing factor: Ministers and parliaments, "once exclusively the instruments of private, financial, and economic interests . . . have today become instruments in the hands of the parties." But does that also mean their democratization? Have the parties not become the tools of those same "private, financial, and economic interests"? M. Duverger does not think so: "This transformation represents an advance of democracy, not a retreat." For "the new party structures ensure an admirable training of the political leading strata as well as closer and more faithful contact of the people and their ruling elites." [10]

This optimistic statement seems to contradict the previous one about the autocratic and oligarchic character of the new party structures. But the contradiction is only verbal, for "all government is by nature oligarchic but the origins and the training of the oligarchs may be very different and these determine their actions."

This is most unlike anything the old elitists ever wrote. Mosca and Michels were agreed that all bureaucracies, regardless of class origin, would tend to be tradition-bound and, hence, conservative, the need for orderly procedure transforming erstwhile revolutionaries into cautious officeholders. Duverger rejects this generalization. His emphasis on class background and habits is a fruitful one. Bureaucracy may be conservative, progressive, even revolutionary, implementing startling changes of the social system, as in Soviet Russia. Bureaucratization need not thwart the democratic, or totalitarian, *ends*.

But what about the means?

Professor Duverger's reply is simple: "The formula 'Government of the people' must be replaced by this formula, 'Government of the people by an elite sprung from the people.'" [11]

The democratic myth is salvaged—at a price. The Gettysburg address has been abridged by Duverger. Rule "by the people" is conspicuously absent from his revamped democratic formula. Like Mosca-Michels, he holds that "the sovereign people" are a fiction, that their choices are manipulated by the politicians and their propaganda experts. Party elites will be "of the people" without necessarily being representative of rank and file opinion.

It might seem to some that Duverger's revision of the formula is still not radical enough for the elitist taste, while it is far too radical for the majoritarian democrat.

Another try to reconcile Rousseau with Mosca has been made by the late Joseph Schumpeter. Without mentioning the author of

The Ruling Class, the great economist defines the democratic method as "that institutional arrangement for arriving at political decisions in which individuals acquire the power to decide by means of a competitive struggle for the people's vote." [12] And Duverger, who does not seem to have read Schumpeter, could not have written differently about the electorate: "Its choice ... does not flow from its initiative but is being shaped, and the shaping of it is an essential part of the democratic process. Voters do not decide issues ... In all normal cases the initiative lies with the candidate ..." [13]

Are there exceptions to that rule? Is there such a thing as an authentic "draft" of candidates who truly represent "the people's choice"? There is: "there are certain cases in which the political engine fails to absorb certain issues either because the high commands of the government and the opposition's forces do not appreciate their political values or because these values are in fact doubtful. Such issues may then be taken up by outsiders who prefer making an independent bid for power to serving in the ranks of one of the existing parties. This of course is perfectly normal politics." [14] But, we may add, not normal politics in the United States, at least not, as a rule, in national elections. Even within the loose framework of our two great parties, mavericks, no matter how well known they are, have very little chance to "buck the party."

So democracy, according to Schumpeter, "does not mean and cannot mean that the people actually rule in any obvious sense of the terms 'people' and 'rule.'" It only means they have the right to accept or reject the men who are to rule them. "But since they might decide this also in entirely undemocratic ways, we have ... to narrow our definition by adding a further criterion identifying the democratic method, viz., free competition among would-be leaders for the vote of the electorate." [15]

The meaning of the term "free competition" is not clear. If it refers to independent candidates soliciting votes outside or against the well-established parties, then free competition would not be a typical mark of the democratic process as we know it. Schumpeter himself feels some uneasiness about this point: though democratic competition "excludes many ways of securing leadership which should be excluded, such as competition by military insurrection, it does not exclude the cases which are strikingly analogous to the economic phenomena we label 'unfair' or 'fraudulent' competition or restraint of competition. And we cannot exclude them because if we did we should be left with a completely unrealistic ideal." [16] Duverger, on his part, grants that in the United States free electoral competition (in Schumpeter's sense) has "to a large extent" been realized through the device of the open primary: "No doubt the present decline of the 'machines' must be partly attributed to it." But then the author qualifies that favorable judgment by saying that the power of the party leaders to select the candidates is "modified rather than suppressed . . . The primary system tends less to encourage the freedom of candidates relative to the leaders than to develop internal factions and rivalries between groups of leaders. At the primaries the electors may judge between such rivalries, but the small number of electors taking part in the primaries takes away much of the significance from this choice . . ." [17] The elitist theory is once more vindicated.

What have we gained from Schumpeter's redefinition of democracy? He claims that it provides us with "a reasonably efficient criterion by which to distinguish democratic government from others . . ." Because the interests of the people (both in the subjective and objective sense) "may be and in many historic instances have been, served just as well or better by governments that cannot be described as democratic according to any accepted usage of the term," Schumpeter decides to omit from his formula all statements about democratic ends and to equate democracy with what he calls "a *modus procedendi* the presence or absence of which it is in most cases easy to verify."

Democracy has been reduced—terminologically—to a mere technique. And if a Hitler comes to power, as he claimed *and did*, by constitutional means, then Schumpeter's second proposition that "the theory . . . leaves all the room we may wish to have for a proper recognition of the vital fact of leadership" assumes a meaning which was certainly far from the author's mind. For he acknowledges, as part and parcel of the democratic process, certain "genuine, groupwise volitions," such as "for instance, the will of the unemployed to receive unemployment benefit or the will of other groups to help." In common parlance, we would speak of their desideratum as a democratic aim in the pursuit of social justice or, to quote a famous document, of happiness. They are aims which, again in common parlance, are called democratic *ends*, to be achieved by democratic *means*. Schumpeter, concentrating on the means, insists that his scheme takes care of the ends as well: "On the contrary we are now able to insert them in exactly the role they actually play." For those volitions of the people, or a part of them, "do not as a rule assert themselves directly." They are sometimes dormant "for decades" and do not become articulate "until they are called to life by some political leader who turns them into political factors." [18]

That is indubitably a true statement of the facts. But the elitist thrust is blunted by the observation that "no leadership is absolute. Political leadership exerted according to the democratic method is even less so than are others because of that competitive element which is of the essence of democracy." [19] That competition, to be sure, takes place between political (and cultural) elites, but as their number multiplies in modern mass society, the element of competition works *in favor of the democratic tendency*.

Thus understood, the theories of the elite and liberal democracy not only do not contradict each other, but are complementary. Essentially, Schumpeter's reappraisal amounts to an integration of elitist elements into a democratic framework which is much more modest than the structure built two hundred years ago, more diffident and more complex, but basically still within the classical tradition.

Croce's Strawman

Others have not been so cautious. Such an unquestionable liberal as Mosca's great contemporary Benedetto Croce, wrote in the last years of Mussolini's rule, which found him so intractable, lines ostensibly directed against Marx and his class struggle doctrine, but in fact aimed at another target: "Politics become altogether unintelligible unless we go back to the concept of a 'classless class,' of a 'general class,' which lays the foundation and rules and governs the State." [20]

That was a safe enough beginning, as the concept of a "classless class" cutting across, and mirroring, all classes was a favorite idea with the fascist movements of both Italy and Germany. From there, the Crocean argument moves on in innocent vacuities, a watered-down version of Mosca: "A political class, or ruling minority, which knows what it wants, is indispensable to the liberal state as to every other form of state, and the rest follows in consequence. And when it is affirmed that liberalism is depressed, or decadent, or exhausted ... this is but to say that these few, the minority, this ruling class is depressed, or decadent, or exhausted, ... that it must rise again and revive itself," or else "a new generation of men will succeed it," who will compose "a new aristocracy, young and vigorous like that of other days." The tone has almost imperceptibly changed; the famous clarity of Benedetto Croce's style is in eclipse, and we no longer know: Are the successors of the decadent old liberals still liberals of the young generation, or no longer liberals—Fascists perhaps? This ambiguity, we suspect, was intentional, contrived to throw the Fascist censor off the scent. But in the end, there is no question about where the author stands, for after taunting the old ruling class for its refusal to reform itself, he finds that it is haunted by a sense of guilt: "an obscure remorse pricks the conscience, and gives an indication of the ever persistent truth that the liberal idea is never outmoded because the moral ideal with which it substantially coincides cannot be out-moded." [21]

Brave words, considering the time when they were uttered. But the reassertion of the liberal ideal is accompanied, quite à la Mosca, by an attempt to detach it from its historical connection with democracy: "The liberal method does not claim to call everybody to politics and the government of the commonwealth, putting them all on the same level, which is the democratic utopia. When people think that they have brought this into existence, it leads to demagogy and tyranny." However, unlike Mosca, Croce does not openly declare himself against the universal suffrage, although he does cite the monk Savonarola's warning against popular assemblies: "the man 'who wants to make a parliament' wants (he said) 'to wrest the government from your hands.' " Here Croce forgets that, according to his own definition, the government is not, and even ought not to be, in the hands of the people in the first place. But having taken our democratic rights away, he instantly restores them to us, under another name, for he concedes that:

... the liberal method does convert all from subjects into citizens, and gives to all, or to as many as possible, the means of sharing power, whether in government and administration, or by criticism and counsel ... Whoso wants to make use of these liberties can do so ... and he can take part in the competition and in the political struggle, whose larger or smaller fruits depend upon the quality, more or less good, of the forces in play, and of the men who share in them and handle the method.[22]

The friend of democratic principles may, at this point, respectfully submit that Benedetto Croce's "democratic utopia" (which is also that of Gaetano Mosca) makes claims far beyond those advanced in the sacred texts of democracy. They do indeed "call everybody to politics," but democratic theory does not assume that government could be by all—unless Vladimir Lenin's *State and Revolution* is considered as a democratic theory. Not even the greatest of them all, not even Rousseau at his boldest, in the *Social Contract*, has the people govern: all he says is that authority to govern comes from them; the people are sovereign but they do not rule. Wherever Rousseau drafted practical proposals for a constitution, as for Corsica and Poland, the result was a model of liberal restraint.[23]

Modern representative democracy assures the voter control of his government, that is, judgment of its actions and the changing of its personnel: the legislature by his vote, and indirectly, through the men of his choice, the executive. To the extent that the elitists can show popular control to be an object of manipulation by an organized minority, they have a talking point; when they forget, or slur over the fact, that these minorities in turn depend, as they compete with one another, on the democratic process, they exaggerate. The "democratic utopia" is such an exaggeration, an *ad hoc* constructed strawman. Once that strawman is destroyed, we find that the emerging liberal utopia "gives to all, or to as many as possible, the means of sharing power ... ,"[24] and that should be good enough for us and all.

There remains an irritant, as any casual perusal of contemporary writing will reveal: a penchant toward an aristocratic view of social and political relationships. Below the summit occupied by such as Mosca and Pareto, Croce, Schumpeter, and C. Wright Mills[25] elitism has become the new snobbery. The term "elite" is being used, in a self-congratulatory way, by those who, to misquote George Orwell slightly, are of the opinion that all men are equal, but some more equal than others.[26] The tendency to view our mobile mass society in the light of a stratified and static past may be a symptom of repression and accompanying overcompensation: hankering for rank in a society which knows, officially, no ranks. Elitism in the present may be a rationalization of the submerged wish for social and political pre-eminence.

No wonder this attitude has caused a great deal of annoyance. And no wonder that much of the protest is aimed at the founding fathers of the theory, blaming the river's source for the vast inundations of the distant plain.

Root-and-Branch Rejection?

One way of giving battle to the whole elitist school is to attack its very premises and to deny the facts which the school takes for granted. Carl J. Friedrich's criticism may serve as a representative example of the kind of root-and-branch rejection. It concerns Pareto rather than Mosca, but since, in Professor Friedrich's view, "Pareto's 'governing elite' seems largely identical with Mosca's 'ruling class,'" the argument applies with equal force to both.[27]

The onslaught, as may be expected from that quarter, is as formidable as its thrust is to the point. The point is, of course, not the basic thesis that in all historically known societies the few ruled over vast majorities. Professor Friedrich does not question that assertion, for the simple reason that it merely states the obvious: nobody will be surprised to find that, in most armies, officers are much less numerous than private soldiers. The theory of the elite makes bigger claims. It rests upon the proposition that the outstanding minority is not just the sum total of the individuals in control of a particular group or organization, but a compact body, conscious of its role and functioning in concert. It is this contention that Professor Friedrich ardently denies: "No attempt is made by Pareto to show that the 'elite,' as defined by him, possesses a distinct group character; if he had made it, it would, no doubt, have failed, for these several exceptional persons do not constitute a cohesive group." The same,

Professor Friedrich says, is true of Mosca's statement that the ruling class is composed of the people who rule: "the argument remains tautological."

Now, to say that Mosca and Pareto failed, or did not even try, to prove that a *cohesive* ruling class exists is not the same as proving that such a ruling class does *not* exist. But that is what Professor Friedrich thinks he has been doing.

He begins by saying that "both writers [Mosca and Pareto] smuggle in as an unproven assumption or major premise what is the most problematical part of all elite doctrines, namely, (*a*) that those who play a role in government constitute a coherent group, and (*b*) that they possess distinguishing characteristics." [28]

This sounds like a denial of the elite doctrine under *all* conditions. However, as the argument proceeds, we find that Friedrich, very reasonably, narrows it down to the mere assertion that elites do not exist in *democratically governed states*:

> In the light of the continuous change in the composition of the majority, it is not possible to say, under conditions such as prevail in a functioning democracy, that those who play some considerable part in government constitute a cohesive group . . . Even granting for the moment that the "facts" were correct, this would merely argue that democratization was incomplete, or, in the light of de Tocqueville's warning, on the retreat.

According to Professor Friedrich, the elitists have produced no evidence of the conspiracy which is supposed to link the ruling individuals and make of them a ruling class acting in unison. What proof they offer is "but historic evidence, drawn mostly from nondemocratic societies." It is in this connection that Professor Friedrich makes use of the *argumentum ad hominem* by referring to Mosca's Sicilian background.

In a democratic system, those possessing superiority of some kind or another are either those who have a "capacity for workmanship in a given field of activity" or "those called upon to formulate public policies." In making this distinction, Friedrich hardly intends to deny the possibility that, in the United States at least, the two "callings" frequently do overlap. At any rate, those with a flair for public office will be called to it only if and *because* "their general outlook coincides with that of the majority." If they have any "merit" at all—in Mosca's mouth that word is merely a "concession to . . . democratic verbiage"—then "only in that they are 'representative.' " [29]

No!, Mosca would reply, it is the other way around: the members of the ruling class are representative because they have some "merit," in the sense that they fulfill a necessary function as the social and political directors of society or else are able to convince the people that their rulers in fact exercise that function. More important, Mosca would insist that this is the case in all social orders, the democracies included.

Professor Friedrich, speaking with some heat, concedes that, in the course of democratic competition, "various individuals" will "achieve leadership." But he maintains that "they cannot stabilize their position because their 'solutions' are likely to be judged inadequate after a trial . . ." Therefore, "they come and go in continuous succession." Satisfied that he has shown conclusively that the turnover in the democratic leadership makes the consolidation of elites into cohesive cliques impossible, Professor Friedrich exclaims on a note of triumph: "Indeed, the most striking thing about such leadership is that it is most usually recruited from among the common men." [30]

But the coming and going of individual leaders need not exclude the existence of consolidated, hierarchically organized groups of great staying power. They recruit and train their future leaders in their own, established cadres which, in turn, are filled by eager applicants from colleges and universities. In that sense, elites become self-perpetuating, superhuman entities which mold all newcomers, regardless of their origin, into a common pattern. Reversing Marx, one might say that it is not the social class which determines the nature of the ruling group, but on the contrary, the nature of the ruling group determines the class character of all its present and prospective members. Thus even if most leaders were "recruited from among the common men," this need not seriously affect the oligarchic forms and *attitudes* of modern bureaucratic institutions.

The disagreement between the elitists and Professor Friedrich can be narrowed down to the one question: Does the democratic system where it functions as effectively as in the United States prevent the

formation and stabilization of elites? Neither Mosca nor Pareto
show proof that a ruling class exists in this country. Professor Friedrich, on the other hand, makes no attempt to prove that it does not
exist. All he says is that it *cannot* exist because leadership in a democracy is (*a*) never stable, and (*b*) merely the representative or pro-
jection of the public will. He might have added that elite formations
in this country are as yet too tenuous, too variegated, and too competitive to solidify into a ruling class in the accepted sense. But this
Professor Friedrich could not do because it would have meant
acknowledging the fact that dominant minorities exist, although they
are still checked, if not checkmated, by the competitive mechanics
of the system in their drive for unified control. But mutual cancella-
tion of minority demands can be no substitute for the decision-
making utterance of the majority, the fulcrum of the democratic
order defended by Professor Friedrich.

The impasse seems complete. To some extent the critic's unrelent-
ing attitude may be related to the fact that at the time he wrote
his book, democracy had to combat the fascist version of totalitarianism. Then it was only natural to suspect anyone who doubted the
eternal values of democracy of plotting against our free institutions.
That such intention was far from Mosca's mind I hope I have
shown to the reader's satisfaction. The possibility that Mosca's writings gave, if only indirectly, an assist to fascist or authoritarian tendencies it would be foolish to deny. Professor Friedrich, I believe, is on
firm ground when he suggests that "the concepts of the 'elite' and
'the ruling class' are useful only in analysing and describing the non-
cooperative patterns of society." [31]

At a first glance, this statement does not seem to be quite fair to
Mosca's doctrine of the ruling class. Nowhere does he deny that it
owes its position and importance to the social humus out of which it
sprang. He knows that "situations form elites at least as much as elites
form situations," and that "domination must be explained as a social
need and not as a desire or intention of the elite." [32] The elite's
raison d'être is only as the instrument of social and political co-operation. But it must be said that Mosca has a tendency to take that fact
for granted and to treat elites as if they had not emanated from, but
were independent of, society, prime movers of its destiny. He could

succumb to that illusion because the elites, while coming from the people, stand as rulers face to face with them, in a relationship of tension. Since that latter aspect was in Mosca's view, denied or simply overlooked by democratic theory, he stressed it, unduly perhaps, but understandably. Thus The Few and The Many appear to confront each other, as it were, across a sharp divide which, in reality, does not exist, and what is a continuum of social and political differentiation may look like a "non-cooperative pattern of society." This observation of Professor Friedrich is, so we believe, extremely fruitful and deserves some further exploration.[33]

The Elite to End All Elites

Carl J. Friedrich's attitude is fairly representative of the American majority opinion: ruling classes may exist in Europe, or in Asia, but it cannot happen here. If there is something like a trend toward a class society ruled by elites, there are still more effective countertrends at work to guarantee this country's democratic character for a long time to come, if not forever.

The writer of this study has so far refrained from trying to fit the United States into the framework of the ruling class doctrine. He has been waiting for a native American to do that. He did not have to wait in vain. The bold American has at long last appeared, just as this study was about to be concluded. C. Wright Mills has been referred to once before; he has been laboring for a long time to prove that the United States is governed by a relatively small, well-integrated ruling class. It is "The Power Elite" to end all elites, and judging from the first reactions to Mills' radical pronouncement, he will have a battle on his hands compared with which the clashes with the old elitist school become mere skirmishes.[34]

The temptation to treat Mills as a rambunctious junior member of that school is almost irresistible. However, while The Power Elite seems to carry Mosca's Ruling Class to its extreme conclusions, it is anything but a late vindication of the older master: "It is not my thesis," Mills writes, "that for all epochs of human history and in all nations, a creative minority, a ruling class, an omnipotent elite shapes all historical events. Such statements, upon careful examina-

tion, usually turn out to be mere tautologies . . ." And in a footnote
Mills makes it clear that this is "the case, quite notably, of Gaetano
Mosca . . ." It is the one and only point on which Professors Fried-
rich and Mills see eye to eye.[35]

While Mosca's ruling class derives its *raison d'être* from the social
force or forces which it "represents," the Power Elite is defined "in
terms of institutional position." [36]

This formula has undeniable advantages. For one, it makes the
proof of the Three C's:—group consciousness, cohesion, and conspiracy—unnecessary; the Power Elite may lack one of these characteristics and still be a genuine ruling class. Mills does not claim that
"the powerful are united, that they fully know what they do, or that
they are consciously joined in conspiracy." What matters to him is
"the structural position of the high and mighty . . ." [37] As James
Burnham and the interesting U.S. fascist, Lawrence Dennis, did before him, Mills (who fails to mention either man) identifies those
"high and mighty" as the virtual—and in wartime, actual—combination of three groups: "the political directorate, the corporate rich
and the high military." [38] Anticipating criticisms à la Friedrich, Mills
is careful to admit that the co-ordination of these three groups may
be neither total nor continuous nor deliberate. However, he insists
that "as the institutional mechanics of our time have opened up
avenues to men pursuing their several interests, many of them have
come to see that these several interests could be realized more easily
if they worked together . . . and accordingly they have done so." [39]
This is, in essence, the position also held by Mosca and his followers:
elites entrench themselves in institutions. But the emphasis is
changed. With Mills, the institution makes the man; the master institutions of a corporate economy and polity determine who shall
wield the power.

The author then proceeds to analyze the power structure of American society, deploying an enormous battery of facts and figures. To
determine whether or not Mills draws the correct conclusions from
his facts and figures is not the purpose of this study. One can only
hope that Mills is wrong when he decides that "organized irresponsibility . . . is today the most important characteristic of the American
system of corporate power." [40] It is no longer "held in check by a

plurality of voluntary associations which connect debating publics with the pinnacles of decision." [41] The result is a regime of "higher immorality" (this is the title of Mills' Chapter 15) which "is sensed by enough people . . . to lead to cynical views of the lack of connection between merit and mobility, between virtue and success." [42] The American myth, Mills suggests, is no longer an unquestioned article of faith. The U.S. ruling class is, speaking morally, a sub-elite.

Before Mills can arrive at this conclusion, he must perform one more feat. While not denying the fact that there are American elites in process of formation, many people will still cling to the belief that the "plurality of voluntary associations" is still operative, that it keeps "the high and mighty" from solidifying their position, that the old mechanics of free, democratic competition makes for a wide scattering of social power. This "idea of the impotent elite" is ridiculed by Mills in the first chapter of his book. The pluralists suppose that "no one has enough power to make a real difference; events are the result of an anonymous balance of power . . ." The capitalist "notion of an automatic economy" is translated into political terms: "there is the leaderless democracy in which no one is responsible for anything and everyone is responsible for everything . . ." [43]

This negative view, as expressed by David Riesman, is subjected to a withering critique in Mills' Chapter 11, called "The Theory of Balance." By implication, the attack upon the author of *The Lonely Crowd* is also an attack upon the author of *The Ruling Class*. Professor Riesman's equilibrium of competing "veto groups" (which corresponds to Mosca's "balance of the social forces") is "romantic pluralism." It describes a situation which exists no longer, or, if it does exist, then only on a lower plane; it is no longer the whole picture. Riesman's thesis is "a recognizable, although a confused, statement of the middle levels of power, especially as revealed in Congressional districts and in the Congress itself." [44]

If Mills is right, then the whole sphere of politics in the traditional sense has lost its primary importance. The political elites have to defer to other forces. "The considerable powers that do remain in the hands of key Congressmen are now shared with other types of political actors": with the heads of the congressional committees whose decisions are in turn "increasingly subject to decisive modification by the administrator ..." The latter becomes the key figure: "Increasingly, the professional politician teams up with the administrator ... to exert power with him against other administrators and politicians, often in a cut-and-thrust manner." [45]

Nor is "democracy by pressure groups" to be relied upon, as in the past, to counteract the process of political collusion and corrosion. "The important pressure groups have either been incorporated in the personnel and in the agencies of the government itself, both legislative and executive, or become the instruments of small and powerful cliques, which sometimes include their nominal leaders but often do not." [46] In consequence, "more and more of the fundamental issues never come to any point of decision before the Congress ..." [47] The incorporation of the erstwhile independent social forces has become complete: "The old lobby, visible or invisible, is now the visible government ... The executive bureaucracy becomes ... the arena within which and in terms of which all conflicts of power are resolved or denied resolution. Administration replaces electoral politics; the maneuvering of cliques replaces the clash of parties." [48]

This is no longer Mosca or Pareto but Spengler: it is the advent of Caesar. Mosca's all-important "second stratum" of the ruling class, the middle level of political and intellectual leaders, is demoted from its key position in the power structure. It could loom so large only in a society in which "as a professor or as a free-lance intellectual, the political analyst [was] generally on the middle levels of power himself." [49] But Mills does not confine himself to this small exercise in the "sociology of knowledge." He relates the status loss of the intelligentsia to the general decline of the old middle class which "became politically, as well as economically, dependent upon the machinery of the state." [50] In addition, "there had arisen, inside the corporate society, a *new* dependent *middle class* of white collar employees ... They are in no political way united and coherent ... The old middle class for a time acted as an independent base of power; the new middle class cannot." [51] The "balance of the social forces" thus becomes a dated notion: it was feasible as long as power was not yet consolidated in the inner circle of the top elite. "When the middle classes decline . . . the balancing society as a system of power declines . . ." [52]

Ideologically, this means that all elitist theories we know have lost their importance for sociological analysis. To put it differently, the elitist myth reflects the aspirations of *ascending* middle classes only. Their decline, however, does not terminate the usefulness of the old myth, as Mills is quick to recognize. The Power Elite will appropriate the theory of balance so as to make itself more acceptable to the defeated bourgeoisie. Mills cites E. H. Carr's observation that " 'the doctrine of the harmony of interests . . . thus serves as an ingenious moral device invoked, in perfect sincerity, by privileged groups in order to justify and maintain their dominant position.' " [53] The "formula" of the professors becomes a device of self-deception.

It is then not true that, with Mills, Mosca has, at last, "arrived" in the United States. Instead, we find him under fire from two directions—not just one, as in the past. The democrats, much as his theory of balance and juridical defense may please them, will continue to loathe Mosca because of his doctrine of the ruling class with its aristocratic overtones. The followers of Mills in turn could adopt Mosca's ruling class as a "romantic" concept badly in need of modernization. But the theory of balance they cannot accept because of its strong liberal flavor.

So, no matter how we look at him, our author remains, as before, in no man's land. Only if Mills should be proven right about the future of American society can we foresee a chance for Gaetano Mosca to become a latter-day John Stuart Mill, a patron saint of liberty for the opponents of the corporate elite. They will have little use for C. Wright Mills' new formula because it is in itself contradictory. On the surface, Mills seems to debunk the Power Elite; actually, he justifies it as a force against which there is no defense. His counsel is one of despair and hate. He magnifies the facts and thereby helps to create something unique: an inverted myth, enhancing, "in perfect sincerity," the very power against which he wants to warn the world. It's a long way from Mill to Mills, but it took us only a hundred years to travel it. At the beginning of the road we find Karl Marx, the dragon-slayer of the bourgeoisie, and at the end, the bourgeois intellectual who has seen through Marx and anti-Marx alike, who has seen it all and has no place to go.

Elitist Revisionism: Dorso

The reader frightened by this picture of America may feel more comfortable in the company of Guido Dorso, an Italian follower of Gaetano Mosca who attempts to reconcile the master's doctrine with the principles of classical democracy without surrendering any positions vital to the theory of the elite.

He starts out with a minor sacrilege by redefining Mosca's "political class" (the totality of all elites, inside and outside government). He calls it *classe dirigente* while reserving Mosca's term, *classe politica* for that part of the ruling class which is in charge of the official government.[54]

Except for this semantic change, which is not too important, it seems to be the old story, faithfully retold. But that is true only of the beginning. There we find again the government with its two strata: one, small, issuing the actual commands, the other, much more numerous, which implements the policies and makes them work. Again the sub-elite would seem to be the more important of the two, since without it the top group could not expect to be obeyed by the people, except in very small and primitive societies. And the secondary elite can reach the people so successfully because it is itself recruited from the people. Inasmuch as not all eligible elements can be absorbed into the government, they will form separate elites expressing social forces not yet represented in it. That way Dorso can dispense with the dividing line between the governing and the nongoverning part of society which Mosca—the one who wrote the *Teorica*—had started out with. The "political class" (Mosca's government) becomes the *classe dirigente*, Dorso's common pool for all elites, political and social. Thus, by starting at the point where the old master ends, the pupil has with one stroke managed to establish the continuum on which to project all elites. He recognizes Mosca's early two-class scheme for what it is: a technical device which had to be discarded, and the sooner, the better:

Between directing and directed class there exist numerous relations and connections which it is not always possible to state precisely . . . For reasons of epistemology and terminology we draw a line between the two great social classes, but we are not able to say where the one starts and the other ends . . .[55]

Dorso tries to drive this thought home by encircling it like a composer writing variations on a theme: we may distinguish the two "classes" but without pretending that they can ever be separate compartments; they "intercommunicate," they are "linked across a grey, intermediate zone which belongs neither to the dominating nor the dominated class but oscillates autonomously between both . . ." The ruling class is called "the mirror of the people, its most delicate elaboration." [56] Interdependence between ruled and rulers is "a constant factor which stands out most clearly in a revolutionary period," when the circulation of elites is fastest. But the same is true, although less ostentatiously, of normal periods. Dorso switches here his similes when he says that in normal times class interaction functions *in sordina*, muted.

If this is the correct approach, it follows that "the study of the ruling class is the first step toward the understanding of a people's history, but not sufficient in itself because it might yield the one-sided, so to speak, official portrait of society." [57] To be a fair approximation of reality, the study would have to be of "a ruling class which functions to perfection, with the opposition having its fair share of constitutionally regulated power. But such an exclusive study of the ruling class would not suffice in situations where it is in conflict with the ruled majority. And since such conflicts are the normal state of affairs, while the perfect functioning of the political elite is the exception, therefore, if one wishes to be sure of accurate results, a study of the whole society is always needed."

Another reason for considering the social pyramid in its entirety and not just the apex is the fact that "ruling classes are recruited from the ruled; they show therefore all the characteristics of the race *in nuce* . . . The continuous renewal of the social cells assures, as far as it is possible, a certain correspondence between ruled and rulers."

The hesitant note reveals the uneasiness of one who wishes but does not quite dare to come out with the ugly truth that in predem-

ocratic times the ruling class did not too closely "mirror" the subjected mass. Indeed, the author is forced to proclaim, a few lines
later, the necessity for the historian "to bring out, in his description
and analysis of class interdependence, its anomalies and aberrations." [58]

It is only too clear: Mosca's predicament is also Dorso's in that
both (*pace* Professor Friedrich) treat the ruling class as basically
representative of the totality of social forces, that is, the majority.
If it is not, that must be due to aberrations and anomalies and not,
as the Marxist would insist, to the essential incompatibility of the
two classes ("non-cooperation"). Mosca-Dorso are utterly incapable
of conceding that incompatibility because of their own, unitarian
vista of society. Their view can hardly be expressed with greater
vigor than in Dorso's statement that "the ruling class has no right
to confine itself to the direction and protection of its own affairs..."
Instead it has "the social obligation to look after the collective interest." [59]

We have here, Dorso remarks sagely, contradictory class interests
between which conflict "is sometimes inevitable." We are faced by
the great issue of Co-operation versus Non-Co-operation. Now, whenever the collective good is disregarded by the dominant minority,
something will have to give, and Guido Dorso leaves no doubt about
the outcome:

When the ruling class in the defense of its own interests has injured
those of the community or has obstructed its advance, the fact of privilege, which always goes with power, stands exposed and lacks justification.
The disequilibrium of functions can be ended only with the end of privilege, the declassation of the ruling class.

Would "declassation" lead to democratization, would it mean
the end of all elites, the coming of a truly classless, though not necessarily communist society? That would no longer be the house that
Mosca built. And Guido Dorso may be thinking that the house
needs some repairs, but he is far from ready to demolish it. Looking
for help, he calls in the post-paradisian Adam, fallen man:

Due to the imperfection of human nature, social life cannot take shape
except in oligarchic forms. They provide the skeleton for the whole
social structure. Oligarchies rule in politics, in economics, in the field of

human culture. They must be endured, indeed, they will have our support as long as they rule in accordance with the public interest.

But even when they do so rule, the various privileges which the members of a ruling class enjoy evoke the envy of the masses. The masses ignore the fact that "those advantages are earned in the performance of severe and complicated tasks—tasks which the masses could not take upon themselves and which, therefore, have to be delegated to the men who find themselves placed on the social heights."

There is no need to comment on this passage, which is a mere paraphrase of Michels' chapter on the indispensability of leaders. When the ruling class is finally admonished "to exact as little as possible in return for its oligarchic services," it becomes Mosca's class of the disinterested leaders, dressed up in pragmatic business suits.[60] Unlike their fathers, Dorso's new elite will charge a service fee but, mindful of his own good advice, they will never charge more than the traffic will bear. In any case, we are back where we started: an elite is of the essence because it is that articulation of society which *ought* to correspond to the collective need.

However, Guido Dorso has not finished saying all he has to say.

The Pacific and the Agonistic Instinct

The first part of the *Elementi* has a chapter headed "Churches, Parties, and Sects," a chapter to which we did not pay too much attention because it did not materially advance our understanding of those human associations beyond the point already reached in the *Teorica*.[61] That should, however, not deter the reader of *The Ruling Class* from paying close attention to the seventh chapter. For it offers some suggestions for a theory of groups and group relations which might well have served the author to expand his doctrine of the ruling class into a general philosophy of social and political behavior. At the same time, there is reason to believe that Mosca, had he pursued those ideas further, might have changed his mind about the role of modern parties and related mass organizations.

What he says there refers back to certain scattered remarks in the third chapter of *The Ruling Class,* where Mosca sees society controlled by two conflicting tendencies. One impels man to join his fellow social type and to combine with him into a single organism; the other urges him on to form separate "and almost always rival" groups.[62] It is a great pity that these observations were to remain unrelated to the central theory of the elite and to the part contemporary mass organizations play as the key agents of elite selection and elite formation.

Guido Dorso sees the possibilities inherent in those hints and makes the most of them. He, too, starts from the proposition that "man is by nature forced to satisfy two contradictory instincts which together constitute the essence of his being: the instinct of human solidarity and the instinct of strife which pits him against his fellow." He adds, with a sigh: "One might have wished the social progress of mankind had not been dominated by these hostile instincts. In that case, however, human history would have been very dull ..." Exciting or dull is, of course, Dorso knows, not the point at all. Much more important is what Mosca did not see: that the agonistic instinct and the instinct of co-operation are, while on the surface contradictory, at the same time also complementary: "that instinct of strife, the first cause of all human struggles, has ideological reasons which, in primitive times, led to uniformities of costume, creed, and superstition, bonds which later widened into ethical and intellectual affinities ..." [63] If we disregard the strange etiology (human struggles are "caused" by the agonistic instinct which in turn is "caused" by ideological differences), what is left amounts to a belief in the essential unity of process. That belief is stated with all necessary clarity in Dorso's statement that "the churches, sects, groups, factions, parties —all the segments into which mankind continuously divides, are the essential instruments for the articulation of collective life ..." Inside these segments takes place "the elaboration of minute controlling nuclei which organize the sectional majorities for the external struggle." [64]

In other words, the rationale of the elite is the need of each social group to unite against other groups. Internal domination becomes necessary for the sake of group survival and, if possible, predominance. The agonistic tendency leads to expansion and thereby to ever-growing integration, until unity has been achieved on a large, super-tribal scale. Put differently, segmentation precedes integration but is in itself already integration on a smaller scale. Not only does it precede large-scale integration but it is its direct condition. There is then no integration without differentiation; but the reverse is also true, no differentiation without integration. Integration here means more or less harmonious coalescence into first small, then large social groups; but beyond that, the statement has teleological significance in that integration on a broader if not higher level might be understood as the sole *purpose* of differentiation. In that case, we fight in order to achieve (impose) *our* kind of unity, thereby promoting *some* kind (if not our own kind) of unity.

If all co-operative actions have in them an element of sheer pugnaciousness and if all agonistic (non-co-operative) actions have an element of the fraternal instinct, then it would appear that integration (unity) and differentiation (pluralistic articulation) are interdependent aspects of one and the same phenomenon.

Considered only by itself, this statement, whose Hegelian character is obvious, tells us very little. But it has some implications which might be worth-while exploring. If we reduce the patterns of democracy and aristocracy to the proportions of a simple chart and then compare them with the theory of the elite, we get the following picture, in which the arrow indicates the direction of choice and control.

CHART I

A. The Democratic Version

Government (Agent)

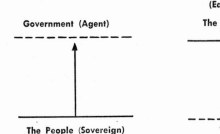

The People (Sovereign)

B. The Aristocratic Version
(Early Mosca)

The Ruling Class

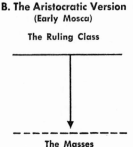

The Masses

C. The Elitist Compro
(Mature Mosca)

The Ruling Class

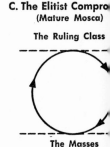

The Masses

A. The democratic order has the sovereign people choose their representatives who, as the government, act as the agents of the whole community.

B. The aristocratic concept, as it appears in the early works of Mosca, has the rulers confront and control the great majority. This is Professor Friedrich's "non-cooperative" situation or, rather, since without a modicum of co-operation society could not survive, co-operation has to be assured by the fact, or ever-present threat, of effective coercion. The latter would be true even of a society in which aristocratic rule is loyally accepted; in that case the people may be said to love the rod which, for that very reason, can be spared.

C. In the elitist order of things, as developed in the later works of Mosca, dominant minorities emerge from the majority by a process of either "natural selection" or political election. They form the "political class," which controls the rest effectively. In their capacity as rulers, the minority confront the masses, as it were, in a "non-cooperative," ostensibly aristocratic role. But this is only one part of the story, for the "circulation of elites" secures, in the long run, the co-operative continuum. The rulers are themselves part of the people, whom they "represent" because they are the outstanding leaders of the social forces. It is difficult to say where sovereignty is located; the concept does not seem to be of much concern to the elitist theorist. In fact, he could not use it without getting into serious trouble: in a co-operative pattern, sovereignty, like power, is not anywhere in particular, but is with the total process. In that respect, we find no disagreement between David Riesman and the later Mosca.

If this is the correct interpretation, then C represents a definite advance beyond the concepts A and B, of which it is the compromise.

We might try to define the power thrusts in the three patterns. A reveals no obstacle which would obstruct or blunt the democratic tendency, unless we agree with Rousseau who recognized that the "corporate will" of the magistrate had a "natural" tendency to thwart the general will of the sovereign (Social Contract, Book III, Chapter ii).

In B, the power of the ruling class must be assumed to have its limits only in the "natural" conditions of the ruled society, such as the vigor of the aristocracy and the docility of the subjects, or in the social power of the government which, in part, is determined by the technological development in general. But in a more advanced civilization, the aristocratic power thrust will also be opposed by strong, self-conscious social forces. The extent of the aristocratic power no longer is equal to the force of the aristocratic will. How much of that will has been realized in any given case is beyond measurement because only a portion of the ruling force will remain "visible," the rest being cancelled by the counter-will of the opposing classes. In turn, their democratic thrust is also blunted and in part submerged by the aristocratic pressure coming from above.

Since C assumes a circularity of the political and social power flow, it should not figure here at all. But since a residue of the aristocratic pattern can be found in even the maturest theories of the elite, what has been said with regard to B, applies to some extent also to C. It is a sad result: in all three instances, a theory of power thrusts would seem to be unworkable. We must try a different approach.

So far, the aristocratic and the democratic tendencies have been considered as two mutually exclusive forces, pitting groups or classes against one another. But as the pacific and the agonistic instincts dwell together in one and the same individual or group of individuals, so the tendencies toward democracy and aristocracy likewise appear together, in one person or one group. That is how Mosca, for one, saw the matter. (In order to avoid confusion, I will not treat as synonymous the "agonistic instinct" and the "aristocratic tendency." Nor are the terms "co-operation" and "democracy" simply exchangeable. Rather, non-co-operation and co-operation are to be conceived as attitudes characteristic of both the aristocratic and the democratic type.)

Assuming, then, that the two tendencies appear conjointly, let us see if it is possible to construct them in such a way that they will fit into one and the same all-comprehensive theory. For that purpose I shall borrow the two Hobbesian concepts, rest and motion. But in contrast to Hobbes' man, who is a creature of incessant motion, finding rest only reluctantly in the Leviathan-ordained "felicity" of outward peace, our man desires repose as much as change, stability after mobility, adventure and security in alternation. Economically speaking, he craves for possession as much as for acquisition. In political terms, man is equally disposed to conquest and to domination. In Freud's language he is son and rebel, and then father and conserver. Sociologically, man will try to climb the social ladder as long and as high as he can reach. He will think and act "democratically" as a low man on the totem pole but step on those who follow on his heels and stand on his "aristocratic" privilege. And he may be both things at the same time, aristocrat and democrat, and "in perfect sincerity" at that.

Now this ambivalence is perfectly expressed by the elitist doctrine, and this may well be its greatest virtue—if there is virtue in an act that lacks intention. We propose to study the result in two convenient stages.

RT II

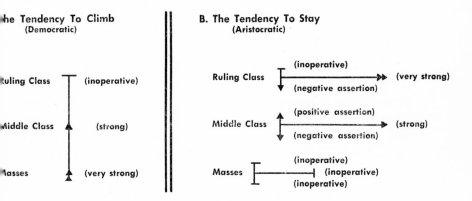

A. The vertical urge (tendency to climb) which is behind the democratic drive will manifest itself as long as there are still "new worlds to conquer." On the lowest, or mass, level, the felt need for self-promotion will express itself as primitive equalitarianism: what we want for ourselves, we grant to the entire group, if only for the reason that we realize how much our own advancement depends on co-operation with the group. Man at the bottom of the social pyramid has many reasons to think and act democratically, hardly any reasons for developing aristocratic notions (some possible reasons will be discussed under B).

Exactly where the democratic aspiration is at its most vigorous (between the lowest and the middle level or between the middle and the top rung) is a question to which there can be no simple answer. The history of revolutions is in that respect a cloudy mirror. In the French case, it was an already potent bourgeoisie which overthrew the old regime, while in the Russian revolution the dynamic impetus came from a petty bourgeois intellectual clique which, under Lenin's leadership, leapfrogged over the bourgeoisie into the vacant seats of power. In general, one might expect the democratic drive to slow down gradually, as the ascending class tries to secure a foothold. When the climbers reach the peak, the democratic drive becomes inoperative, though its rhetoric may be retained for reasons pointed out by C. Wright Mills.

B. The tendency to stay will generate the wish for positive assertion of one's "rights" against those who try to monopolize them; that wish, turned against the class next in line, may turn into the negative resolve to deny equal rights and to repress, by violence if necessary, those who claim them. Both reactions may occur together (the French bourgeoisie in 1848). The tendencies to stay will be weakest on the lowest level, because that is a most unattractive proposition. On the middle level the aristocratic tendency is already pronounced but kept from being all-pervasive by the prospect of still higher heights to conquer. However, the equalitarian aspect of the democratic creed becomes suspect, the radical schemes of the past are disavowed as childish dreams, their advocates outlawed as enemies and wreckers of society. At last the tendency to hold on altogether overshadows the acquisitive plebeian urge, the *bourgeois* becomes *gentilhomme* and closes ranks and club doors against the gate-crashing upstart.

The statement that assertive or repressive action could not possibly occur on the mass level needs qualification. In some societies, a race or class that finds itself below the social floor may play a useful, even an important role within, but is not a part of, the community. In that case, the group *on* the ground floor may try to keep the submarginals from rising in the social scale: the underdog has found his under-underdog and evolves an aristocratic attitude toward him. In relation to the middle class above him, the superior underdog maintains his democratic attitude (we are as good as you, if not better!) unless the barrier of admission becomes insurmountable. There are historic instances of a plebeian class withdrawing into a hard shell of isolation, forming its own sub-community which has the same sodalities and hierarchies as the society from which it is excluded. When the house above the surface crumbles, they are ready to rebuild it.

The strength of middle-class repressive action will depend on the degree of democratic pressure generated by the masses. It will normally not be as vigorous as the resistance of the top group to bourgeois ascendancy is apt to be. The need for self-assertion, on the other hand, with regard to the ruling classes, may transform parts of the bourgeoisie, into a self-styled caste, analogous to what may, *in extremis*, happen on the lower levels of society. The French *gens de la robe* who under the *ancien régime* monopolized the *parlements* as a hereditary class of jurists are a good example of that process of "aristocratization."

That the ruling class will try to prevent infiltration by the middle class by all means, fair or foul, goes without saying.

We are now ready for the last step: placing the aristocratic and the democratic tendencies (*A* and *B*) on the same system of co-ordinates:

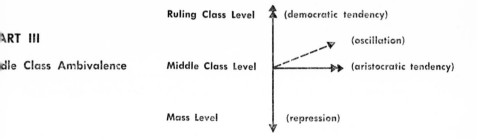

The chart takes account only of the middle class because it is the only one whose attitudes show a great measure of ambivalence under all conditions. Its democratic drive against the ruling class continues strongly, but the notion of aristocratic superiority is hardly less pronounced. At first it will assert itself only against the lower classes, but in the event that middle class ambition finds itself frustrated by the ruling class, the process of "aristocratization," referred to earlier, transforms what is left of the democratic tendency into a hybrid type in which the sense of superiority would be extended to the—conquered—mass and the—unconquered—ruling set alike.

It can be seen now why the would-be elite of the middle classes should evolve the kind of myth in which the actual blends with wish-dreams of the unachieved potential. The annoying snobbery of the elitist myth is only the most superficial aspect of that *junctim*, which combines both the aristocratic and the democratic preference. It can be seen now why the former should so strongly reassert itself precisely at the stage when the elite is facing the test which unmasks all ambiguity, when power is almost within its grasp and nothing is more deadly than equivocation. But equivocation is the fate of all elites, because they are pulled, irrevocably, in opposite directions which cannot be reconciled. They are, ironically, reconciled only when a great Tribune of the People becomes Caesar. Then the democratic drive still appears to continue with increasing fury against the defeated and, sometimes fictitious, enemies of freedom and equality, while the hard fact of domination is still in the future. How sad that this should be the *only* time in history when people feel that glowing satisfaction which is caused by the reconciliation, in one action, in one man, of their most potent social urges: to be rulers and be ruled in one mysterious consummation. Final triumph, ultimate defeat are bound together indissolubly.

These are some of the airy speculations which are stimulated by the simplifying magic of a chart, and it is with an overwhelming sense of guilt that we return now, for a last time, to our sober text.

Political Parties: Their Special Function

Still following the lead of Gaetano Mosca, Guido Dorso moves on to a study of that master institution of the agonistic instinct in our time: the political party. Like his master, he refuses to see any *fundamental* difference between a party and a church or sect, but he will grant that "political parties ... are particular human formations organized for the ideological-political struggle. While having much in common with the great religious institutions, they pursue a different objective, their field being politics." [65] But do they really? Was Mosca not perhaps right when he lumped together churches, sects, and parties? Cannot at least one of the contemporary parties be called an agnostic sect, a church of infidels? Mosca's well-known dislike and distrust of political parties in general may be explained, if only in part, by the fact that the only modern mass organization he knew was the Socialist Party—which most certainly had all the marks of a sectarian movement. As a liberal, Mosca had a lively fear of any human group which claimed to know the whole and only truth; it did not matter to him whether that claim was made by a church or by the followers of Marx.[66]

Not so the pupil. Although Dorso applies Mosca's observations about the great world religions to the modern parties—they too operate as "interclass organizations held together by a common ideology and built up into immense human associations comprising factions both of the political class and the masses ..." [67]—he, unlike Mosca, does not feel that parties disrupt the organic pattern of the social forces. If "in our time the ruling class comes on the whole from the efficient matrices of the political party," [68] the reason is not difficult to see: "The parties have become the generators of the ruling class simply because the various social groups or classes cannot possibly fulfill that function." [69]

Dorso knows, of course, that this is an exaggeration and that government by party does not exclude other screening methods used to parallel and supplement the democratic choice of leaders: "Many offices of decidedly political character are assigned to men who, strictly speaking, have not risen through the party cadres. It is true that there are ecclesiastical, bureaucratic, and military hierarchies which seem to rule the state all by themselves ..." But that appearance, Dorso believes, is deceptive. "All those governmental bodies, powerful as they may be, will function, as a rule, only through co-optation with that section of the ruling class which has directly crystallized out of the contest between parties ..." From the "political confessional" to the official masters of the state run lines of compromise which, be they ever so subtle, will rarely escape the attention even of the uninstructed common man.

Between "the regimes of permanent institutional compromise" (where the executive branch has retained its constitutional autonomy, as for example in the United States) and those of "a more outspoken democratic character" the only difference is this: in the first case, the party-born elite only enacts and promulgates the law which represents a compromise between that segment and all other segments of the ruling class, while in the second case the party cadres furnish the whole ruling personnel, including that of the bureaucracy, the foreign service, and the army.

Mosca was convinced that a regime in which the civil services and the judiciary become "politicized," in which collusion between legislators and administrators is the order of the day, could no longer maintain "juridical defense." Dorso, on the contrary, can see no reason why this should be so. He takes a highly optimistic view of the ability of the full-fledged democracies to maintain a superior level of political organization. In that respect, "these countries are indubitably more advanced." The way in which they manage to supply the kind of leadership essential to the conduct of affairs proves that "their masses have superior education and more influence, and also that the evolution of the ruling class encounters fewer obstacles." [70]

These obstacles would, in our democratic age, be insurmountable if the selection of elites were still left to the distinct social forces and their human counterparts, the various interest or pressure groups: "a conservative party, composed merely of aristocrats and grand bourgeois, could never rally a majority and would be, therefore, kept forever out of government." But political history shows that, on the contrary, conservative parties have held office, in all countries, for long periods. This was possible, and only possible, because they managed to attract broad strata who would normally not vote for the conservative *class* interest. However, "through the mechanism of the party" the conservatives "succeed in launching programs of political and social conservation which enlist the interests of the majority."

The best historical example of this new kind of conservativism is

Disraeli's reform of the Tory party. In our time, the Conservatives of England or the Christian-Democratic parties of post-fascist Italy and Germany might serve as equally good illustrations. Dorso could have proved his point equally well by reference to modern labor governments such as existed in Great Britain until recently and still exist in Scandinavia. Everywhere we would find the new phenomenon so ominous to Mosca's mind: massive political machines obliterating all class barriers, collaring the masses, *activating them for the first time in human history.* What Dorso says of the conservatives applies to all political organizations acting in the name of representative democracy:

The ideological formula of the party enlists not only the ruling oligarchies which have most at stake in the preservation of the social fabric, but also vast numbers of the middle and lower-middle class, as well as large portions of those masses who normally have nothing to hope and nothing to fear from the changes taking place within the ruling class.

In broadening its basis the elite gives up its class identity without surrendering its leader function. Nothing is lost. On the contrary, only through full democratization can the process of elite formation operate with full efficiency:

It is clear that the political class is an offshoot of the ruling class, the technico-political instrument for the administration of the country. Its formation takes place constantly and normally through the medium of the political party which has the specific task of sifting from the masses the potential leaders of the nation.[71]

The elitist and the democratic routes have merged.

Guido Dorso even has a happy explanation for that absence of initiative by which the doctrinaires of the elite like to distinguish the ruled from the rulers: "through the political party, elements of the governed class achieve a rapid passage into the political or ruling classes, and in the process they bleed the governed class." They leave it behind in an "anemic" state. And that, adds Dorso, is not due to any "diabolic intrigue" of the ruling class. It simply means that "the governed class is all the time supplying new cells to the ruling class. It has a function similar to the process of blood circulation."

So much about political physiology. But something else is said on behalf of the governed class: "In the last sense it rules itself." [72]

This is no longer the authentic gospel. It is Gaetano Mosca's seen in a new, brighter light. Not merely the reconciliation of democracy and aristocracy (in liberal disguise), it is—great music to our ears!—a clear reaffirmation of the democratic faith that We, The People, indeed rule ourselves, although that is a fact not always easy to discover.

The Debate Goes On

Guido Dorso expressed the cautious optimism of a nation which had just emerged from fascist domination and wartime occupation into what looked like a new era of democratic freedom tempered by bold leadership. One may wonder whether Dorso would still write in the same vein today. But, then, he might, because his Italy has still a long way to go before she will have reached the stage of mass civilization.

Contemporary England, on the other hand, has become one gigantic suburbia without the benefit of the economic dynamism of its counterpart in America. That fact perhaps explains the remarkable urgency which characterizes the debate of elites and elitism among the English intelligentsia, both of conservative and laborite persuasion. The reaction for the most part is one of recoil from elitist ideas. So one reads, for instance, in the most distinguished English literary review, which only some years ago found very kind words for Gaetano Mosca's particular brand of aristocratic liberalism, a rather trenchant attack on theorists, all theorists, of the elite, particularly of "power elites"—an attack which almost amounts to a declaration of love for, of all people, Karl Marx. And this in an organ of unquestionably conservative leanings. The occasion is a review of C. Wright Mills' new book. Not only is he made to suffer the supreme ignominy of being treated as one more elitist, albeit a most radical one—what is worse, he is not even given a fair hearing. "The elite theory," one reads, "seeks to identify those who actually rule. It is an altogether less refined and less far-reaching instrument than the class theory which, whatever abuses and exaggerations occurred in its application, sought to explore the social and economic basis of the whole group from which the rulers were drawn and in whose behalf they acted." But, is not Mills' argument precisely that the new "power elites" draw their strength from the key institutions they control and that they no longer have to act responsibly on behalf of anyone? [73]

The necessary reappraisal of both the old class and the newer elite theories is carried on with particular vigor in the pages of another British journal. There one finds the young Labour M.P., Anthony Crosland, addressing himself to the problem of an elite of intellectual merit. He flatly states that "people do not want to be ruled by a select elite. To be sure, an aristocracy of talent is an obvious improvement on a hereditary aristocracy ... [But] any selection must in practice be based on a limited number of more or less known and measurable aspects of character." Now, "why should [intelligence] be singled out for such an exceptional treatment?" Crosland asks. "Why should no marks be given for saintliness, generosity, compassion, humor, beauty, assiduity, continence, or artistic ability?" This is what the writer calls "the fundamental ethical case against any elite or aristocracy." [74]

Crosland's and the *Times* writer's viewpoints are combined in an essay by Peregrine Worsthorne, who exclaims: "An upper class may feel superior and a lower class may feel inferior; but how much more rigid and unfraternal would a society be in which those at the top not only felt but *were* superior and those at the bottom not only felt but *were* inferior—and knew it! The very evils of a society stratified by money or birth at least avoid the worst danger of all—a society dominated by men whose privileges are invulnerable because entirely deserved." [75]

The new elite rejecting the idea of elites: this is, at least to this writer, a good omen.

THE FINAL VERSION OF
THE THEORY OF THE RULING CLASS

by Gaetano Mosca *

The two traditional classifications of the forms of government are those of Aristotle and Montesquieu. The former distinguished between monarchies, aristocracies, and democracies, depending on whether sovereign power was vested in a single person, a restricted class, or in the totality of the citizens. Montesquieu defined as despotic those regimes in which the power of the sovereign was unrestrained by any custom, local or class privilege, or his own law; a monarchy, he said, was a state in which the ruler was subject to those restraints, and all organizations with non-hereditary heads of state he labeled as republics of the democratic or aristocratic type, depending on whether sovereignty belonged to all or only a part of the citizens.

These classifications have this common defect, that they are based

* This is a translation of the fortieth (last) chapter of the author's *Storia delle dottrine politiche* of 1933 (see above, Chapter 11). Reproduced by special permission of Dr. Bernardo Mosca, Rome.

Footnotes omitted, except one which has been incorporated in the text.

on observation of a single moment in the evolution of political organisms. In the case of Aristotle, the model was the Greek polis of the fifth and fourth centuries b.c.; Montesquieu considered only the conditions which existed in the Europe of his time, when Venice, Genoa, and Switzerland did not have a hereditary chief of state, when France was governed by a monarchy which to a certain extent was limited by custom, a relatively independent judiciary, and by the privileges of the upper classes and the corporations, and Turkey was ruled by a unique despot who, apparently, did as he pleased. Between the lines, the author of *The Spirit of the Laws* let it be known that his ideal was the tempered monarchy as it existed at the time in England.

The other, more important, defect of the two traditional classifications is the superficiality of the criteria on which they are based. They take into account the formal rather than the really substantial differences between the various political organisms. Speaking of Montesquieu, it is not difficult to prove that there is more dissimilarity between the governments he calls republics than between some of them and certain monarchies. For instance, the United States has today surely less in common with the French Republic than the latter has with the Kingdom of Belgium; it is hardly necessary to mention the great differences between the republics of our time and those of medieval times or of antiquity. If we consider Aristotle's scheme, we see at once that it is quite impossible for one man to rule over millions of subjects without the assistance of a hierarchy of officials or a ruling class, and equally impossible for a democracy to function without a co-ordinating and directing body which again will be an organized minority, another ruling class.

Today, a whole new method of political analysis attempts to draw attention to that very fact; its major purpose is to study the formation and organization of that ruling stratum which in Italy is by now generally known by the name of *political class*—an expression which together with the term *elite*, used by Pareto, begins to find international acceptance.

To be exact, the method is not altogether new, for the importance of, and the need for, a ruling class had already been intuitively recognized in isolated instances in antiquity, and later by such men as Machiavelli, Guicciardini, and Rousseau. Even more authors had that intuition in the nineteenth century, foremost among whom was Saint-Simon. But it was only toward the end of that century and afterwards that the new vision became diffused.

One of the first results of the new method was the notion of what, since 1883, has been known as the *political formula*, meaning that in all societies, be their level ever so mediocre, the ruling class will justify its power by appealing to some sentiment or credence generally accepted in that period and by that society, such as the presumed Popular or Divine Will, the notion of a distinct nationality or Chosen People, traditional loyalty toward a dynasty, or confidence in a man of exceptional qualities.

Of course, every political formula must reflect the specific intellectual and moral maturity of the people and the epoch in which it is adopted. It must closely correspond to the particular conception of the world prevailing at that time in that particular society, in order to cement the moral unity of all the individuals who compose it.

Any indication that a political formula has become "dated," that the faith in its principles has become shaky, that the ardent sentiments which once inspired it have begun to cool down is a sign that serious transformations of the ruling class are imminent. The French revolution came when the great majority of Frenchmen ceased to believe in the divine right of kings, and the Russian revolution broke out when virtually the whole intelligentsia, and perhaps also the majority of the Russian workers and peasants, had stopped believing that the Tsar had received the right from God to govern Holy Russia autocratically.

Vice versa, when a political formula is in harmony with the mentality of the epoch and in tune with the prevailing sentiments of the nation, its utility is undeniable: it often serves as a check on the power of the ruler and ennobles somewhat the subjection of the ruled, making it appear less the result of merely brute coercion.

Given the fact that a ruling class is necessary to the functioning of all political organisms, it is evident that the study of political phenomena must focus upon the examination of the various ways in which the ruling class is formed and organized.

As concerns organization, one may say that, up to now, three types existed: the feudal, the bureaucratic, and the third, less frequent but with an impressive intellectual heritage and quite important in its times, the Greek-Italian city-state.

The system which, in accord with the historical tradition, we call feudal is the simplest and most primitive of the three. It is also the least satisfactory because it rarely succeeds in co-ordinating all the forces of a people in pursuit of one and the same end, in peace or war. Its main characteristic is the fragmentation of the state into small parts, in each of which the representative of the supreme lord appropriates to himself all sovereign powers. That is what happened in medieval Europe when the baron was at the same time the military chief and the chief civil magistrate and also had the right to levy taxes and all kinds of tributes in his fief.

The result was to make each part of the state so independent of the center that complete secession became relatively easy. Accordingly, the unity of any feudal state and the cohesion between its component parts could be maintained only when the central organ was administered by a superior ruler of enough prestige and energy to overawe the local chieftain, or else when the national sentiment was sufficiently developed to hinder the dismemberment of the state, as was the case in Japan prior to the *Tokugawa Shoguns* early in the eighteenth century.

The bureaucratic system is characterized by the fact that the governmental functions are distributed not geographically but according to their nature. The military tasks thus become separated from the administrative-judicial duties, and these from financial operations. Each attribute of sovereignty is now entrusted to as many special hierarchies of officeholders, each of which receives its impulse from the central organ of the state. With the various activities of government distributed among different persons, the action of the small group which presides over the state becomes much more efficient and secure; conversely, there is little chance for any part to break away and achieve independence from the state.

The ancient oriental monarchies and the Mohammedan states usually retained a feudal character. In contrast, we can find in ancient Egypt traces of an evolution toward state bureaucracy. Bureaucratization can be likewise ascertained during the happier periods of Chinese civilization, although the provincial governors retained great power. Even greater was the independence of the Persian satraps, and there is no doubt that excessive local independence was one of the main causes of the, relatively rapid, dissolution of the Caliphate of Baghdad and of the Moghul empire.

The transition from the feudal to the bureaucratic stage is usually quite slow. A typical example is the development of France, where the struggle between central monarchy and feudalism lasted almost seven centuries, from Hugh Capet to Louis XIV. Disintegration of a bureaucratic state is rarer than the dissolution of a feudal organism, but when it happens, as for instance in the case of the Western Roman Empire in the fifth century A.D., the collapse is likely to be more complete and more enduring than that of a feudal system, and the breakdown of the political machinery will be accompanied by a change of the moral forces and by the deterioration of the economic strength which that society had previously enjoyed.

We have already mentioned the characteristics that distinguished the old city-states of Greece and Rome from the two other types of government—characteristics which can also be discovered in the medieval communes rising throughout Western Europe after 1000 A.D. In these as in the old city-states the ruling class was, at least in appearance, very large, including (given the short tenure and the fast rotation of all public offices) a good-sized portion of the citizenry. In fact, however, the important offices were almost always controlled by the members of a certain number of illustrious families. That was particularly so in Rome; in Greece the democratic current triumphed in imposing absolute equality on all the citizens, but the accompanying civil wars, and the spoliation of the rich that went with them, prepared the ground for the formation of tight oligarchies, which in turn produced the tyrant.

In the medieval commune, too, the most important offices were as a rule reserved for the heads of the major craft guilds or, as in Venice, for a certain number of distinguished families. Where such a power concentration in a limited group did not occur, the commune almost invariably gave way to a *signoria*, the equivalent of the ancient tyranny.

It is a well-known fact that hardly ever did the old polis or the medieval commune manage to extend its boundaries and at the same time keep intact the principles on which the state was based. Only the political wisdom of Rome could partly overcome that difficulty, but when her dominion had expanded to all corners of the Mediterranean, even Rome was finally forced to adopt a bureaucratic form of government.

Still, the strength and the resilience of the city-state in an emergency surpassed by far the limitations of its size. Thus Athens, after having lost all but a few of the forty thousand men sent on the ill-fated Sicilian expedition, remained strong enough to withstand the Peloponnesian League for almost another decade. Rome's immense losses did not prevent her from winning the first and second Punic wars, and Pisa, which in the thirteenth century never had more than eighty thousand inhabitants, suffered no less than five thousand casualties and eleven thousand prisoners in the battle of La Meloria alone. The Athenian, Florentine, Venetian contributions to the arts and sciences are too well known to require more than a brief mention.

The intellectual influence exerted by this form of government was, in conjunction with some other factors, favorable to the evolution of that type of social and political organization which may be called liberal, in distinction from that other type which may be labeled autocratic. The main characteristic of the liberal system consists in the fact that in it power is transmitted from the bottom to the top. That is, the functionaries are elected by the citizens who subsequently are expected to obey them, whereas in the autocratic system the supreme chief appoints his immediate aides who in turn appoint the lower officials.

The last-named system was in force in the old oriental monarchies, the Moslem states, the Roman and Byzantine empires and, with certain limitations, also in the Western European monarchies from the sixteenth to the early nineteenth century. As examples of the liberal regime we may list, in addition to the ancient city-states and medieval communes, the various republican governments and parliamentary monarchies, although they may as well be classified as a mixed type, since their bureaucracies, which control a good part of the effective power, are almost always recruited along autocratic lines.

In general, the autocratic regimes may be said to have a greater staying power than the liberal regimes. The organism of the latter is so delicate that it will function only under suitable conditions, preferably in periods of economic prosperity and of great intellectual flowering. It would be naive to assume that the regimes called liberal are actually based, as their political formula claims, on the explicit consent of the popular majority. As I have demonstrated elsewhere, the electoral contest takes place between organized minorities controlling the disorganized majority of voters, who may choose between a small number of candidates presented by those minorities.

Still, the necessity to make a bid for the allegiance of the vast, unorganized majority obliges each of those groups to adapt itself, if only in appearance, to the thoughts and sentiments prevailing among the masses. That necessity sometimes enables liberal regimes to display an amazing vigor, but it has also the effect of forcing the ruling class to play up to the great majority of people who are less aware of the true interests of the society. And that is why the greatest threat to liberal institutions comes from the extension of the suffrage to the most uncultured strata of the population.

Even more important than the examination of the various types of ruling class organization is the study of the various methods by which ruling classes are recruited. What criteria are they using to admit some individuals while keeping out the rest?

The predominant criterion, all but indispensable to the formation of a ruling class, is the ability to rule. It is, as Saint-Simon already knew, the sum of all the personal characteristics most appropriate to the direction of a certain people in a certain period. Add to it the will to rule and the conviction of possessing the right qualities —qualities which undergo continuous change as the conditions of each people in intellectual, moral, economic, as well as in military matters change continuously, with the result that each people's political and administrative arrangements also need appropriate modifications.

These modifications may take place gradually, in which case the new elements who infiltrate the ruling class will not effect a radical change in its attitude and structure. If, on the contrary, the changes in the composition of the ruling class take place in a tumultuous and rapid fashion, the replacement of the old minority by the new elements may be almost completed in the course of one or two generations. In the first case, the prevailing influence is, as we called it elsewhere, the aristocratic tendency; in the second it is the one which we called the democratic.

It is rather difficult if not impossible to nullify completely either one of these two tendencies. The absolute predominance of the aristocratic tendency would presuppose that the ideas and conditions of human association never change; experience shows the absurdity of that assumption. On the other hand, the democratic tendency could absolutely triumph only on condition that the sons would not inherit the means, contacts, and advantages in training which enabled their progenitors to capture all the choice positions.

The private ownership of land and capital has been regarded as the major cause responsible for the hereditary nature of political control. Now I shall not deny the modicum of truth contained in that assertion. But we have already seen, to our satisfaction, that the state control of the means of production would leave the administrators of the state—who are sure to be a minority—in a position where they should be able to combine all economic and political power in their hands and to appropriate the largest share in such a manner as would advance the career of their own sons and protégés.

In the remote past, rapid and almost complete renewals of the ruling class took place not infrequently in the wake of an irruption of barbaric tribes which had not yet found a fixed habitat. They established themselves in the conquered country and supplanted there the previous rulers. Very often the success of the invaders was due to the discord and the decadence of the old dominant minority, and almost always to the apathy, sometimes to the connivance, of the lower class in the invaded territory.

These political cataclysms were not at all rare events in the oriental empires of antiquity. The Mesopotamian civilization suffered several of them, and the havoc which the Hyksos worked in Egypt is a well-known story. Invasions of the same type were, at various intervals, the ruin of the Chinese and Indian civilizations; the fall of Rome and the invasions of the Arabs and Turks are all part of the same chronicle.

With the progress of civilization, the zone populated by barbarians became more and more restricted, while the densely settled areas of industrious, peaceful agriculturers and artisans increased apace. A much improved technology put into their hands weapons of defense which had not been available against the raiders led by Genghis Khan and Tamerlane. Catastrophes caused by external forces have thus become more and more unlikely, if not utterly impossible.

In our time, the violent convulsions of the social order are the product of internal factors. The ruling class, attacked by a political force from below, disintegrates. Instead of invasions, we have today revolutions. It will suffice to mention here the great French revolution; what took place in Japan between 1853 and 1886 may well be called a revolution too. And there is finally the Russian revolution, the most violent of all. But no matter how violent and whatever the causes of the cataclysms that revolutionize the composition and the structure of the ruling class, almost invariably some elements, more or less numerous, of the old ruling class will enter the ranks of the new.

From an objective study of historical events one may draw this conclusion: The best regimes, that is, those lasting a long time and able to avoid the violent convulsions which have plunged mankind back into barbarism, are the mixed regimes. We call them mixed because in them neither the autocratic nor the liberal principle rules supreme, and the aristocratic tendency is tempered by a gradual but continuous renewal of the ruling class, enabling it thus to absorb the better elements into its ranks. But in order that such a regime may long endure, conditions must exist which not even the wisest legislator can create by fiat. The necessary multiplicity and balance of the ruling forces, if they are to function well, require a highly civilized community. Also, the church ought to be separated from the state; economic decisions must not be monopolized by the political decision-makers; the means of violence must never be controlled by any single faction of the people; last, men of cultural and technical accomplishment ought to be given access to the ruling class.

But more is needed: a great deal of education, which is always a slow process, and long experience in devising the most practical means of domesticating the base instincts which so often are joint to the will to power—instincts which again and again reasserted themselves after a protracted period of political and social peace, just when they seemed to be extinct forever.

NOTES

Abbreviations

TE for *Teorica dei governi e governo parlamentare* (2d ed.; Turin, 1925).
EL " *Elementi di scienza politica* (4th ed.; Bari, 1947).
RC " *The Ruling Class (Elementi di scienza politica)* (New York and London, 1939).
ST " *Storia delle dottrine politiche* (6th ed.; Bari, 1951).
PS " *Partiti e sindacati nella crisi del regime parlamentare* (Bari, 1949).
For other editions, see the Bibliography

Preface

1. Carl J. Friedrich, *The New Image of the Common Man* (2d ed.; Boston, 1950), p. 246.

Introduction

1. James Burnham, *The Machiavellians: Defenders of Freedom* (New York, 1943). See Chap. 12 of this work.
2. Isaac Deutscher, "Russia in Transition," *Dissent*, II, No. 1 (Winter, 1955), 32.
3. Robert Michels, *Political Parties* (Glencoe, Ill., 1949), pp. 401, 407.
4. Max Nomad, "Masters—Old and New," in *The Making of Society*, ed. V. F. Calverton (New York, 1937), pp. 893, 891.
5. For a good account of the two schools of democracy, see H. B. Mayo, *Democracy and Marxism* (New York, 1955), pp. 254 ff.; also Harold J. Laski, *The Prospects of Democratic Government* (Williamsburg, 1939), p. 4.

394 Notes to Pages 6–14

6. Karl Marx, *Capital* (London, 1920), I, 29.

7. Gaetano Mosca, RC, pp. 332–37. See also p. 193 of this work.

8. That is, in any case, the line which Georges Sorel took in his *Réflexions sur la violence* (Paris, 1908); translated as *Reflections on Violence* (London and New York, 1914).

9. Vilfredo Pareto, *The Mind and Society* (New York, 1935), IV, 1926, Sec. II-u; III, 1422, Sec. 2027; 1424, Secs. 2035–36; and 1426, Sec. 2043.

10. Karl Mannheim postulated "a nonpartisan body of highly esteemed and disinterested men . . . which might gain great moral prestige and become the 'conscience of the country.' The members should represent the diverse social and intellectual currents of the community, so that their agreement and joint resolve would represent a high-level mediation of tensions at large." *Freedom, Power and Democratic Planning* (New York, 1950), p. 166. See also the same author's *Ideology and Utopia* (New York: Harvest Books, n. d.), pp. 185 ff.

11. But the Marxian influence is still much in evidence when Mosca writes: "One might say, indeed, that the whole history of civilized mankind comes down to a conflict between the tendency of dominant elements to monopolize political power . . . and the tendency toward a dislocation of old forces and an insurgence of new forces . . ." RC, p. 65.

12. Pareto, *op. cit.*, III, 1430, Sec. 2053.

13. "In der einen oder anderen Form schlugen überall die Massen durch, wie in einer geistigen Völkerwanderung, die von unten aufsteigt" (the universal triumph of the masses was "a spiritual barbarian migration from below"). Alfred Weber, *Kulturgeschichte als Kultursoziologie* (2d ed.; Munich, 1951), p. 444. See also the Supplement to the present study, p. 390.

14. Ludwig Gumplowicz, *Der Rassenkampf*, Preface to the 1st ed. (1883), in *Ausgewählte Werke* (Innsbruck, 1928), III, viii. The theory is far from dead: see Franz Oppenheimer, *Der Staat* in *System der Soziologie*, Vol. II (Jena, 1926), a work which carries Gumplowicz's philosophy into the twentieth century (originally published in Frankfurt a. M., 1908; translated as *The State*, Indianapolis, 1914). A contemporary member of the school is Alexander Rüstow with his theory of "Überlagerung" (superimposition), *Ortsbestimmung der Gegenwart* (Zurich, Vol. I, 1950; II, 1952; III, 1955). About Rüstow, see Carl J. Friedrich, "The Political Thought of Neo-Liberalism," *American Political Science Review*, XLIX, No. 2 (June, 1955), 509–25.

15. RC, Chaps. V ("juridical defense") and XVI, pp. 456 f. ("relative justice").

16. See p. 154 of this study.

17. See Sorel, *op. cit.* (Glencoe, Ill., 1950), Chap. 7, "The Ethics of Producers."

18. For Mosca's strictures on Machiavelli, see Chap. 12 of this work.

19. E.g., such a standard work as Francis W. Coker's *Recent Political Thought* completely ignores Mosca; so does John H. Hallowell in his *Main Currents of Modern Political Thought*. The *Encyclopaedia of the Social Sciences* (1933) has a long article on Pareto by Talcott Parsons; an article on Mosca will be sought in vain, though Mosca was one of the contributors to the *Encyclopaedia*.

See Robert Michels, *First Lectures in Political Sociology,* translated with an introduction by Alfred de Grazia (Minneapolis, 1949).

20. An excellent beginning has been made by H. Stuart Hughes: "Gaetano Mosca and the Political Lessons of History," *Teachers of History* (Ithaca, 1954), pp. 146–67.

21. RC, Chap. XII. For the controversy between Mosca and Pareto, see my discussion in Chap. 8.

22. The following four writers agree on this point: Arthur Livingston, Intro. to RC, xiv, xxxviii; Benedetto Croce, review of RC which became the Preface to the 4th Italian ed. (see my Chap. 6, p. 129); Mario delle Piane, *Bibliografia di Gaetano Mosca* (Florence, 1949), p. 52, where he speaks of the author's "epistemological and . . . methodological deficiencies"; Ferruccio Pergolesi, *Mosca* (Brescia, 1950), pp. 99 f.

23. See *The Comparative Study of Elites: An Introduction and Bibliography* by Harold D. Lasswell, Daniel Lerner, and C. Easton Rothwell (Stanford, 1952). Also: Donald R. Mathews, *The Social Background of Political Decision-Makers* (Garden City, N.Y., 1954), and E. Digby Baltzell, *Philadelphia Gentlemen: The Making of a National Upper Class* (Glencoe, Ill., 1957). About Mosca's interest in Lasswell's work and method, see my Chap. 6, p. 130.

24. Else Frenkel-Brunswik in *Totalitarianism,* ed. Carl J. Friedrich (Cambridge, Mass., 1954), p. 174. See also Karl Loewenstein, "Political Systems, Ideologies and Institutions: The Problem of Their Circulation," *Western Political Quarterly,* VI, No. 4 (December, 1953), 689: "It is submitted as the . . . major premise of this study that in any political system it is the underlying political ideology which actually conditions the function and shapes the operation of the political institutions and techniques."

25. "Prerogative del Capo del Governo," in Mosca, PS, pp. 277–84. See also Chap. 10 in the present work, pp. 224 f.

26. That source is Arthur Livingston in RC, p. xiv. My own account is influenced by Pergolesi, *op. cit.,* pp. 5–12.

27. The *Teorica dei governi* . . . of 1884.

28. "Pensieri inediti di Gaetano Mosca," *Ethos,* I, No. 3 (December, 1945), 3; Eccles. i:18.

Chapter 1

1. In addition to TE and EL: *Dei rapporti fra il Parlamento ed il potere giudiziario* . . . (Palermo, 1885); the précis of Mosca's lectures on constitutional law, "Studi ausiliari del diritto costituzionale," *Il Circolo giuridico,* XVII (1886), 101–10, which, according to Mario delle Piane (*Bibliografia di Gaetano Mosca,* Florence, 1949, p. 9) shows the influence of Achille Loria's economic materialism; and *Le costituzioni moderne* (Palermo, 1887), which foreshadows Mosca's key conception of "juridical defense." See also my Chap. 6, and n. 1, Chap. 6.

2. "Gaetano Mosca and the Political Lessons of History," *Teachers of History* (Ithaca, 1954), pp. 146–67.

3. My working copy of TE is a photostat of the 2d ed. For the reproduction President Einaudi kindly placed the facilities of the Italian government at my disposal.

4. TE, pp. iii, iv, v.

5. *Ibid.*, p. 5.

6. Rubashov and Gledkin are, of course, the well-known protagonists of Arthur Koestler's novel, *Darkness at Noon*.

7. For Italian critics of the parliamentary regime in Mosca's youth, see TE, p. 259, n. 1. Cf. also Bruno Brunello, *Il pensiero italiano dal Romagnosi al Croce* (Bologna, 1949), pp. 189–211; Michele Dipiero, *Storia critica dei partiti italiani* (Rome, 1946), p. 9; and Mario delle Piane, *Gaetano Mosca, Classe politica e liberalismo* (Naples, 1952), pp. 63 f. The salient figures are A. Cantalupi (*Politica in Italia*, Turin, 1880); P. Turiello (*Governo e governati in Italia*, Bologna, 1882); and R. Bonghi (*Opere*, Vols. I and III, Milan, 1933).

8. *Lezioni di storia delle istituzioni e delle dottrine politiche* (Rome, 1933). With the 2d ed. the title was changed to *Storia delle dottrine politiche* (Bari, 1937). See my Chap. 11.

9. TE, p. 16.

10. EL., Intro. to the 2d ed. (Turin, 1923), p. 2.

11. TE, p. 7.

12. *Ibid.*, p. 9. Eduard Fischel, constitutional lawyer, author of *Die Verfassung Englands* (Berlin, 1862); Heinrich Rudolf von Gneist, *Das heutige englische Verfassungs und Verwaltungsrecht* (Berlin, 1857–63), an authoritative study of British constitutional and administrative law; Joseph Kaspar Bluntschli, Swiss conservative publicist, author of the influential *Lehre vom modernen Staat* (Stuttgart, 1875). For Taine's works, see n. 14 to Chap. 4, below.

13. TE, pp. 12, 13, and 14, n. 1. In his review of EL, which became the Preface to the 4th Italian ed., Benedetto Croce expressed the belief "that Mosca apparently did not know [Vico], otherwise he surely would have drawn upon his thoughts in support of his own thesis" (*La Critica*, XXI, Nov., 1923).

14. TE, p. 14, n. 2. Mill has: "It often happens that the universal belief of one age of mankind—a belief from which no one *was*, nor, without an extraordinary effort of genius and courage, *could* at that time be free—becomes to a subsequent age so palpable an absurdity, that the only difficulty then is to imagine how such a thing can ever have appeared credible." In *Principles of Political Economy* (1848), ed. W. J. Ashley (London, 1909), p. 3.

15. TE, p. 15. This is Taine with a vengeance. "The question . . . as to the truth or falsity of Taine's theory in purely methodological respects, is whether he would have succeeded . . . had he depended exclusively on the form of scientific description and explanation which, as a philosopher, he had set up as the standard . . . Obviously this is not the case. He naively yielded himself to a sort of shrewd wisdom about man and a kind of 'physiognomics' that had grown out of quite other ground than that of scientific analysis." Ernst Cassirer, *The Problem of Knowledge* (New Haven, 1950), p. 253. Words which equally apply to Gaetano Mosca.

16. See p. 129.

17. TE, pp. 15–16. A pilot study of Mosca's attempt to replace Aristotle's scheme of governments has been made by Renzo Sereno: "The Anti-Aristotelianism of Gaetano Mosca and Its Fate," *Ethics*, XLIII, No. 4 (July, 1938), 509–18.

18. TE, p. 16.

19. RC, p. 50. This whole idea has been beautifully expressed by Trevelyan:

"When men collectively are very poor some few must be made rich if there is to be any accumulation of wealth for civilized purposes. When men collectively are very ignorant, progress is only possible through the endowment of an educated few. In such a world, organization can only begin through personal ascendancy and can only be rendered permanent through privilege." *History of England* (Garden City, 1953), I, 73.

20. "Piccola polemica," PS, p. 117.

21. TE, p. 16.

22. *Ibid.*, p. 18.

23. *Ibid.*, p. 19. This strongly reminds one of Machiavelli's "in all republics, however organized, there are never more than forty or fifty citizens who attain a position that entitles them to command" (*The Discourses*, Bk. I, Chap. 16, in *The Prince and the Discourses*, New York, 1940, p. 165), cited in RC, p. 329.

24. TE, p. 19.

25. See p. 35.

26. TE, pp. 20, 21.

27. Ludwig Gumplowicz, *Geschichte der Staatstheorien, Ausgewählte Werke* (1st ed; Innsbruck, 1926), I, 43–44. But Gumplowicz had expressed the same view on pp. 204–5 of *Der Rassenkampf*, first published in 1883, and even earlier in *Rasse und Staat* (Wien, 1875; also in *Ausgewählte Werke*, I, 397). Cf. also the same author's *Outlines of Sociology* (Philadelphia, 1899; trans. from *Grundiss der Soziologie*, Wien, 1885), p. 115: "Private property ... presupposes, first of all, an organized control, with power to compel obedience."

28. TE, p. 21.

29. Gumplowicz himself explains the origin of middle classes as due, not to force and subjugation, but to immigration and slow infiltration, that is, to a peaceful process placing that class somewhat outside of the two-class system of the rulers and the ruled (*Rasse und Staat, Ausgewählte Werke*, pp. 365–68). Thus, Gumplowicz escapes the narrow dualism which vitiates Mosca's institutional analysis in the *Teorica*. See also my Chap. 3.

Chapter 2

1. TE, p. 21.

2. *Republic*, I, 11. (351–52).

3. TE, p. 25.

4. In *The Mind and Society*, IV, 1950. (The index lists: Classes, social; Class-circulation.)

5. TE, p. 26.

6. *Ibid.*, p. 27. *Politics* vi. 7. 1321^{a}15 (Mod. Lib. ed.; New York, 1943), p. 271.

7. TE, pp. 28, 29.

8. Cf. RC, pp. 53–54: "In primitive societies ... military valor is the quality that most readily opens access to the ruling, or political, class. In societies of advanced civilization, war is the exceptional condition."

9. TE, pp. 30, 31.

10. *Ibid.*, p. 31, n. 2.

11. *Ibid.*, p. 32.

12. Mosca's source for facts about England is Eduard Fischel, *Die Verfassung Englands* (Berlin, 1862); see TE, p. 32.

13. RC, p. 419. This idea was further developed by Karl Mannheim; see Conclusions of this study and note 1 to Conclusions.

14. Oral communication from Dr. Bernardo Mosca.

15. See Conclusions hereinafter and note 1 to Conclusions.

16. TE, pp. 32, 33.

17. RC, pp. 404, 405. Saint-Simon's famous "Parable" first appeared in his and Auguste Comte's publication, "L'Organisateur" (*Oeuvres de Saint-Simon et Enfantin*, XX, 17–26); the English text is reproduced in Frank E. Manuel's recent monograph, *The New World of Henri Saint-Simon* (Cambridge, Mass., 1956), p. 211. "Mosca lauded him as a brilliant forerunner of his own theory of the élite" (p. 3). See also Herbert Marcuse, *Reason and Revolution* (New York, 1954), pp. 330 ff.; and Albert Salomon, *The Tyranny of Progress* (New York, 1955), *passim*.

18. TE, p. 34; RC, p. 335.

19. TE, p. 34. Mosca's high opinion of British local government as a liberal institution is not quite shared by Trevelyan, who has this to say about the situation under George III: "The Justices of the Peace were autocrats of the countryside and represented one class alone." *History of England* (Garden City, 1953), III, 145–46.

20. TE, p. 35.

21. RC, Chap. III.

22. Georges Sorel, *Introduction à l'économie moderne* (Paris, 1903), pp. 396–97.

23. TE, pp. 36, 37.

24. Karl Marx and Friedrich Engels, *Selected Works* (London, 1950), I, 356.

25. TE, p. 39.

26. See Chap. 1, and n. 23 to Chap. 1.

27. ST, pp. 9, 265. Saint-Simon's theory of social classes, an integral part of his doctrine of historical phases, is developed in "L'Organisateur" (*Oeuvres de Saint-Simon et Enfantin*, XX, 77 ff.). See Manuel, *op. cit.*, Chap. 19.

28. RC, p. 444.

29. See above, p. 57, and n. 23 to this chapter.

Chapter 3

1. TE, p. 53, n. 1. *The Ancient City*, by Numa Denis Fustel de Coulanges, was first published in 1864; the English translation, in 1873.

2. Julius Wellhausen, *Geschichte Israels* (Berlin, 1878); Simon Dubnow, *Weltgeschichte des juedischen Volkes*, 10 vols. (Berlin, 1925–29); Elias Auerbach, *Wueste und Gelobtes Land* (Berlin, 1932); Oscar Goldberg, *Die Wirklichkeit der Hebraeer* (Berlin, 1932). Adolf Erman, *Ägypten und ägyptisches Leben im Altertum* (Tübingen, 1885–87); J. H. Breasted, *A History of Egypt from the Earliest Time to the Persian Conquest* (New York, 1905); Gaston Maspero's *Études égyptiennes* were published in 1879–82, but his *Lectures historiques, histoire ancienne, Égypte, Assyrie* did not appear until 1890.

3. TE, p. 43 and n. 1; Judg. xxi: 25.

4. TE, p. 44.

5. *Ibid.*, p. 45. See Max Weber, *Gesammelte Aufsätze zur Religionssoziologie* (4th ed.; Tübingen, 1947), III., 108, 122 f.; trans. as *Ancient Judaism* (Glencoe, Ill., 1952; pp. 103, 113).

6. TE, pp. 46, 47.

7. *Ibid.*, p. 47.

8. *Ibid.*, pp. 48, 49.

9. *Ibid.*, p. 50.

10. *Ibid.*, p. 51.

11. See Oswald Spengler, *Decline of the West* (New York, 1939), II, 353, 427, 435; also A. J. Toynbee, *A Study of History*, I, 45–46, 137 ff.; IV, 85, 224, 413, 421, 516; V, 695–96.

12. TE, p. 57.

13. *Ibid.*, p. 56.

14. *Ibid.*, pp. 58, 59.

15. *Republic*, VIII, 1, 560.

16. TE, p. 61.

17. *Politics*, v. 4. 1304^a 41; v. 6. 1306^a 26 (Mod. Lib. ed.; New York, 1943), pp. 219 and 225.

18. Toynbee, *op. cit.*, IV, 201.

19. G. B. Grundy, *Thucydides and the History of His Age* (2d ed.; London, 1948), I, 113; II, 162.

20. See Joseph A. Schumpeter, *Capitalism, Socialism and Democracy* (2d ed.; New York and London, 1947), p. 364; Vernon V. Aspaturian, "The Contemporary Doctrine of the Soviet State and Its Philosophical Foundations," *American Political Science Review*, XLVIII, No. 4 (December, 1954), 1037 ff.

21. TE, p. 63.

22. Grundy, *op. cit.*, II, 163.

23. TE, p. 64.

24. Toynbee, *op. cit.*, IV, 200 ff.

25. See his *Imperialism, The Highest Stage of Capitalism* in *Selected Works* (London, 1947), I, 635, 708–10.

26. Grundy, *op. cit.*, II, 193–201.

27. TE, p. 65.

28. Grundy, *op. cit.*, II, 205–12.

29. TE, p. 65.

30. *On Power* (New York, 1949), title of Book IV.

31. TE, p. 67.

32. For the important distinction between the concept of revolt of the poor and that of class revolution, see Michael Freund, *Georges Sorel: Der revolutionaere Konservativismus* (Frankfurt a. M., 1932), pp. 84–85.

33. TE, p. 68.

34. *Ibid.*, p. 69.

35. See R. E. Smith, *The Failure of the Roman Republic* (Cambridge, 1955), Chaps. IX and X.

36. TE, p. 70.

37. Spengler, *op. cit.*, II, 506.

38. TE, pp. 71, 72.

39. See Mikhail I. Rostovtsev, *The Social and Economic History of the Roman Empire* (London, 1926), Chap. XI.

40. TE, p. 75.

41. In A.D. 275 the Senate's choice fell on old M. Cornelius Tacitus (killed by the soldiers one year later). A similar "return to constitutionality" occurred during the English Great Rebellion, when the ruling army clique restored the old Rump under its Speaker, William Lenthall (1659).

Chapter 4

1. *The Prince*, Chap. XIX, in *The Prince and the Discourses* (Mod. Lib. ed.; New York, 1940), p. 69.

2. This is, of course, an allusion to Lenin's famous fragment, *The State and Revolution*, in *Selected Works* (London, 1947), II, 141 ff.

3. TE, pp. 92, 93.

4. *Ibid.*, p. 85.

5. *Ibid.*, p. 101.

6. *Ibid.*, p. 106.

7. *Ibid.*, pp. 102–4.

8. *Ibid.*, pp. 105, 107.

9. See Franz Mehring, *Der brandenburgisch-preussische Staat*, in *Historische Aufsaetze zur preussisch-deutschen Geschichte* (Berlin, 1946).

10. See J. Salwyn Schapiro, *Liberalism and the Challenge of Fascism* (New York, 1949), pp. 328 ff.

11. TE, p. 105.

12. *Ibid.*, p. 108. The number of all families presented at Court was estimated at 4,000. That would make the "ruling class" 18,000 to 20,000 members strong. See Martin Goering, *Weg und Sieg der modernen Staatsidee in Frankreich* (Tübingen, 1946), p. 16.

13. TE, p. 107.

14. Hippolyte A. Taine, *Les origines de la France contemporaine* (Paris, 1877–85; *The Origins of Contemporary France*, New York, 1878–85). Mosca's other important source is Alexis de Tocqueville's *L'Ancien régime et la révolution* (Paris, 1855; *The Old Regime and the Revolution*, New York, 1856).

15. TE, p. 131.

16. *Ibid.*, p. 129. Cf. Trevelyan, *History of England* (Garden City, 1953), I, 321: "It was not so much that the clergy had sunk as that the laity had risen."

17. TE, p. 111.

18. See Goering, *op. cit.*, p. 22; also Franz Neumann, Intro. to Montesquieu, *The Spirit of the Laws* (New York, 1949), p. xxii; cf. further Albert Mathiez, *La révolution française* (10th ed.; Paris, 1948), I, Chap. 11.

19. TE, p. 131. See Daniel Mornet, *Les origines intellectuelles de la révolution française* (4th ed.; Paris, 1947), pp. 469–77.

20. TE, pp. 136, 134, 135.

21. *Ibid.*, pp. 135–36.

22. *Ibid.*, p. 137.

23. Clarence C. Brinton, *Anatomy of Revolution* (2d rev. ed.; New York, 1952).
24. TE, p. 139.
25. About the Jesuits, see RC, pp. 26, 169, 194–95.
26. Toynbee's term. I am thinking of the curious underground existence which the communist conspiracy of Gracchus Babeuf led in the history of the French bourgeois revolution, until Buonarroti linked it to the incipient tradition of the proletarian movement. See J. L. Talmon, *The Rise of Totalitarian Democracy* (Boston, 1952), *passim*.
27. TE, p. 139.
28. *Ibid.*, pp. 140, 141.
29. *Ibid.*, p. 142.

Chapter 5

1. TE, p. 147.
2. *Ibid.*, p. 148.
3. *Ibid.*, p. 250.
4. *Ibid.*, pp. 250–51.
5. RC, p. 154
6. *Ibid.*, p. 155.
7. TE, p. 251.
8. Aristotle, *De anima*, III.
9. TE, p. 251, again almost identical with RC, p. 154.
10. TE, p. 252.
11. *Ibid.*, pp. 253, 254.
12. Michels, *Political Parties* (Glencoe, Ill., 1949) pp. 377 ff.
13. TE, p. 255.
14. *Ibid.*, p. 256.
15. *What Is To Be Done?*, in Lenin, *Selected Works* (London, 1947), I, 167–68; Georges Sorel, *Reflections on Violence* (Glencoe, Ill., 1950), Chap. 6.
16. TE, pp. 256, 257, 258.
17. *Ibid.*, p. 259, n. (1925). See also Chaps. 6, 9, and 10 of the present work.
18. See Chap. 8 of the present work.
19. See above, p. 9.
20. TE, p. 263.
21. *Ibid.*, p. 280.
22. *Ibid.*, p. 281.
23. *Ibid.*, pp. 294–95.
24. *Ibid.*, p. 292.
25. Max Weber, *Gesammelte Aufsätze zur Religionssoziologie* (4th ed.; Tübingen, 1947), I, 4, and the same author's *Wirtschaft und Gesellschaft*, in *Grundriss der Nationalökonomik* (3d ed.; Tübingen, 1947), Pt. III, I, 96. Cf. Weber, *The Theory of Social and Economic Organization* (New York, 1947), pp. 279 f.
26. TE, p. 288.
27. *Ibid.*, p. 292.
28. *Ibid.*, p. 293.

29. From the large literature on this subject I cite: Emil Lederer and Jakob Marschak, *The New Middle Class* (New York, 1937); Lewis Corey, *The Unfinished Task* (New York, 1942); and Peter Drucker, *The Future of Industrial Man* (New York, 1942).

30. TE, pp. 294, 295.

31. *Ibid.*, pp. 297, 298.

32. *Ibid.*, p. 298, n. 1 (1925).

33. *Ibid.*, p. 300.

Chapter 6

1. *Le costituzioni moderne*, 1887. Delle Piane, in his *Bibliografia di Gaetano Mosca* (Florence, 1950, p. 7), discovers the same concept even earlier, in *Dei rapporti fra il Parlamento ed il potere giudiziario* ... of 1885, See n. 1 to Chap. 1, above.

2. EL (2d ed.; "with a second, unpublished part"; Turin, 1923). Mosca's autobiographical remark occurs on the first page of Vol. I.

3. RC, p. xl.

4. *Ibid.*, p. 52.

5. *Ibid.*, pp. xxxvi–xxxix.

6. The subject of Gumplowicz and Comte is taken up in Chapter VI of the first ed. of EL; in the RC it is moved up into Chapter III, "where it logically belonged." (Arthur Livingston, ed., RC, p. xl.)

7. RC, pp. 29, 30.

8. Friedrich Nietzsche, *The Joyful Wisdom*, No. 349, in *The Complete Works* (London, 1910), X, 289–90. Reinhold Niebuhr made the same discovery in *The Children of Light and the Children of Darkness* (New York, 1944): "Man being more than a natural creature, is not interested merely in physical survival but in prestige and social approval ..." and therefore in "enhancing his power, individually and collectively" (p. 20).

9. RC, p. 47.

10. *La Critica*, XXI (November 20, 1923), 377. See also n. 13 to Chap. 1, above.

11. RC, p. 337.

12. Renzo Sereno, "Note on Gaetano Mosca," *American Political Science Review*, XLVI, No. 2 (June, 1952), 605. Cf. also n. 23 to my Introduction.

13. RC, p. 51.

14. *Ibid.*, p. 116.

15. *Ibid.*, pp. 61, 62–63.

16. *Ibid.*, pp. 71–72.

17. *Ibid.*, p. 73.

18. *Ibid.*, p. 163.

19. See Ludwig Gumplowicz, *Der Rassenkampf* in *Ausgewählte Werke* (Innsbruck, 1928), III, 238 ff. Cf. also his *Outlines of Sociology* (Philadelphia, 1899), pp. 11 f.

20. RC, pp. 75, 76.

21. *Ibid.*, p. 80.

22. *Ibid.*, pp. 81, 83, 84, 86. "The term 'bureaucratic political system' was

probably first used systematically by Mosca, who contrasted it with feudal systems," S. N. Eisenstadt, "Political Struggle in Bureaucratic Societies," *World
Politics*, IX, No. 1 (October, 1956), 15. Eisenstadt cites as his authority one of
the very earliest students of Mosca, Fritz Morstein-Marx, "The Bureaucratic
State: Some Remarks on Mosca's Ruling Class," *Review of Politics*, I (October,
1939), 457–72. About Byzantium, see Toynbee, *A Study of History*, IV, 72–75,
392, 398.

23. RC, p. 98.

24. *Ibid.*, p. 100.

25. *Ibid.*, p. 89.

26. *Ibid.*, p. 88. About weather-magic, as an example of "non-logico-experi-
mental action," cf. Pareto, *The Mind and Society*, I, 111, Secs. 186 ff. Mosca's
formulation is safe from such criticisms as have been advanced against Pareto
in this regard. Cf. Morris Ginsberg about magical practices: "There is always
an element of experience behind them, though this is too readily generalized and
no adequate means are available for disentangling the subjective and objective
factors." *Reason and Unreason in Society* (Cambridge, Mass., 1948), p. 92.

27. RC, p. 90.

28. Title of 1st ed. of EL, Chap. IV, shortened in the English text to "Ruling Class and Social Type."

29. RC, p. 103.

30. *Ibid.*, pp. 105–7. When Mosca observes that the use of "large numbers
of Greeks, Armenians and even Europeans in her ruling class . . . provided
[Turkey] with some of the resources of a superior civilization; but it deprived
the Turkish ruling class of much of its savage vigor, and in fact did not save
the sultan from losing considerable portions of his territory," he fails to utilize
his own theory, which would suggest that the original Turkish ruling class remained unable to perform the administrative and economic tasks required of
classes ruling over, and no longer conquering, an empire. In co-opting subjects
of the conquered races to its ranks, the Ottoman elite opened the door for some
essential social forces which, according to our author, ought to have been represented in the ruling class. Its decadence and fall should not be blamed, by him,
upon a policy which merely meets the requisites of his own theory.

31. RC, pp. 110–12.

32. This problem has been treated by Max Weber, *Wirtschaft und Gesellschaft*, in *Grundriss der Nationalökonomik* (3d ed.; Tübingen, 1947), Pt. III,
II, 659–60; in English: *From Max Weber: Essays in Sociology*, eds. H. H. Gerth
and C. Wright Mills (New York, 1946), pp. 212–13. About the cultural and
educational presuppositions of bureaucracy, see also Chester I. Barnard, *The
Functions of the Executive* (Cambridge, Mass., 1938), pp. 163 ff.

33. RC, p. 116.

34. *Ibid.*, p. 117. In Pareto's terms: the ruling class appeals to the "residue
of group-persistence" in the lower classes, where it is usually intense. See *The
Mind and Society*, III, 1185, Sec. 1723.

35. RC, pp. 116–17.

36. *Ibid.*, p. 119.

37. *Ibid.*, p. 120.

38. *Ibid.*, p. 127.

39. *Ibid.*, p. 126.
40. *Ibid.*, p. 130; "Guicciardini, *opere inedite*, Vol. II, p. 169."
41. RC, pp. 138, 139.
42. Montesquieu, *L'esprit des lois*, Bk. IX, Sec. 6; *The Spirit of the Laws* (New York, 1949), p. 152.
43. RC, p. 134.
44. Franz Neumann, Intro. to *The Spirit of the Laws*, p. lviii.
45. RC, p. 139.
46. For the contrary opinion see Hans Kelsen, "Foundations of Democracy," *Ethics*, LXVI, No. 1, Pt. II (October, 1955), 26: "The parallelism which exists between philosophical and political absolutism is evident."
47. RC, pp. 143–44; EL, 1st ed., p. 189.
48. EL, 1st ed., p. 201, n.(a).
49. RC, p. 143.
50. *Ibid.*, pp. 150–52.
51. *Ibid.*, p. 147.
52. *Ibid.*, p. 260.
53. *Ibid.*, p. 157. Mosca conceives of the party elites as extraneous forces working upon and against the government instead of treating them as just another *section* of the ruling class.
54. RC, p. 256.
55. *Ibid.*, p. 258. This contradicts what Mosca wrote before: see above, p. 150; RC, p. 260.
56. RC, p. 327. See Walter Lippmann's *Essays in the Public Philosophy* (Boston, 1955); and Eric Voegelin's much-discussed work, *The New Science of Politics* (Chicago, 1952).
57. RC, p. 291.
58. See David Riesman, Nathan Glazer, Reuel Denny, *The Lonely Crowd* (New Haven, 1950), Chap. X.
59. RC, p. 292.
60. James Burnham in *The Machiavellians: Defenders of Freedom* (New York, 1943), p. 110. He might have made the same discovery by reading Montesquieu, who knew that "power can be checked only by power." *Spirit of the Laws*, Bk. XI, Sec. 4, p. 150, and Franz Neumann's Intro., p. lvii.
61. RC, p. 291. "Mean moral level" is in the original (EL, 1st ed., p. 423) as "medio," average.
62. RC, p. 125. Cf. Hume's similar but more reserved opinion on this subject in *A Treatise of Human Nature*, Bk. III, Pt. II, Sec. II (London, 1949), p. 500.
63. Pareto, *op. cit.*, IV, 1918, Sec. I-m.
64. RC, p. 144. See p. 36, above, and n. 24 to Chap. 1.
65. EL, 1st ed., p. 202, n.(b). The same idea is restated in EL, 2d ed., p. 92 (RC, p. 392): "Once everybody has acquired the right to vote, it is inevitable that a clique should detach itself from the middle classes and, in the race to reach the better posts, try to seek leverage in the instincts and appetites of the more populous classes . . ."
This is a rather narrow view of the sectarian type in politics as well as a dim echo of Marx's prophecy that, "when the class-struggle nears the decisive hour

...a small section of the ruling class cuts itself adrift and joins the revolutionary class ..." (*Manifesto of the Communist Party*, in Karl Marx and Friedrich Engels, *Selected Works*, I, 41.)

Chapter 7

1. RC, p. xl.
2. "Il programma dei liberali in materia di politica ecclesiastica," PS, pp. 61–62. First published in *Giornale degli economisti*, XV (1897), 458–71.
3. PS, p. 83.
4. *Ibid.*, p. 65. For Guicciardini, see p. 247 of this study. J. V. Stalin, *Marxism and Linguistics* (New York, 1951), pp. 10–11.
5. PS, pp. 66–67.
6. *Enquiries Concerning Human Understanding, and the Principles of Morals* (2d ed.; London, 1902), p. 275, Sec. 224. See also my Chap. 6.
7. PS, p. 70.
8. *Ibid.*, p. 75. Cf. RC, p. 158: "The state is nothing more than the organization of all social forces that possess political significance." Marx would have no quarrel with that statement. Cf. Engels: "The state is ... by no means a power forced on society from without ... Rather, it is a product of society at a certain stage of development" (*The Origin of the Family* ..., in Karl Marx and Friedrich Engels, *Selected Works*, II, 288–89). Mosca would take exception to the last part of the sentence, because in his view states and ruling classes will be with us always.
9. PS, pp. 75–76.
10. *Ibid.*, p. 76.
11. *Ibid.*, p. 77.
12. *Ibid.*
13. TE, pp. 250, 254, see my Chap. 5, p. 109.
14. "Il principio aristocratico e il democratico" (1902), PS, p. 5.
15. *Ibid.*
16. *Ibid.*, p. 12.
17. *Ibid.*, p. 13.
18. *Ibid.*, pp. 19–20.
19. *Ibid.*, p. 22.
20. *Ibid.*, p. 23.
21. *Ibid.*, p. 24.

Chapter 8

1. See Chap. 13.
2. Delle Piane, *Bibliografia* (Florence, 1950), p. 27.
3. "Pensieri inediti," *Ethos*, I, No. 3 (Dec., 1945), 3.
4. See n. 14 to Chap. 7, above.
5. PS, p. 11.
6. *Ibid.* Reference is to Pareto's two volumes, *Les systèmes socialistes* (Paris, 1902).
7. PS, p. 18. *Systèmes* (2d ed.; Paris, 1926), II, 399–400.

8. Pareto, *ibid.*, pp. 400–401. *Engels to Starkenburg* (1894) in Karl Marx and Friedrich Engels, *Selected Works*, II, 457.

9. PS, pp. 18–19. Mosca refers to his essay, "Il programma dei liberali . . . ," discussed in Chap. 7, above.

10. Pareto, *Manuale di economia politica* (Milan, 1906), pp. 403–4, n. 3. As examples are listed, among others, E. Fournier, *L'esprit des autres* (1856), p. 83; Balzac, *Physiologie due mariage*; Sumner Maine, "Popular Government," cited from the *Quarterly Review*, April, 1883. Gabriel Tarde is mentioned as the author of "volumes demonstrating that the civilizing process is exclusively the work of a few people."

11. "Piccola polemica," PS, pp. 116–17. First published in *La riforma sociale*, XVII (1907), 329–31.

12. PS, p. 117.

13. EL, II, 177. (Omitted in the corresponding Chap. XVI of RC.)

14. Pareto, *Systèmes*, I, 28.

15. PS, pp. 118–20.

16. His contribution, "Dove si dicorre di Pareto, di Mosca ed anche di de Viti," appeared in *La riforma sociale*, XLI (1934), 707–11.

17. RC, pp. xxxvi–xxxix; see also Delle Piane, *Bibliografia di Gaetano Mosca* (Florence, 1950), pp. 31–32.

18. He wrote the letter upon receipt of Sereno's Mosca study (see n. 17 to Chap. 1, above).

19. See n. 12 to Chap. 6, above.

20. In *Rivista italiana di sociologia*, IV (July–Aug., 1900), 401–56.

21. Sereno, "Note on Gaetano Mosca," *ibid.*, pp. 604–5.

22. Pareto, *Cours*, II, 29.

23. *Ibid.*, p. 56.

24. *Ibid.*, p. 372.

25. *Ibid.*, p. 57.

26. *Ibid.*, p. 347. Cf. *The Mind and Society*, IV, 1918, Sec. I-m.

27. See my Chap. 14.

28. Pareto, *Cours*, II, 57.

29. *Ibid.*, p. 66, Sec. 682.

30. *Ibid.*, p. 351.

31. *Ibid.*, p. 356.

32. *Ibid.*, pp. 385–86.

33. *Ibid.*, p. 387. Written in the heyday of Tammany rule.

34. *Cours*, p. 388. "Admired I am of those that hate me most. Though some speak openly against my books, Yet they will read me, and thereby attain To Peter's chair: and when they cast me off, Are poisoned by my climbing followers." Marlowe, Prologue to *The Jew of Malta*, cited by Ernst Cassirer in the first chapter, on Machiavelli, of his *Myth of the State* (Garden City, 1955), p. 148.

35. Pareto, *Cours*, II, 394, 395.

36. ". . . Pareto, though he has freed himself from many prejudices, has certainly not succeeded in freeing himself from all of them. This can be seen in nearly every page he writes, especially, of course, where he speaks of what he describes not inappropriately as 'the humanitarian religion.' His own prejudice

is the anti-humanitarian religion. Had he seen that his choice was not between prejudice and freedom of prejudice, but only between the humanitarian prejudice and the anti-humanitarian prejudice, he might perhaps have felt a little less confident of his superiority." K. R. Popper, *The Open Society and Its Enemies* (London, 1945), II, 303.

37. For instance Guido Dorso (see my Conclusions) and Mario delle Piane.

38. *Political Parties* (Glencoe, Ill., 1949), p. 391. The original German text was entitled *Zur Soziologie des Parteiwesens in der modernen Demokratie: Untersuchungen über die oligarchischen Tendenzen des Gruppenlebens* (Leipzig, 1910; Italian translation, Turin, 1912).

39. "La sociologia del partito politico nella democrazia moderna," PS, pp. 26–36. First published in *Il pensiero moderno*, I (1912), 310–16.

40. PS, p. 27.

41. *Ibid.*, pp. 28–30; RC, p. 187.

42. PS, p. 31. This is, of course, Max Weber's term, not Mosca's.

43. *Ibid.*, p. 33.

44. Georg Lukacs, *Die Zerstörung der Vernunft* (Berlin, 1955), p. 498.

45. Alvin W. Gouldner, "Metaphysical Pathos and the Theory of Bureaucracy," *American Political Science Review*, XLIX, No. 2 (June, 1955), 506.

46. See my Chap. 5.

47. PS, pp. 33, 34.

48. The standard work on the subject is Graham Wallas' *The Great Society* (London, 1914). Recently, the problem of mass organization has been treated in some valuable studies, e. g., Philip Selznick, *The Organizational Weapon* (New York, 1952); and C. Wright Mills, *The Power Elite* (New York, 1956). For a discussion of the last-named work, see my Conclusions, pp. 360 ff.

49. The argument will be continued (see Conclusions).

Chapter 9

1. *Questioni pratiche di diritto costituzionale* (Turin, 1896), *Le dottrine di Locke ed il pensiero e le istituzioni politiche moderne* (Turin, 1898), *Appunti di diritto costituzionale* (Milan, 1908), *Italia e Libia* (Milan, 1912).

2. See M. delle Piane, *Bibliografia di Gaetano Mosca* (Florence, 1950), pp. 70–72; about Mosca's parliamentary activities, *ibid.*, pp. 73–80.

3. See Chap. 6, p. 125, and n. 2 to Chap. 6.

4. EL, II (3d ed., 1939), 245. The passage cannot be found in the English text, although *The Ruling Class* was published that same year.

5. See Chap. 7, p. 168, and n. 20 to Chap. 7.

6. RC, p. 329: "*Deca.* XVI." More exact: Bk. I, Chap. xvi, already referred to above; see Chap. 1 and n. 23 to Chap. 1.

7. RC, p. 329.

8. *Ibid.*, p. 330. A more detailed account of Mosca's indebtedness to his precursors is found in Chaps. 11–13 of this work. Bagehot was apparently unknown to Mosca. See David Easton, "Walter Bagehot and Liberal Realism," *American Political Science Review*, XLIII, No. 1 (1944), 20–21.

9. RC, p. 331. See above, Chap. 1 and n. 27 to Chap. 1.

10. RC, p. 331.

11. Karl Marx, "Theses on Feuerbach," in Friedrich Engels, *Ludwig Feuerbach and the End of Classical German Philosophy*, Karl Marx and Friedrich Engels, *Selected Works* (London, 1950), II, 367.

12. RC, pp. 332, 333–34.

13. Robert Michels, *Political Parties* (Glencoe, Ill., 1949), pp. 5 ff.

14. RC, p. 334.

15. *Ibid.*, pp. 336, 337.

16. Francesco de Sanctis, *Storia dei Romani* (Turin, 1907); Guglielmo Ferrero, *Grandezza e decadenza di Roma*, 5 vols. (Milan, 1902-7). (*The Greatness and Decline of Rome*, 5 vols., London, 1907-9). Mosca's particular interest in Ferrero's work is attested by two critical essays: "Il fenomeno Ferrero," *La riforma sociale*, VII (1897), 1017–31, 1135–64, and "La nuova opera di Guglielmo Ferrero," *La letteratura*, 1902, 908–15.

17. ST, p. 361. See also the Supplement to the present study, pp. 384–86.

18. Toynbee, A *Study of History*, III, 354.

19. RC, pp. 375, 376.

20. *Ibid.*, pp. 374, 375.

21. Toynbee, *op. cit.*, III., 356, 345–50.

22. RC, pp. 389–90.

23. *Ibid.*, p. 147; see Chap. 6. of this study, p. 149.

24. EL (3rd ed., 1939) II, 89, n. 1.

25. The term is Toynbee's. See *op. cit.*, I, Chap. 1.

26. RC, p. 336; see p. 31 of this study.

27. "The Aristocratic and the Democratic Principle"; see Chap. 7 of this work.

28. RC, pp. 394, 395.

29. *Ibid.*, p. 413.

30. *Ibid.*, p. 395.

31. *Ibid.*, p. 397.

32. *Ibid.*, p. 398.

33. *Ibid.*, pp. 403–4.

34. *Ibid.*, p. 405.

35. See n. 32 to Chap. 6 above; cf. also C. Wright Mills, *White Collar* (New York, 1951). The most recent study of this kind is William H. Whyte's *The Organization Man* (New York, 1956).

36. See Chap. 4, of this study, p. 91.

37. RC, p. 406.

38. *Ibid.*, p. 408. And from the upper middle class at that. See the recent study showing the "over-representation" of Oxford and other public schools in the English bureaucracy: R. K. Kelsall, *Higher Civil Servants in Britain* (London, 1955).

39. RC, p. 406.

40. *Ibid.*, p. 407.

41. Toynbee, *op. cit.*, IV, 133 ff.

42. RC, p. 407.

43. *Ibid.*, p. 408.

44. See Bertrand de Jouvenel, *On Power* (New York, 1949), pp. 220 f; also Hannah Arendt, *The Origins of Totalitarianism* (New York, 1951), p. 244.

45. See Chap. 8, p. 186.

46. RC, p. 409.
47. *Ibid.*, p. 355.
48. *Ibid.*, p. 410.
49. *Ibid.*, p. 487. See J. L. Talmon, *The Rise of Totalitarian Democracy* (Boston, 1952). The notion of "totalitarian democracy" is, by the way, not quite as recent as one would think: it can be found in Max Weber's work: see *Wirtschaft und Gesellschaft*, Chap. III, on "plebiscitarian democracy," in *Grundriss der Sozialökonomik*, Pt. III, I, 156–58; cf. *From Max Weber: Essays in Sociology*, 103–4. But the same idea had been well developed by Marx in his study of "Bonapartism," see *The Eighteenth Brumaire of Louis Bonaparte*, in *Selected Works*, I, 221 ff.
50. Cf. Chap. 8, and the Conclusions.
51. RC, p. 411.
52. *Ibid.*, p. 412.
53. *Ibid.*, p. 450.
54. *Ibid.*, p. 413.
55. *Ibid.*, p. 414.
56. *Ibid.*, pp. 415, 416.
57. *Ibid.* A footnote of the author refers to his essay on "The Aristocratic and the Democratic Principle," discussed in Chap. 7 of this study.
58. RC, p. 418.
59. RC, p. 420.
60. *Ibid.*, p. 421.
61. *Ibid.*, p. 422.
62. *Ibid.*, p. 423. See Otto Ammon, *Die Gesellschaftsordnung* (Jena, 1895), Chaps. XX–XXI. Pareto (*The Mind and Society*, IV, 1542, Sec. 2206) calls him, for some strange reason, "Hamon" (*Il Hamone*).
63. RC, pp. 424, 425.
64. *Ibid.*, p. 426.
65. Pareto, *The Mind and Society*, IV, 1515, Sec. 2178; 1555, Sec. 2227.
66. RC, pp. 426, 427.
67. *Ibid.*, pp. 428, 429.

Chapter 10

1. RC, p. 430.
2. *Ibid.*, p. 433.
3. *Ibid.*, p. 434.
4. *Ibid.*, p. 437.
5. See above, pp. 132–34.
6. RC, p. 415.
7. *Ibid.*, p. 430.
8. *Ibid.*, pp. 431, 432.
9. Cf. above, p. 85.
10. RC, p. 433.
11. RC, p. 434.
12. *Ibid.*, p. 122.
13. *Ibid.*, p. 434.

14. *Politics* iii. 4. 1276ᵇ 30 (Mod. Lib. ed; New York, 1943, p. 131).
15. RC, pp. 177, 178.
16. *Ibid.*, p. 435. Cf. Pareto, *The Mind and Society*, III, 1422–23, Secs. 2027–28.
17. RC, p. 456.
18. *Ibid.*, p. 435. *The Prince*, Chap. XVIII in *The Prince and the Discourses* (Mod. Lib. ed.; New York, 1940, p. 65).
19. RC, p. 436.
20. But cf. what Mosca said before about the virtues necessary for maintaining high positions in society: see above, p. 221.
21. RC, p. 450. Already quoted in EL, I; see RC, p. 193. For the other, anti-Machiavellian Mosca, see Chap. 12 of this work.
22. "The Crisis in Parliamentarism" in *The Development of the Representative System in Our Times* (Lausanne, 1928). The Italian text of Mosca's contribution appeared as "Cause e remedi della crisi del regime parlamentare" in PS, pp. 87–115.
23. "Prerogative del capo del governo," PS, p. 281.
24. *Ibid.*, p. 282.
25. *Ibid.*, pp. 282–83.
26. *Ibid.*, p. 283.
27. *Ibid.*, p. 284. *Iliad*, trans. Andrew Lang and others (London, 1903), vi. 1. 480.
28. RC, p. 473.
29. *Ibid.*, p. 474.
30. *Ibid.*, p. 475.
31. *Ibid.*, EL, II, 213.
32. Willmoore Kendall, *John Locke and the Doctrine of Majority-Rule* (Urbana, Ill., 1941).
33. RC, p. 476.
34. Daniel Halévy, *Essai sur l'accélération de l'histoire* (Paris, 1948).
35. RC, p. 477.
36. *Ibid.*, p. 478. See Sorel, *Reflections on Violence* (Glencoe, Ill., 1950), pp. 99 f.
37. RC, p. 482.
38. Cf. Arthur Livingston on Prezzolini and Papini, RC, p. xii. About the unsuccessful attempt to enlist Mosca for their brand of nationalism, see Pietro Piovani, *Momenti della filosofia giuridico-politica italiana* (Milan, 1951), p. 105, n. 17; see also the rather negative interview which the writer Mario Calderoni had with Mosca on behalf of the nationalist organ *Regno*: "Aristocrazie e democrazie" (published in that journal on January 24, 1904; reprinted in PS, pp. 331–37).
But Corradini was, according to Giovanni Prezzolini, greatly influenced by Mosca and Pareto: see "L'Aristocrazia dei briganti" in G. Prezzolini and G. Papini, *Vecchio e nuovo nazionalismo* (Milan, 1914), p. 38.
39. RC, p. 482.
40. *Ibid.*, p. 484. About Mosca and syndicalism, see Chap. 14 of this study.
41. EL, II, 242, n.(c).
42. RC, pp. 487, 488.

43. *Ibid.,* p. 391.

44. *Ibid.,* p. 490.

45. *Ibid.,* pp. 491, 492.

46. *Ibid.,* pp. 493, 494. Cf. Walter Lippmann, *Essays in the Public Philosophy* (Boston, 1955), p. 178: "I do not contend, though I hope, that the decline of Western society will be arrested if the teachers in our schools and universities come back to the great tradition of the public philosophy. But I do contend that the decline, which is already far advanced, cannot be arrested if the prevailing philosophers oppose this restoration and revival . . ."

47. E. M. Forster, "What I Believe," in *Two Cheers for Democracy* (London, 1951), pp. 82–83.

Chapter 11

1. These notes, taken faithfully by L. Donato and A. Fedele, were published as *Corso sintetico di storia delle dottrine politiche* (Rome, 1929). The "Course" quickly became Mosca's most popular work. Renamed *Lezioni di storia delle istituzioni e delle dottrine politiche* (Rome, 1933), it received its final title in 1937, *Storia delle dottrine politiche* (the official 2d ed. of ST). Our quotations are from the 6th ed. (1951). See Delle Piane, *Bibliografia di Gaetano Mosca* (Florence, 1950), p. 61.

2. According to Delle Piane (*op. cit.,* p. 62), Mosca was perturbed by the great vogue which the book enjoyed; he wondered what it might do to his reputation as a scholar.

3. See the Supplement, pp. 382 ff.

4. "Encore quelques mots sur 'Le Prince' de Machiavelli," in *Revue française de sciences politiques,* XLVIII (1925), 481–509, XLIX (1926), 5–27; "Machiavelli," in *Encyclopaedia of the Social Sciences* (New York, 1933), IX, 655–57 (for a discussion of both pieces, see my Chap. 12); "L'utopia di Tommaso Moro ed il pensiero communista moderno," in *Scritti della Facoltà giuridica di Roma in onore di Antonio Salandra* (Milan, 1928), 259–72 (see Chap. 13 of this study); "Cenni storici e critici sulle dottrine razziste," in *Rendiconti della R. Accademia Nazionale dei Lincei Classe di scienze morali, storici e filologiche,* XI (1933), 455–70.

5. *History of Western Philosophy* (New York, 1945).

6. ST, p. 9.

7. *Ibid.,* pp. 12–15.

8. *Ibid.,* pp. 15–31.

9. *Ibid.,* pp. 31–39.

10. *Ibid.,* p. 46.

11. *Ibid.,* p. 51.

12. *Ibid.,* p. 57.

13. *Ibid.,* pp. 62–63.

14. *Ibid.,* p. 64.

15. See n. 16 to Chap. 9 of this study.

16. ST, p. 73.

17. *Ibid.,* p. 69.

18. *Ibid.,* pp. 74–75.

19. *Ibid.*, p. 88. See R. W. and A. J. Carlyle, *A History of Medieval Political Theory in the West* (4th ed.; New York, n.d.), III, 110.

20. ST, pp. 89–96.

21. *Ibid.*, p. 101.

22. *Ibid.*, pp. 103, 104.

23. *Ibid.*, p. 105. *The Prince*, Chap. XV, in *The Prince and the Discourses* (Mod. Lib. ed.; New York, 1940), p. 56.

24. ST, p. 106.

25. See Chap. 12 of this work.

26. ST, p. 138.

27. See p. 159.

28. ST, p. 139: "*Ricordi politici e civili*, 134."

29. J. W. Allen, *Political Thought in the Sixteenth Century* (3d ed.; London, 1951), p. 498.

30. ST, p. 139. Allen, *ibid.*, p. 499.

31. ST, p. 140. Cassirer, *The Myth of the State* (Garden City, N.Y., 1955), p. 147. Mosca's cautious pro-Machiavellian, Placidus Schouppe, is, in all probability, the German Kaspar Schoppe (Gaspard Scioppius, 1576–1649) whose *Paedia politices* (1622) was much read in his time. About him, consult pp. 138 ff. in Friedrich Meinecke's *Machiavellism* (London, 1957), a translation of the great German historian's *Die Idee der Staatsraeson* (Munich, 1924).

32. ST, p. 140, and n. 1. Mosca cites Giuseppe Ferrari's *Corso sugli scrittori politici italiani* (Milan, 1862) and Camillo Giardina's monograph, *La vita e l'opera politica di Scipione di Castro* (Palermo, 1931).

33. ST, p. 142.

34. *Ibid.*, p. 143. Curzio Malaparte, *Coup d'Etat: The Technique of Revolution* (New York, 1932).

35. ST, p. 145. Paolo Sarpi, *Opinione del come abbia a governarsi internamente ed esternamente la Repubblica di Venezia per conservare il perpetuo dominio.* Probably written 1610, published 1683.

36. ST, pp. 152–53.

37. *Ibid.*, pp. 155–56. As for the much-disputed authorship of the *Vindiciae*, see George H. Sabine, *A History of Political Theory* (2d ed.; New York, 1950), p. 377.

38. ST, pp. 156–57.

39. *Ibid.*, p. 160.

40. Georges Sorel, *Matériaux d'une théorie du prolétariat* (3d ed.; Paris, 1929), p. 138.

41. ST, pp. 160–61. Allen, *op. cit.*, p. 509.

42. ST, pp. 162–66.

43. *Ibid.*, p. 167.

44. François Guizot, *Historie de la république d'Angleterre et de Cromwell* (Paris, 1854); Samuel R. Gardiner, *History of the Great Civil War, 1642–49*, 3 vols. (London and New York, 1886–91).

45. ST, pp. 214–15.

46. *Ibid.*, pp. 218–19.

47. *Ibid.*, pp. 222–24. About Dubos, see Franz Neumann in Montesquieu, *The Spirit of the Laws* (New York, 1949), p. xxv.

48. ST, pp. 226–31.

49. *Ibid.*, pp. 232–33. About Croce's Preface, see Chap. 1 of this study, and n. 13 to Chap. 1.

50. ST, p. 247. Mosca's italics. See Rousseau, *The Social Contract*, Bk. III, Chap. IV, in *Social Contract*, ed. Ernest Barker (New York and London, 1948), p. 232. Mosca might have also quoted the concluding remarks of the same chapter: "Were there such a thing as a nation of Gods, it would be a democracy. So perfect a form of government is not suited to mere men" (*Ibid.*, p. 233).

51. *Ibid.*, p. 232.

52. In a note to RC, p. 416, repeated in ST, p. 270, Gaetano Mosca refers to "Il pensiero di Saint-Simon considerato dopo un secolo," an article by one of his sons, Bernardo Mosca (published in *La riforma sociale*, Fasc. 10–12, Oct.–Dec. 1921).

53. ST, p. 265. Cf. *ibid.*, p. 2. See also Chap. 2 of this study, and n. 27 to Chap. 2.

54. ST, p. 267.

55. RC, p. 278.

56. *Ibid.*, pp. 278–79.

57. *Ibid.*, p. 416.

58. *Ibid.*, pp. 454–55.

59. See Chap. 6 of this study. ST, pp. 293 ff.

60. *Ibid.*, p. 296.

61. See Arthur Livingston, RC, pp. xxxvii–xxxix; see also Chap. 8 of this work.

62. ST, pp. 290–92.

63. *Ibid.*, p. 256.

64. *Ibid.*, p. 289.

65. *Ibid.*, p. 282.

66. See Bruno Brunello, *Il pensiero italiano da Romagnosi al Croce* (Bologna, 1949), p. 9.

67. ST, pp. 328–33. Mosca's view of Sorel is discussed in Chap. 14 of this study.

68. See last entry in n. 4, in this chapter.

69. ST, p. 337.

70. *Ibid.*, p. 334.

71. *Ibid.*, pp. 338–39. Julius Langbehn, *Rembrandt als Erzieher*, 1890; Paul Anton de Lagarde, *Deutsche Schriften*, 2 vols., 1878–81; Jacob Burckhardt, *Weltgeschichtliche Betrachtungen*, 1905, transl. as *Force and Freedom* (New York, 1943).

72. ST, pp. 340, 343.

73. *Ibid.*, p. 342.

74. *Ibid.*, p. 345.

75. *Ibid.*, pp. 345–53. In a note on p. 346, the author refers to EL, I (RC), Chap. I, perhaps with the intention of showing that his views of racialism had remained unchanged.

Chapter 12

1. Also, according to Mario delle Piane, "he remained, throughout his life, essentially a stranger to the work that, in his lifetime, was done on the subject of the theory of history." *Bibliografia di Gaetano Mosca* (Florence, 1950), p. 52.

2. Cassirer, *The Myth of the State* (Garden City. N.Y., 1955); R. G. Collingwood, *The New Leviathan* (London, 1942); Collingwood's *Idea of History* (London, 1946) and *Idea of Nature* (London, 1945) may also be considered works in political philosophy; Cyril E. M. Joad, *Guide to the Philosophy of Morals and Politics* (London, 1948); Bertrand Russell, *History of Western Philosophy* (New York 1945); A. R. M. Murray, *An Introduction to Political Philosophy* (London, 1953); Abraham Kaplan (with Harold D. Lasswell), *Power and Society* (New Haven, 1950).

3. Morris R. Cohen, "The Conception of Philosophy in Recent Discussion," in *Studies in Philosophy and Science* (New York, 1949), pp. 41, 38.

4. Leo Strauss, *Political Philosophy of Hobbes* (London and New York, 1936); D. G. James, *The Life of Reason* (London, 1949).

5. "Encore quelques mots sur 'Le Prince' de Machiavelli," *Revue française de sciences politiques*, XLVIII (1925), 481–509, XLIX (1926), 5–27. In Italian published as "Il Principe di Machiavelli quattro secoli dopo la morte del suo autore," in Mosca, *Saggi di storia della scienza politica* (Rome, 1927).

6. Subtitle of James Burnham, *The Machiavellians* (New York, 1943).

7. *The Prince*, Chap. XIX, in *The Prince and the Discourses* (Mod. Lib. ed.; New York), pp. 69 f.

8. Burnham, *op. cit.*, pp. 29, 30, 31. Cf. Chap. 11 of this study.

9. Burnham, *op. cit.*, pp. 38–39.

10. *Ibid.*, p. 31.

11. *Ibid.*, pp. 40, 41.

12. *Ibid.*, pp. 51–52. *The Prince*, in *op. cit.*, pp. 66–67, 61.

13. Burnham, *op. cit.*, p. 52; *Disc.*, Bk. I, Chap. 44 (*op. cit.*, p. 228).

14. Burnham, *op. cit.*, pp. 53–54; *Disc.*, Bk. I, Chap. 57 (our edition, p. 260, reads differently; see the following discussion in the text, p. 268.

15. Burnham, *op. cit.*, p. 55; *Disc.*, Bk. I, Chap. 58 (*op. cit.*, pp. 262–63).

16. Burnham, *op. cit.*, p. 58; *Disc.*, Bk. II, Chap. 13 (*op. cit.*, p. 318).

17. Burnham, *op. cit.*, pp. 60, 61; *The Prince*, Chaps. XVIII and XXV (*op. cit.*, pp. 63 ff., 91 ff.).

18. Burnham, *op. cit.*, pp. 62, 63 (*Hist. of Florence*, Book V).

19. *Disc.*, Bk. I, Chap. 57 (*op. cit.*, p. 260).

20. Burnham, *op. cit.*, p. 69.

21. *Ibid.*, p. 70.

22. *Ibid.*, p. 71; *Disc.*, Bk. I, Chap. 4 (*op. cit.*, p. 119).

23. *Disc.*, Bk. I, Chap. 4 (*op. cit.*, p. 119). J. W. Allen, *A History of Political Thought in the Sixteenth Century* (3d ed.; London, 1951), p. 461.

24. *The Prince*, Chap. XIX (*op. cit.*, p. 69).

25. *Disc.*, Bk. I, Chaps. 2, 7, 50.

26. Antonio Gramsci, *Note sul Machiavelli* (Turin, 1952), p. 14. Gramsci wrote this in 1932, in a Fascist prison where he died in 1935.

27. "Cicero, *De Republica*, III, 13." Cited from José Ortega y Gasset, *Concord and Liberty*, trans. Helene Weyl (New York, 1946), pp. 14–15.

28. Gramsci, *op. cit.*, p. 3.

29. James Burnham, *The Managerial Revolution* (New York, 1941).

30. Max Lerner, Introduction to *The Prince and the Discourses* (Mod. Lib. ed.; New York, 1940), p. xxxvi.

31. RC, pp. 202–3.

32. See above, n. 5. (Mosca's Machiavelli essay will hereafter be identified by the symbol MM; page numbers will refer to the two issues of the French review in which the essay ran, marked according to their years of appearance.)

33. MM (1925), p. 483, n. 1. About Ferrari, see n. 32 to Chap. 11 of this study. Alfredo Oriani, *Fino a dogali* (Bari, 1918).

34. MM (1925), p. 498.

35. *Ibid.*, p. 500.

36. *Ibid.*, p. 501.

37. MM (1926), p. 12.

38. *Ibid.*, p. 13.

39. This passage from Mosca's article on Machiavelli in the *Encyclopaedia of the Social Sciences* (IX, 656) sums up most succinctly thoughts expressed at greater length in "Quelques mots . . ."

40. MM (1926), p. 14.

41. *Ibid.*, p. 15.

42. *Ibid.*, pp. 16–17.

43. Allen, *op. cit.*, p. 447. Lerner, *op. cit.*, xl.

44. Allen, *op. cit.*, p. 448.

45. Toynbee, *A Study of History*, III, 306.

46. MM (1926), p. 17.

47. Cassirer, *op. cit.*, p. 183.

48. MM (1926), pp. 17–18.

49. *The Prince*, Chap. III (*op. cit.*, pp. 7–9).

50. MM (1926), pp. 18–21.

51. *Ibid.*, pp. 21–22.

52. *The Prince*, Chap. XVII (*op. cit.*, p. 61).

53. MM (1926), p. 22.

54. *Ibid.*, p. 23.

55. *Disc.*, Bk. I, Chap. 18 (*op. cit.*, p. 171).

56. MM (1926), p. 23. Cf. *Mein Kampf* (New York, 1939), Pt. I, Chap. VI.

57. MM (1926), p. 24.

58. *Ibid.*

59. *Ibid.*, p. 25. About the Machiavelli legend, see Cassirer, *op. cit.*, pp. 144–60.

60. MM (1926), p. 26.

61. *Ibid.*, p. 27.

62. *The Prince*, Chap. XV (*op. cit.*, p. 56).

63. *Ibid.*, Chap. XVIII (*op. cit.*, p. 64).

64. For a recent interpretation (at variance with the one given in the text) of Machiavelli as a doctrinaire who wrote an operational code, see Herbert Butterfield's brilliant essay, *The Statecraft of Machiavelli* (New York, 1956), p. 115.

65. RC, pp. 50, 329.

Chapter 13

1. "L'utopia di Tommaso Moro ed il pensiero communista moderno," *Scritti della Facolta giuridica di Roma in onore di Antonio Salandra* (Milan, 1928), pp. 259–72. (In the following identified as UT.) *The Prince* and *Utopia* both appeared in 1516.

2. ST, Chap. 20, pp. 145 f.; Chap. 31, pp. 248 f.

3. RC, pp. 271, 442.

4. Gerhard Ritter, *Machstaat und Utopie* (Munich, 1940). Retitled after four editions *Die Daemonie der Macht*. Quotations will be from the 6th ed. (1948).

5. UT, p. 265.

6. Ritter, *op. cit.*, p. 88.

7. UT, p. 266, and n.2.

8. *Ibid.*, p. 267.

9. *Ibid.*, pp. 268–9.

10. Karl Marx and Friedrich Engels, *Manifesto of the Communist Party*, in *Selected Works*, I, 58; Joseph A. Schumpeter, *Capitalism, Socialism and Democracy* (2d ed.; New York, 1947), p. 307; cf. also Martin Buber, *Paths in Utopia* (London, 1949), pp. 16–18; and Bertrand Russell, *Roads to Freedom* (London, 1918), p. 26. n. 1.

11. UT, p. 269.

12. Schumpeter, *op. cit.*, p. 307.

13. UT, pp. 270–71.

14. *Ibid.*, p. 272. *Utopia*, end of Bk. I.

15. Cf. J. W. Allen, *A History of Political Thought in the Sixteenth Century* (3d ed.; London, 1951), pp. 136–37.

16. RC, p. 191.

17. Mosca, "The Crisis in Parliamentarism," in *The Development of the Representative System in Our Times* (Lausanne, 1928), p. 77. Lenin, *What Is To Be Done?*, in *Selected Works*, I, 167.

18. RC, pp. 269–70.

19. *Ibid.*, p. 247.

20. Cassirer, *The Myth of the State* (Garden City, N.Y., 1955), p. 282.

21. RC, p. 283.

22. *Ibid.*, p. 284.

23. Cf. Rudolf Hilferding, "State Capitalism or Totalitarian Economy," *Modern Review*, June, 1947, 267–71 (written in 1940). See also Anton Ciliga, *The Russian Enigma* (London, 1940). These and quite a few other authors long ago discovered what the Yugoslav communist heretic Milovan Djilas finally proclaimed to the world from his Yugoslav prison in *The New Class* (New York, 1957).

24. RC, p. 286.

25. *Ibid.*, pp. 287–88, n. 1. Mosca refers to Albert Schäffle's *Quintessenz des Sozialismus* (Gotha, 1875), and to Maurice Block's *L'Europe politique et sociale* (Paris, 1869).

26. This chapter of *The Ruling Class* has been rather freely edited. A long reference to Achille Loria's "*Teoria economica della Costituzione politica,*" in EL, I, 435 (an early edition of *Le basi economiche della costituzione sociale,* 3d ed.; Turin, 1902) has been omitted altogether from RC, p. 300; a long footnote (EL, I, 442) in turn appears in the text of RC, p. 305.

Saverio Merlino, briefly mentioned in "Il programma dei liberali" of 1897 (PS, pp. 79–80), is the author of *Pro e contra il socialismo* (Milan, 1897), a work which played a considerable role in its time. Merlino was an inspiration to Sorel. So was Napoleone Colajanni with his book, *Il socialismo* (Catania, 1884). Mosca mentions his (and I. Scarabelli's) *Il socialismo e la lotta di classe* (Ferrara, 1895), in EL, 1st ed., p. 444 (RC, p. 307). See my *Genesis of Georges Sorel* (Ann Arbor, 1951), pp. 113–17.

Croce's important *Materialismo storico ed economico marxista* (Palermo, 1900; *Historical Materialism and the Economics of Karl Marx,* New York, 1914) seems to have eluded Mosca altogether.

27. RC, p. 298.

28. *Ibid.*, p. 299.

29. *Ibid.*, pp. 300, 304.

30. *Ibid.*, p. 305. Mosca's italics. (Marx, *Capital,* Bk. I, Chap. 23.)

31. Cf. Chap. 3 of this study and n. 24 to Chap. 3.

32. Max Weber, *Wirtschaft und Gesellschaft* in *Grundriss der socialökonomik* (3d ed.; Tübingen, 1947), Pt. III, I, 181 ff.

33. Engels, *Feuerbach and the End of Classical German Philosophy,* in Karl Marx and Friedrich Engels, *op. cit.,* II, 360–61. A good, non-Marxist summary of the whole argument can be found in M. M. Bober, *Karl Marx's Interpretation of History* (2d ed.; Cambridge, Mass., 1948), pp. 356 ff.

34. Karl Marx and Friedrich Engels, *op. cit.,* I, 409.

35. N. I. Bukharin, *Historical Materialism* (New York, 1925), p. 213.

36. Karl Marx and Friedrich Engels, *op. cit.,* II, 457. In the sentence preceding the one cited in the text, Engels even states explicitly: "It is not that the economic condition is the *cause* and *alone active,* while everything else only has a passive effect." Stalin, *Marxism and Linguistics* (New York, 1951).

37. Jack Lindsay, *Marxism and Contemporary Science* (London, 1949), p. 26; Sidney Hook, *Towards an Understanding of Karl Marx* (London, 1933), p. 140.

38. Cited more completely on p. 298. RC, p. 298.

39. *Manifesto, op. cit.,* I, 44.

40. "Il programma dei liberali," PS, pp. 71–72. See also Chap. 7 of this study.

41. PS, p. 72.

42. *Ibid.*, pp. 72–73.

43. *Ibid.*, p. 73.

44. *Ibid.*, p. 74.

45. *Ibid.*

46. Max Weber in his *Gesammelte Aufsätze zur Religionssoziologie,* 3 vols.

418   Notes to Pages 305–312

(4th ed.; Tübingen, 1947). See also Chap. 3 of this study and n. 5 to Chap. 3; also Chap. 5 and n. 25 to Chap. 5. On Pareto's theory of interdependence and Mosca's claim to priority, see Chap. 8 of this work.

47. See p. 301.

48. Modern philosophies of the subconscious go back to Schopenhauer. His disciples were Nietzsche and Eduard von Hartmann, whose *Philosophie des Unbewussten* ("Philosophy of the Unconscious"), 1869, greatly influenced Sorel.

49. "Il principio aristocratico e il democratico," PS, p. 15.

50. *Ibid.*, pp. 16–17.

51. Spengler, *The Decline of the West* (New York, 1939), II, 432, 464, 506–7.

52. PS, p. 17.

53. *Ibid.*, p. 18.

54. See p. 48. Cf. also p. 318.

55. RC, p. 439.

56. *Ibid.*, pp. 440–41.

57. *Ibid.*, p. 441.

58. *Ibid.*: "Ferrero, *Grandezza e decadenza di Roma*, Vol. III."

59. See Toynbee, *A Study of History*, III, 200 ff.; also Sorel, *Reflections on Violence* (Glencoe, Ill., 1950), pp. 306 f.

60. RC, p. 442.

61. *Ibid.*, p. 443.

62. *Ibid.*, p. 446.

63. "He introduces the mode of economic production as the fundamental conditioning factor of only the general and most pervasive characters of a culture. He does not overlook what is specific and unique to each country and to each of its historical situations." Sidney Hook, *op. cit.*, p. 133. In his later writings, though, Professor Hook did not quite maintain this charitable point of view. Cf. his recent work, *The Ambiguous Legacy: Marx and the Marxists* (Princeton, 1955), pp. 36–38.

64. See pp. 301, 302 and notes 33, 35 to this chap. Cf. Bukharin, *op. cit.*, p. 268: "The ruling classes, maintained by the slaves conquered in countless wars, became parasites, also a portion of the burghers. Their technology permitted them to wage wars, thus conditioning a corresponding economy, which produced a specific state order; but the material condition of the classes also determined their being, their social psychology (a mentality of parasitic degeneration among the rulers; of degeneration by stupefaction and oppression among the oppressed). Such a superstructure was too heavy for its basis, the productive forces, which ceased to grow, ultimately becoming a negative quantity."

By emphasizing technology rather than economics, Bukharin offended Marxist orthodoxy. But it was not for that reason that Stalin had him executed.

65. "The need of protection against foreign invaders or against oppressive administrators drove many of the remaining small proprietors to surrender their holdings to their wealthier neighbors, who could provide shelter against marauders in their fortified villas ..." M. Cary, *History of Rome* (5th ed.; London, 1949), p. 735; Max Weber goes still further, maintaining that Roman society was never anything but feudal, organized along "patrimonial lines of economic relationships." See *Wirtschaft und Gesellschaft* in *op. cit.*, II, 599–600.

66. RC, p. 442.

67. Bukharin, "Marx's Teaching and Its Historical Importance," in *Marxism and Modern Thought* (New York, 1935), p. 70.

68. A. I. Tiumeniev, "Marxism and Bourgeois Historical Science," in *Bukharin and others*, *op. cit.*, pp. 277, 314.

69. Georg Lukacs, *Die Zerstörung der Vernunft* (Berlin, 1955), pp. 478–79.

70. *Ibid.*, pp. 485, 496–97. Cf. Leo Strauss, *Natural Law and History* (Chicago, 1953), pp. 36 ff.

71. Carl J. Friedrich, *The New Image of the Common Man* (2d ed.; Boston, 1950), pp. 264–65. Mosca's Sicilian cradle had already been rocked by A. Livingston in RC, p. xxxv.

72. Antonio Gramsci, *Note sul Machiavelli* (Turin, 1952), p. 140.

73. Gramsci, *Gli intellettuali e l'organizzazione della cultura* (4th ed.; Turin, 1952), p. 4, n. 1 (written in 1932).

Chapter 14

1. RC, p. 480.

2. See Robert Goetz-Girey, *La pensée syndicale française: Militants et théoriciens* (Paris, 1948), p. 31.

3. RC, p. 481. The same idea is developed in Mosca's essay, "Lo Stato-città antico e lo Stato rappresentativo moderno," *La riforma sociale*, XXV (1924), 97–112; reprinted in PS, pp. 37–60. See there particularly pp. 57–58.

4. RC, p. 488. *The Social Contract*, Bk. II, Chap. 3, in *Social Contract*, ed. Ernest Barker (New York and London, 1948), p. 194.

5. RC, p. 481.

6. See my *Genesis of Georges Sorel* (Ann Arbor, 1951), pp. 292 ff.

7. ST, pp. 331–32.

8. See Alexandre Zévàes, *Histoire du socialisme et du communisme en France* (Paris, 1947), p. 326.

9. "Feudalismo funzionale," *Corriere della Sera*, October 19, 1907.

10. "Stato liberale e stato sindacale," PS, pp. 302 ff. (first published in *Rinascita liberale*, January, 1925); "Il problema sindacale" (conference held at the Consiglio Nazionale Liberale, 1925) in PS, pp. 316 ff.

11. PS, pp. 304–5.

12. *Ibid.*, p. 306.

13. See "Three Evils," Chap. 10 of this study, p. 231.

14. Benedetto Croce, *Politics and Morals* (New York, 1945), pp. 119–20.

15. "An Italian Political Philosopher," *The Times Literary Supplement* (London, March 17, 1950). A brilliant review of Mosca's *Partiti e sindacati*.

16. "Il programma dei liberali," PS, p. 78. See Chap. 7 of this study, pp. 157 ff.

17. PS, pp. 310–11.

18. RC, p. 480.

19. *The Intelligent Woman's Guide to Socialism and Capitalism* (Garden City, N.Y., 1928), p. 186: "Trade Unionism is not Socialism: It is the Capitalism of the Proletariat." Cf. Lenin, *What Is To Be Done?*, in Lenin, *Selected Works*. (See Chap. 5 of this study.)

20. PS, p. 307.

21. *Ibid.*, p. 312.
22. *Ibid.*, pp. 313, 314.
23. *Ibid.*, p. 323.
24. *Ibid.*, p. 322.
25. *Ibid.*, p. 315.
26. RC, p. 317.
27. See n. 29 to Chap. 5 of this study.

Chapter 15

1. "Pensieri inediti," *Ethos*, II, No. 1 (February, 1946), 4.
2. *Ibid.*, p. 2.
3. "Encore quelques mots sur 'Le Prince' de Machiavelli," *Revue française de sciences politiques*, XLIX (1926), 22.
4. "Pensieri," *op. cit.*, No. 2, 4–5.
5. "Pensieri," *op. cit.*, I, No. 3 (December, 1945), 1–2.
6. *Ibid.*, p. 2: "Stubbs, *Histoire constitutionelle d'Angleterre.* Preface . . . by Charles Petit Dutailles."
7. RC, p. 458.
8. "Ciò che la storia potrebbe insegnare," in *Studi in onore di Francesco Scaduto*, II (Florence, 1936), 195–207. Essentially identical with RC, Chap. XVI, Sec. 6 (pp. 457–64).
* 9. RC, p. 39, and n. 1.
10. Engels, *Feuerbach*, in Marx-Engels, *Selected Works*, II, 328. Dwight Macdonald, "The Root Is Man," Pt. 2, *Politics* (July, 1946), pp. 199–200.
11. RC, pp. 80–81.
12. RC, p. 165. This is, if not Marx, then in any case not very far from Hegel (whose name is conspicuously absent from the *Elementi*); see also Chap. 11 of this study. Cf. Cassirer, *The Myth of the State* (Garden City, N.Y., 1955), p. 333: "Hegel's unity is a dialectic unity; a unity of contraries. It not only allows but even requires the strongest tensions and oppositions."
13. RC, p. 397.
14. See Conclusions.
15. "Il problema sindacale," PS, p. 323.
16. RC, p. 459.
17. *Ibid.*, p. 360.
18. *Ibid.*, p. 41.
19. *Ibid.*, p. 463.
20. "Ciò che la storia . . ." in *op. cit.*, p. 196.
21. *Ibid.*, p. 200. See my Chap. 13, p. 305, and RC, p. 304.
22. "Ciò che la storia . . . ," p. 200.
23. "Pensieri," I, No. 3 (December, 1945), 3. The source is given as: "Gautier, *Moeurs et coutumes des Musulmans* (Paris, 1931), pp. 254–55."
24. RC, pp. 35, 34.
25. *Ibid.*, p. 320.
26. "Pensieri," p. 3.
27. Toynbee, *A Study of History*, VII, 420 ff.
28. RC, pp. 248, 249 (EL, I, 363).

Conclusions

1. About Mosca's fear of frenzied competition in a completely equalitarian society, consult RC, p. 419; quoted in Chap. 2 of this study. According to Karl Mannheim (*Man and Society in an Age of Reconstruction*, London, 1940, pp. 86 ff.) four processes can be asserted of contemporary mass society:

1) The great increase in the number of elites leads to diffuseness; the elites end up by canceling each other out.

2) With too many elites existing, they are deprived "of the exclusiveness which they need for the sublimation of the [creative] impulse." The slow, deliberate formation of taste and style "becomes impossible." New intuitions can no longer mature and are "apprehended by the masses as mere stimuli. As a result . . . we find constantly increasing hunger after ever new sensations."

3) The *principle* governing the selection of elites has changed. "These groups should be reasonably accessible as well as exclusive if culture is to flourish." But mass democracy, emphasizing selection by achievement, strengthens the dynamic element to the detriment of "social continuity." Lately, however, mass society has "shown a tendency to renounce the principle of achievement . . . and has suddenly established blood or other criteria as the major factors . . ." [The reference to the Third Reich is obvious; another criterion that comes to mind is of a social or religious kind: the class in Soviet Russia.] This is "negative democratization . . . the populace as a whole now becomes a privileged group . . ."

4) The elites are undergoing "artificial changes" inasmuch as they tend to become parochial; the internationally minded, "mobile type" gives way to "intellectual provincialism." [One thinks of Stalin-Zhdanov's tirades against "cosmopolitanism" and of similar know-nothing movements.] This "negative selection gives a position of pre-eminence to those who were unable to live up to the standards of modern culture . . ." The older elites [the liberals] "begin to be ashamed of their slowly acquired cultural and moral values and come to regard them as the expression of weakness and as a form of cowardice . . ." [This is the anti-intellectualism of the intellectuals, they discover that they are, when all is said, neo-conservatives, a negative elite united only by the lingering, malingering fear of contemporary mass society. The only way out seems to be destruction of the hated thing]: "The chaotic and undisciplined elements of the psyche come . . . into the open."

2. Lawrence Dennis, *The Dynamics of War and Revolution* (New York, 1940). See also his *Coming American Revolution* (New York and London, 1936). James Burnham, *The Managerial Revolution* (New York, 1941), Chaps. X, XI, and XVI; *The Machiavellians* (New York, 1943), p. 233, n.

According to one critic (Bernard Rosenberg, "The 'New American Right,'" *Dissent*, Winter 1956, p. 49), Talcott Parsons, the distinguished American sociologist, who devoted a chapter of his *Structure of Social Action* (1937) to Pareto, would be another 'elitist' (in the bad sense) because he wrote recently: "Broadly, I think, a political elite in the two main aspects of 'politicians' and of 'administrators' in both civil and military services, must be greatly strengthened" [in this country]. But if read in context, the statement, which appears in *The New American Right*, ed. by Daniel Bell (New York, 1955, p. 139–40), merely echoes Mosca's criticisms of democratic muddle. Daniel Bell himself talks Mosca in the language of our decade when he says that "two 'silent' revolutions in the relations between power and class position in modern society seem to be in process. One is a change in the *mode of access* to power insofar as inheritance alone is no longer all-determining; the other is a change in the *nature of power-holding itself* insofar as technical skill rather than property, and political position rather than wealth, have become the basis on which power is wielded." In this connection, Bell delivers himself of a very able definition of "ruling class." It is "a power-holding group which has both an established *community* of interest, and *a continuity* of interest." ("The Break-Up of Family Capitalism," *Partisan Review*, Spring 1957, p. 320.)

3. RC, p. 154. Already quoted on p. 106, above.

4. Cf. Franz Neumann, *Behemoth* (2d ed.; New York, 1944), pp. 8–17.

5. See Chaps. 5 and 8 of this study.

6. C. Wright Mills, "On Knowledge and Power," *Dissent*, II, No. 3 (Summer, 1955), 205–6.

7. Maurice Duverger, *Political Parties* (London and New York, 1954), pp. 422, 423. (*Les partis politiques*, Paris, 1951.)

8. *Ibid.*, pp. 87–88.

9. Joseph A. Schumpeter, *Capitalism, Socialism and Democracy* (2d ed.; New York, 1947), p. 285.

10. Duverger, *op. cit.*, pp. 425, 426, 427.

11. *Ibid.*, p. 425.

12. Schumpeter, *op. cit.*, p. 269.

13. *Ibid.*, p. 286.

14. *Ibid.*, p. 281.

15. *Ibid.*, p. 285.

16. *Ibid.*, p. 271.

17. Duverger, *op. cit.*, p. 364.

18. *Ibid.*, pp. 269–70.

19. *Ibid.*, p. 280.

20. Benedetto Croce, *History as the Story of Liberty* (New York, 1955), p. 195.

21. *Ibid.*, pp. 254–55.

22. *Ibid.*, pp. 253–54.

23. About Mosca and Rousseau, see Chaps. 11 and 14, pp. 254 and 318, in this study.

24. Croce, *op. cit.*, p. 254.

25. *The Power Elite* (New York, 1956). Discussed on my pp. 360 ff.

26. George Orwell, *Animal Farm* (New York, 1946), p. 112: the original refers to "animals" not men.

27. *The New Image of the Common Man* (2d ed.; Boston, 1950), p. 370, n. 12.

28. *Ibid.*, pp. 257–58. The unity of the elite is strongly denied also by Raymond Aron in his "Note sur la stratification du pouvoir," *Revue française de sciences politiques*, IV, No. 3 (July–Sept., 1954), 469–83.

29. Friedrich, *op. cit.*, pp. 256–60. See Chap. 13 of this study, and n. 71 to Chap. 13.

30. Friedrich, *op. cit.*, p. 269.

31. *Ibid.*, p. 265.

32. Franz Borkenau, *Pareto* (New York, 1936), pp. 11, 114–15.

33. See pp. 368 ff.

34. See n. 25 of the Conclusions. For earlier work of the same author, see n. 6 of the Conclusions, and n. 35 to Chap. 9.

35. *The Power Elite*, pp. 20, and 367, n. 7.

36. *Ibid.*, p. 366, n. 6.

37. *Ibid.*, p. 18.

38. *Ibid.*, p. 19. About Burnham and Dennis, see n. 2 to the Conclusions.

39. *The Power Elite*, p. 20.

40. *Ibid.*, p. 342.

41. *Ibid.*, p. 361.

42. *Ibid.*, p. 349.

43. *Ibid.*, p. 17, n. This sounds like a parody of Rousseau's "Whoso gives himself to all gives himself to none." *The Social Contract*, Bk. I, Chap. VI, in *Social Contract*, ed. Ernest Barker (New York and London, 1948), p. 181.

44. *The Power Elite*, p. 244. David Riesman, Nathan Glazer, Reuel Denny, *The Lonely Crowd* (New Haven, 1950), Chap. X.

45. *The Power Elite*, pp. 257–58. Alfred de Grazia too finds in our time an "absolute decrease in the freedom to 'politick'... traditional democracy is being slowly crushed in the gigantic pincers of depolitization and totalitarianism." However, he finds also that "the changes occurring in the politists themselves make of them at one and the same time a group more vulnerable to extinction, because of their loss of traditional status and function, and a more fitting instrument for a radical movement that, in a flare of indignation, can infuse the ranks of politists and re-politize for a fleeting moment the arena of politics before it settles finally into a new bureaucratic civilization with a new elite." "Research on Voters and Elections," in *Research Frontiers in Politics and Government* (Washington, D.C., 1955), pp. 133, 134.

46. *The Power Elite*, p. 247.

47. *Ibid.*, p. 255.

48. *Ibid.*, p. 267.

49. *Ibid.*, p. 245.

50. *Ibid.*, p. 260. One might even envision "the shadowy outline of a new society, which is markedly no longer the old bourgeois society... a society which can apparently go on without an elite. So far as power goes, the bureaucracy of the new ruling institutions has to some extent taken the place of the old bourgeoisie, but culturally it lacks the independence and confidence to become a new elite." This is a description, not of Soviet society, but of the present British welfare state by T. R. Fyvel: "The Stones of Harlow. Reflections on Subtopia" (which is the English term for Suburbia), *Encounter*, VI, No. 6 (June, 1956), 16.

51. *The Power Elite*, pp. 261–62.

52. *Ibid.*, p. 268.

53. *Ibid.*, p. 248. E. H. Carr, *The Twenty Years' Crisis* (London, 1949), pp. 82–83.

54. Guido Dorso, *Dittatura, Classe politica e classe dirigente* (Turin, 1949), pp. 126–27.

55. *Ibid.*, p. 128.

56. *Ibid.*, pp. 129, 130.

57. *Ibid.*, p. 131.

58. *Ibid.*, p. 132.

59. *Ibid.*, pp. 132–33.

60. *Ibid.*, p. 133. Cf. Michels, *Political Parties* (Glencoe, Ill., 1949), Pt. III.

61. RC, VII (pp. 163–98). Cf. Chaps. 5 and 8 of this study.

62. RC, p. 73; see Chap. 6 of this study.

63. Dorso, *op. cit.*, pp. 168, 169.

64. *Ibid.*, pp. 170, 168. Appearing too late to be considered in this section is a study of Lewis Coser, *The Functions of Social Conflict* (Glencoe, Ill., 1956). The author develops, in a very stimulating manner, ideas of Georg Simmel with which I should have been, but was not, familiar.

65. Dorso, p. 172.

66. See Chap. 7 of this work. "It would seem that the features of human psychology which make possible collaboration between individuals who are not in [face to face] company with each other are the same as those which give rise to religious activity . . . It would be possible to . . . talk of politicians as a priesthood . . ." Peter Laslett, "The Face to Face Society," in *Philosophy, Politics and Society*, ed. Peter Laslett (Oxford, 1956), p. 177.

67. Dorso, *op. cit.*, p. 173. Cf. Chap. 6 of this study (RC, p. 75).

68. Dorso, *op. cit.*, p. 174. For Mosca's negative attitude toward "the various party organizations in which the ruling class is divided" (RC, p. 411), see Chap. 5 of this work.

69. Dorso, *op. cit.*, pp. 175–76.

70. *Ibid.*, pp. 174, 175.

71. *Ibid.*, pp. 176, 177.

72. *Ibid.*, p. 179.

73. "Elites and Classes," *The Times Literary Supplement* (London, July 6, 1956), p. 409. Cf. Chap. 14 of this study and n. 15 to Chap. 14. Mills answered his critics in *Dissent* (Winter 1957), pp. 22 ff.

74. ". . . About Equality" (II), *Encounter*, VII, No. 2 (August, 1956), 46–47. The essay forms part of a series, now published as a book, entitled *The Future of Socialism* (London, 1956).

75. "The New Inequality," *Encounter*, VII, No. 5 (Nov., 1956), 29.

SELECTED BIBLIOGRAPHY

Books by Gaetano Mosca

Sulla Teorica dei governi e sul governo parlamentare: Studi storici e sociali. Turin, 1884. 2d ed., *Teorica dei governi e governo parlamentare: Studi storici e sociali.* Turin, 1925.

Dei rapporti fra il Parlamento ed il potere giudiziario, in specie in relazione ai giudizi di costituzionalita delle leggi, alla verifica delle elezioni ed al sindacato delle Camere sull'azione del potere giudiziario. Palermo, 1885.

Le costituzioni moderne. Palermo, 1887.

Elementi di scienza politica. Turin, 1896. 2d ed., with a second unpublished part, 2 vols., Turin, 1923. 3d ed., Bari, 1939. 4th ed., with a Preface by Benedetto Croce, Bari, 1947. English translation, in one volume, *The Ruling Class (Elementi di Scienza Politica).* Translated by Hannah D. Kahn. Edited and revised, with an Introduction by Arthur Livingston. New York and London, 1939. German translation, *Die Herrschende Klasse: Grundlagen der politischen Wissenschaft.* 1 vol. Preface by Benedetto Croce. Translated from 4th Italian ed. by Franz Borkenau. Bern, 1950.

Questioni pratiche di diritto costituzionale. Turin, 1898.

Appunti di diritto costituzionale. Milan, 1908.

Italia e Libia: Considerazioni politiche. Milan, 1912.

Saggi di storia della scienza politica. Rome, 1927.

Lezioni di storia delle istituzioni e delle dottrine politiche. Rome, 1932. Preface dated June, 1933. 2d rev. ed., *Storia delle dottrine politiche.* Bari, 1937. 3d ed., 1939. 4th ed., 1942, 5th ed., 1945. 6th ed., 1951. French translation, *Histoire des doctrines politiques depuis l'antiquité jusqu'à nos jours.* Translated with an introduction by Gaston Bouthoul. Paris, 1936.

Partiti e sindacati nella crisi del regime parlamentare. Bari, 1949.

Essays, Articles, and Reviews by Mosca

"Studi ausiliari dell diritto costituzionale," *Il Circolo giuridico*, XVII (1886), 101–10.

"Intorno al parlamentarismo," *Il rinnovamento economico-amministrativo*, I (1885), 199–204.

* "Il programma dei liberali in materia di politica ecclesiastica," *Giornale degli economisti*, XV (1897), 458–71.

"Il fenomeno Ferrero," *La riforma sociale*, VII (1897), 1017–31, 1135–64.

"La nuova opera di Guglielmo Ferrero," *La letteratura*, 1902, pp. 908–15.

* "Il principio aristocratico ed il democratico nel passato e nell'avvenire." Inaugural address, Turin, 1903.

* "Piccola polemica," *La riforma sociale*, XVII (1907), 329–31.

* "La sociologia del partito politico nella democrazia moderna," *Il pensiero moderno*, 1912, pp. 310–16.

* "Lo Stato-città antico e lo Stato rappresentativo moderno," *La riforma sociale*, XXV (1924), 97–112. Included in *Saggi di storia della scienza politica*, Rome, 1927.

* "Stato liberale e stato sindacale," *Rinascita liberale*, January 20, 1925.

* "Il problema sindacale," address delivered at the Consiglio Nazionale liberale, 1925.

* "Le forze sindacali e gl'interessi sociali," *Corriere della Sera*, October 23, 1925.

* Sul disegno di legge relativo all 'Attribuzioni del Capo del Governo.' " Rome, 1925.

"Encore quelques mots sur 'Le prince' de Machiavelli," *Revue française de sciences politiques*, XLVIII (1925), 481–509; and XLIX (1926), 5–27. In Italian as "Il Principe di Machiavelli quattro secoli dopo la morte del suo autore," in *Saggi di storia della scienza politica*, Rome, 1927.

* "The Crisis in Parliamentarism," in *The Development of the Representative System in Our Times* (Lausanne, 1928).

"L'utopia di Tommaso Moro ed il pensiero communista moderno," in *Scritti della Facoltà giuridica di Roma in onore di Antonio Salandra* (Milan, 1928), pp. 259–72.

"Machiavelli, Niccolò," in *Encyclopaedia of the Social Sciences*, IX (New York, 1933), 655–57.

"Cenni storici e critici sulle dottrine razziste," in *Rendiconti della R. Accademia Nazionale dei Lincei—Classe di scienze morali, storiche e filologiche*, XI (1933), 455–70.

"Ciò che la storia potrebbe insegnare," in *Studi in onore di Francesco Scaduto* (Florence, 1936), II, 195–207.

"Pensieri inediti di Gaetano Mosca," *Ethos*, I, No. 3 (December, 1945), 1–3; II, No. 1 (February, 1946), 1–4.

* These articles were reprinted in *Partiti e sindacati nella crisi del regime parlamentare*. Bari, 1949.

INDEX

427